D1548653

THE SHAPE OF INCA HISTORY

THE SHAPE OF INCA HISTORY

Narrative and Architecture in an Andean Empire   Susan A. Niles

UNIVERSITY

OF IOWA PRESS

IOWA CITY

University of Iowa Press, Iowa City 52242

Copyright © 1999 by the University of Iowa Press

All rights reserved

Printed in the United States of America

Design by Omega Clay

http://www.uiowa.edu/~uipress

No part of this book may be reproduced or used in any form or by any means, electronic or mechanical, including photocopying and recording, without permission in writing from the publisher. All reasonable steps have been taken to contact copyright holders of material used in this book. The publisher would be pleased to make suitable arrangements with any whom it has not been possible to reach.

Figures 6.42, 9.4, and 9.15 are reproduced from *Inca Architecture and Construction at Ollantaytambo* by Jean-Pierre Protzen with drawings by Robert N. Batson. Copyright © 1993 by Oxford University Press, Inc. Used by permission of Oxford University Press, Inc.

Figures 3.5, 8.4, 8.8, and 8.9 are reproduced from *Inca Architecture* by Graziano Gasparini and Luise Margolies, translated by Patricia J. Lyon. Copyright © 1980 by Indiana University Press. Used by permission of Indiana University Press.

Printed on acid-free paper

Library of Congress Cataloging-in-Publication Data

Niles, Susan A.

The shape of Inca history: narrative and architecture in an Andean empire / by Susan A. Niles.

  p. cm.

Includes bibliographical references and index.

ISBN 0-87745-673-9 (cloth)

1. Inca architecture—Peru—Yucay Region. 2. Incas—Peru—Yucay Region—Historiography. 3. Incas—Peru—Yucay Region—Kings and rulers. 4. Huayna Capac, Inca, d. ca. 1525—Contributions in architecture. I. Title.

F3429.3.A65N56   1999

985'.37—dc21   98-51181

99 00 01 02 03 C 5 4 3 2 1

For the people of Urubamba,
most especially Señora Elizabeth,
Angel, and my friends on the
Barrios Altos de Urubamba
soccer team, with affection
and gratitude.

Contents

Acknowledgments

This work is the product of twenty years of thinking about Inca architecture and history. For all that time, John Rowe has been a valued mentor and colleague. Ever generous with his knowledge, John suggested I see what was in Urubamba when I was casting about for a new project in 1986. His enthusiasm for my work (along with, surely, his puzzlement at my reports of such weird architecture) brought him to visit Quispiguanca, and to make observations that he shared with me. He also generously gave me copies of his own transcriptions of various sixteenth-century legal documents related to lands on Huayna Capac's estate.

In preparing this work I have benefited from the help and support of many friends. Above all, I am grateful to Robert Batson for bringing his architect's eye and artist's hand to the project. Many of the ideas that appear in chapters 6, 7, and 9 were refined in conversations with him and are represented in the plans and drawings that present the visual argument about the design of Huayna Capac's estate. Most of the drawings in those chapters were made by Robert. In the field, Robert uncomplainingly bounded over terrace walls to pull a tape across fields as we checked and rechecked measurements and, back in Texas, faithfully faxed sketches across the country when I wanted to test out yet another hunch about the site's design. Always able to find the right mix of humor, architectural reasoning, and patience, Robert managed to pull me back to the real world when I proposed ideas that were unrealistic and coaxed me farther out on a limb when my suggestions were too earthbound. I am fortunate to have him as a friend and colleague.

Christopher Blechschmidt pushed me to think more about Inca great halls as he prepared a thesis on Inca roofing techniques. With creativity and energy he modeled the roof structure of Quispiguanca's great hall, providing information that is central to the discussion of that building provided in chapters 6 and 9. I am grateful to Chris for his interest in Inca architecture and his continuing willingness to spend time thinking about Inca engineering and design issues.

Catherine Julien commented on an earlier version of this book, offering insightful suggestions that have sharpened its focus and bibliographical references that have improved it.

My ideas about Inca architecture have been shaped over the years by conversations with many friends and colleagues, among them Jean-Pierre Protzen, Margaret MacLean, Vince Lee, Anne Paul, and Ann Kendall.

Other people gave me ideas that sparked a notion that found its way into this book. For their help, I thank Horacio Villanueva Urteaga, Alan Dundes, Patricia J. Lyon, Ed Franquemont, Vince Viscomi, Peter Palmieri, Joan O'Donnell, Linda Schele, Bill Conklin, Maarten Van De Guchte, Stella Nair, Frank Salomon, Ned Dwyer, and Elisabeth Bonnier.

I was helped in the field by friends who usually didn't know what they were getting into when they agreed to hold the end of a tape measure. Thanks are due to Claire DeFoor, Cynthia Allen, Sara Steck, Angel Mejía, Eloy Mejía, Fredy Rada, Emilio Puma, Marcos Pacheco, Feliciano Mayhua, and the late Ed Lamb.

Sra. Elizabeth Hammer de Figueroa's warm hospitality and delicious meals sustained me during two seasons of fieldwork. Her kindness is acknowledged with affection.

While this book incorporates insights I have gained in a number of episodes of fieldwork at various archaeological sites, the argument advanced in the latter half of the book is based on my investigations of Huayna Capac's estate near Urubamba, carried out in 1986, 1987, 1996, and 1997. I am grateful to the directors of the Instituto Nacional de Cultura in Cuzco for their generosity in providing permission for me to work at the site. The 1987 field season was supported by a grant from the H. John Heinz III Charitable Trust and by a summer fellowship from Lafayette College's Committee on Advanced Study and Research. Research grants from Lafayette College's Academic Research Committee in 1997 and 1998 made it possible for me to return to Quispiguanca with Robert Batson to finish the study.

I was fortunate to receive support for writing up the material as well. Much of that work was done while I was a resident fellow at the School of American Research, supported by the National Endowment for the Humanities. I completed the book as a resident fellow at the John Carter Brown Library, again helped by a fellowship from the National Endowment for the Humanities. I appreciate the vision of the directors of these institutions, Doug Schwartz at the SAR and Norman Fiering at the JCB, that has made their fellowship programs a source of support for anthropologists. I am grateful to the staff of both of these institutions for their help and their friendship, as well as to my fellow fellows, with whom I shared long conversations about obscure ideas and even more obscure sources. Among the latter I acknowledge, especially, Karen Graubart and Jorge Cañizares, who spent some of their reading time at the JCB in my corner of the sixteenth century and rigorously debated ideas with me.

A Note on the Orthography and Translation

It is never easy to decide how to spell a word in a language spoken by people without a tradition of writing. Many recent researchers have chosen to adopt one of the orthographies devised to represent the full range of sounds in Quechua when writing about the Incas (or the Inka, as such researchers might prefer). However, I have elected to spell most Quechua personal names, place-names, and loan words using Spanish orthography. Thus readers will note that I write the Late Inca king's name as Huayna Capac, rather than Wayna Qhapaq, and that I write Urubamba and Yucay with *b*'s and a *c*, letters not generally used in the Quechua systems of spelling. I have chosen to do this because most places indicated on Peruvian maps are spelled using Spanish orthography, and I think it is more important to be able to locate places on maps than to adhere to a desirable, if not consistently applied, set of spelling rules. In exceptional cases I use Quechua orthography when that is the spelling most commonly used for a place or site (e.g., Huch'uy Qozqo). Because my argument draws so heavily on early written sources, I have opted to use the sixteenth-century version of some Inca words that are commonly used by the chroniclers, as well as in cases where there is no consensus on the spelling of a term in modern Spanish. Thus readers will see *mitimaes* rather than *mitmaqkuna* or *mitmacuna* and *yanacona* rather than *yanakuna* or *yanacuna*. While my solution may not be ideal, it does reduce the number of variant spellings within the text. I also follow the sixteenth-century convention of pluralizing terms like *mamaconas*, a word which is already plural in Quechua (*mamakuna*). Similarly, I preserve the sixteenth-century Spanish spelling for place-names that appear in early documents but that are no longer in use or that do not appear on modern maps.

Except where otherwise noted, all translations are my own. Long or ambiguous passages are presented in their original language as well as in English. Short and unambiguous passages are presented in translation only. I have retained the Spanish convention of using Inca in the singular to refer to the *sapa Inca* (unique Inca), ruler of the people who disseminated their religious, economic, and political beliefs over much of the Andean world in the fifteenth century; I use Incas in the plural to refer to these people. The Spanish chroniclers of Inca elite life employed familiar paradigms to understand the institutions they observed and the people they met. Thus they liken the *huar-achicuy* male puberty ritual to ceremonies that armed young men as knights and used words that we might gloss as "king" to refer to the *sapa Inca* and "lords" to refer to the *apus* who were his closest associates. I have chosen to use the term "royal" to refer to the individuals who were members of the twelve *panacas* of Cuzco that were believed to have been founded by Inca rulers; the rulers will sometimes be called "kings." While surely the original Inca understanding of these concepts does not map neatly onto the terms as used in modern English, I choose them to remind readers that these most highly ranked families, like their contemporaries in European royal families, believed themselves to be different from ordinary people, supported their belief by enforcing sumptuary laws and engaging in activities designed to substantiate that belief, and practiced theoretical endogamy (manifested at its extreme by the brother-sister marriage attributed to their mythical ancestors and required of the later Inca rulers).

A Note on the Illustrations

In this book I suggest that Inca architectural style is dynamic, changing over time to reflect the concerns of architects and their patrons.
This is an argument that rests, ultimately, on an understanding of
what Inca sites looked like. In some cases it is possible to visualize an
ancient building from architectural remains. In the case of the principal site discussed here, Huayna Capac's country palace, its large scale
and relatively poor preservation make it difficult to show what the
magnificent compound must have been like. In order to allow readers
to envision the site, I have chosen to present the visual argument in
plans and photographs supplemented by drawings that suggest how
the site may have appeared in antiquity. The drawings were created by
Robert N. Batson based on measurements and observation of standing architectural remains. They were roughed out in the field after
much checking, rechecking, and redrafting and were refined in our
discussions of the site. The resulting drawings reflect our understanding of this site, interpreted in light of our experience with the other
Inca sites—chiefly near Cuzco and in the Urubamba Valley—that we
have each studied over the years.

A decision to represent a now-fallen structure entails a host of
questions: How high were the original walls? What sort of roof did it
have? What color were its niches? In creating visual answers to these
and other questions we were governed by a set of principles.

First, the reconstruction had to fit all the evidence available from
the physical remains.

Second, any feature shown in the drawing had to have a precedent
at another Inca site in the region.

Third, the final result had to be architecturally sound. In the absence of any clear Inca precedent or structural consideration, we relied
on aesthetic considerations: If we felt that gable roofs looked better
than hip roofs or that they framed a more dramatic view, that is the solution we chose. We believe that all of the drawings present plausible
views of the site, although we acknowledge that some of our decisions
about architectural details that may have been present are arbitrary.

In plans of the site, walls that preserve such architectural details as
niches or door jambs are indicated with solid lines and diagonal

hatching. Walls that are visible but not sufficiently well preserved to show detail are represented in solid lines without hatching. Broken lines are used to indicate walls or other features that may have existed but for which there is no above-ground evidence.

Introduction

This book got its start in a casual conversation with a gringo anthropologist on a street corner in Cuzco in the early 1980s. My friend congratulated me on a book I had written on South American Indian narrative folklore, but he chastised me for not including much discussion of the Andes. In half-hearted defense of my omission, I commented that the Andean material, based on the sixteenth- and seventeenth-century chronicles, was hard to treat as folklore, for it was, in some ways, better considered as history.

My friend's off-hand remark had hit a sore spot with me: How was one to treat the stories of Inca kings that appeared as histories in the standard Colonial accounts of Andean culture? Like more easily identified examples of folk narratives, they had at one point been part of an oral tradition. Yet I had a feeling that if we could conjure up one of the dead Incas who was the subject of a story, he would swear that the narrative was a straight historical account. I wasn't ready to tackle the problem, so I pushed it into the background as I turned my attention again to Inca architecture, a subject that—I thought—would be more straightforward.

When I began to study the architecture attributed to Huayna Capac, I was impressed not only by the originality of the style devised for his estate in the Yucay Valley but also by the wealth of documentary sources that I could use to understand that style. The relatively good preservation of remains near Urubamba and Yucay made it possible to document the physical organization of Huayna Capac's estate, and the abundant legal documents related to claims for properties within the estate's boundaries made reference to the tribute status and ethnicity of its residents, so I could discuss its social organization as well. Further, as the last Inca to complete his reign before the arrival of the Spaniards, Huayna Capac was a known historical personage: There were many natives who had known him personally and gave eyewitness accounts of his activities to Spanish scribes; there were women in Cuzco who claimed to have been his wives or daughters; and his sons and grandsons were granted positions in the Colonial hierarchy established by the Pizarro brothers due to their descent from him. By focusing on Huayna Capac and his handiworks, I thought I could sidestep the ongoing debate among Andeanists about the historicity of Spanish accounts of Inca kings.

As I tried to characterize the distinctive style of architecture seen on the estate, I found I could not separate it from its historical context: In order to account for what was unusual about the buildings, I had to account for what was unusual in the life of Huayna Capac. That got me straight back into Inca royal histories.

Anyone who has looked at the Spanish presentations of Inca royal history in search of a single truth has encountered a morass: There is clear disagreement among the sources. Some of the disagreement is due to the specific rhetorical or political strategies of the Spanish writer. For example, Viceroy Francisco de Toledo's hired historian, Pedro Sarmiento de Gamboa, set out to prove that the Incas were brutal latecomers with only two generations of rule in a land previously governed by warlords, while Miguel Cabello Balboa sets Inca history against royal and papal dynasties that would be familiar to a European readership. But other disagreements emerge from the Inca informants themselves. Sometimes we have textual hints about the varying traditions. For example, Juan de Betanzos notes that the old men who served with Atahuallpa's army at Cajamarca denied parts of the account of the Spanish Conquest told by Spanish soldiers, their Cañari allies, or members of Huascar's party. Imagine the job of Sarmiento de Gamboa, a man charged with the difficult task of getting the one true history of the Incas, who resorted to sitting down with hundreds of descendants of the royal families to check the histories he had elicited point by point, trying to achieve consensus where he could and apologizing to his readers where he couldn't.

Scholars have disagreed on how to make sense of the varying accounts of Inca history.[1] Some choose to privilege the works of mestizo or Amerindian sources, such as the *Relación de quipucamayos*, or accounts by Pachacuti Yamqui, Titu Cusi Yupanqui, Guaman Poma de Ayala, or Garcilaso de la Vega, arguing that these sources present an indigenous view of the Andean past. Yet, no less than the Spanish chroniclers, the indigenous writers had their own rhetorical and personal axes to grind. Other scholars have assumed that there is little historical validity to the early accounts, as the Spanish writers tried to stretch a nondynastic indigenous system to fit their own dynastic expectations. Some have tried to compensate for the sixteenth-century error by imposing theoretical constructs devised in the Northern Hemisphere in the twentieth century to get at an underlying mythical truth that, it is claimed, eluded the early Spanish writers. Another approach has been to do close reading of the competing versions of history to discern the points of convergence, to screen out the obvious bias, and so to arrive at something approaching a valid and unitary history of the Incas.

I have benefited from reading the work of scholars coming from these varied approaches but have found none of them fully satisfying. I believe there is a logic and a truth to the stories told by the Spanish and the Amerindian sources, but that what is most interesting about the stories is what they tell us about Inca attitudes about history. I am not really concerned about whether the stories were, in fact, true, though there is fairly good evidence that the stories told about Huayna Capac, the last Inca to rule before the Spaniards arrived, are, perhaps, more faithful records of his actions than are the more stylized stories told about some of his predecessors. I am interested that the stories were told as true and accepted as true by their auditors, indigenous as well as Spanish. In this regard, my approach is informed by my reading in folklore: These stories are like legends (told as true, believed as true).[2] Like legends, they are set in the real world and tell of people considered to be human, though sometimes with superhuman attributes. They chronicle the protagonists' interactions with other humans and with supernatural forces. Often the stories include etiological motifs, accounting for the origin of certain practices or names. And, much as the royal families may have wished they could control the content of these narratives, they clearly existed in multiple versions and variants.

These legends were shaped into narrative histories which, punctuated by songs and the rhythm of drums, were performed on ritual occasions and served to validate the claims to an ancestor's greatness on the part of his descendants. The performance of these histories had more than an abstract importance for the families who preserved the cult of their ancestor: The prestige of the living was directly related to the reputation of the dead, and claims for property or favors could be framed in terms of just compensation for the glorious deeds of the family's founder.

Reciting the formal histories that told of their rulers is not the only way in which the Incas recalled and displayed historical events. In funerary and military rituals personal and public histories were created and performed, often on an historicized landscape. Most importantly, events were memorialized in monuments and works of commemorative architecture. I argue that in royal architecture, no less than in their narratives, the Incas shaped historical events, giving material form to claims based on victories in battle, encounters with gods, and deeds carried out by their kings. I depart from some scholars who have considered Inca architecture to be essentially ahistorical, anonymous, and directed to the administrative needs of the state. I suggest that in considering royal Inca architecture, it is critical to be cognizant of the historical setting of a building and of the claims about historical importance that may be attributed to it. I focus on the works attributed to Huayna Capac, for whom we have documented buildings and historical accounts that are rich and varied.

In this book, I propose a way to read Inca history and a way to read Inca architecture in light of that history. If there is a punchline to my argument it is this: The royal histories of the Incas are pieces of propaganda, intentionally created to depict ancestors in a flattering light. We might see royal architecture as propaganda, too, designed not only to serve the domestic and ritual needs of its creator but also to enhance his reputation and to confirm his place in Inca dynastic succession. In the absence of an unambiguous system of writing, a recognizable architectural style could be an Inca ruler's claim to legitimacy and greatness. It was a tangible way to shape his place in history.

THE SHAPE OF INCA HISTORY

Map of the central Andean area indicating the sites mentioned in the text. Diagonal hatching shows the maximum extent of the Inca empire.

GENRE AND CONTEXT
IN INCA HISTORICAL NARRATIVES

Inca history is known to us primarily through chronicles written by Spanish witnesses to the Conquest and its aftermath. Their records, written for a Spanish readership and often directed to a specific rhetorical end, were based on information reported by Inca informants. The situations in which the histories were gathered vary, and their utility to us likewise differs, depending on such factors as the rapport the writers had with their informants, the willingness of the informants to share their knowledge, and the skill with which they were translated from Quechua to Spanish. Even the chronicles written by individuals who defined themselves as mestizos or Amerindians cannot be used uncritically as expressions of indigenous historical thought, as their authors likewise followed the canons of Spanish historical writing and, no less than the Spanish chroniclers, had a specific rhetorical agenda.

Despite the problems that confront us as we use the chronicles to reconstruct Inca historical process, it is possible to use these and other documents to gain insight into Inca notions of history.

The Structure of Royal History

The standard chronicles of Inca history left by Spanish writers were prepared to tell their compatriots about the riches and marvels of a world that was new to them. They heard about the Inca kings who had directed impressive armies and collected nearly unimaginable quantities of gold and silver in tribute, and they repeated versions of these stories in the books, reports, and reminiscences they would write. As presented in most of the sources, the histories are structured to tell of the lives of individual kings. The stories generally begin with the rituals of accession to the throne and conclude with the death of the king. Between these two points are episodes that tell of military conquests and administrative innovations of the ruler and that name his loyal kinsmen and his most important enemies. The narratives are rich with detail on military encounters and the pageants in which victories are celebrated, and they include stories of piety to earthly parents and encounters with the gods who favored the Incas in battle. They describe ceremonies of marriage, funerals, and festivals that celebrate the birth of sons. In short, they present the stories of the rulers whose lives they exalted in a most flattering light.

But as much as the histories are stories about individuals, they are also stories about the founding of *panacas*, the patrilineal descent group established by each Inca. In the narratives, the rites of fasting, commemoration of the old ruler's death, official marriage to the legitimate sister-wife, and installation as Inca generally happen simultaneously. The ritual of succession is thus also a ritual of initiation of the royal descent group. In Inca kinship theory, each ruler established his own descent group separate from that of his father; the founder of the *panaca* worked to acquire property to enrich it and to bring prestige to himself and to its members. At his death, the members of the *panaca* served as curators of the founder's mummy and his reputation, working to provide for his food and drink and preserving and performing the narratives that told of his deeds. It is these stories—formalized, partisan histories conserved by an Inca's descendants—that are the basis of our understanding of Inca history.

The standard sources on Inca dynasties delineate a sequence of rulers and relate each to the *panaca* he founded. While the Incas did not provide years for the reigns of their rulers, some of the Spanish chroniclers imposed dates for them. Table 1.1 presents the traditional list of Inca succession, following Rowe (1944: 57–58), who, in turn, based dates for the reign on Cabello Balboa's chronicle (1951).[1]

However much they may have stretched the historical facts, the royal histories maintained by and elicited from Inca informants in Cuzco were believed to be true. As the Spanish chronicler Sarmiento noted when he collected a story told about Mayta Capac:

> Esto todo parece que se puede contar con las demás fábulas, pero yo escribo lo que los naturales tienen de sí y de sus mayores, y esto tienen por tan verdad, que se mataran con quien otra cosa les dijese. (Cap. 17; 1960: 221)

> All of this seems as though it should be told with the rest of their tall tales, but I write what the natives have heard from each other and from their elders. And they hold it to be so true that they would kill whoever said otherwise.

In making reference to the royal histories, I take the point of view that they may or may not have been faithful to the facts, but what is important is that they were told as true and believed as true: I accept them—with all the versions, variants, distortions, and exaggerations—as representations of Inca history.

We do have some other sources that allow us to check the historical claims, at least for the later Inca rulers. Administrative, ecclesiastical, and legal investigations that took place in the decades after the Spanish conquest of the Andes included inquiries about landownership, succession, and ritual that often bear upon claims that are historically grounded. Further, information about the witnesses to investigations of legal proceedings can sometimes provide a cross-check for claims made in other sources. These anecdotes and reports of family traditions are in their own right valuable evidence of the events that formed the basis of the elaborate stories maintained by the royal *panacas*.

Regrettably, there are few examples of intact Inca historical narratives; indeed, we have *no* narrative that can be proven to date to the years before Conquest. The degree to which the stories that are pre-

TABLE 1.1. Traditional List of Incas[a]

Ruler's Name	Presuccession Name	Reign	*Panaca*
Manco Capac		mythical	Chima *panaca*
Sinchi Roca		unknown	Raura *panaca*
Lloque Yupanqui		unknown	Ahuayni *panaca*
Mayta Capac		unknown	Usca Mayta *panaca*
Capac Yupanqui		unknown	Apu Mayta *panaca*
Inca Roca		unknown	Vicaquirau *panaca*
Yahuar Huacac	Titu Cusi Huallpa	unknown	Aucaylli *panaca*
Viracocha Inca	Hatun Topa Inca	until 1438	Socso *panaca*
Pachacuti Inca Yupanqui	Inca Yupanqui	1438–71	Iñaca *panaca*
Topa Inca Yupanqui		1471–93	Capac *panaca*
Huayna Capac	Titu Cusi Huallpa	1493–1525	Tomebamba *panaca*
Huascar Inca	Topa Cusi Huallpa	1525–32	Huascar *panaca*
Caccha Pachacuti Inca Yupanqui Inca[b]	Atahuallpa	1532–33	none
Topa Huallpa		1533	none
Manco Inca Yupanqui		1533–45	unknown
Topa Amaro		1545–72	none
Sayri Topa		1545–58	none
Titu Cusi Yupanqui		1558–71	none

[a] Dates for pre-Conquest Incas are based on Cabello Balboa after Rowe (1944).
[b] This succession name of Atahuallpa is given by Betanzos, who claims he was named for the war idol Caccha and to honor Pachacuti, whose world-transforming innovations he hoped to emulate (parte II, cap. VI; 1987: 221). As he is conventionally known as Atahuallpa, I use this presuccession name to refer to him.

served in the early chronicles may represent pastiches of earlier narratives, embellished to suit the taste and the ritual or economic needs of Colonial elites, is an open question. Still, I will argue that it is possible to reconstruct some of the narrative devices by which these histories were originally shaped and so, perhaps, to reconstruct part of the story that was told. In the succeeding chapters, I explore the ways in which the Incas arranged events into the formalized narratives that became their histories. I will argue that the remembrance of history was central to Inca royal politics and that events believed to be historical were commemorated in the built and imagined landscape of Cuzco and reenacted in the rituals that took place in these spaces. Because members of Inca royal families saw themselves as active participants in the creation of their histories, we can view their handiworks as testimonies to those histories.

The analysis I present will move from the oral tradition to the built one, from stories to architecture. I believe that the argument I advance is valid for the culture shared by members of the Inca royal families and that it explains much of the architecture that they created. Still, there is much that took place in the Inca empire that I do not address. This is not a story about provinces or state politics. While it is likely that the elite families of important provinces shared their own flattering histories and similarly had a tradition of building commemorative monuments, the lives of their enemies—except insofar as they put up a good fight against the Incas—did not matter to the royal Inca men whose stories have come down to us. The narratives of conquest told by victorious Inca kings may imply an efficient infrastructure of roads to move the armies and storehouses to provision them, but the stories themselves are more likely to focus on the feather headdresses they wore and the drums made from the hides of important enemies than on the logistics of moving soldiers from one end of the empire to the other.

The Remembrance of History

The Incas did not document their actions or genealogies in writing as Euro-Americans are accustomed to doing, and so their histories are not remembered as were ours. Still, they were deeply concerned with remembering actions, events, and relationships and with reporting them. In royal histories, particularly, these matters were important as reflections of an individual's relationship to the past, to other populations, and to members of other royal families. All of these relationships were critical in advancing claims to prestige and property—claims which were validated in the historical narratives that were told.

Some Inca historical information was recorded on and recalled from the *quipu*, a system of mnemonic reckoning based on patterned knotted cords (fig. 1.1). In contrast to a written record, wherein information can be recorded in any degree of detail and in any order, the *quipu*, while lending itself to a number of applications, is bound by its structure: Information must be stored and remembered in relational categories. The structure is premised on nested hierarchies and permits comparison both within a category and across categories. To choose an analogy to a system of writing, recording information on a *quipu* would be like having to write using only an outline structure. To "write" this way, information would have to be remembered in a particular way; it would still be possible to say almost anything, but the information would have to be organized carefully, and much of the detail in any given recitation would have to be created anew or added from memory.

There are a number of aspects of Inca culture that lend themselves to recording on a *quipu* (Ascher and Ascher 1981). For example, the shrines of the Inca capital were conceived of as sacred spots arrayed on lines which were cared for by royal descent groups; they comprise a conceptual system with an obvious analogue to the knots on cords that are the physical basis of the *quipu*. Similarly, *quipus* were devised to record tribute records and labor obligations (Murra 1982: 239–262) and to keep the census (Rostworowski de Diez Canseco 1990; Julien 1982; *Relación de Chincha* 1934). Even the patterns of architectural complexes (cf. Lee 1996) and textiles could be recorded this way, as Inca material culture is based on patterns that repeat in seemingly standardized ways. Garcilaso also reports that *quipus* were used to record "laws and ordinances, rituals, and ceremonies" (parte I, lib. V, cap. VIIII; 1609: 137 v.).

The *quipu* imposes restrictions on the recording of information because the data can only be stored as a knot. This makes it possible easily to store, retrieve, sum, and modify numerical information, such as would be useful for organizing tribute and census information, but creates challenges to the recording of narrative information, such as we associate with histories. We assume the *quipus* were organized mnemonically, in a system where the size, style, and grouping of knots were meaningful, as were the colors and relationship of cords to one another. Presumably these patternings jogged the memory of an expert who kept the *quipu* and recited the information it contained upon request. Ascher and Ascher (1981: 18–21) report on the importance of color and texture in distinguishing cords; Urton adds that it is also important to note the spin and ply of fibers and the direction in which the knots are tied (Urton 1995). The arrangements of cords relative to one another, too, was significant. In describing the structure

FIGURE 1.1. Topa Inca consults a *quipucamayo* about tribute goods kept in the storehouses (Guaman Poma f. 335 [337]; 1980: 309).

of *quipus* used to record tribute and census information, Garcilaso notes that "things . . . were arranged in order, beginning with those of the highest quality and proceeding to those of least quality" (parte I, lib. VI, cap. VIII; 1609: 136 r.).

Experts in the creation and reading of *quipus* were called *quipucamayos* by the Incas and by early Colonial authorities. It is clear from the early Colonial record that the knowledge of deciphering *quipus* was privileged; that is, the *quipucamayo* knew his own work and could read it, but others did not unless they were specifically taught by him. For example, a 1567 investigation of the Spanish tribute system in the old Lupaca kingdom near Lake Titicaca required the native *caciques* to report on the census and tribute of their district. Most of these communities were still using the figures from the last Inca census (Julien 1982: 127). The *caciques* brought in aging *quipucamayos* to have them read off the tribute figures for their *parcialidad*, though in some cases they reported that since the old *quipucamayo* had died, there was no one who kept records or could decipher their community's *quipus* (Diez de San Miguel 1964: 89).

These data remind us that, with a mnemonic system such as the *quipu*, the person who records the information has enormous control over its content and over the context in which it could be shared. One would assume that the official *quipucamayos* who kept information vital to Inca state interests must have demonstrated their honesty and loyalty, in addition to their ability to record and remember such data.

While there was clearly a bureaucratic and administrative use for *quipus* as record-keeping devices, they were used for storing historical information as well, such as the recording of military victories (Rowe 1985b) and, in the Colonial Period, at least, genealogies (see, e.g., Callapiña, Supno y otros Khipukamayuqs 1974). There is reason to believe, too, that they were used to record histories.

Garcilaso tells of the *quipus* used to recall "historical events or facts or the existence of any embassy, speech, or discussion made during times of peace or times of war" (parte I, lib. VI, cap. VIIII; 1609: 137 r.) and that "such speeches were memorized by the *quipucamayos*, summarized in a few words. And they were committed to memory and, by tradition, taught to their successors and descendants from father to son" (parte I, lib. VI, cap. VIIII; 1609: 137 r.). Sarmiento, too, notes the ability of Inca informants to remember long and complex histories and distinguishes rote memorization from the *quipus* (cap. 9; 1960: 211–212).

While *quipus* were surely used for keeping records relevant to remembering histories, there were other ways in which the Incas recalled historical events. The raw facts of history were worked into complex narratives that formed the basis of a vital Inca oral historical tradition. The narratives, in turn, had a place in royal and public ritual performances.

Genre and Context in Historical Performance

In addition to reporting the job of *quipucamayos* as historians, Garcilaso tells us of *amautas*, who had the job of turning historical events into short stories (parte I, lib. VI, cap. VIII; 137 r.), and of *harauicus*, who wrote poems

> en los quales encerraban la historia, o la embaxada, o la repuesta del Rey,
> en suma dezian en los versos todo lo que no podian poner en los ñudos: y

aquellos versos cantauan en sus triumphos, y en sus fiestas mayores, y los
rescitauã a los Incas noueles, quando los armauan caualleros. (Parte I, lib.
VI, cap. VIIII; 1609: 137 r.)

containing the history or an embassy, or the king's reply, saying in those
verses all that they couldn't put in the knots of the quipus. And these verses
were sung in their triumphs and in their principal festivals and recited to
the young nobles when they were armed as knights.

Garcilaso's mention of the experts who recorded or reworked historical events into narratives allows us to discern some of the dimensions of genres that the Incas devised to shape their histories. Turning
to the early Inca dictionaries for additional insight, we can explore
some of these terms. Gonçalez Holguin defines *amauta* as a sage or
wise man of good judgment ("sabio prudente, cuerdo") (1952, lib. I:
24). This entry does little more than confirm that there was such a
word. In considering the poets that Garcilaso calls *harauicu*, Gonçalez
Holguin offers the related term *haraui*, with its synonyms *yuyaycucuna*,
and *huaynaricuna ttaqui*, which he defines as "songs of the deeds of
others, or the memorial of absent loved ones, also songs of love and
affection. And now they use these terms for religious and spiritual
songs" (1952, lib. I: 152). But in the reverse translation from Spanish
he contrasts *llumpacta harauicuni*, "to sing true songs from the soul,"
with *harauicuni*, "[to sing] false or off-color songs" (1952, lib. II: 446).
Exploring the synonyms *yuyaycucuna* and *huaynaricuna*, we enter a series of related words that have to do with managing memories. Most
interesting is *yuyani*, which Gonçalez Holguin defines as "to remember, to think about and take care of something, to be in charge of it"
(1952, lib. I: 372–373). *Huaynaricuna* is defined as "something that
fills the heart and doesn't let you think about anything else" (1952, lib.
I: 194). The 1603 *Arte de la lengua general* . . . omits any reference to the
preservation of memory but does include the relationship of those
terms to mourning and love: It defines *haraui* and *harauicuy* as "Indian
songs sung like dirges, or about love" (*Arte de la lengua general* . . . 1603;
cf. *Arte y vocabulario* . . . 1614).

In discussing Inca formalized histories, the Spaniards who wit-
nessed their performance most commonly call the genre *cantar*. In sixteenth-century Spain, this term was used to describe epic poems of
praise, sometimes set to music. Chroniclers also use the terms *canto*,
loa, *historia*, and *romance*. The *cantar* included praise for the protagonist, and for Inca men, that meant telling the story of his victories in
battles. Gonçalez Holguin does not provide a direct translation for
cantar in the general sense, but he does define the special *cantar* or
canto of triumph as "*Haylli haylli*, victory victory," which was sung to

celebrate military victory or when fields were completed (1952, lib. II: 445–446).[2]

If we consider the sixteenth-century Inca terms that relate to Inca formalized histories, we can suggest that the Inca notions that were captured in the Spanish term *cantar* included the idea of formalized memories, perhaps rendered in song and verse, that were managed (presumably by the custodian of the family's history) and that were designed to fill listeners' minds with the deeds of the person or with thoughts of the person memorialized in the *cantar*. Because one of the principal contexts for the performance of these narratives included funerals and rituals commemorating the life of a dead ancestor, it is not surprising that the notion of love for an absent family member would be included in the term, along with the comparison of the song to the Spanish dirge.

Context of Performance

The Inca *cantar* embedded the notions that were important to the protagonists of the narratives, that is, to the royal men of Cuzco. They were performed pieces, involving recitation, musical accompaniment, and audience response. They were praise-narratives, focused on the admirable deeds attributed to an individual. The chroniclers tell us of the performance of the *cantar* at celebrations of military victories and at funerals.

For example, Murúa describes the solemn entrance into Cuzco of Huayna Capac's corpse, which had been carried on a litter from the northern frontier in the company of his victorious army and captives from the northern campaigns. The entrance into Cuzco was by way of the fortress, and

> venían con el cuerpo de Huaina Capac mucho número de señores y gente que hauían salido del Cuzco a sólo a compañar el cuerpo y entrar con él en el triumpho. Y todos cantaban cantares tristes y de melancolía, refiriendo las hazañas famossas de Huaina Capac y rogando al açedor por él. También venían infinitas mugeres y doncellas delas que le hauían servido y hauían sido fauorecidas y regaladas suyas en su acompañamiento, cantando con triste son al modo de quien llora, que causaba a los que las oyan por las calles dolor y prouocaba a lágrimas. (Cap. 42; 1962, vol. 1: 119)

> accompanying the corpse of Huayna Capac were many people who had left Cuzco just so they could accompany the body and enter triumphantly with it. Everybody sang sad and melancholy *cantares* which told of the noteworthy deeds of Huayna Capac, and they prayed to the Creator for him. In addition, the retinue included an infinite number of ladies and maidens who had served him, and had been favored by him, and had received gifts from him. They were singing sadly, like people who were crying, which

caused great pain to those who heard them singing in the streets and drove them to tears.

The procession was both a funeral and a victory celebration, and the praises and prayers were part of the *cantar*. Some of the performances were, according to legend, recorded on *quipus* or on colored sticks, set out by the dying Huayna Capac to specify the order of the triumphal parade into Cuzco (Murúa cap. 49; 1962, vol. 1: 108; Cabello Balboa cap. 24; 1951: 394).

Our most complete reference to a performance of a victory *cantar* comes from Betanzos' account of a six-day recitation held at the conclusion of Pachacuti's rebuilding of Cuzco (parte I, cap. XII; 1987: 59–63). Pachacuti invited the nearby notables to come enjoy a big party in Cuzco.[3] The plaza was filled with reeds, flowers, and live birds, and the lords of Cuzco and the local *caciques*, in their finest clothes, entered the plaza, followed by the ladies of Cuzco and the wives of the *caciques*. Food and drink were provided, and they performed the *cantar* of Pachacuti's victory over the enemy Chanca captain, Uscovilca:

> el Ynga mandó sacar cuatro atambores de oro e siendo allí en la plaza mandáronlos poner a trecho en ella e luego se asieron de las manos todos ellos tantos a una parte como a otra e tocando los atambores que ansi en medio estaban empezaron a cantar todos juntos comenzando este cantar las señoras mujeres que detrás dellos estaban en el cual cantar decían e declaraban la venida que Uscovilca había venido sobre ellos e la salida de Viracocha Ynga e como Ynga Yupangue le había preso e muerto diciendo que el sol le había dado favor para ello como a su hijo e como después ansi mismo había desbaratado y preso e muerto a los capitanes que ansi habían hecho la junta postrera e después deste canto dando lores e gracias al sol e ansi mismo a Ynga Yupangue saludándole como a hijo del sol se tornaron a sentar e ansi mesmo comenzaron a beber de la chicha que allí tenían que a según ellos dícen había muy mucha que allí tenían que a según ellos y en muy gran cantidad e luego les fue traído allí muy mucha coca y repartida entre todos ellos y esto ansi hecho se tornaron a levantar e hicieron ansi mesmo como habeis oído su canto e baile la cual fiesta duró seis días. (Betanzos parte I, cap. XII; 1987: 61)

the Inca ordered them to bring out four gold drums and to place them at intervals on the plaza, and then they all joined hands and playing the drums that were in their midst, they began to sing in unison, with the ladies who stood behind them starting the *cantar*. In this *cantar* they told of Uscovilca's advancing against them and of the departure of Viracocha Inca and of how Inca Yupanqui had captured and killed [Uscovilca], saying that the Sun had favored him because he was his son. And [they told] how he had routed the army and captured and killed the captains who had assembled the last forces. After this *canto* giving praise and thanks to the Sun and also to Inca Yupanqui, greeting him as the Son of the Sun, they sat down again and began to drink the corn beer that they had in great abundance. Then they were brought much coca which was divided among them, and, this done, they arose again, and again performed their *canto* and dance. This celebration went on for six days.

This passage gives us particular insight into the nature of the text and its performance. The *cantar* recounted Pachacuti's success in the Chanca War, along with his father's disgrace. The style of performance included singing led by the women and joined by the men, accompanied by drumming and dance. The story is closed by praise to the Sun and to the ruling Inca.

The story of the Chanca War is one of the most detailed set pieces we have in the Inca histories that have come down to us. Lengthy and detailed versions by Betanzos, Sarmiento, and Pachacuti Yamqui, especially, allow us to see it as both a story unto itself and as a story set within the narrative of the life of Pachacuti Inca. It is likely that the story formed part of the overall performance of Pachacuti's deeds recounted to Huayna Capac when he was installed, as will be discussed in a succeeding section. The story had clearly maintained its integrity long after conquest, when it was recorded by Betanzos (around 1551) and by Sarmiento (around 1572). It is probable that the *cantar* tradition stayed vital among some of the nobles of Cuzco until at least 1560, when the bulk of the Inca mummies was rounded up by Licenciado Polo, as the recitation of their deeds was an important part of the cult of these ancestors. Pachacuti's mummy was found in Tococachi in Cuzco, guarded and well cared for (Sarmiento de Gamboa cap. 47; 1960: 253); presumably the custodians carried out some of the commemorative rituals, including retelling the story of his victory over the Chancas. Even after this date, the popularity of depictions of Chañan Cori Coca, a supernatural heroine of the Chanca War, on wooden cups and in paintings attests to the vitality of at least part of the tradition (Jorge Flores Ochoa, personal communication; see also Flores Ochoa 1995; Damian 1995: 127). Perhaps the dwindling population of nobles found refuge in their oral tradition and in painted images that depicted a time when their ancestors bested any enemies who dared to invade their homeland.

Variation in the Remembrance of History

The histories of the Incas written down by Spanish chroniclers have a remarkably similar structure: They include a succession of stories about individual rulers. Each includes scant detail about the boyhood of the prince but fairly rich description of the rituals of accession and subsequent military campaigns and victory celebrations. The stories generally end with the death rituals of the king, sometimes followed by a listing of the descendants of the king or his properties. It is likely that most of these individual stories were based on *cantares* of the ancestors who were remembered by the *panacas* of the dead kings, supplemented at times by bureaucratic detail and, for the latest rulers, eyewitness accounts. Still, though the histories were based on formalized narratives—narratives that were maintained by a relatively small number of surviving nobles—there are many discrepancies among them. It is interesting to explore some of the sources of variation among the chronicles that tell of Inca history. (An alternative explanation of the variation is offered by MacCormack 1991: especially 80–138.)

Cieza de León encountered variation among the traditions reported by living informants but attributed it to the lack of an unambiguous system of recording history:

> Como estos yndios no tienen letras, no quentan sus cosas sino por memoria que dellas de hedad en hedad y por sus cantares y quipos: digo esto, porque en muchas cosas varían, diciendo unos uno y otros otro. (Parte II, cap. LII; 1985: 150)

> Because these Indians lack writing, they record their history only by memorizing events from the past and in their *cantares* and in their *quipus*. I say this because in many cases they offer varying accounts, some saying one thing and others another.

Another kind of variation among the histories reflects the perspectives of different protagonists in those histories. Murúa comments on the relationship between the narratives of the Inca kings and those of other valiant individuals. After presenting his history of the ruling Incas, which he collected from "elderly Indians, with their *quipus* and their memories" (cap. 86; 1964, vol. 2: 3), he turns to the lives of nobles who did not succeed to the throne but who were valiant in war, "whom the Indians still memorialize, telling of the things worth remembering and which they celebrate among themselves, with no less energy and pleasure than they do for their kings" (cap. 86; 1964, vol. 2: 3).

There were also varying traditions held by people from different regions. Cieza, for example, notes differences of opinion about Inca history among people from other provinces but defers to the stories he heard from nobles in Cuzco for his own history of the Incas (parte II, cap. XLI; 1985: 121). Garcilaso was aware of competing provincial traditions, particularly concerning matters of history and conquests. In the interest of preparing a complete history of Inca life, he wrote to his old mestizo schoolmates whose mothers came from different provinces to solicit their memories of the stories they had heard from their mothers' families so that they could be included in his chronicle (parte I, lib. I, cap. XIX; 1609: 18 r.).

Other variants reported by Spanish chroniclers center on the legitimacy of rival claims to the throne. Such accounts are framed in terms of the pedigree of the claimant's mother: whether she was a legitimate wife, and, if not, how highly ranked she was. For example, varying assertions about the status of the mother of Huascar and the mother of Atahuallpa appear in different stories about the brothers, a point to be more fully explored in chapter 4. Pro-Huascar stories assert that his mother was a legitimate, if secondary, sister-wife of Huayna Capac (see, e.g., Murúa cap. 38; 1962, vol. 1: 105; Guaman Poma ff. 111, 113; 1980, vol. 1: 91, 93; Cieza parte II, cap. LXX; 1985: 202), while anti-Huascar stories claim she was a low-ranked noblewoman of Hurin-saya moiety (see Betanzos parte I, cap. XLVI; 1987: 194). Stories that promote Atahuallpa's cause identify his mother as a noblewoman of Cuzco's Hanansaya moiety (Betanzos parte I, cap. XLVI; 1987: 194; Sarmiento cap. 63; 1960: 265), while his enemies asserted that his mother was a provincial from Cuzco at best or a woman from the northern frontier at worst (e.g., Garcilaso parte I, lib. IX, cap. XXXVI; 1609: 258 v.; Zárate lib. I, cap. XII; 1947: 473; see also Cieza parte II, cap. LXX; 1985: 202).

Reconciling Inca Histories: Two Rhetorical Strategies

While a number of chroniclers acknowledge variation among Inca histories, they rarely do more than suggest that there are rival stories in circulation. In two cases, we can discern the writer's rhetorical strategy and how that strategy influenced the way he contended with rival versions and variants in the oral tradition. It is useful to consider the accounts of Inca history by Pedro Sarmiento de Gamboa, written around 1572, with that of Juan de Betanzos, written between 1551 and 1557.

Achieving Consensus: Pedro Sarmiento de Gamboa's
Historia índica

Of all the Spanish chroniclers, Pedro Sarmiento de Gamboa is the most straightforward about his relationship to his informants and their relationship to the histories they presented. Sarmiento was commissioned by Viceroy Toledo to write a general history of the Incas, a task which he must have found frustrating when he realized that his Inca informants did not share the Spanish penchant for composing a unitary, general history.

In telling readers how he researched his work, Sarmiento takes issue with those who assert the Incas had no history because they lacked a tradition of writing. He had great respect for the ability to record historical information on knotted cords. Sarmiento comments with admiration on the way in which histories were passed from father to son, noting that

> Y así cada uno a sus descendientes iba comunicando sus anales por esta orden dicha, para conservar sus historias y hazañas y antigüedades y los números de las gentes, pueblos y provincias, días, meses y años, muertes, destrucciones, fortalezas y cinche. Y finalmente las cosas más notables, que consisten en número y cuerpo, notábanlas, y agora las notan, en unos cordeles, a que llaman quipo. (Cap. 9; 1960: 212)

> Each one of his descendants kept the record in the established order, in order to preserve his history and his deeds and the antiquities and the number of people, towns, and provinces, the days, months, and years, the deaths, destruction, fortresses conquered, and warlords vanquished. And finally the most noteworthy things, remembered as numbers and substance, were noted (just as they are now) on cords called quipus.

In this passage, Sarmiento reminds us that history was memorized and recorded in quipus and that custody of an ancestor's history passed from father to son. His implication that the memory of an individual was to be preserved by his descendants is made clear when he says that "the true history is kept by their descendants" [quedó la verdadera memoria con sus ayllos] (Sarmiento, Fe de la prouança; 1960: 277). Such histories were certainly not general histories; they were the privileged property of the descendants of the protagonist.

Sarmiento's task of composing a general history was further complicated because these partisan histories were often in conflict with one another and balanced praise for their ayllu's founder with condemnation of the founders of other panacas. Sarmiento devised a way to cross-check the royal histories:

> saqué y recopilé la presente historia, refiriendo las declaraciones y dichos de unos a sus enemigos, digo del bando contrario, porque se acaudillan por bandos, y pidiendo a cada uno memorial por si de su linaje y del de su contrario. Y estos memoriales, que todos están en mi poder, refiriéndolos y corrigiéndolos con sus contrarios y últimamente ratificándolos en presencia de todos los bandos y ayllos en público, con juramento por autoridad de juez, y con lenguas expertas generales, y muy curioses y fieles intérpretes, también juramentados, se ha afinado lo que aquí va escrito. (Cap. 9; 1960: 212)

> I collected and compiled the present history by repeating the material I had elicited from one group to their enemies, that is, the opposite faction (because here they are governed by factions) and asking each one for the history of its own lineage and that of its opposite number. And I took the histories I had collected and corrected them by talking to their opposite

numbers. Finally I verified them in public, in the presence of all the factions and *ayllus*, sworn by a judicial authority, and with expert translators, and with very careful and faithful interpreters, also sworn, and thus I perfected what I have written here.

Despite his rigorous cross-checking, Sarmiento was aware that his history was not identical to histories presented by others (cap. 9; 1960: 212), and he was careful to include a *Fe de la prouança*, written by his secretary, which included a list of his informants and the royal families to which they belonged, along with a restatement of the method used to collect the testimony (1960: 277–279).

Despite Sarmiento's attempts to reconcile variations in the histories told by royal families by cross-checking to get at the "true" story, he was too careful an historian to obviate all traces of variation; likewise, he tells us when the story he has recorded seems unusual in Inca terms or implausible given his own frame of reference or the one that he attributes to his audience.

For example, in recounting the life of Mayta Capac, the fourth Inca (cap. 17; 1960: 221–223), Sarmiento presents the tradition that the young Inca had a supernatural birth and childhood, an account that he clearly does not find entirely convincing as history. In order to present the story, he likens the strange birth and youthful deeds of Mayta Capac to those of Hercules, familiar to his Spanish audience. He then grounds his account of the miraculous conception in its universal acceptance by descendants and others:

dicen estos indios de su linaje y todos los demás en general que su padre, cuando lo engendró, era tan viejo y sin virtud natural, que todos le tenían por inútil del todo para generación, y así tuvieron por cosa de maravilla que engendrase. (Cap. 17; 1960: 221)

the Indians of his lineage and everybody else say that when he sired him, his father was very old and without natural virtue, and that everyone thought he couldn't procreate. Thus they considered it a miracle that he fathered the child.

This is a theme he repeats when he describes the preternatural growth of the prince:

afirman todos que de a tres meses que su madre se hizo preñada, lo parió y nació con dientes, y rebusto, y que iba creciendo tanto, que de un año tenía tanto cuerpo y fuerzas como otro de ocho y aún más, y que siendo de dos años peleaba con los muchachos muy grandes y los descalabraba y hacia mucho mal. (Cap. 17; 1960: 221)

they all agree that after a three-month pregnancy, his mother gave birth to him. He was born with teeth and was strong, and he grew so quickly that in a year he had the body and strength of a boy at least eight years old. At the age of two he fought with much bigger boys and beat them and did much mischief.

Sarmiento then reaffirms that this story, although it seems more akin to the *fábulas* of the Indians, is believed as so true that his informants would kill anybody who said it wasn't (cap. 17; 1960: 221).

Similarly, Sarmiento warns us that the story of the life of Yahuar Huacac (cap. 20; 1960: 224–226) is unusual because it details the childhood of the king. He proceeds to tell us a story of political intrigue involving the Incas and two rival groups, the Ayarmacas and Guayllacanes, whose dispute over marriage rights culminated in the abduction of the prince. Sarmiento then interjects that there is another version of the account of the prince's kidnapping which involves intrigue among the elite families of Cuzco:

> Otros dicen que esta traicion fué de esta manera: que como el tío del muchacho le regalase y diese muchas cosas, sus primos, hijos de Inga Paucar, tuvieron envidia y por esto trataron con Tocay Capac que se le entregarían en las manos. (Cap. 20; 1960: 225)

> Others say that the treachery happened this way: Because his uncle gave him so many nice things, his cousins, the sons of Inca Paucar, became envious, and so they arranged with Tocay Capac that they would deliver their cousin to him.

Sarmiento de Gamboa attempts to present a unitary version of Inca history, one that would support the administrative and political agenda of Viceroy Toledo, for whom the history was prepared. Toledo would assert in his *informaciones* that the Incas were an upstart government, with legitimate kings for only two generations (*Informaciones de Toledo*; Levillier 1940). In the letter to King Philip of Spain introducing his work, Sarmiento echoes the sentiment that the Incas deceived the Spaniards into thinking they were legitimate kings and the local *curacas* the natural lords of their people, when, in fact, the Incas were "inhuman tyrants" and the local lords given power only during Topa Inca's reign (1960: 198). In the histories he shaped, he includes comments that support the point of view that the southern Andean region was ruled by *sinchis*, or warlords, prior to the time of Inca rule (see especially his comment on Chuchi Capac, the Colla lord; cap. 37; 1960: 242), and he is happy to include stories of fratricide and succession disputes (see especially cap. 50; 1960: 274–275). But despite the attempt to frame the history as the viceroy wanted, he presents the stories he heard from the noble informants of Cuzco, and they do not entirely provide support for Toledo's claims. Certainly they do not support the view that there was consensus among Inca informants on what happened in their past. Perhaps this is why Sarmiento's history remained unpublished until the beginning of the twentieth century.

A Purely Partisan View: Juan de Betanzos' *Suma y narración de los incas*

As Sarmiento discovered, Inca informants giving their stories to Spanish writers presented narratives of the glorious deeds of their ancestors that were, in essence, family traditions, used in partisan ways to exalt the prestige of their lineage. A clear example of the presentation of a partisan history comes from the account of Juan de Betanzos. Betanzos, married to Doña Angelina (known before Conquest as Cusirimay Ocllo), presents an account of events in the lives of Huayna Capac and Atahuallpa that is far more detailed than that of most other chroniclers, largely because he had access to informants from his wife's family and, as he was fluent in Quechua, could collect their histories directly from them, rather than working through translators as Sarmiento did. Intercalated with the histories of Pachacuti, Topa Inca, Huayna Capac, and Atahuallpa is the story of Doña Angelina's patriline. As presented by Betanzos, the men of his wife's family were practically kings: Her grandfather, Yamqui Yupanqui the elder, is a grand conqueror and is chosen by his father, Pachacuti, as his own successor. But in view of his own advancing age, he cedes the position to his brother, Topa Inca. His own son, also named Yamqui Yupanqui, is given a position of overseeing the royal herds which parallels the position of overseer of the Sun's herds that is given to the young Huayna Capac. The younger Yamqui Yupanqui's son, Cusi Yupanqui, and daughter, Cusirimay Ocllo, are similarly favored by Huayna Capac: The son is given custody of Caccha Inca, a statue carried into battle, and the daughter is betrothed to Huayna Capac's son, Atahuallpa. Later, Cusi Yupanqui serves as Atahuallpa's trusted assistant, overseeing the slaughter of nobles loyal to Huascar's cause and ultimately spiriting Atahuallpa's body toward Quito. A leitmotif in the stories Betanzos presents is that members of the glorious lineage served their kings loyally and came quite close to ruling in their own right: Yamqui Yupanqui the elder places the *borla* on Topa Inca's head; at his death, Topa Inca places a *borla* on Yamqui Yupanqui's statue.[4] Cusi Yupanqui places the *borla* on Atahuallpa's head and, it is intimated, would probably have been crowned as his successor had Rumiñahui not killed him out of jealousy. But for the arrival of the Spaniards, Cusirimay Ocllo would have consummated her marriage to Atahuallpa and been the mother of the next Inca.

The presentation of this history gives us insight into the way that Inca royal families were organized and the way that the histories they presented reflected that organization. In Betanzos' overall history of the Incas, it is clear that his informants have but the dimmest memory of or interest in any of the Incas between the founding ancestor, Manco Capac, and Pachacuti. By contrast, they provide rich detail from what must have been a *cantar* of Pachacuti's life and similarly present rich but somewhat formalized detail on the lives of Topa Inca and Huayna Capac (see the comments by Hamilton, "Introduction" to Betanzos 1996: xi). On the life of Atahuallpa, there is again a great deal of detail, but it seems anecdotal; at times Betanzos is presenting competing eyewitness accounts of the life and death of that last autonomous Inca king.

Doña Angelina's family traced their descent from Pachacuti and from one of his sons who presumably was part of his father's descent group, Iñaca *panaca*. It is likely that members of their family would have known the *cantares* of Pachacuti's life and, perhaps, performed them in the rites surrounding the upkeep of his mummy. But Doña Angelina's branch of the family descended not through Topa Inca and Huayna Capac but through two Yamqui Yupanquis who were important in their own right. The formalized stories of the deeds of their family's immediate ancestors suggests the possibility that the informants were presenting family *cantares* about their illustrious but nonruling ancestors. The stories of the Yamqui Yupanquis, elder and younger, overlap the stories of Topa Inca and Huayna Capac because their interactions with these kings were demonstrations of the family's prestige. The stories her relatives tell about the lives of Topa Inca and Huayna Capac can also be seen as the histories of their immediate ancestors, whose luster came in part from their association with the two great kings.

The anecdotal quality of the stories having to do with Atahuallpa's life may reflect, in part, Betanzos' own conflicted loyalties about the horrific events that took place at the end of the Inca civil war and the beginning of the Spanish regime: In telling the story of the Spanish conquest of the Andes, should he identify with his compatriots, who deceived and butchered Atahuallpa's party in Cajamarca, or with his in-laws, who slaughtered Huascar's in Cuzco? As Betanzos reiterates in the letter to Viceroy Mendoza that accompanied his work, "I write here to state the facts since I am under orders to translate what used to happen" (Betanzos, *Prologue*; 1996: 4). The narrative strategy he uses in the part of his history that deals with events in Cajamarca is based on alternating chapters, showing the Inca and Spanish points of view on the pivotal events in the conquest of the Incas. I would surmise that there were few Incas left in Cuzco willing or able to prepare *cantares* that formalized the life of Atahuallpa. In any event, he left no descent group in Cuzco whose duty would have included preserving his memory. It is for these reasons that we have only eyewitness testimony to report his history in Betanzos' otherwise pro-Atahuallpa version of the Inca civil war.[5]

The version of royal history that Betanzos presents glorifies the family of his wife. The story of Yamqui Yupanqui the elder is surprisingly similar to the story told about Amaro Topa Inca by Sarmiento (caps. 42–43; 1960: 246–248) and Pachacuti Yamqui (1968: 300). Yamqui Yupanqui and the other brothers are also mentioned in the chronicles of Murúa and Cabello Balboa.[6] In Sarmiento's history, Amaro Topa Inca is the older son and designated heir of Pachacuti who marries a full sister but ultimately does not become king. Amaro Topa Inca's existence and prominence are attested by the fact that he held a great deal of property in and around Cuzco and that both he and his wife are associated with shrines on Cuzco's official devotional system (Niles 1987: 19–20). His importance as an ancestor is shown by the fact that eight men claimed to be his grandsons in 1569 and joined in a petition of the other men of Capac Ayllu seeking restoration of lands to the *ayllu* on the basis of descent from this great conqueror (Rowe 1985b).

Amaro Topa Inca does not appear at all in Betanzos' chronicle, nor does Yamqui Yupanqui appear in the 1569 petition listed among the brothers who were the grandfathers of the men of Capac Ayllu. If he was indeed as accomplished and loyal a son of Pachacuti and brother of Topa Inca as Betanzos' account would suggest, Yamqui Yupanqui's children might well have been incorporated into Capac Ayllu, as were the children of Amaro Topa Inca and Topa Yupanqui. I suspect that Betanzos' informants appropriated the story that other chroniclers attribute to the life of Amaro Topa Inca because there was no one around to argue against them. Capac Ayllu (the *panaca* that included all the descendants of Topa Inca and his brothers Topa Yupanqui and Amaro Topa Inca) took Huascar's side in the Inca civil wars. All the adults of the *ayllu* and the women married into it were killed by Atahuallpa's generals; if we believe Betanzos, this act of slaughter was overseen by Yamqui Yupanqui's grandson. One goal of Inca reprisal against traitors was to wipe out the living members of a family and to destroy all memory of that family's name by erasing the history borne by the living and manifested in the dead mummy of its founder (see, e.g., Atahuallpa's threat to the translator who seduced his wife, Betanzos parte II, cap. XXVI; 1987: 284). In the case of Capac Ayllu, it seems, Yamqui Yupanqui's descendants took this one step further by appropriating part of the slaughtered family's history and making it their own.

I assume here that the appropriation of the story was done by his informants, rather than by the Spanish chronicler. Betanzos had every reason to glorify his wife's lineage, as he needed to establish her right to property that came to her due to her descent from Inca royalty.[7] Her rights were not critical in 1551 when he began to write the history but became so a few years later. In 1558 Betanzos launched a claim on his wife's behalf (Rostworowski 1962: 143–151) for land near Yucay—a claim certainly motivated by the imminent departure of Sayri Topa Inca from the jungle and the promise by the viceroy that control of the lands would become his as last heir to the Inca empire. In the legal documents, Doña Angelina presents a different history of her family. Several of the informants are prompted to tell that the lands she sought are hers by right as heiress to the natural lords, specifically naming Topa Inca and Mama Anahuarque as her ancestors. In fact, the lands in question belonged to Huayna Capac (they are part of his estate near Yucay, which will be explored in chapter 6), and even Betanzos' glorified history of his wife's family did not claim she was descended from Topa Inca or that he was married to Mama Anahuarque. Still, neither Betanzos nor his wife corrected their witnesses, and the petition sped through the courts. I assume that by claiming right to the land through descent from Topa Inca (even though other documents make it clear he never owned these lands), Doña Angelina felt she could trump Sayri Topa's claim to legitimate ownership by a generation, as his claim was based on descent from Huayna Capac (who had, in fact, owned the properties). In the alternative, it may be that Betanzos had enough friends in high places so that any more or less substantiated claim on his wife's behalf was more likely to be successful in the courts than a claim by an Inca dignitary—especially one that had only grudgingly been coerced to leave his forest capital-in-exile.

The way that Betanzos presents the narratives of Inca kings and nobles reminds us that ultimately they were individual and partisan stories. Where Sarmiento was frustrated in his attempt to write a unitary history by the varying opinions of his informants, Betanzos did not do this because his informants (presumably a smaller set) did not have a full history to give him. Still, there are hints that, long before Conquest, Inca kings intervened to regularize stories of their people's past and, perhaps, to edit out the personages or events that did not support their own agenda.

Reshaping History

We often think of the Spanish writers reshaping Inca narratives to fit a model of dynastic succession and linear history that was more at home in the European than in the Andean tradition. But it is important as well to consider the ways in which the Incas themselves revised the history that told of their people. Because histories were privileged, there were perforce rival ways in which the larger history of the Incas may have been reported or remembered. We have several references to the attempt by individual rulers to reshape the history of their people.

Sarmiento asserts that Inca history was regularized by Pachacuti, who brought expert historians into his presence, had them tell the stories of the past, and then painted some of the histories on tablets, placed in the Temple of the Sun, which were then used to transmit the histories of these *ayllus* (cap. 9; 1960: 212; *Fe de la prouança*; 1960: 279) and which formed the body of knowledge transmitted by certain experts (cap. 9; 1960: 212). Betanzos, too, tells a story of Pachacuti rearranging the mummies of the ancestral kings to place them in chronological order and appointing custodians for them. At the same time,

> mandó a estos mayordomos e a cada uno por sí que luego hiciesen cantares los cuales cantasen estas mamaconas y yanaconas con los lores de los hechos de cada uno destos señores en sus días ansi hizo los cuales cantares ordinariamente todo tiempo que fiestas hubiese cantasen cada servicio de aquellos por su orden y concierto comenzando primero el tal cantar e historia e loa los de Mango Capac e que ansi fueron diciendo los tales mamaconas e servicio como los señores habían sucedido hasta allí adelante para que de aquella manera hubiese memoria dellos e sus antigüedades. (Parte I, cap. XVII; 1987: 86)

> he ordered each of these custodians to compose *cantares* which would be sung by the *mamaconas* and *yanaconas* to tell of the praiseworthy deeds each lord had carried out when he was alive. They performed these *cantares* every time there was a festival, each in order, beginning with the *cantar* and history and praise story of Manco Capac. And so the *mamaconas* told what the lords had done from then onward, and in this way the memory of their lords and their ancient times would be known.

This conscious revising of history is in keeping with Pachacuti's other actions as reported in his own histories: He is portrayed as reformer of ritual, reshaper of the landscape, and organizer of the royal families of Cuzco. By organizing the histories that told of ancient dignitaries, whether real or mythical, he further legitimized his own claim to rule, as well as his claim to the cultural and physical superiority of his people, by extending the Inca pedigree into the mythical past. The proof of their pedigree was the spoken history and its physical manifestations: the tablets in the Temple of the Sun, the mummies or *huauques* of his predecessors, and the places associated with their actions that he ordered to be included on Cuzco's devotional circuit.

It is possible that Atahuallpa, too, hoped to rewrite Inca history.

The rather problematic *Relación de quipucamayos* includes this claim as part of its statement of legitimacy:

> con la venida de Challcochima e Quisquis, capitanes tiranos por Ataovallpa Inga que destruyeron la tierra, los cuales mataron todos los quipocamayos que pudieron haber a manos y les quemaron los "quipos", diciendo que de nuevo habían de comenzar (nuevo mundo) de Ticcicápac Inga, que ansí le llamaban a Ataovallpa Inga. (Callapiña, Supno y otros 1974: 20)

> with the arrival of Chalcochima and Quisquis, Atahuallpa Inca's tyrannical captains who destroyed the world, they killed all the *quipucamayos* that they could get their hands on and burned all the *quipus*, saying that everything should start over with Ticcicapac Inca, as they called Atahuallpa Inca.

We do not know how Pachacuti or Atahuallpa may have revised history, though there are a few hints from the Spanish accounts. One way in which the Incas reshaped their history is to exclude parts of it from Inca historical performance. For example, Pachacuti Yamqui tells us of the singing of the praise songs of war at the death of Viracocha Inca, but he also tells us that was unusual: Relations had ruptured between Viracocha and his son, Pachacuti, who had usurped power after the Chanca War. Viracocha was allowed to live out his life in exile, but at his death, Pachacuti did not mourn. Rather, he celebrated the death of the old man by ordering his soldiers to group up in military formation (Pachacuti Yamqui 1968: 299). The soldiers, in full military dress, sang a war song and beat slowly on drums. However, the relatives and wives of the dead man said that Pachacuti was really singing songs of joy and celebrating the death of his father, and they arranged a counterdemonstration of their grief. Pachacuti mocks the women for their expressions of grief, confronting his father's wife: "Oh, my mother! Such love you have for my father! You have cried well; and when you die, who will cry for you this way?" (Pachacuti Yamqui 1968: 299–300).

In this passage, Pachacuti attempts to supplant the performance of his father's history with the story of his own military victory. The unflattering image of Pachacuti presented in this account suggests that it may have been elicited from what Sarmiento calls "the enemy band," that is, from historians not of Pachacuti's descent group but rather, most likely, of his father's. There could have been little love lost between these two *ayllus*, as Pachacuti not only usurped rule from his father but also banished him from Cuzco. Nonetheless, his descendants did preserve the stories of Viracocha's life, and there certainly were flattering accounts of it in circulation which were presented by some of the chroniclers. Such was not always the case for disgraced royals. The life of Inca Urcon is a good example.

There are several accounts of the life—and, especially, the death—
of Inca Urcon. The chroniclers who mention him agree that he was a
son of Viracocha Inca but differ on the closeness of their relationship.
Some accounts assert that he was the first son and designated heir
(Cieza parte II, cap. XLIII–XLIV; 1985: 127–131); others claim that he
was an illegitimate son (Pachacuti Yamqui 1968: 296) whose mother
was from Ayauilla (Sarmiento cap. 24; 1960: 229). Sarmiento states
flatly that "although the descendants of Inca Urcon say he was legitimate, everybody else says he was a bastard" (cap. 24; 1960: 229). The
more flattering accounts mention that he was in charge of military
conquests for his father, noting that he was responsible for a number
of successful campaigns (Murúa cap. 87; 1964, vol. 2: 5; Pachacuti
Yamqui 1968: 296). Most of the accounts concur that Viracocha Inca
had earmarked him as his successor; some suggest that Inca Urcon
actually had assumed rule while his father was still alive (Cieza parte
II, cap XLIV; 1985: 129; Pachacuti Yamqui 1968: 296; and see Betanzos' account of Viracocha according Inca Urcon all the perquisites of a
ruling Inca, parte I, cap. VIII; 1987: 31–32).

While the chroniclers agree that Inca Urcon's death was linked to
the circumstances of the Chanca War, they disagree on exactly how.
Most suggest that there was a dispute over succession between Pachacuti and Inca Urcon, focused on the latter's cowardly actions in the
Chanca War, and that Inca Urcon was killed. The site of his death is
usually singled out as Cache, in the Yucay Valley, where one of Pachacuti's captains saw to it that Inca Urcon was killed in battle (Murúa
cap. 19; 1962, vol. 1: 46; cap. 87; 1964, vol. 2: 6). One account tells that
Pachacuti's other brother, Inca Roca, pitched him into the river and
that he was finished off by others loyal to Pachacuti (Sarmiento cap.
33; 1960: 238). In a unique version of the story, Pachacuti Yamqui
claims Inca Urcon was killed by a Collasuyu captain named Yamqui
Pachacuti prior to the Chanca War, but that on the conclusion of that
war, Pachacuti personally thanked the Collasuyu captain for his action
and honored him by taking his name (1968: 296–297).

Clearly, there were several vital, and quite different, versions of the
Inca Urcon story in circulation at Conquest. Cieza, the only chronicler
to give a full account of the life of Inca Urcon as a ruler, notes:

> Los orejones, y aun todos los más naturales destas provinçias, se ríen de
> los hechos deste Ynga Urco. Por sus poquedades quieren que no goze de
> que se diga que alcançó la dinidad del reyno; y ansí vemos que en la quenta
> que en los quipus y romançes tienen de los reyes que reynaron en el Cuzco
> callan éste, lo qual yo no haré, pues al fin, mal o bien, con viçios o con vir-
> tudes, governó y mandó el reyno algunos días. (Parte II, cap. XLIV; 1985:
> 129)

> The *orejones*, and, for that matter, all the other natives of these provinces laugh at the actions of Inca Urcon. Due to his inadequacies they don't want to admit that he ever ruled. Thus we see that in the story told in the *quipus* and *romances* that tell of the kings that ruled in Cuzco they are silent about this one. But I will speak of him because, for good or bad, with all of his vices or virtues, he did govern the realm for a few days.

Cieza concludes his discussion by saying: "I have nothing further to say about Inca Urco, because the Indians never talk about him except to laugh at him" (parte II, cap. XLVI; 1985: 136).

In the stories told about Inca Urcon, we have a case of a man written out of history. While he is remembered by his descendants,[8] others, presumably accepting the revised history of the Incas promulgated by Inca Urcon's victorious brother, omit the story of his rule (if, indeed, he ruled) and have nothing to say about him.

History, Remembrance, and Prestige

The reshaping of history by the *panacas* of Cuzco was more than an exercise in the management of reputation. For the Incas, the deeds of an ancestor were related to the prestige accorded his living descendants, and prestige could be marked in tangible ways. We have many accounts of the relationship of remembrance and prestige to property rights. Perhaps the clearest demonstration of the relationship among history, remembrance, and prestige comes from documents used to support claims for rights and property made by Colonial Inca dignitaries.

The first document is a *probanza* dated 1569 that inventories the military victories of Topa Inca and his brothers (Rowe 1985b). The *probanza* verifies that historical records were kept on *quipus* and shows that they were used to support a family's claim to privileges. In that year, the men of Capac Ayllu, descendants of Topa Inca and of his brothers, Amaro Topa Inca and Topa Yupanqui, prepared a petition to be granted properties that had been lost to their *panaca*. The request was based on their claim that their grandfathers had conquered vast parts of the Andes; for their glorious deeds, their descendants should receive some of the property they had lost in the Inca civil war and in the Spanish war of conquest. The *memorial* that they prepared in support of their cause reflects its incorporation on a *quipu*, which was organized by *suyu* (quadrant of the Inca empire), with pendant cords for provinces in each quarter of the empire which were conquered and subsidiary cords naming the fortresses and enemy kings vanquished (Rowe 1985b: 197). The resulting text does little more than inventory the conquests in a set order. The minimal narrative that is provided can be interpreted as set phrases to explain the conquest or as detail on the location of fortresses for a Spanish audience that would not know Andean geography (Rowe 1985b: 197–198).

In the Colonial Period, members of the Inca royal families and other dignitaries used or created histories to validate their pedigrees and to seek perquisites afforded them as nobles or notables. In addition to the *probanza* launched by the men of Capac Ayllu, for example, there was a narrative purporting to be based on the testimony of four elderly *quipucamayos* which was tailored by a priest, "Fray Antonio," to glorify the family of Paullu Inca. The document was almost certainly used by his son, Don Melchor Carlos Inca, to seek a grant from the Spanish court (Callapiña, Supno y otros Khipukamayuqs 1974; see also commentary on the document by Duviols 1979; Rowe 1978: 84–85; and Urton 1990: 43–46).

The interest in proving pedigrees led to many strategies for representing them in ways that the Europeans would understand. A claim for exemption from tribute as native nobles was prepared by provincial elites from Pacarictambo in 1569 (Urton 1990, see also the document in his Appendix: 129–140) in Andean narrative form which framed a European-style pedigree that would prove noble descent from both the father's and the mother's *ayllus*. In 1603 a number of the surviving Inca nobles commissioned a genealogy to be painted on a panel of silk which they hoped would be used to prove their descent from Inca royalty so that they would be granted exemption from tribute (Garcilaso parte I, lib. IX, cap. XL; 1609: 263 r.).

These and other examples suggest that Andean dignitaries saw clearly the link between their family history and access to property and prestige. While the presentation of their pedigrees in written court documents and in painted genealogies may have been a post-Conquest invention,[9] the use of narrative histories to exalt an ancestor's name and thus to enrich his descendants has deeper Andean roots.

Betanzos' account of Huayna Capac's accession suggests that the *cantar*, or praise-narrative, and the bureaucratic accounting both had a place in pre-Conquest royal succession and in royal ritual (parte I, caps. XL–XLI; 1987: 179–183). Shortly after he assumes the throne, Huayna Capac sends his accountants out to the provinces to figure the census and tribute and then installs new governors in the provinces on the basis of this accounting. He then goes to the Temple of the Sun along with his cousin Yamqui Yupanqui and his governors (or regents), Lord Hualpaya and Lord Oturunco Achachi, to get an accounting of the Sun's property. The fidelity of the overseer of the Sun is rewarded, as is the care with which the *mamaconas* have served the Sun. Betanzos implies an on-the-spot accounting of the property in the presence of highly placed witnesses—and witnesses who could be

held accountable, as regents or cogovernors, had shortages appeared—that culminates in the granting of people (*mamaconas* and *yanaconas*) and goods dedicated to the Sun.

After seeing to the provisions of the Sun, Huayna Capac proceeds
to an accounting of the goods that belonged to his dead ancestors
because

> quería ver y visitarlos y saber de qué manera se desprendían los bienes de
> los tales bultos y de qué manera se les hacían los sacrificios todo lo cual
> hecho y aderezado el Ynga comenzó a tomar cuenta a los que ansi tenían
> cargo e administración del servicio y destos bultos y comenzó a visitarlos y
> verlos desde el bulto de Mango Capac hasta el de su padre Topa Ynga Yu-
> pangue que era el postrer señor que a lo sazón había muerto. (Betanzos
> parte I, cap. XLI; 1987: 182)

> he wanted to see and visit [the dead lords and their custodians] and know
> how the goods that belonged to the dead lords were being used and how
> the custodians were carrying out the sacrifices [to the dead lords]. And
> when everything was ready, the Inca began to take an accounting from ev-
> eryone who was in charge of the service and of the *bultos* of the dead lords.
> And he began to visit and inspect the *bultos*, from that of Manco Capac
> through that of his father, Topa Inca Yupanqui, who was the last lord to
> have died.

As he inspected the mummies, he granted them additional *mamaconas*,
yanaconas, clothing, and gold and silver serving vessels, "and he ordered that as he was entering into the things that belonged to each
lord that their *mamaconas* and servants should sing his history and tell
of his past deeds" (Betanzos parte I, cap. XLI; 1987: 182).

Clearly, the accounting involves an inventory of property, of rituals,
and of the deeds of the dead lords. When Huayna Capac came to the
house where the mummy of his grandfather Inca Yupanqui (Pachacuti) was displayed, "seeing in the *cantar* of his history the great deeds
he had done and the large herds of this lord, he spent a month there
making great festivals and sacrifices to the image of his grandfather
Inca Yupanqui" (Betanzos parte I, cap. XLI; 1987: 182). In honor of his
great history, Huayna Capac dedicated more *mamaconas*, *yanaconas*,
and property, singling out the Soras, Lucanas, and the Chancas of Andahuaylas to serve the mummy as the first peoples conquered by his
grandfather. He then proceeded to the mummy of his uncle Yamqui
Yupanqui and, hearing the *canto* of his accomplishments, granted him
property in Vilcas. He finished at the house of his dead father, where
again he spent a month listening to the formal performance of his history and carrying out sacrifices in his honor. The ceremonial nature of
the accounting of the dead is implied by the amount of time spent with

some of the mummies (one month each for Pachacuti and Topa Inca), as is the fact that Huayna Capac is receiving formal instruction in the history of his ancestors. The passages also make an explicit comparison between praise and property and remind us that in the pre-Conquest Andes, exalting the name of the ancestor could have important repercussions for the material well-being of his descendants.

Conclusion

Inca praise-narratives, devised by his descendants to report the life of a king at rituals important to his descendants and to other members of the royal families of Cuzco, represent a privileged and idealized version of historical events. They are examples of propaganda that shaped a religious and historical reality to achieve a particular end. When they were elicited and recorded by Spaniards, the narratives were reshaped to support their recorders' own agenda.

The shaping of historical events into formalized praise-narratives that in turn were used in partisan ways leads to difficulty for modern readers in discerning the true events through the Inca propaganda. Another level of difficulty is imposed by the Spanish chroniclers, who often did not understand the language and in any event, whether or not they understood Inca history, wished to tailor it to its intended audience. Regrettably, they weren't writing for the anthropologist or historian of the twentieth century but usually for an ecclesiastical or administrative officer. But it is not impossible to use these narratives to explore Inca history.

Understanding the partisan nature of the presentation of their histories helps us at one level to see how the Incas gave shape to the past. In order to consider how Andean people composed their histories, it is important to be able to discern the Inca narratives within the Spanish ones. In the next chapter I will address some of the stylistic devices used by Inca historians to create the narratives that constituted the formal histories of their kings.

2

STRUCTURING
REMEMBERED HISTORY

As we have seen, accounts of Inca history written by Spanish chroniclers give us some insight into the performance of histories by the Incas. It is important, too, to consider the narrative strategies used by Inca historians as they created the stylized narratives that would be performed. Surely they chose to edit the content, selecting some episodes from the lives of the protagonist and omitting others. Because in most cases we cannot check the formalized histories against data derived from other sources, we can only suggest by comparison among royal histories the kinds of episodes that were an expected part of these narratives. We can also discern some of the stylistic conventions by which Inca historians composed and recalled these histories. Fundamentally, the Inca royal histories were works of oral literature: They are not dry recitations of historical fact but intentionally composed elaborations of it, incorporating music, poetry, and metaphor. By identifying ways in which histories were remembered, we might notice these strategies in the narratives as they are restructured by chroniclers coming from a different literary tradition.

Shaping Remembered History

The Spanish chroniclers, encountering examples or reports of Inca narrative performance, likened them to their own familiar genres of literature and folklore. Bearing in mind Garcilaso's interest in crediting his Inca forebears with a literary tradition at least as exalted as that of the Spaniards he hoped to impress, he does offer some useful comments on literary devices. He reports that the deeds of Inca kings were rendered in blank verse, likened by Garcilaso to the Spanish *redondilla* (parte I, lib. II, cap. XXVI; 1609: 52 v.). Noting the relationship of verse to music, he says that "love poems had short lines so that they could be more easily played on the flute" (parte I, lib. II, cap. XXVII; 1609: 52 v.). He also reports:

> Las canciones que componian de sus guerras y hazañas no las tañian, porque no se auian de cantar a las damas, ni dar cuenta dellas por sus flautas, cantauanlas en sus fiestas principales, y en sus victorias y triunfos en memoria de sus hechos hazañesos. (Parte I, lib. II, cap. XXVI; 1609: 52 v.)

The songs they made to tell about their wars and their deeds were not played on instruments, because they shouldn't be sung to ladies, nor should they be played on flutes. They sang them at their principal festivals and in their victory celebrations and triumphs held to commemorate their noteworthy deeds.

This latter comment contrasts with descriptions offered by Betanzos and other chroniclers that show that women were active participants in the performance of victory celebrations.

In addition to inventorying a range of narrative forms that would validate the gentility of the Inca royal families, Garcilaso's accounts of Inca oral literature suggest that there were a number of devices that helped to structure the remembrance of history. He highlights the use of verse to record and recall parts of the history and music, or at least a beat, to facilitate its performance. He comments that memorized speeches were an important component of remembrances. Finally, he notes the structuring of *quipus'* logical categories arranged by prestige. Fortunately, Garcilaso does not stand alone in noting such narrative devices; other Spanish chroniclers report aspects of narrative performance that support his claims. Further, the texts of some of the narratives themselves permit the identification of these and other narrative devices.

Inca Poetic Conventions

Garcilaso characterizes the poetry used in royal histories as premised on meter rather than rhyme. In a handful of cases, we have Quechua text that purports to be a *cantar*. In one example, Pachacuti mandates that the wives of the lords of Cuzco come out to sing praise after the victory over the Soras peoples. The text of that *cantar*, given by Betanzos, is presented here, breaking the phrases differently:

Ynga Yupangue yndin
Yocafola ymalca
Chinboleifola ymalca
Axcoley Haguaya guaya
Haguaya guaya. (Parte I, cap. XIX; 1987: 93–94)

This verse might be translated as "Inca Yupanqui, son of the Sun, conquered the Soras and put fringes on them." The fringes here refer to the red tasseled garments worn by prisoners to humiliate them described elsewhere in Betanzos' story.

In this *cantar*, the repetition of "ymalca" gives a kind of rhyme. A poetic meter can be achieved by considering the number of syllables per line: As I have broken the lines, they have 7, 7, 8, 8, and 5 syllables. Similar principles of word or final-syllable repetition in succeeding lines is seen in Garcilaso's presentation of a long verse recorded by Blas Valera (parte I, lib. II, cap. XXVI; 1609: 53 v.), which Garcilaso likewise divides into lines of similarly numbered syllables.

Elsewhere Betanzos includes verses in Quechua in his narration of history without mentioning whether they were sung or not. One of these passages justifies the request of Inca warriors that their dead be returned to their homeland from the battlefield at Hatuncolla. Betanzos reports their belief as

> Caypacha tu coptin
> Atarixunxi llapanchic
> Runa caurispa aichantin
> U manamcuna canchic. (Parte I, cap. XX; 1987: 101)

which can be translated as "When this world comes to an end we will all rise up with life and with this flesh as we are now" (Betanzos chap. XX; 1996: 94). In this passage we see, again, syllables providing the meter (6, 8, 8, 7) and lines that use end-rhyme in an A B A B pattern.

As a final example, Betanzos uses a repeating phrase in Quechua to illustrate Pachacuti's choice of a successor: "Caiñoc aprandicanga / Caiño caprandicachun" (parte I, cap. XXVII; 1987: 131), which I translate: "This one will take my place; may this one take my place." In this passage the two lines are nearly identical but for the end, which conveys the tense of the verb phrase.[1] In this case the meter is based on phrases of seven syllables, with the rhyme being formed not at the end of the word but at the beginning.

The incorporation of these Quechua texts in Betanzos' narrative perhaps reflects the structure of at least parts of the original. Betanzos was fluent in the language, having served as an official translator. There are parts of his own chronicle where the texts he records from his informants seem to be directly translated from the Quechua. Betanzos does not tell us why he chooses to include these passages and not others in Quechua; perhaps he was struck with the beauty of the verse. It is worth noting that all of Betanzos' examples of poetry come from the account of the life of Pachacuti. There is other internal evidence to suggest that his account follows the text of an Inca *cantar* of Pachacuti's life quite closely, and it is likely that he was faithfully presenting portions of the text as he heard them.[2]

Music

Music was a part of some historical performances. Many of the chroniclers, in choosing familiar Iberian models for Inca narratives, describe them as a *canto*, *cantar*, or *cantar y loa*. In some cases, they may be using the terms to describe poetry; in others, it is clear they refer to songs, for they tell us of some of the variations that exist in the musical performances, depending on the subject matter and context of the *cantar*. For example, Sarmiento and Betanzos both tell of Pachacuti singing after a deathbed oration. Sarmiento tells us that the song was sung "in a low and sad tune" (cap. 47; 1960: 252) in Quechua, which he translates:

> Nací como lirio en el jardín,
> y ansí fuí criado,
> y como vino mi edad, envejecí,
> y como había de morir, así me sequé y morí. (Cap. 47; 1960: 252)

> I was born like a lily in the garden,
> and thus was I raised,
> and as I aged, I grew old,
> and as I must die, thus I dried up and died.

Betanzos provides us with a parallel text described as Pachacuti's deathbed *cantar*, which he tells us was still being sung in his day by that lord's descendants. The text, which he presents only in Spanish, reads:

> Florecía como la flor del huerto
> hasta aquí he dado orden y razón en esta vida y mundo
> hasta que mis fuerzas bastaron
> y ya soy tornado tierra. (Parte I, cap. XXXII; 1987: 149)

> I have thriven like a flower in the garden until now;
> I have given order and reason in this life and world
> until my strength was depleted.
> And now I am returned to earth.

The existence of these two texts not only verifies that a *cantar* tradition existed, it also confirms Garcilaso's comments on the importance of short verses in the Inca narrative tradition. Although Sarmiento and Betanzos offer different translations of their text, it seems likely that they are two verses from the same *cantar* or that they are alternative translations of the same verse.

The triumphant melody of the *cantar* of victory contrasted with the dirgelike melody of songs of mourning or defeat. Recall that at his funeral, Viracocha's body was carried through the streets of Cuzco by his son's warriors, who sang a *canto de guerra* as they played the drums slowly. The bad blood between Pachacuti and his dead father, however, made Viracocha's descendants accuse Pachacuti of "cantando alegrías" instead of mourning their relative (Pachacuti Yamqui 1968: 299). By contrast, at his own death, Pachacuti's life was commemorated with mournful dirges that recounted his deeds and feats (Cabello Balboa cap. 18; 1951: 337). A dirgelike melody was also used for a *cantar* that commemorated the slaughter of Inca nobles orchestrated by the lord of the Island of Puná (Cieza parte I, cap. LIII; 1986: 173).

Melody was also used in certain phrases within a narrative. It is not possible to tell from the descriptions whether a repeating melody was used like a refrain within a chanted or sung performance or whether the melody constituted a sung refrain within a prose narrative, as in the European *cante fable* tradition. Cabello Balboa describes the celebratory rituals that followed Pachacuti's punitive expedition against the Chancas. The captured enemies are ordered to lie face down, and Pachacuti steps on them "while they sang a refrain that translates, 'I tread on my enemies'" (Cabello Balboa cap. 15; 1951: 305).

Speeches

There is abundant evidence from the Spanish records of Inca history that speeches were an important part of the royal narratives. The Inca language had no way of indicating indirect discourse, so it is probable that the original narratives incorporated a good deal of speech.[3] As reworked in Spanish, however, some Inca speeches are rendered into indirect discourse.

A brief illustration of how this occurs comes from Guaman Poma's presentation of an Inca war song. In Spanish, he describes the punishment of traitors: "they were punished by making a drinking cup from their heads, necklaces from their teeth, flutes from their bones, and drums from their skin" (Guaman Poma f. 34[316]; 1980, vol. 1: 287). By contrast, the Quechua passage that he presents obeys the conventions for Inca poetry, that is, it is short, told in the first person (here plural), and with all lines end-rhymed:

> Aucap umanuan upyason
> Quironta ualcarisun
> Tullunuan pincullusun
> Caranpi tinyacusun
> Taquecusun. (Guaman Poma f. 34[316]; 1980, vol. 1: 287)

The Inca text might be translated: "We will drink from the enemy's skull, we will wear necklaces made of his teeth, we will play the flute on his bones [and] the drum on his hide, and we will dance." The presentation of a Quechua verse juxtaposed with Guaman Poma's Spanish description of the subject matter is suggestive of the relationship of Inca oral text to Spanish written text in the chronicles. Writing in Spanish, Guaman Poma describes what the text is about; in the Quechua passage, which presumably was from a story or song that he had heard, the singer or teller is proclaiming what the victors will do to the enemies. This passage shows a shift in person (Spanish: *they* made drinking cups of the skulls of traitors vs. Quechua: *Let us* drink from the skull of the traitors), and a shift from description to direct discourse.

Evidence that direct speech is part of an Andean narrative tradition comes from the way that texts in the Inca language are incorporated into the Spanish-language chronicles. In some cases small utterances are included as terms of address or pieces of praise. Cieza de León, for example, tells that after the death of Topa Inca, Huayna Capac was hailed by the people of Cuzco:

> "Guaynacapa Ynga çapalla tuquillata oya" que quiere dezir: "Guaynacapa sólo es el rey; a él oyan todos los pueblos". (Parte II, cap. LXII; 1985: 179)

> "Guaynacapa Ynga çapalla tuquillata oya," which means: "Huayna Capac alone is king; all people listen to him."

It is illustrative to see how different sources handle the matter of speeches. For example, there is an incident from the life of Pachacuti where he names Topa Inca as his successor. In Sarmiento's version of the story, Pachacuti chooses his successor over the previously named older son, Amaro Topa Inca. The announcement of Topa Inca as his choice is presented by Sarmiento in a long speech directed by the king to his relatives (cap. 42; 1960: 247). Murúa, too, includes a speech by Pachacuti naming his successor; he delivers it first to the Sun and then to his counselors (cap. 22; 1962, vol. 1: 54).

In another case, Cabello and Murúa, basing their chronicles on a common source,[4] describe an instance in which disgruntled nobles from Cuzco decide to abandon Huayna Capac and his army in Tombamba. The story unfolds in speeches by the rebel leader to Huayna Capac, by Huayna Capac to the rebel captain, and ultimately by the statue of Mama Ocllo to the rebels (see Murúa cap. 34; 1962, vol. 1: 90–93; Cabello Balboa cap. 22; 1951: 371–376). Though both chroniclers use direct speech in their presentation of the story, the speeches they present differ in their length and, to a lesser degree, their content. It is reasonable to assume that the lost common source included direct discourse in this scene, but the Spanish writers evidently did not feel compelled to present a word-for-word speech, as Garcilaso's account of Inca narratives might suggest would be the Andean way to tell the story.

The accounts of the Chanca War illustrate the way in which reported speech is used in the overall narrative structure, at least in the stories as reported by the Spanish. The story is presented in its greatest complexity in the accounts of Sarmiento (caps. 26–29; 1960:

230–235) and Betanzos (parte I, caps. VI–X; 1987: 23–47), which must have been told by informants sharing the same version of the life of Pachacuti Inca. Shorter versions of this narrative are presented by Pachacuti Yamqui (1968: 295–297) and by Cieza de León (parte II, cap. XLV; 1985: 132–134). The stories told by Cabello Balboa and Murúa differ in their presentation of some of the episodes (Cabello Balboa cap. 14–15; 1951: 296–312; Murúa cap. 19; 1962, vol. 1: 44–47).

In the accounts of the Chanca War, speech is used to propel the action. As reported in its most complete versions, there are a number of episodes involving many changes of venue and of characters. The Chancas come toward Cuzco; Viracocha Inca flees the capital; the prince, Inca Yupanqui, determines to stay in Cuzco; the Chanca captains make their demands known to Viracocha Inca and to Inca Yupanqui; Viracocha (and, in some versions, the lords of nearby towns) refuses to send help to Inca Yupanqui; Inca Yupanqui petitions a deity and speaks with the apparition; the Chancas are repelled and retreat to regroup; Inca Yupanqui informs his father of his success; Inca Yupanqui wins a second battle against the Chancas; in the aftermath of the victory, Inca Yupanqui assumes the throne, banishes his father from the capital, and defeats a brother who disputes his claim to the throne.

The setting changes from Cuzco to Viracocha's retreat above Calca, to the Chancas' camp where they prepared to fight, and to the battleground itself. In some versions of the story, the matter of the change of setting is handled by visits from messengers or from main characters in the story who deliver speeches from characters at one place to characters at another. For example, before the first battle, the Chanca captains send a messenger to Viracocha Inca asking him to surrender (one version reported by Sarmiento), telling him that Inca Yupanqui is planning to fight rather than surrender (Betanzos), or in order to negotiate (Cieza). Elsewhere in the story messengers or the protagonists themselves plead with Viracocha Inca to support Inca Yupanqui's stand (Betanzos) or to celebrate his victory in the first battle (Betanzos, Pachacuti Yamqui, Sarmiento). Visits also appear in Betanzos' accounts of Inca Yupanqui's attempts to gather the support of local lords for his stand and in their subsequent support of his victory.

The stories of the Chanca War nicely validate Garcilaso's claim that speeches of historical importance were committed to memory. The speeches included in the narratives also give immediacy to the action: Tellers can propel the story by shifting the scene of the action and using direct assertions, thus avoiding the distancing from verifiable truth that is implicit in the reportive marker that would have been used for descriptive passages in the original stories.[5]

The Deathbed Oration

A special kind of speech that is frequently incorporated into Inca royal narratives is the deathbed oration. Perhaps the best passage showing the relationship of a Quechua text to its Spanish paraphrasing comes from Betanzos' account of the imminent death of Pachacuti. Like Sarmiento's parallel account, Betanzos' story includes a speech made by the dying king. This story includes a very long episode based on Pachacuti's preparations for his death (Betanzos parte I, caps. XXIX–XXXI; 1987: 137–148). Pachacuti gathers his counselors to repeat instructions for his succession and to arrange the marriage of his daughters. He then mandates the rituals that are to take place upon his death and the sacrifices that are to mark the *purucaya* held on the anniversary of his death. Throughout these chapters, Betanzos describes Pachacuti's actions in Spanish, using the third person and past and subjunctive tenses:

> la cual fiesta mandó que le hiciesen en la ciudad del Cuzco y por otra parte y la cual fiesta estuviesen un mes y la cual hiciesen los señores y señoras del Cuzco en esta manera. (Parte I, cap. XXXI; 1987: 145)

> he ordered that they observe that celebration in the city of Cuzco and elsewhere, and that the festival should last a month and that the lords and ladies of Cuzco should carry it out in this manner.

Betanzos goes on to detail the elaborate rituals that are set out for the *purucaya*, including the costumes, the sacrifices, and the dances that are to be done, followed by a long passage that begins, as does most of his description, in the third person:

> y mandó Ynga Yupangue como esto acabasen que fuesen a lavar todos del luto que ansi tenían puesto todo el año. (Parte I, cap. XXXI; 1987: 146–147)

> and Inca Yupanqui ordered that once the ceremony was completed they should all go to wash away the signs of mourning they had worn all year.

As his narrative continues with the list of offerings that are to be part of the ritual, Betanzos slips into the first person and the future tense, taking the perspective of Pachacuti setting out the order for the ritual:

> y traerán luego allí mil ovejas vestidas con sus vestimentas de todos colores y allí en aquel fuego me serán sacrificadas y luego traerán otras dos mil ovejas sin vestimenta las cuales serán allí degolladas y a mí ofrecidas y carne destas será repartida entre todos los de la ciudad que por mi han hecho sentimiento . . . y esto hecho todo mi servicio de oro y plata será metido debajo de tierra conmigo y en mis casas y todo mi ganado y depósitos será quemado en las partes do yo le tuviese diciendo que todo iba con él y que aquello acabado estas fiestas ya acabadas el nuevo señor hiciese de su

cuerpo un bulto y lo tuviese en su casa do todos le reverenciasen y ado-
rasen. (Parte I, cap. XXXI; 1987: 148)

and they will then bring a thousand sheep dressed in garments of all
colors, and they will be sacrificed to me in that fire, and then they will
bring another two thousand sheep without garments, which will be
slaughtered there and offered to me, and the meat of these animals will be
divided among all citizens who grieved for me . . . and when this is done,
all my plates of gold and silver will be placed below ground with me and in
my houses, and all my livestock and storehouses will be burned wherever
they are, saying that everything went with him. And once that was done,
the rituals were over. The new lord should make of his body a statue and
put it in his house where everyone should worship him.

In most of the chapter, Betanzos' description of an Inca death ceremony replaces Pachacuti's prescription for the ceremony. In contrast
to other chroniclers who report the obsequies of Pachacuti but place
the rituals, appropriately to Spanish sensibilities, after the death of
that king (see, e.g., Murúa cap. 22; 1962, vol. 1: 55; Sarmiento cap. 48;
1960: 253–254), Betanzos places the description of the ritual before
the death. There is no stylistic reason for Betanzos to include the passage he did in the first person. This chapter shows Betanzos' sloppy
editing, fortunately for us, because it allows us some insight into the
way Inca historical narratives were told.

Betanzos is echoing his informants in this passage rather than
paraphrasing their performance. It seems reasonable to assume that
the rest of Pachacuti's deathbed speech, elsewhere presented as description by Betanzos, was his rephrasing of the informants' telling of
the episode in the first person, as Pachacuti's words. Such a stylistic
convention makes a good deal of sense when we think of the Incas' attitude about their kings. In this narrative Pachacuti, the great religious
and social reformer, takes credit for devising a ritual. The pomp of
royal ritual life is presented in the description of the *purucaya* ritual.
Further, the focus of the *purucaya*, the soon-to-be-dead Pachacuti, is
present in the narrative: He organizes the ritual. For people who expected that their dead ancestors would continue to intervene in their
world, this is a wonderful narrative solution to the problem of how to
describe a ritual. Not only does the leader not cease to exist, but his funeral takes place (at least in the story) before his death. With every telling, the king is brought back to life, and the ritual dispatching his soul
is held again.

The oration by a dying Inca king is a convention we see in other
presentations of the royal histories; indeed, Garcilaso calls it "the
usual discourse which the Inca kings were accustomed to give instead
of a will" (parte I, lib. VIII, cap. VIII; 1609: 206). For example, Sarmi-

ento's life of Pachacuti, similar in many ways to Betanzos', though abridged, includes the disposition of his property, instructions to his successor, ordering arrangements for his funeral and *purucaya* ritual, and, finally, the deathbed song (cap. 47; 1960: 252–253). Topa Inca is described as calling his counselors to Chinchero when he feels that he is mortally ill so that he can make arrangements for his death rituals and his succession. In Sarmiento's short rendition of the episode, he addresses his counselors to announce his impending death and to name his successor (cap. 54; 1960: 258). In Betanzos' longer version of the episode, the dying king names Huayna Capac as his successor, charges his son and a nephew with certain religious obligations, and appoints regents to help his young successor rule; he concludes with a brief charge that his counselors should look after his widow and should carry out his *purucaya* celebrations (parte I, cap. XXXVIII; 1987: 175–177). Cieza alludes to a deathbed oration (parte II, cap. LXI; 1985: 177), while Garcilaso includes a didactic speech instructing the successor to govern well and similarly cites this king's "sententious sayings" (parte I, book 8, cap. VIII; 1966: 496–497).

Most versions of the life of Huayna Capac include a dramatic deathbed selection of an unfortunate heir (Sarmiento cap. 62; 1960: 264; Betanzos parte I, cap. XLVIII; 1987: 200; Cieza parte II, cap. LXIX; 1985: 199–200). Garcilaso's version of the deathbed testament includes instructions for the disposition of his body and a spurious prophecy about the arrival of the Spanish (parte I, lib. IX, cap. XV; 1609: 241 r.–v.; he also cites López de Gómara for this latter point; cf. Cieza parte II, cap. LXIX; 1985: 200 on this prophecy). In the story told by Murúa and by Cabello Balboa, Huayna Capac also spends his last minutes setting out the order for the triumphal procession of his body, its retinue, and the victorious warriors from Tomebamba to the Inca capital (Murúa cap. 39; 1962, vol. 1: 107–111; Cabello Balboa cap. 24; 1951: 393).

A final example of a deathbed oration comes from Titu Cusi Yupanqui's account of the death of his father, Manco Inca, in his jungle stronghold. Betrayed by Spaniards he had befriended some years earlier, he is stabbed and, in his son's account, lives for three days after the attack. On his deathbed he addresses his captains, asking them to care for and obey his son Titu Cusi Yupanqui, and then addresses the son, asking him not to surrender to the Spaniards and giving him charge of his family and his subjects (Titu Cusi Yupanqui 1992: 60–62). Although the account was set down nearly forty years after the Spanish Conquest, the presentation of the story obeys many of the conventions of Andean historical narratives, appropriate for a narrator who maintained his opposition to European values.

Repetition

Repetition occurs as a narrative device in several ways in the Inca histories. Repetition may occur within a narrative, such as the story of the Chanca War, in which phrases or sequences of actions are repeated in different contexts. In addition, a narrative may describe an action or address that is repeated several times, for example, when variations on the deathbed speech are directed to different audiences. It is worthwhile to consider some examples of repetition in the narratives to see how the Incas present it and how the chroniclers handled the matter as they rewrote the Andean narratives to suit Iberian taste.

In some cases we are told that an Inca story includes repetition, but the chronicler declines to include it in the written account. For example, Pachacuti Yamqui gives an account of the attempt to usurp power from Huayna Capac that was spearheaded by his uncle Hualpaya. The plot is revealed to another uncle in a vision; this uncle immediately calls a council of authorities to tell them of his vision, "and he reported what had happened, telling them everything, and they made him repeat it three times" (Pachacuti Yamqui 1968: 306). Pachacuti Yamqui mentions the fact of repetition and presents abbreviated reactions to each of the three reports: The advisors first say that Hualpaya's minions should be taken secretly, then they say that the captains should be seized, and finally they report that fifty men should be sent out as spies.

In other cases, we are given more detail on repetition. Betanzos describes a rebellion of the Collasuyu provinces that occurred during Pachacuti's reign in which Ruquicapana, a dignitary from Hatun Colla, began declaring himself son of the Sun (parte I, cap. XX; 1987: 100). Pachacuti calls together the nobles of Cuzco and tells them that he plans to marshal forces against the Colla upstart and that he wants to send messengers to tell the provincial administrators to call up troops. The messengers arrive and are given the message; then the messengers depart and deliver the message. Betanzos repeats parts of the message, telling us at one point that the messengers were sent out to carry the mandate "that you have already heard" [que ya habeis oído] (parte I, cap. XX; 1987: 100). This is Betanzos' standard phrase to tell readers that he is omitting a repetition. One assumes from his recounting that the Inca original included three slightly differing presentations of the same message: once in an address to the nobles, once to the messengers, and once as given by the messengers to the provincial administrators.

Just as speeches can be repeated, so can actions. Betanzos gives an account of Topa Inca's response to another Collasuyu uprising. He ul-

timately raises an army for this campaign and to keep order in Chinchaysuyu and Antesuyu provinces (parte I, cap. XXXI; 1987: 155–156).
When the troops arrive in Cuzco, he divides them into groups and dis-
patches one group to Chinchaysuyu and one group to Antesuyu; the
rest go with him to Collasuyu. As the narrative is repeated, the troops
included in each group are described, as are their selection, separation,
and departure. The rituals that follow successful military campaigns
are often described in the narratives as having a repeating sequence of
actions, a point that will be explored in a succeeding chapter.

 In light of Garcilaso's comment that administrative *quipus* were organized using logical categories that ranged from noblest to least noble, one might wonder if, in complex narratives, the ordering of passages followed some similar logic. In fact, the texts of some narratives
do suggest that incorporating prestige categories might have been
part of the strategy used in reporting Inca history. The arrangement is
related closely to the device of repetition, where certain phrases or
passages are presented with slight variations within a complex narrative. As will be shown, the order of the repetition does, in some cases,
relate to Inca prestige categories.

For example, Cabello Balboa describes the festival held to celebrate
the Inca victory over the Chancas, noting: "Each one went along singing of the deeds the king had done, and then the deeds of the captains
and commanders, and finally his own, adding lies and fables in the
telling of the verses" (cap. 15; 1951: 305–306). The repetition implied
by the account includes noblest (the deeds of the king), less noble (the
deeds of the captains and commanders), and least noble (the soldier's
own deeds). Cabello does not repeat the full story but summarizes it,
noting that the account included the tripartite structure.

In another case, Pachacuti Yamqui describes the review of the victorious troops entering Cuzco from the first northern campaigns as they
pass before the triumvirate:

> & en donde Pachacutiyngayupangui sienta con su hijo Topayngayupangui,
> y Amaro Ttopaynga, todos tres con iguales *tiyanas* de *ruua*, hechas de oro;
> todos los tres vien bestidos con sus *capacllaottos y mascapachas*, y el viejo con
> su septro de *suntorpaucar*, hecha de oro, y el Topayngayupangui con su sep-
> tro de *ttopayauri*, y el otro sin septro, sólo con *cambis* pequeños de oro.
> (1968: 302)

> [and they pass by where] Pachacuti Inca Yupanqui sits with his son Topa
> Inca Yupanqui and Amaro Topa Inca, all three on equal thrones made of
> gold; all three well dressed in their fringes and headdresses, and the old
> one with his *suntur paucar* scepter made of gold, and Topa Inca Yupanqui
> with his *t'opa yauri* scepter, and the other without a scepter, but with small
> swords of gold.

Although Pachacuti Yamqui does not present separate descriptions of the review of the troops by each of the witnesses, the order in which they are mentioned and the attributes each is given suggest they were seated in order from noblest (the reigning king), to less noble (his designated successor), to least noble (the successor's brother).

In some cases the relationship of prestige to the repetition of the action is obvious, as, for example, in the accounts of the toppling of forts, the victory parades from different provinces, and the ordering of rituals and military pageants. In other cases, the relationship of prestige categories to a threefold repetition is not obvious. It is interesting, though, that the repetition so often occurs three times. Perhaps Inca auditors liked the drama of repetition and expected that incidents would be repeated three times. It is also possible that such a stylistic device may have served as a formula which facilitated the remembrance of the narratives.

Metaphors and Refrains

Just as ancient Greek epics include familiar phrases and the Norse *eddas* use kennings as conventional metaphors to refer to things, the versions of the Inca narratives that have come down to us include certain repeated phrases or actions that may have filled analogous purposes. Warfare and victory pageants are frequent subjects for the narratives, and perhaps it is not surprising that these activities seem also to have inspired some of the Incas' most colorful imagery. A reading of the chronicles reveals a number of motifs that appear with some frequency and that must have referred to Inca practices. Their repetition certainly serves to punctuate the stories and to define episodes in them.

TURNING THE ENEMY INTO A DRUM   There are many references in their narratives to the victorious Inca celebrating his success by making a drum with the skin of an enemy captain. One example of a war song that promises to use a traitor's hide for a drum was presented elsewhere in this chapter in the discussion of Guaman Poma's conversion of Inca direct discourse into indirect speech. As will be explored in the next chapter, making war trophies of the body parts of their enemies was a practice by which the Incas made history visible. In the narratives, though, the reference seems to be used as a way to bring closure to the story of a battle and to end an episode. It may also have served as a validating motif to assert that the drum actually used in Cuzco for a particular festival, whose beat was heard by the auditors of the history, was made of an enemy vanquished in a battle far removed in time or space.

TREADING ON THE BOOTY   In Inca military victories, the symbolic affirmation of victory and the granting of credit for the defeat were marked by the act of treading on captured enemies, booty, or the insignia (standards, banners, emblems) of foreign armies, as Betanzos explains (parte I, cap. IX; 1987: 35). Reference to this practice appears frequently in the histories. Cabello Balboa reminds us that the phrase was sung or chanted (cap. 15; 1961: 305) within the story.

In the story of the Chanca War, much of the narrative's drama turns on Inca Yupanqui's attempts to get his father, Viracocha Inca, to step on the captive Chanca captains, their weapons, and emblems and Viracocha's insistence that his designated heir, Inca Urcon, be accorded that honor (after the first victory, Betanzos parte I, cap. IX; 1987: 35–37; Sarmiento cap. 27; 1960: 233; after the second battle, Sarmiento cap. 28; 1960: 234). In that story, the request stands for the Inca victory over the Chancas and also illustrates Inca Yupanqui's fealty to his father and obedience to authority. References to treading on the booty and insignia of enemies appear in accounts of other Inca victories, among them the request by his captains that Pachacuti claim victory over the Condesuyu and Antesuyu (Betanzos parte I, cap. XIX; 1987: 95). There is an intriguing reference to Inca Yupanqui being so old and infirm that he could not stand, but still the booty from the first Quito campaign was put in front of him by his sons (Betanzos parte I, cap. XXVI; 1987: 128). On another occasion the aged man asked two of his sons to hold him up so he could tread on the booty from Topa Inca's Antesuyu campaign; he also invited another son to join him in stepping on these items (Betanzos parte I, cap. XXVIII; 1987: 136). Finally, Huascar's commemoration of his father's victories in Quito included a symbolic treading on the emblems by the principal deities and the cured bodies of two important lords; in addition, the Inca ladies who had accompanied their now-dead husbands to the war stomped on captives to mark their victory (Murúa cap. 42; 1962, vol. 1: 120).

The act of stepping on the enemies or the objects that represent them was a way to restate the relationship of conqueror to conquered and was, further, a way for the Inca captains to restate their relationship to the ruler or to the gods in whose name the victory was made. As with the reference to turning a vanquished captain into a drum, the reference to stepping on the booty often appears near the end of a war story. A short reference to the act must have recalled, to an Inca listener, the full ritual and its meaning. Its placement at the close of a war story may have provided a sung or narrative closure to the episode.

I WAS BORN FREE AND WILL DIE RATHER THAN BE SUBJUGATED Another phrase which appears in several of the histories certainly reflects an Inca sentiment and may also be based on an Inca refrain. It is articulated in a statement that a warrior facing a hopeless battle would rather die free than be subjugated. The best example of the use of this phrase in a narrative comes again from Betanzos' account of the Chanca War, where the refrain is repeated in different contexts. When the Chancas first arrive and Viracocha Inca decides to abandon Cuzco to them, Inca Yupanqui decides to stay and face the enemies with whatever allies he can find. In facing the Chanca captain, he decides "not to give in to him, and that he would die before saying that he lived in subjugation" (Betanzos parte I, cap. VI; 1987: 25). Inca Yupanqui enlists the aid of three young friends, describing his plans and telling them that they "should expect and welcome death rather than living in subjugation and infamy, as they had not been born subject peoples" (Betanzos parte I, cap. VI; 1987: 25). Later in the story, the Chanca captain sends a message to Inca Yupanqui and his friends, advising them to surrender. Inca Yupanqui responds that "he was ready to die fighting rather than be subjugated because he had been born free and was a lord" (Betanzos parte I, cap. VII; 1987: 28). The phrase recurs, with slight variations, when the prince chastises his father for abandoning Cuzco, in the speech as delivered to the father, and in the prayer offered by the prince to the creator god on the eve of battle. The fact that the phrase appears so often suggests that it was part of the original Inca text, though whether it was delivered as a speech, as a verse, or as a sung refrain is impossible to discern from the story as set down by Betanzos.

The sentiment expressed here is one that appears in other Inca histories, but in no other case is it possible to discern a fixed-phrase refrain. For example, in Sarmiento's account of Topa Inca's campaign to Collasuyu, the Collas are said to prefer to die fighting rather than to surrender to the Incas (Sarmiento cap. 40; 1960: 246). In his campaign to Quito, the prince sends messengers to the local captains, advising them to surrender; they respond that they were free and did not want to serve anybody or to be tributaries (Sarmiento cap. 46; 1960: 250). In Sarmiento's report on Huayna Capac's campaigns in the same area, we are told that the Cayambis vow to die or win (cap. 60; 1960: 262). However much the phrase might have expressed the idealized sentiments of an Andean warrior, the way it is used in the narratives suggests that it punctuated the stories, serving as a conventional way to introduce episodes that culminate in battle.

PUTTING FRINGES ON THE ENEMIES A motif that appears in several accounts of Inca victories describes the enemies being made to wear long red tunics or wearing garments decorated with tassels or fringe. The practice that underlies the motif is explained by Betanzos. He tells a story about Pachacuti's treatment of the Soras captives, noting that he made them wear special long red tunics with red tassels or fringes on them as a sign of the Inca victory (parte I, cap. XIX; 1987:

93). Betanzos' story of the treatment of the Chicha captives after Amaro Topa Inca's hard-won battle similarly refers to the fringed red garments they were forced to wear (parte I, cap. XXIII; 1987: 120). Without noting the tassels, Murúa states also that after Huayna Capac's Quito campaign, the captives "wore long red tunics that reached to their feet and wore their heads uncovered, without headbands or any other headdress, the hands placed across their chests in the attitude of prisoners" (cap. 41; 1962, vol. 1: 116). Fortunately these sources give us the full explanation of the reference to "putting the fringes on the Soras" that appears as an otherwise puzzling victory *cantar* sung by the ladies of Cuzco, discussed as an example of Inca poetry (Betanzos parte I, cap. XIX; 1987: 93).

The presence of the abbreviated reference in the *cantar* itself reminds us that the fringing of captives was well-enough understood so that a short reference to it in a narrative or in a *cantar* could bring to mind the action and its meaning to auditors.

Genre, Text, and Performance

Working through the Spanish reports of Inca historical performance and their attribution of genre terms, it is difficult to reconstruct those aspects of performance that might allow us to characterize Inca historical genres. It is clear that in likening the Inca texts to their *cantar*, the Spaniards were commenting on narratives that, in at least some cases, were based on poetry and in some on song. Some of the performances involved dance, and others surely included prose recitations. Finnegan's discussion of the gradation of performative and textural modes in oral literature (1992a: 139) reminds us that even if the *cantar* represented a single genre, it may well have involved a rich and varied texture which is all but lost in the accounts of the texts and their performance that we have.

Nor do we know how Inca historical narratives were composed or performed. If, as may have been the case for some histories, the skeletal facts were recorded mnemonically on *quipus*, much would have been left to the memory and creativity of the composer or reciter of the narrative. Alternatively, the complex stories may have been memorized—in whole or in part—and recited by experts. Ascher and Ascher suggested that formulas for narratives could have been stored on *quipus*, facilitating the telling or creation of the history by a *quipucamayo* (1981: 75). I have suggested some of the textual evidence that recurring metaphors, prosody, and patterned repetition may have been part of the structure of the narratives, perhaps to make them more elegant or accessible as oral literature or perhaps to facilitate their remembrance. Reports of the shrine system of Cuzco and the accounts of

Inca death commemorations, to be discussed in the next chapter, bring to mind the importance of points on an historicized landscape in inspiring the recitation of stories, none of which, regrettably, are preserved. Because the Inca texts have come to us only through translation, and incompletely, it is not possible to comment more fully on structure or its meaning to the composers of the narratives or to their performers or audience.

While we can only speculate on why such devices as repetition, rhythm, and traditional metaphors appear in their narrative histories, it is intriguing to offer some speculations. The Inca repetition of narratives (or rituals) in threes has an analogue in the traditional narrative expectations of Euro-Americans familiar with fairy tales, where sequences of events often repeat three times (Propp 1965). Further, Dundes has argued that a culture can have a propensity for a number which might underlie not just its narratives but other aspects of it as well, and that the number might be subject to analysis in its own right (Dundes 1980). Because the Inca narratives purport to describe activities that took place, it is not possible to tell whether the structure seen in the stories is a narrative device or whether it reflects events that unfolded in real time. For example, when we read that in certain battles the army made three attempts to conquer a fort or that the army was divided into three parts to surround and conquer an enemy, are we seeing conventional narrative representations of the actions of conquest in terms of prestige categories (*collana, payan, cayao*), or did the Incas in fact formalize or ritualize actions that are reported more or less faithfully in their accounts? While there is no definitive answer to this question, it is interesting to contemplate the possibility of the underlying structures of both history and the remembrance of history.

Conclusion

We have considered the way in which Inca oral literary devices helped to shape events into narrative histories which were remembered, repeated, and performed. It is also important to consider other ways in which the Incas gave shape to their history. In the next chapter I turn to the ways in which historical events were made tangible and visible in rituals and monuments.

3

MAKING HISTORY VISIBLE

Much of Inca ritual and architecture is intimately tied to an oral historical tradition. Places, objects, and actions become manifestations of history; as such, they are like visible etiological motifs or like the mnemonic knots on a *quipu*: An appreciation of their meaning relies on the shared knowledge of a narrative/historical reality. The performance of a ritual or action, the viewing of a work of architecture, or the experience of an important place serves to confirm the truth of the narrative and to validate its historical claims.

Ritual Performance of History

Death Rituals

The intimate tie of the narrative historical tradition to action and object is exemplified in part of the commemoration of the deaths of members of the royal families. A royal death was commemorated in several stages (fig. 3.1). To close mourning and dispatch the soul of the departed, the one-year anniversary of the death was marked by the performance of an elaborate ritual known as the *purucaya*.

In part of the ritual, the relatives of the deceased made pilgrimages to the places the person had visited in life and to the properties the person had owned. The places they visited and objects they carried with them were used to spur the recounting of the deeds of the person. We have several generic reports of this ritual, including mention by Pedro Pizarro (cap. XII; 1986: 70) and Bernabe Cobo:

> Salía todos los días el acompañamiento bailando con atambores y flautas y cantando con sones tristes, y daba vuelta por todas aquellas partes por donde el difunto solía en vida festejarse más a menudo, diciendo en sus cantares todas las cosas que le sucedieron siendo vivo, remontando sus proezas y hazañas, si fué valiente, y cuanto hizo digno de memoria y fama, para mover a llanto a los circunstantes. (Lib. 14, cap. XIX; 1964: 274)

> They went out every day dancing, playing drums and flutes, and singing in sad tones. And they went around to all the places where the dead person had gone to enjoy himself most often during life, telling in their *cantares* all the things that happened to him in life, recounting his actions and deeds, if he was brave, and all the actions that contributed to his reputation, so that they would all cry.

FIGURE 3.1. Guaman Poma's depiction of an Inca mortuary ritual shows men and women at the site of a tomb, preparing drinks and offerings of corn beer (f. 287 [289]; 1980: 262).

For the death of a king, the mourning lasted longer, but again,

> Visitaban los lugares donde solía ir a sus recreaciones, llevando sus deudos en las manos los vestidos y armas del difunto, diciendo en las endechas y cantos tristes las hazañas que con ellas había hecho, y las victorias y trofeos que había alcanzado, refiriendo sus loable costumbres, sus virtudes y liberalidad para con todos. (Cobo lib. 14, cap. XIX; 1964: 274)

> They visited all the places where he was accustomed to go for his enjoyment, carrying in their hands the clothing and weapons of the deceased, recounting in their dirges and sad *cantos* the deeds that he had done with those things and the victories and trophies that had been his, referring to his praiseworthy habits, his virtues, and his liberality with everyone.

Betanzos describes in some detail the kind of performance Cobo mentions, noting that it took place on the one-year anniversary of the death as a prelude to the *purucaya* ritual. He presents it as one of the customs prescribed by Pachacuti for his own death ceremonies and to be performed ever after by the Incas.[1] In the steps of the ritual outlined in this narrative, the actions are very clearly designed to limn out a re-membered history, using objects and places that were associated with the deceased:

El primer día que comenzasen que saliesen todos los del Cuzco hechos sus escuadrones ansi hombres como mujeres embadurnados los rostros con una color negra y que fuesen a los cerros de entorno de la ciudad e ansi mismo fuesen a las tierras do él sembraba y cogía y que todos ansi andu-viesen llorando y que cada una destos que trujesen en las manos las ropas de su vestir y arreos de su persona y armas con que peleaban y que llegados que ansi fuesen todos ellos en las partes do se paró y sitios do se sentó cuando el vivía y andaba por allí que le llamasen a voces y le preguntasen donde estaba y que le relatasen allí sus hechos y que cada uno dellos ha-blase con la cosa que tuviese en las manos suya que si tenía alguna cam-iseta que dijese ves aquí el vestido que te vestías y según que fuese el ves-tido que si era el que se vestía en las fiestas que ansi lo dijese y si eran armas con que peleaba que dijesen ves aquí tus armas con que venciste y sujetaste tal provincia y tantos caciques que eran señores dellas y ansi por el consiguiente le relatasen y dijesen lo que hacía cuando vivo era con cada cosa que en las manos trajese y que esto habían de hacer quince días desde la mañana hasta la noche por los cerros y tierras y casas y calles de toda la ciudad y acabado de relatar lo que ansi cada uno dijese según que lo que llevaba en las manos que le llamasen en alta voz y que a estas voces respon-diese el señor más principal de los que allí iban y que dijese en el cielo está con su padre el sol y que luego respondiesen a esta voz que acordase dellos y les enviase buenos temporales y les quitase enfermedades y todo mal que les viniese pues era en el cielo. (Betanzos parte I, cap. XXXI; 1987: 145)

[He ordered that on the first day of this commemoration] everybody from Cuzco should come out in formation, men as well as women, with their faces painted black. And they should go to the mountains surrounding the city and to the lands where [the dead lord] had planted and harvested. And everyone should walk along crying, and each should carry the clothing and ornaments that had belonged to [the dead lord] and the weapons with which he had fought. When they arrived at the places where he had stopped and the sites where he had sat in life, they should walk around cry-ing out to him aloud and asking him where he was, and [he said] that they should relate to him his deeds in that place. And each one of them should speak about the object that he held in his own hands. If he had a shirt he should say, "You see here the clothing that you wore," and if it was one he wore to festivals he should say that. If they were carrying weapons with which the dead lord fought, they should say, "You see here your weapons with which you conquered and subjugated such and such province and the however many *caciques* who were its lords." Thus they should report to [the dead lord] and tell him what he had done when he was alive with each thing they carried in their hands. This should take place for fifteen days from morning until night on the mountains and lands and houses and streets of the entire city. And when each had done telling what he had to say about the object he carried, they should cry out to [the dead lord] in a loud voice. The principal lord among them should answer them, saying that he was in heaven with the Sun, his father. And then they should answer this voice, saying that he should remember them and send them good weather and take away sickness and all evil that might come to them since he was in heaven.

In the ritual outlined in the story of Pachacuti's death, the actions (visiting places and calling out deeds) are designed not merely to repeat a history but to link past events to the life of the dead lord through the agency of the relatives who participate and the objects themselves. The places they visit and the items they carry are mnemonic devices, used, in Betanzos' account, to spur the memory of the descendants of the dead lord and thereby to build his history. The crying out of his deeds piecemeal, implied in the account, is perhaps a predecessor to the narratives that will be carefully preserved as the property of the dead man's descendants and that will be repeated on selected occasions.

The linking of a dead king's history to the sacred places described by Cobo and Betanzos may also have taken place far away from the ritually charged landscape of Cuzco. Murúa reports that when Topa Inca died, Huayna Capac marked his *purucaya* in Cajamarca, visiting all the places where his father had walked and mourning him there (Murúa cap. 30; 1962, vol. 1: 76). It would be very interesting to know whether the histories pieced together in these locations made reference to the sacred places of Cuzco or whether they focused on the campaigns carried out in the province where the ritual was conducted.

The Performance of Royal History

While some of the mourning rituals and the propitiation of shrines on *ceques* maintained by particular royal *panacas* might be seen as family histories, the tie to the shared ethnic history of the Incas was made tangible in particular ritual events. A report credited to Miguel de Estete describes the mummies of the past kings being arranged on the main plaza of Cuzco where their deeds were recounted to all present:

> En los cantares trataban de lo que cada uno de aquellos señores había conquistado y de las gracias y valor de su persona, dando gracias al Sol que les

había dejado ver aquel día, y levantándose un sacerdote amonestaba de parte del Sol al Inga, como a su hijo, que mirase lo que sus pasados habían hecho y que así lo hiciese él y que sirviese y obedeciese mucho a aquel Emperador, cuya gente les había conquistado. (Larrea 1918: 334)

The *cantares* tell what each one of those lords had conquered and speak of his kindness and his personal benevolence and valor, giving thanks to the Sun that he had permitted them to live to see that day. And, rising, a priest playing the part of the Sun addressed the Inca as if speaking to his son, admonishing him to look at what his ancestors had done and do the same and telling him to serve and obey that Emperor well whose people he had conquered.

The description notes that the festival in which these histories were performed went on for thirty days. The apparent address to a still-living Inca brings to mind Betanzos' description of Huayna Capac's preparation to assume rule in which he spent much of his time before his installation learning about the accomplishments of his ancestors. His instruction included visitation to the places where they had lived, where their stories were repeated over a period of days or weeks:

el Ynga comenzó a tomar cuenta a los que ansi tenían cargo e administración del servicio y destos bultos y comenzó a visitarlos y verlos desde el bulto de Mango Capac hasta el de su padre Topa Ynga Yupangue. . . . y mandó que ansi como fuese él entrando en las cosas destos señores que sus mamaconas y servicidores del tal señor cantasen su historia y hechos pasados y ansi como iba visitando los bultos y casas dellos como viese que le faltase alguna cosa íbasela dando y proveyendo y llegó a la de Ynga Yupangue y viendo el cantar de su historia los grandes hechos y ganados deste señor estúvose un mes haciendo grandes fiestas y sacrificios a este bulto de Ynga Yupangue su abuelo. . . . y esto hecho entró en la casa do estaba el bulto de su tío Yamque Yupangue y oída su historia en su canto y loa con mucho acatamiento le reverenció y le hizo sacrificios y proveyéndole y ofreciéndole grandes dones estuvo allí diez dias. . . . y de allí entró en la casa de su padre y en su historia y loa de su canto vio y supo sus hechos tan granados y de buen señor amigo de sujetar tierras y provincias que allí estuvo un mes haciéndole grandes sacrificios y servicios. (Betanzos parte I, cap. XLI; 1987: 182–183)

the Inca began to take account of those in charge of the service [of his ancestors] and of the *bultos*, and he began to visit them and see them, starting with the *bulto* of Manco Capac and going up to that of his father, Topa Inca Yupanqui. . . . As he embarked on learning about the deeds of these lords, he commanded the *mamaconas* and those who served them to sing his history and his past deeds. As he was visiting the *bultos* and the houses of the lords, he would see if it was lacking anything, and he would provide it. And he arrived at the house of [Pachacuti] Inca Yupanqui and seeing the *cantar* of his history of that lord's great deeds and his conquests, he passed a month in the rituals and sacrifices dedicated to the *bulto* of Inca Yupanqui, his grandfather. . . . When this was done, he entered the house where the *bulto* of his uncle Yamqui Yupanqui was kept and listened with great attention to his story in his *canto* and dirge. He honored him and made sacrifices and endowed his service, spending ten days there. From there he went to the house of his father, and in his history and *canto* he learned of his great accomplishments and of his fondness for conquering new lands and provinces. And he spent a month there making great sacrifices to him.

Perhaps as a young man about to be named Inca, it was important for a young Inca to become familiar with the glorious deeds of the Inca people and to see his own place in that history. A recounting of the praiseworthy acts of his ancestors would also serve as an additional lesson in appropriate kingly comportment. The passage seems to describe a private performance of royal history as part of the rites of accession. We do not know how such privately performed histories may have been related to the narratives that were presented in public fora.

The passage is interesting for its depiction of a context for the performance of royal histories. It also highlights quite clearly the association of the history with prestige and, more tangibly, with the material rewards of such prestige, a theme introduced in chapter 1. Huayna Capac uses his visit to his dead ancestors as an opportunity to inspect their holdings and to increase the service dedicated to them. This is a point that will be explored more fully in a later chapter. The passage is also valuable for the suggestion that women—in this case the *mamaconas* of the dead lord—were in part responsible for the performance of his history.

In addition to general references to the importance of women in maintaining the mummies of dead kings, we have a few other suggestions that women were custodians of parts of their histories. In Cajamarca, Pedro Pizarro observed that "after Atahuallpa's death . . . two sisters remained, and they walked around crying, beating drums, and singing, recounting the deeds of their husband" (cap. 12; 1986: 69–70).

Pachacuti Yamqui gives a similar report about the role of women mourning the dead Viracocha Inca. In opposition to the victory songs sung by Pachacuti Inca's male followers,

> al fin las yndias salen otra procesión todas, haziendo llantos y lloros, tresquilados y con fajas negras, y el rostro, todo hechas negras . . . y desnudas hasta medio cuerpo. . . . y otras yndias con tamborçillos pequeñuellos, y chandose con sinezas en las cabeças. (Pachacuti Yamqui 1968: 299)

> finally, all of the women went out in procession, crying and wailing, their hair shorn and wearing black sashes, with their faces [painted] black . . .

and naked to the waist. . . . and [there were] other women with tiny drums, tossing ashes on their heads.

Pedro Pizarro also points out the importance of women in the anniversary celebrations of the dead, offering this general statement:

> Era costumbre entre estos yndios que cada año llorauan las mugeres a sus maridos, y los parientes, lleuando sus bestiduras y armas delante, y muchas yndias cargadas con mucha chicha detrás, y otras con atambores teñiendo y cantando las haçañas de los muertos, andauan de çerro en çerro y de lugar en lugar donde los muertos siendo viuos auían andado, y después que estauan cansados, sentáuanse y beuían, y descansados tornauan al llanto hasta que acauáuase la chicha. (Cap. 12; 1986: 70)

> It was customary among these Indians for women to cry each year for their husbands. And their relatives, carrying their clothing and weapons before them, followed by many women carrying corn beer and other women beating drums and singing the deeds of the dead, walked from hill to hill and place to place where the dead had walked around when they were alive. When they got tired, they sat down and drank. And when they were rested, they returned to the mourning until the beer was all consumed.

When the Spaniards present histories of the Incas, the informants they name as their sources are invariably male. Surely there were men in charge of reporting aspects of official Inca history—some of those histories recorded on *quipus* and read by male *quipucamayos*. But the passages cited here make it clear that women, too, as custodians of the reputations of the relatives they mourned, also knew and performed histories in the context of death rituals. These histories were spoken and sung, punctuated by drumbeats, and they were inscribed on the landscapes in the paths they walked. The shape that they gave to those histories is now, regrettably, lost to us.

Mapping an Historical Landscape

The recounting of anecdotes, memorates, or legends at specific places brings to mind the stories told about the shrines in the ritual circuit of the Inca capital. Just as the personal relics of the dead Inca are mnemonics of his actions, so the shrines within the ritual district of Cuzco were mnemonics of Inca myth and both personal and public history. Set down in their best-known form by Bernabé Cobo, following lists made by Polo de Ondegardo and Cristóbal de Albornóz, the system included more than 340 sacred places which were organized on *ceques*, or lines, and which were given offerings by the royal families of Cuzco.[2] For many of the shrines, we are given a short legend accounting for the reason it is sacred; in other cases we are told that a legend exists, but the Catholic recorder declines to present it. For example, of the shrine Matoro (Co-7:5), sacred as the houses in which the ancestors who emerged after a flood first slept, Cobo tells us, "In this connection they allude to other absurdities" (book I, chap. 15; 1990: 75).

The shrine system was not static; rather, it appears a number of places important to his ancestors or to his neighbors were organized into a system at the behest of Pachacuti (Sarmiento cap. 37; 1964: 242). Later, his grandson Huayna Capac oversaw the revision and expansion of the system (Rowe 1980, 1985a). An inventory of the shrines associated with the life of Pachacuti stands as a striking affirmation of the actions credited to him in the narratives that tell of his life. The salient points of that history include his role in the Chanca War, his rebuilding of the Cuzco region and reformulation of its shrines, and his subsequent acts of war and civilization. Among the shrines of Cuzco are a number that affirm his life and deeds. Cusicancha, his birthplace, is a shrine (Ch-5:1), as is Tambo Machay (fig. 3.2), a house "where he lodged when he went hunting" (An-1:9; Cobo book I, chap. 14; 1990: 80). A house in which he lived, Condorcancha (Ch-3:4) is designated as a shrine, along with Coracora (Ch-5:5), a building in which he slept, Patallacta (Ch-1:2), the house in which he died, and Pilcopuquio (Ch-1:3), an adjacent fountain. The gold idol named Inti Illapa he took as his *huauque* (Ch-2:3) had a house in Totocache and was kept with his body (Cobo book I, chap. 13; 1990: 54). In his role as religious reformer, Pachacuti Inca Yupanqui designated a number of shrines around Cuzco, among them Marcatampu (Ch-7:3), Mollaguanca (Ch-3:6), Macasayba (Ch-2:6), Rondoya (An-5:9), and Colcapata (Ch-4:4). Perhaps as testaments to his claimed resculpting of the Cuzco Valley and its provision with water, several canals and fountains were designated as shrines under his aegis, among them Viroypacha (Ch-2:4), Pilcopuquio (Ch-1:3), Quinoapuquio (Ch-3:1), and Aspadquiri (Ch-8:11). His personal encounters with the gods were marked at Cugiguaman (Ch-3:9), a "stone that had appeared to him shaped like a falcon" (Cobo book I, chap. 13; 1990: 56), and Illanguarque (Ch-8:1), a "small house . . . in which were kept certain weapons which they said the Sun had given to Inca Yupanqui; with them he conquered his enemies" (Cobo book I, chap. 13; 1990: 60). This latter legend almost certainly refers to the Chancas, the invaders who were defeated by Pachacuti and his supernatural reinforcements. This battle was commemorated in several shrines around Cuzco. A number of other shrines were *pururaucas*, stones that were the evidence of supernatural reinforcements sent by the gods to assist the Inca cause; a full discussion of these battle shrines is presented in the succeeding section.

Thus a number of the places on the ritual district of Cuzco were associated with the events that were part of the stories told about Pacha-

FIGURE 3.2. The site now known as Tambo Machay, near Cuzco, was probably Quinoa-puquiu, An-1:10, a fountain with two springs (Cobo lib. 13, cap. XIV; 1964: 175).

cuti, as reported in so many Spanish sources. Again, they serve as confirmation of the truth of the story and could well be the kind of places in which the remembrance of history, reported by Betanzos to have been decreed by Pachacuti, was repeated.

The shrine list of Cuzco includes places that are similarly associated with other members of royal families, again suggestive of the kinds of places that were remembered in their histories. For example, a pass (Ch-2:8) where Viracocha Inca rested was sanctified, as were a house (Amarumarcaguaci, An-1:7) and field (Chacuaytapara, Ch-8:5) that had belonged to Amaro Topa Inca, brother of Topa Inca; Topa

Inca himself was venerated in a house (Calispuquio Guasi, Ch-3:7). Huayna Capac was remembered at Pomacorca (Ch-3:5), a house he had owned; Cajana (Casana, Ch-6:5), his city palace; and Cugitalis (Ch-8:4), a place where he had had a dream that foretold a war. Huayna Capac had also ordered sacrifices to his mother, Mama Ocllo, at a small house where she used to sleep (Ch-9:2). This lady was also venerated at Anyapampa (Co-3:5), a field she had owned, and Ticicocha (Ch-3:3), a fountain that belonged to her. The house of Curi Ocllo, wife of Amaro Topa Inca, and its adjacent fountain were shrines (Ch-4:3), as was Pomamarca (An-6:6; figs. 3.3-3.4), the house where Pachacuti's wife's body was kept. Managuañunca Guaci (Cu-8:9) was a house that belonged to an unidentified queen, and Chamanchanca (Ch-5:8) was the tomb of a brother of Huayna Capac who had died young.

Other shrines were associated with events in the lives of Incas who are not specified, for example, Cunturpata (Cu-2:1), "a seat on which the Inca rested when he went to the festival of the Rayme" (Cobo book

FIGURE 3.3. An interior wall with fitted masonry and body-size niches from Pumamarca (Pomamarca), above San Sebastián, Cuzco, where Mama Anahuarque's mummy was kept.

FIGURE 3.4. Detail, a double-jambed doorway at Pumamarca, San Sebastiàn. The narrow opening and small jambs are characteristic of relatively early imperial Inca style.

I, chap. 16; 1990: 82); Rauaypampa (Cu-14:3), "a terrace where the Inca lodged" (Cobo book I, chap. 16; 1990: 83); Capipacchan (Ch-6:6), a fountain "in which the Inca used to bathe" (Cobo book I, chap. 13; 1990: 58); and Pacha (An-1:5) "a fountain . . . in which he washed himself a certain time" (Cobo book I, chap. 14; 1990: 63); Caynaconca (An-2:7), "a resting place of the Inca on a flat place near Tambo Machay" (Cobo book I, chap. 14; 1990: 64). Other places seem to have been important because of their association with the presence of royalty on important days, for example, Pirpoypacha (Co-3:3), a fountain "in which the Incas washed themselves on certain days" (Cobo book I, chap. 15; 1990: 71); Pomapacha (Co-4:1), "a fountain where the Incas bathed, with a house next to it into which they retired when they came out of the bath" (Cobo book I, chap. 16; 1990: 72); Sabacurinca (Ch-

5:6), a carved seat used by the Incas; and Quinoacalla (Ch-9:3), a hill where Inca nobles rested during the Raymi festival.

Such shrines, and the fact of the regular offerings made at them, confirm the existence and the importance—both religiously and historically—of members of Inca royal families. They were remembered after death at the places where they slept, farmed, rested, dreamed, drank, or lived.

In a similar way, the activities of ancestors of the Incas were commemorated at shrines. The point of emergence of the ancestors at Pacarictampu was one of the most important Inca shrines (Cobo book 13, cap. 15; 1990: 74, discussion of Huanacauri). Near the main temple in Cuzco were commemorated the first place where the ancestor Manco Capac settled (Caritampucancha, Cu-5:1), a hut that was his residence (Tampucancha, Co-6:1), and the small house where his sisters lived (Inticancha, Cu-7:1). Other shrines marked the buildings where ancestors slept after a cataclysmic flood (Matoro, Co-7:5) and the nearby fountain in which they drank (Co-7:6). A field called Sausero (Co-8:9) was used for ritual plantings and was dedicated to Mama Guaco, the sister-wife of Manco Capac and the lady who first sowed maize (Molina 1916: 86). The lives of two very early and possibly mythical Inca kings were also marked in shrines: Acoyguasi was the house in which Sinchi Roca's body was kept (Co-6:3); a prison attributed to Mayta Capac (Sancacancha, Co-8:1) was sacred, as was a seat where he planned a successful battle against enemies (Tampucancha, Co-9:1).

The Incas identified points important in the lives of both real and mythical rulers and ordered these places into a system where offerings were governed by kinship and calendrics. In this way, the Incas linked myth and history, making both real and tangible, by localizing action, event, and narrative at places on their sacred landscape. The shrines were points of remembrance of their sacred narratives—legends as well as myths—which helped to tie the Inca royal families to their remembered ancestors and to a past that they claimed to share.

Mnemonics of War

The narratives that tell of the lives of Inca kings invariably revolve around the theme of the defeat of enemies in battle. It would seem that distinguishing himself in war was the principal way by which an Inca man could achieve glory. Individual Incas took credit for the conquests they made and incorporated the stories of their victories into the chants and songs that told of their lives. The Inca narratives give great detail on the nature of military campaigns, the strategies employed, and the celebratory rituals that followed successful campaigns. Clearly, war was an endeavor important to Inca men, one that was remembered in the histories associated with the lives of kings. It should not surprise us that the oral testimony of victory is made visible in the places, buildings, and objects that served to commemorate Inca military prowess and legitimize the claims of victory.

Place and Remembrance of the Chanca War

The most explicit linking of place and military event comes from the shrines that commemorated the Inca defeat of the Chanca invaders erected by Pachacuti when he established or reformulated the shrine system of Cuzco. Cobo lists three shrines at the site of the Chanca rout: the battlefield (Cutirsaspampa, Ch-9:7), a pass (Queachili, Ch-9:8), and the spring where the victors refreshed themselves (Quishuarpu-quiu, Ch-9:9). Albornóz identifies two battlefield shrines: Omo chill-iguas (probably Cobo's Queachili), "a flat place where the Ingas had a battle with the Changas and defeated them; the Changas fled, and they say they turned into condors and escaped" (Albornóz' shrine 12; Rowe 1980: 73), and Suchique, "an altar where they sacrificed people . . . and . . . animals, in the said pampa [Oma chilliguas]" (Albornóz' shrine 13; Rowe 1980: 73). Betanzos reports on the way Pachacuti sanctified the site right after battle:

> y que en el sitio de la batalla y para que della hubiese memoria en presencia de todos los de su campo mandasen hincar muchos palos de los cuales fuesen ahorcados y después de ahorcados les fuesen cortadas las cabezas y puestas en lo alto de los palos e que sus cuerpos fuesen allí quemados y hechos polvos y desde los cerros más altos fuesen aventados por el aire para que desto hubiesen memoria y ansi mismo mandó que ninguno fuese osado de enterrar ningún cuerpo de los enemigos que ansi habían muerto en la batalla porque fuesen comidos de zorros y aves y los huesos de los tales fuesen allí vistos todo el tiempo. (Parte I, cap. X; 1987: 45)

> and on the site of the battle, in order to commemorate it and in the presence of his followers, he ordered them to erect many poles from which [the enemies] were hung, and after hanging their heads were cut off and stuck on top of the poles. Their bodies were burned and the ashes were blown into the air from the tallest mountains to commemorate the battle. He ordered that no one should bury the corpse of an enemy killed in battle, bur rather it should be left to be eaten by foxes and birds and the bones left there to be seen forever.

In addition to this treatment of the site, Cieza tells of a free-standing building erected at the battle site which he describes as

> una casa larga a manera de tanbo en la parte que se dio la vatalla, adonde para memoria fuesen desollados todos los cuerpos de los muertos y que

hinchesen los cueros de çenizas o de paja de tal manera que la forma
umana pareçiese en ellos, haziéndolos de mill maneras, porque a unos,
pareçiendo honbre, de su mismo vientre salía un atanbor y con sus manos
haziá[n] muestra de le tocar, otros ponían con flautas en las bocas. (Parte
II, cap. XLVI; 1985: 135–136)

> a long house like a *tambo* built at the site of the battle where, in memory of
> it, all the bodies of the dead were flayed and stuffed with ashes or straw so
> that they looked like people. They were placed in a thousand positions:
> Some were in the shape of a man with a drum protruding from his belly
> and with his hands arranged to play the drum; others were positioned with
> flutes in their mouths.

Especially intriguing are the references to the shrines that were *pururaucas*. These shrines were stones which were evidence of the divine
troops sent to help the Incas in battle. The origin of the *pururaucas* is
given in several versions. Some chroniclers heard that the very stones
rose up from the battlefield to join the Inca army (Garcilaso parte I,
lib. V, cap. XVIII; 1609: 116 v.); others heard that the supernatural soldiers who sacrificed themselves in battle turned into stone at death
(Cobo book I, chap. 8; 1990: 35–36; see also Acosta, lib. 5, cap. XXI;
1954: 201). Pachacuti Yamqui tells that a priest in the main temple of
Cuzco lined stones up in military formations and put weapons by
them so that they would appear to be soldiers; Inca Yupanqui, mistak-
ing them for laggard troops, urged them to rise up and follow him
into battle, which they did (Pachacuti Yamqui 1968: 296–297). Whatever their origin, Cobo reports that the *pururauca* stones were gathered
up after the battle and placed in the Temple of the Sun and elsewhere
by Pachacuti (Cobo book I, chap. 8; 1990: 35–36). The location and
description of these shrines accords with his account (table 3.1).

An examination of the location of these *pururauca* shrines shows
that they are clustered in several places (fig. 3.5). Assuming that the
starting point for the lines on which the shrines were arrayed would
have been the Temple of the Sun, we can assume that a shrine that is
the first on its line (e.g., Ch-6:1, the first shrine of the sixth *ceque* of
Chinchaysuyu) was in or near the Temple of the Sun. Such *pururauca*
shrines included Catonge (Ch-6:1), Pururauca (Ch-4:1), Sabaraura
(Cu-1:1), and Apian (Cu-6:1). Others were probably also in this general
area: Araytampu (Ch-4:1), identified as next to the house of Benito de
la Peña; and Tanancuricota (Chañan Cori Coca, Cu-8:1), which is likewise the first shrine on its *ceque*. Oman amaro (Ch-7:1) was located in
the doorway of Juan de Figueroa's house; this house would have been
near Inti Pampa, the plaza in front of the Temple of the Sun (Garcilaso
parte I, lib. VII, cap. IX; 1609: 175 v.). Albornóz' identification of the
location of Uman Amaro, clearly the same shrine, as "in the plaza"

TABLE 3.1. *Pururauca* Shrines of Cuzco

Number	Name	Description
Ch-4:1	Araytampu	"a large stone with four other small ones" (Cobo book I, chap. 13; 1990: 56)
Ch-5:3	Cuzcocalla	"A fair quantity of stones . . . all *pururaucas*" (Cobo book I, chap. 13; 1990: 57)
Ch-6:1	Catonge	"a stone of the *pururaucas*" (Cobo book I, chap. 13; 1990: 58)
Alb. 20	Catunqui	"a squadron of stones like men of war" (Albornóz, in Rowe 1980: 74)
Ch-7:1	Omanamaru	"a long stone . . . [one] of the *pururaucas*" (Cobo book I, chap. 13; 1990: 59)
Alb. 5	Uman amaro	"a stone shaped like a ninepin which was in the plaza" (Albornóz, in Rowe 1980: 72)
Co-1:1	Pururauca	"a window which opened onto the street . . . in it was a stone of the *pururaucas*" (Cobo book I, chap. 15; 1990: 70)
Co-7:2	Cotacalla	"a stone . . . which was one of the *pururaucas*" (Cobo book I, chap. 15; 1990: 75)
Co-9:2	Tancarvilca	"a small round stone . . . [one] of the *pururaucas*" (Cobo book I, chap. 15; 1990: 76)
Cu-1:1	Sabaraura	a stone; "an officer of the *pururaucas*" (Cobo book I, chap. 16; 1990: 78)
Cu-4:1	Pururauca	a stone; "on a stone bench next to the Temple of the Sun" (Cobo book I, chap. 16; 1990: 79)
Cu-5:2	Tiucalla	"ten stones of the *pururaucas*" (Cobo book I, chap. 16; 1990: 80)
Cu-6:1	Apian	"a round stone of the *pururaucas*" (Cobo book I, chap. 16; 1990: 80)
Cu-6:3	Ocropacla	"some stones of the *pururaucas*" (Cobo book I, chap. 16; 1990: 80)
Cu-8:1	Tanancuricota	"A stone into which . . . a woman who came (Chañan Curi Coca) with the *pururaucas* turned" (Cobo book I, chap. 16; 1990: 81)

must refer to the plaza of Inti Pampa rather than the main plaza of Cuzco. Other *pururaucas* must have been located near the main plaza, among them Cuzcocalla (Ch-5:3), located on a street leading to the Hawkaypata, and possibly Co-1:1, located at the site of Mancio Serra's house; Garcilaso locates this house as on the main plaza (parte I, lib. VII, cap. IX; 1609: 175 v.). Two groupings of *pururauca* stones were found in the district of Cayocachi (Tiucalla, Cu-5:2, and Ocropacla, Cu-6:3), which was to the southeast of Inca Cuzco. One *pururauca* was near the town of Quiçalla (Cotacalla, Co-7:2), also southeast of Cuzco, and another (Tancarvilca, Co-9:2) was located in the house lot of Antonio Pereira (Rowe 1980: 51), which Garcilaso places in Carmenca (parte I, lib. VII, cap. VIII; 1609: 173 r.).

These placements are in accord with some of the principal sites described in the narratives of the battles in which the Incas defeated the Chancas with the aid of the supernatural forces. Before their first battle, the Chancas camped above Carmenca (Cieza parte II, cap. XLV; 1985: 133). When they tried to invade Cuzco, they entered through

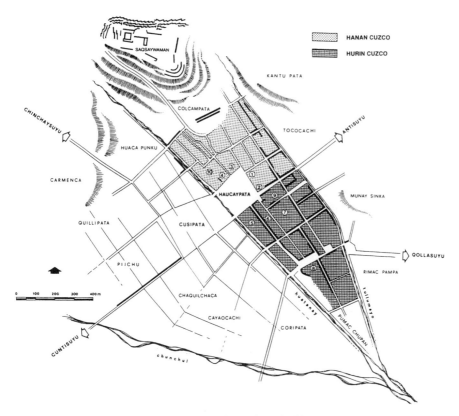

FIGURE 3.5. Plan of Inca Cuzco. Numbers that refer to buildings mentioned here include 2, Cuyusmanco; 4, Casana; 5, Amarucancha; 8, Coricancha. Reproduced from Gasparini and Margolies (1980: 46, fig. 35).

Carmenca but were repelled by twenty squadrons of previously unseen (and perhaps supernatural) soldiers that had come to the Incas' aid from Collasuyu and Condesuyu (Betanzos parte I, cap. VIII; 1987: 32–33). Chañan Cori Coca (Cu-8:1) was heroine of the battle at Choco and Cachona (Sarmiento cap. 27; 1964: 233); from these towns, one could enter Cuzco by way of Quiçalla and Cayocachi.

The shrines that commemorated the Inca victory over the Chancas—battlefield shrines and altars, buildings in which vanquished captains were displayed, the stones that were the *pururaucas*—were mnemonics of war. Their presence in the shrine system of the Inca capital would have been a constant reminder, to the Incas as well as to potential invaders, of the Inca defeat of the Chanca troops. They similarly stood as evidence of the favor of the gods who sent the supernatural aid to Inca troops in their hour of need. The *pururaucas*, especially, testified to Pachacuti's personal relationship with the Sun or with Viracocha and the fact that he won the battle, which propelled him to rule because he was favored by the gods. The placement of the *pururaucas* in the environs of the ancient capital commemorated the physical arrangement of the supernatural troops as reported in the stories of the Chanca War, both in their arrangements and in their locations. Cobo tells us that the *pururauca* shrines were given special offerings when the Incas went to or returned from war, and that when they were shown to visitors, the name and story of each of the *pururaucas* was recounted by special individuals whose job was that alone (lib. 14, cap. VIII; 1964: 162). His report reminds us that the physical evidence of the divine help (the stone) was associated with the narrative that told of the event.

The system of war shrines in Cuzco was like a *quipu*: Each shrine, like a knot on a *quipu*, could bring to mind the event that occurred in that place. The arrangement of the shrines relative to one another, like the relative positioning of knots on a *quipu* cord or of the cords on the *quipu* itself, made it possible for the full story of the divine grace that gave the Incas their victory to be recalled and repeated.

Battlefields and Body Parts

Other Inca military victories were similarly made visible in actions, places, and objects. Weapons given by the Sun and used in an Inca victory were displayed in Illanguarque, a building used when young Inca men were initiated (Cobo's Ch-8:1; Albornóz' shrine 3, Yllanguaiqui; Rowe 1980: 72). But not all displays involved Inca weapons. An important part of Inca warfare was taking distinguished captives and the weapons, standards, and insignia of the defeated armies. One of Cuzco's buildings was dedicated to the display of such treasures. Known as Llaxaguasi, this house was used for the display of weapons and insignia of defeated enemies (Betanzos parte I, cap. XIX; 1987: 96). The heads of defeated enemy captains, such as that of Chuchi Capac, a Colla rebel, were also kept there (Sarmiento cap. 37; 1960: 241).[3]

The most important enemy leaders, or, perhaps, those of whom it was most important to make an example, were turned into artifacts. The Incas made drums of human hides, which they called *runa tinya* (Guaman Poma f. 164; 1980, vol. 1: 143). Pinto, an especially brave and recalcitrant leader of the Cayambis, was killed and flayed and his skin turned into a drum; the drum was sent to Cuzco so the Incas could dance for the Sun (Murúa cap. 36; 1962, vol. 1: 98; Sarmiento cap. 60; 1960: 263). The story of his bravery is an episode of the narrative that told of Huayna Capac's hard-won conquests on the northern frontier. Similar fates befell two Colla captains at the hands of Topa Inca (Murúa cap. 24; 1962, vol. 1: 60; Sarmiento cap. 50; 1960: 255). According to Guaman Poma, the traitor Rumiñahui killed Inca Illescas, a son of Huayna Capac, and made a drum from his skin; further, his bones were made into panpipes, and his teeth were strung into a necklace (Guaman Poma f. 164; 1980, vol. 1: 143).

References to war monuments and trophies are more than a literary device used to bring closure to Inca stories of victory. A handful of the first conquerors of Cuzco were interviewed in 1572 as part of Viceroy Toledo's inquiry into Inca history. Toledo's investigator was only too happy to record evidence that the Incas had been cruel and barbarous warlords, and the old soldiers seemed similarly to relish the opportunity to tell their own stories. Alonso de Mesa reported that in order to make these drums of their enemies

> los mataua y dexaba la cabeça y los braços enteros e sacandoles los guesos de dentro y hinchiendolos de ceniza y de la barriga hazian atambores y las manos y la cabeça les hazian poner sobre el propio atambor por que en dando el viento en ellos se tañian ellos proprios. (*Informaciones de Toledo*; Levillier 1940: 200)

> [the Incas] killed them and left the head and arms intact. Removing the bones and stuffing them with ashes, they made drums of the belly. The hands and the head were placed on the drum itself so that when the wind blew, they would beat the drum made of their own body.

De Mesa also had a story to tell about his personal experience with other Inca war trophies:

> entro en una cassa y hallo una cabeça sacados los sesos dello y aforrado los cascos en oro y en la boca tenya un canuto de oro e que tomo esta cabeça y se la lleuo al marques y estando comyendo le pregunto a atabalipa que qué hera aquello y él le dixo *esta es cabeça de un hermano mio que venya a la guerra contra my y auia dicho que auia de beber con mi cabeça y matele yo a el* y bebio con su cabeça y mandola henchir de chicha y bebio delante de todos con ella. (*Informaciones de Toledo*; Levillier 1940: 200)

> [Alonso de Mesa] entered a house and found a head with the brains removed and with its skull plated with gold. There was a gold drinking straw in its mouth. And he took the head and carried it to the Marquis. As he was eating he asked Atahuallpa what the thing was. Atahuallpa told him, "This is the head of one of my brothers who came against me in war. He had said that he would drink from my head. And I killed him and I drink from his head." And he ordered it to be filled with corn beer and he drank from it in front of everyone.

The display of the trophies of war was, in some sense, the public business of royal Inca men. The trophies were stored in the building used for part of the male initiation rituals and in the fortress in a building that could only be entered by members of the Inca ethnic group. Such objects as trophy heads (fig. 3.6), drums made of a vanquished captain's skin, a drinking cup made of the skull of an enemy, or captured enemy insignia were similarly mnemonics of history, tangible reminders of the victory of the Incas as a group and of the ruling Inca as an individual.

Battlefields

In the cases of certain military victories, the Incas left a visible record of the defeat of their enemies at the site of the decisive battle. On these battlefields we see the interplay of the commemoration of an event and the employment of military strategy. As noted in an earlier sec-

FIGURE 3.6. An Inca soldier presents the head of a defeated enemy to his captain (Guaman Poma f. 153 [155]; 1980: 130).

tion, the sites important to the Inca victory over the Chanca invaders were incorporated on the official devotional circuit of Cuzco. The Chanca were the only enemies bold enough to fight the Incas near their capital; therefore, most of the other reports we have of commemorating battlefields come from the provinces. For example, Betanzos tells us the story of Atahuallpa creating a monument to commemorate his defeat of the Cañaris, who had taken his brother's side in the civil war:

> dicen que como pasase de la provincia de los cañares que fueron presos ciertos indios e señores que él mucho deseaba haber y se mandó volver con ellos al sitio do la batalla se había dado y que en un cercado que allí havía los enterrasen vivos debajo de tierra y que fuesen puestos a manera de plantas y árboles bien ansi como cuando lo plantan en los huertos e dijo que hacía sembrar aquel cercado de gentes de corazones de mala disistión y que querían ver si producían allí con sus malos frutos y obras y este cercado mandó que se llamase Collanachacara estremada sementera todo lo cual dicen haber él hecho para memoria de aquella batalla. (Parte II, cap. IX; 1987: 230)

> they say that as [Atahuallpa] was passing through the province of the Cañaris there were certain Indians and lords imprisoned there that he very much wanted to see. He ordered that they be returned to the site of the battle and that they be buried alive in an enclosure that was there, planted as if they were plants and trees in a garden. He said that he was sowing that enclosure with people with bad hearts and evil intentions and that he wanted to see if they would produce bad fruit. He ordered that this enclosure be called Collanachacra, "superior field." They say he did all of this to commemorate the battle.

Even nobles of Inca blood could become part of a battle monument. After he defeated Huascar's troops at the pass to Gampato in the north, Atahuallpa ordered the bodies of all those who had fought against him to be left on the battlefield as a monument to his victory (and, surely, as a warning to any other armies his brother might send against him). Two piles of bodies were made there: one for the nobles of Cuzco who had led the troops, and the other for the commoners who had supported them (Betanzos parte II, cap. IV; 1987: 214).

There was one civil war monument near Cuzco which commemorated the decisive battle over troops loyal to Huascar. When he was interviewed for Toledo's *informaciones*, Juan de Pancorbo recalled that when the Spanish party was making its first entrance into Cuzco, about a day's march before they reached it they saw a plain on which were set fifty or a hundred stools which had belonged to the nobles killed by Atahuallpa's general for their support of his brother (Levillier 1940: 198). Although Pancorbo is imprecise about the location of this monument, it was probably at Xaquixaguana, near the edge of the Pampa de Anta, where Huascar (who had been captured in the battle) was forced to watch the execution of the soldiers of high rank who had supported him (Garcilaso parte I, lib. IX, cap. XXXVI; 1609: 259 r.–v.). We do not know if the stools (seats which symbolized authority to the Incas) were placed there by Atahuallpa's troops to show their victory over the royal regime of Cuzco or whether they were placed there by surviving members of the royal families to commemorate the loss of their relatives.

The civil war battlefields might be thought of as a combination of keen military strategy and history in the making. There is no doubt that the frightful prospect of bodies heaped up at an important pass through the mountains would be daunting to enemies marching up from either direction, and that a field planted with their native lords may have discouraged disgruntled Cañari subjects from further subversive acts. But the commemoration of the victories is also a way to impose history on a landscape that the young Inca was just beginning to claim. The gruesome monuments would be evidence of the glorious victories that surely would have been part of the *cantares* sung in his praise had his own defeat by the Spaniards not come so soon.

War Rituals

Many of the narratives that tell of the lives of the Incas allude to the rituals that celebrate the victory of their conquests. As presented by the Spanish chroniclers, the rituals are generally mentioned in a very abbreviated form and seem to punctuate the rhythm of the story that tells of a king's conquests. Sarmiento summarizes the victory celebration in generic terms:

> Llevaban la gente de guerra en orden por sus escuadras, lo más bien aderezados que les era posible, con muchas danzas y cantares, y los cautivos presos, los ojos en el suelo, vestidos con unas ropas largas con muchas borlas; y entraban por las calles del pueblo, que para esto estaban muy bien aderezadas. Iban representando las victorias y batallas de que triunfaban. Y en llegando a la Casa del Sol echaban en el suelo los despojos y prisioneros, y el inga pasaba sobre ellos pisándolos y diciendo: "A mis enemigos piso". Y estaban los presos callando sin alzar los ojos. Y este orden guardaban en todos los triumphos. (Cap. 33; 1960: 238)

> The warriors lined up in order by unit, dressed with as much ornament as possible, and they went along with many dances and songs. Their captives were with them, eyes cast down, and dressed in long clothing decorated with many tassels. They entered the city through streets that had been well decorated, and they went along depicting the victories and battles that they celebrated. When they reached the House of the Sun, they threw the booty

and the prisoners on the ground, and the Inca stepped on them, saying: "I step on my enemies." And all the prisoners remained silent without raising their eyes. This is how they carried out all their victory celebrations.

Abridged references to victory celebrations appear frequently in the stories of the kings, and elements of the general description provided by Sarmiento may also appear as motifs in these stories. The act of treading on the enemy's clothes or insignia is found frequently, for example, as discussed in chapter 2. We also have at least three accounts that incorporate a fuller description of victory celebrations: Betanzos' description of Pachacuti's first campaigns; Pachacuti Yamqui's presentation of Topa Inca's Quito campaign; and Murúa's account of the return of Huayna Capac's mummy to Cuzco and the celebration of his victories on the northern frontier. These descriptions give us a sense of how the rituals may have been carried out and certainly show how they are reported in the stories that tell of the lives of the kings.

The story of Pachacuti's war rituals is incorporated into the much longer and very formulaic version of his life presented by Betanzos. In this episode, Pachacuti is depicted inventing the kind of military celebration that will take place to celebrate all future victories; the account is parallel to the stories that tell of his invention of the ceremony to initiate young men, his organizing of the rituals to worship mummies, and the orchestration of his own funeral. The war ritual takes place to celebrate three victories which are presented as having taken place simultaneously: Pachacuti's own campaign against the Soras people in Chinchaysuyu, a campaign against Condesuyu led by one of his captains, and the first campaign into Antesuyu led by another. The celebration starts with what might be thought of as a private ritual: The armies meet, and the captains show the booty to Pachacuti and give him the formal right to step on the prizes of the battle, claiming the victory in his name. This more private military celebration feeds into the public commemoration that will be held for a larger audience. The story works out the logistics of getting all the victorious armies and parades of captives back to Cuzco, then picks up with preparations for the march into the capital:

> ya que llegó a vista de la ciudad mandó que los capitanes fuesen allí todos juntos con él e que ansi entrasen en la ciudad cantando por su orden cada uno dellos las cosas que les habían acaecido en las jornadas que ansi havía hecho todo lo cual iban cantando comenzando primero los que con Ynga Yupangue habían quedado el cantar que ya oísteis del vencimiento de los soras y éstos ya que havían acabado comenzaron lo que ansi les había acaecido en la provinicia de Condesuyu e lo mismo hicieron los otros capitanes que ansi habían sujetado a los Andes e ansi mismo mandó que los prisioneros fuesen llorando y diciendo en alta voz sus culpas y delitos y como eran

sujetos y vasallos del hijo del sol y que para contra el tal no había fuerzas comenzando los de los soras primero y luego los demás por su orden. (Betanzos parte I, cap. XIX; 1987: 95)

as they arrived within view of the city, he ordered all his captains to gather together with him so they could enter [Cuzco] singing, each in his turn, about the things that had happened in the campaign and all the deeds that each had done. So they went along singing, beginning with the ones who remained with Inca Yupanqui, who sang the *cantar* that you have heard about the conquest of the Soras. And after they had passed, there came the group that had conquered Condesuyu, and then the other captains that had conquered the Andes. And he ordered the prisoners to walk along crying and proclaiming their guilt and sins in a loud voice and saying that they were the subjects and vassals of the son of the Sun, and that resistance to him was futile. And they were to proceed with the Soras first, and the others afterward, each in order.

The parade of victorious captains and captives enters Cuzco singing and telling the story of their victory (on the Inca side), punctuated by the cries of the vanquished enemies—proof of the stories of the Inca victory. The order that Pachacuti sets up for the entrance exemplifies Inca prestige categories: Chinchaysuyu was the richest and largest quarter of the empire, and the captives from that province, the Soras, march first. Condesuyu had less wealth and prestige, and Antesuyu had the least. The order of the march of the armies and captives thus follows the categories of *collana* (most prestige), *payan* (less prestige), *callao* (least prestige) that underlie much of the ordering of Cuzco's ritual life and the narratives that tell of it.

A similar structure is seen in the procession in honor of Huayna Capac's victories in the north. As presented by Murúa, the celebration takes place after Huayna Capac's death, accompanied by a *bulto* of the dead king carried in a litter. It should be noted that this kind of celebration could well be presented during a king's lifetime, with the statue standing in for the king in Cuzco if he were to be engaged in a campaign elsewhere.

Los delanteros entraban representando las batallas puntualmente como hauía passado; venía toda esta gente repartida en tres compañías y detrás dellas entraron los orejones del Cuzco cantando vnas como endechas de placeres. Venían éstos pomposamente vestidos, con los más ricos adrezos que cada uno podía, con sus armas en las manos y delas lanzas colgadas las cabezas de algunos que hauían muerto, delos más principles y delos más preciosos despoxos que en la guerra hauían ganado. Otros trayan colgadas de las puntas delas lanças las patenas de oro y plata y algunas camiestas labradas de oro y plata. Duró entrar la gente de vrincuzco, por esta orden, todo un día. (Murúa cap. 41; 1962, vol. 1: 116)

The advance guard entered, depicting the battles exactly as they had happened; all the people came divided into three companies, and after them the *orejones* of Cuzco marched in, singing of their triumphs. They marched in ostentatiously dressed, each one wearing the richest ornaments he could find, with his weapons in his hands. From their lances were suspended the heads of some of the most important enemies who had died and some of the most important spoils that they had earned in the war. Others had disks of gold and silver hanging from their lances, and some had shirts worked with gold and silver. The people of Hurin Cuzco took a whole day to enter [Cuzco] in this manner.

The next day a similar parade takes place led by the Hanan Cuzco captains and their armies and captives. The final day there is a parade led by the *orejones* of both Hanan and Hurin Cuzco that dedicates the win to the Sun (Murúa cap. 41; 1962, vol. 1: 116). In this case, the sections of the parade are divided into three groups (advance guard, *orejones*, captives), and the event itself is organized into three days, each devoted to one of three groups: Hurin Cuzco, Hanan Cuzco, and the day dedicated to the reigning Inca and the Sun. In contrast to Betanzos' account, here the three-day ritual seems structured to proceed from lowest to highest prestige.

Our final description of an Inca war ritual comes from Pachacuti Yamqui and is rather different from the others. In this account, he describes the celebration held in Cuzco to commemorate Topa Inca's conquest in the north during Pachacuti's reign. The victorious Incas, along with captives (male and female), approach Cuzco. They march toward Cuzco in two armies; Pachacuti places two generals in symbolic charge of one army and his young grandson Huayna Capac in charge of the other. Dressed in all their finery, the armies enter Sacsahuaman and stage a mock battle, replaying the conquest of the Cayambis and Pastos:

> y entrando a la fortaleza, saca a todos los Cayambis y Pastos y gente habido en guerras, y las cabeças cortadas, que estauan para esse efecto hechas, les unta con sangre de llamas y pone en las lanças. Al fin, a los bencidos hazen *haylle* de ellos, triumfándoles hasta Coricacha, por aquella principal calle. (Pachacuti Yamqui 1968: 302)

> entering the fortress, they took all the Cayambis and Pastos and others who had been taken in the wars and the trophy heads that had been prepared for this reason, and they covered them with llama blood and stuck them on their lances. Finally, they performed the *haylli* of victory, celebrating it all the way to the Coricancha as they passed along the main road.

In the ritual battle and replay of the triumph over the armies of the north, the Incas made the history of that conquest vivid and real. The public display of captives, booty, and victorious army was designed to maximize the contrast between the children of the Sun and their less-favored enemies. In these rituals, the Inca nobles and generals wore their finest outfits and carried the trophies—human and otherwise—that celebrated their victories. They shouted out their victory and sang of their prowess in battle. The live human prisoners, in contrast, wore the long fringed tunics of Inca captives and looked down at the ground. In dress and demeanor they were separated from the Incas. In the performance of the history, too, they had a different role to play. While the victors sang out the narrative of the battle, the captives responded with the chorus, admitting their own faults and verifying the inevitability of their conquest by the Incas.

The random events of the actual military encounter were shaped into stories told in prose, poetry, and song in the months or years that intervened between the battle and its commemoration in Cuzco. The performance of these histories was punctuated by actions of the soldiers and the words of their captives. The captives, like the other trophies of war, were testimony to the histories that were performed, validating their truth. In battle celebrations, the Incas gave form to the history that would be incorporated into the *cantares* of the victorious king and the praise-narratives remembered and performed by the descendants of a brave soldier.

The Spoils of War

A frequent motif in the Inca narratives is that booty brought back from conquest is used to enrich the principal temples of Cuzco. Such accounts remind us that the fabulous wealth of the Inca capital must have come, at least in part, from treasures brought from other places.

Inca historical narratives frequently describe the booty taken from conquered peoples. Betanzos, for example, makes much of Pachacuti's victory parade from his first campaign, which included as trophies from Antesuyu huge snakes coiled on litters and large "tigers" (parte I, cap. XIX; 1987: 94). The unfed animals were put in Sancahuasi, a house into which enemy captains were thrown for several days; if they survived, it was taken as a sign of grace, and they were freed (Betanzos parte I, cap. XXVIII; 1987: 136; Sarmiento, cap. 37; 1960: 241; Cobo, in Rowe 1980: 25; Albornóz, in Rowe 1980: 72; Guaman Poma de Ayala 1980: 276–277). In Topa Inca's difficult Antesuyu *entrada*, snakes and tigers are again brought to Cuzco as trophies to replenish the feral population of the prison (Betanzos parte I, cap. XXVIII; 1987: 136).

While the booty from the relatively poor province of Antesuyu was put to Inca religious use in its placement in the sanctified prison of

Sanca, expeditions to the rich Chinchaysuyu quadrant yielded trophies more appropriate to Cuzco's principal temples. Topa Inca removed the gold- and silver-plated wood beams of the palace of the
Chimu leader and had them carried to his camp at Cajamarca and then
to Cuzco (Sarmiento cap. 46; 1960: 252; Murúa cap. 22; 1962, vol. 1:
52). The accounts of Murúa and Sarmiento both assert that Topa
Inca's expedition to offshore islands resulted in such curiosities as a
brass chair, black people, and a horse's skin and jawbone that were
safeguarded in Cuzco as trophies from that campaign (Murúa cap. 25;
1962, vol. 1: 62; Sarmiento cap. 46; 1960: 251).

Murúa is explicit on the reason why such curiosities were brought
to Cuzco:

> fué costumbre antigua entre estos yngas traer de todas las cosas vistosas y
> que podían causar admiración y espanto al Cuzco, para que las viessen y
> engrandeciesen sus hazañas y para memoria de las cosas que hauía en las
> demás prouincias apartadas. Todos estos tropheos se entiende quemaron
> después Quesques y Chalco Chuma, Cappitanes de Atahualpa, quando to-
> maron al Cuzco, hauiendo preso a Huascar Hinga [sic], y allí quemaron el
> cuerpo de este Tupa Ynga Yupanqui, porque no se halló memoria de todas
> estas cosas quando vinieron los españoles. (Cap. 25; 1962, vol. 1: 62)

> it was the former custom of these Incas to bring back to Cuzco all the
> things they had seen that might cause admiration and wonder, so that the
> sight of these objects would enhance the fame of their deeds and would
> memorialize their accomplishments in distant provinces. I understand
> that all these trophies were burned when Quisquis and Chalcuchima,
> Atahuallpa's captains, having taken Huascar prisoner, entered Cuzco and
> burned the body of Topa Inca Yupanqui, because there was no memory of
> these things to be found when the Spaniards entered.

Murúa links the objects with the memory of events. He also reminds
us that without the objects—trophies and mummies—there was no
history. Atahuallpa's generals punished Topa Inca's panaca for taking
Huascar's side in the civil war by removing their ancestor and by de-
stroying the tangible evidence of his deeds. Had the Spaniards not arrived to set down the history told by his few surviving descendants, it
is likely that the story of the remarkable military achievements of the
Inca who had built the largest empire in the world would have been
eradicated.

The wealth of Cuzco's temples was also in part due to the conspicuous display of the spoils of war. The Temple of the Sun, the principal
shrine of the empire, was the chief beneficiary of the gifts. Originally
built (Betanzos parte I, cap. XI; 1987: 50–51) or redesigned (Sarmiento
cap. 31; 1960: 236–237) by Pachacuti after the Chanca War, the Temple
of the Sun was reendowed after a number of successful military cam-

paigns. For example, stories assert that Pachacuti brought booty from Collasuyu after putting down a revolt; it was given to the temple and to the mummies of his ancestors (Sarmiento cap. 37; 1960: 242). Gold statues of the principal deities were made from the loot brought back from the campaign against the Chimu (Murúa cap. 22; 1962, vol. 1: 53).

Several stories tell of the provision of a band of gold that adorned the Temple of the Sun (fig. 3.7). In Sarmiento's version, Pachacuti, after carrying out his initial conquests in Soras and Lucanas, his punitive raid against the Chancas, and some conquests in Condesuyu, re-endowed the Temple of the Sun, including providing it with a band of gold two spans in width around its patio (cap. 36; 1960: 240). Murúa claims that the gold and silver brought back from the Chinchaysuyu campaigns orchestrated by Pachacuti went to enrich the Temple of the Sun and to make the gold band on the temple wall (cap. 20; 1962, vol. 1: 48). Betanzos tells of a band of gold which was made from the gold dust brought back by Topa Inca from his Antesuyu campaign; this band was put around the exterior of the house of the Sun, just below the thatched roof, and was two and a half spans in width (parte I, cap. XXVIII; 1987: 136). Pachacuti Yamqui tells of gold plaques made for the Temple to be used for the Capac Raymi festival; Topa Inca had them made from gold brought from the southern frontier after putting down a rebellion of the Chillis at Coquimbo and Tucumán (1968: 305). Zárate attributes the gold plaques on the temple to Huayna Capac's booty from the defeat of Chimu Capac (cap. XI; 1947: 472).

The gold plaques from the Temple of the Sun may have come from any or all of these campaigns. Several eyewitnesses to the ransom of Atahuallpa describe astonishing amounts of gold in the important buildings of Cuzco. Cristobal de Mena, for example, reports that the buildings in the compound were covered with large plaques of gold, with gold of lower quality on the side that did not face the sun (1957: 93). Pedro Sancho is more specific:

> Pasaban de quinientas las planchas de oro que se trajeron, arrancados de los muros del templo cuzqueño. Entre ellas, las de menor tamaño pesaban cuatro o cinco libras cada una; otras láminas de hasta diez o doce libras completaban el revestimiento de todas las paredes del dicho templo. (Arocena 1986: 63)

> They brought back more than five hundred plaques of gold, yanked from the walls of Cuzco's temple. Of these, the small ones weighed four or five pounds each; other sheets of up to ten or twelve pounds completed the covering of the walls of that temple.

According to Francisco de Jerez, Pizarro's scribe, seven hundred plaques of gold were taken from the layer of gold applied to one build-

FIGURE 3.7. The austere stone walls of one of the buildings of the Corican-cha (Temple of the Sun) in Cuzco, which was once adorned with a band of gold.

ing alone, and five hundred pieces came from another (Jerez 1947: 343). That such reports are not just the exaggerations of greedy men besotted by gold fever is suggested by the amount of gold distributed to Pizarro's party (Sancho de la Hoz 1557). It is also shown in the inventory of the pieces taken in ransom that were sent back to Spain as the king's royal fifth, which includes, in addition to many portable items made of gold, plaques stripped from temple doors and from benches (*Relación francesa . . .* 1967: 76).

It is significant that the narratives of Inca conquest incorporate details on the spoils of war. The description of booty and, especially, the use to which it is put closes the story of particular military campaigns. The reference to treasures used to reendow a particular temple serves two purposes. First, the motif validates the religious mission of Inca conquest: War is not a selfish enterprise but one carried out with divine support and to sustain the Inca cults. Second, the enrichment grounds the building or its improvement in an historical moment: An informed Inca visitor would know that this part of the building's decoration came from the conquest of Tucumán, while that part came from the palace of the vanquished Chimu Capac. As with other Inca practices, endowing a temple with the spoils of victory was a way to make the historical event tangible; visiting the building would bring to mind and validate the claim of conquest and the fact of Cuzco's hegemony over other wealthy provinces.

The Mnemonics of Myth

The physical plan of the Inca capital at Cuzco and many of the shrines that surrounded it served as visual reminders of the relationship of the Incas to their mythical as well as their historical past. The narratives they told, too, linked the living Incas to the past of their founding ancestors and the deities that governed their universe.

According to Sarmiento, the Inca Pachacuti revised the mythical and legendary history of his people, crafting the narratives so that his contemporaries could trace their ancestry back seven generations to the beginning of time and ordering the history to be set down permanently (Sarmiento cap. 30; 1960: 236). His revision of Inca history probably included both mythical and real personages, whom he embodied in *bultos* which were placed in the Temple of the Sun and whose descendants were provided with lands and privileges in accordance with the supposed deeds of their ancestors (Sarmiento cap. 31; 1960: 236).

In aggrandizing the origins of the Inca people, Pachacuti included on the official devotional circuit several places associated with Cuzco's mythical founding ancestors. Of these, the emergence cave at Pacarictampu was among the most important shrines (Cobo book I, chap. 15; 1990: 74), and Pachacuti elaborated it appropriately by putting gold doors on the opening through which the ancestors had entered this world (Sarmiento cap. 30; 1960: 236).

In addition to providing his own people with a pedigree and a mythical charter for their hegemony over others, Pachacuti promoted a number of the peoples in the surrounding area to the status of Incas-by-privilege. These were the groups with which skirmishes were fought and marriages were contracted prior to Pachacuti's regime and from whom aid was sought in repelling the Chanca invaders and reshaping the Cuzco valley. The real or mythical ancestors of some of these groups were similarly accorded a place on the shrine system of Cuzco, including Autviturco (An-1:4), a cave which was the origin place of the natives of the town of Goalla (Cobo book I, chap. 14; 1990: 63); Cinca (Ch-5:9), the origin stone of the Ayarmacas (Cobo book I, chap. 13; 1990: 58); and Intirpucancha (Cu-6:5), the house of the first lord of the town of Choco (Cobo book I, chap. 16; 1990: 80). Also, tombs of their ancestors were incorporated in the capital's system of devotion: Ayavillay (Co-4:5) was the tomb of the lords of the *ayllu* Ayavillay (Cobo book I, chap. 15; 1990: 72); Cutimanco (Cu-8:2),

Cauas (Cu-8:3), and Cicui (Cu-8:10) were tombs in or near the town of Cachona (Cobo book I, chap. 16; 1990: 81); and Llipiquiliscacho (Cu-12:3) was a tomb near the town of Choco (Cobo book I, chap. 16; 1990: 82).

By including places sacred to neighboring peoples on the capital's ritual circuit, Pachacuti was incorporating their histories and the spaces that validated them into the mythical landscape of Cuzco. By taking a location that was sacred to others and making it nominally Inca, he was setting a pattern for the co-optation of sacred places that would govern the Inca conquest of idols, temples, and shrines of more distant parts of the empire at such places as Tiahuanaco, Titicaca, Pachacamac, and Cacha.

As the frontiers of the Inca world expanded, so did their myths. The sacred places that they elaborated in Collasuyu became part of Inca mythography: Some Incas claimed that Titicaca was the true place of origin of the siblings who were their ancestors (Cabello Balboa cap. 21; 1951: 363). In one myth, the Creator makes all things at Tiahuanaco and sends the Sun, the ancestors, and others to Titicaca; the Incas' ancestors made their way underground to the Inca point of emergence at Pacarictampu (Cobo book II, chap. 3; 1979: 104–107; Betanzos parte I, caps. I–II; 1987: 11–15; Cieza parte II, cap. V; 1985: 8–12). In such a narrative the Incas link the sacred places of their world, reconciling their own myths with those of the other peoples they encountered. The temples, shrines, and idols at these sacred places served to link the Incas to their mythical past and to the past of other peoples.

Commemorative Architecture

One class of commemorative architecture includes the structures commissioned by an Inca king for his own use. Each ruler from Viracocha on owned palaces; most had a city palace in Cuzco, as well as a palace on a country estate that had lands for agriculture and recreation. The act of building these palaces was of both practical and symbolic importance. The creation of palaces, monuments, and public works was an important part of being a good Inca ruler. The stories that tell of Pachacuti praise him for being a tireless builder, both in Cuzco and away from the capital. His stories contrast with the brief mention that is made of his brother and rival to the throne, Inca Urcon, who is characterized as so inadequate to the task of rule that he didn't build a single building.

As a practical matter, ruling Incas had to create property for themselves. The rule of Inca inheritance in place at least after Pachacuti decreed that a ruler's property belonged to his *panaca*, to sustain the cult

of his mummy as its members' common ancestor. The son who succeeded his father founded his own descent group and was also responsible for acquiring the property that he would bequeath to its
members for the care of his mummy. One repercussion of this rule
was that the later Incas had a hard time finding unclaimed property
near Cuzco that they could develop: Huayna Capac resorted to moving
a river and draining a swamp to build his country estate at Yucay (Betanzos parte I, cap. XLIII; 1987: 187), and Huascar scandalized the nobility of Cuzco by threatening to take property from his ancestors (P.
Pizarro cap. X; 1986: 53–54). The symbolic value of building palaces
and developing lands was also important: It established the new
ruler's claim to legitimacy and was equated in Inca narratives with the
founding of a descent group. We have records for specific property
owned by ruling Incas from Pachacuti on, with some additional evidence for buildings that belong to other members of the royal families (table 3.2).

In addition to verifying that royalty owned buildings, we can discuss in part how they used them and the circumstances in which they
were built. Some of the properties were particularly important as sites
for the display, maintenance, and offerings to the mummy of the dead
ruler. For example, Pachacuti built the palace at Patallacta in Cuzco for
his death (Sarmiento cap. 47; 1960: 252), anticipating that his body
would be kept there along with a gold statue (Betanzos parte I, cap.
XXXII; 1987: 149) and that sacrifices would be offered to his body
there (Cobo lib. 13, cap. XIII; 1964: 169). The fingernails and hair that
had been cut from him in life were made into a *bulto* which was kept in
the houses of his son and successor, Topa Inca, so that it could be pa-
raded around Cuzco during its main festivals (Betanzos parte I, cap.
XXXII; 1987: 149). Huayna Capac also took responsibility for preparing the house in which his dead father was to be kept (Sarmiento cap.
57; 1960: 260) and took charge of placing the mummy of his mother
in the house where devotions to her were to be observed on the anniversary of her death (Betanzos parte I, cap. XLIV; 1987: 189). Huayna
Capac's body was taken first to his city palace of Casana and then to
his estate at Yucay in a facility he had built for this purpose during his
lifetime (Betanzos parte II, cap. I; 1987: 208). As discussed in a previous section, some of the performances of the *cantares* that told of the
dead king's accomplishments took place in these death houses (Betanzos parte I, cap. XLI; 1987: 182). Pedro Pizarro reports that the
mummies of the dead could visit the houses of other mummies or of
the living, as their volition was reported by the couple who served as
their custodians (P. Pizarro cap. X; 1986: 52–53), and there is evidence
that in the Colonial Period, at least, royal mummies and the statues

TABLE 3.2. Inca Palaces

Inca	Kind of Palace	Name of Palace	Sources
Viracocha Inca	Town palace	unknown	
	Country palace	Caquia Xaquixaguana	Sarmiento (cap. 35; 1960: 230; cap. 32; 1960: 237); Betanzos (parte I, cap. XVII; 1987: 85)
Pachacuti Inca	Town palaces	Condorcancha	Cobo (lib. 13, cap. XIII; 1964: 170–171)
		Coracora (slept here)	Cobo (lib. 13, cap. XIII; 1964: 172)
		Cusicancha (birth house)	Cobo (lib. 13, cap. XIII; 1964: 171)
		Patallacta (death house)	Cobo (lib. 13, cap. XIII; 1964: 168; lib. 12, cap. XIII; 1964: 82); Betanzos (parte I, cap. XXXII; 1987: 149); Sarmiento (cap. 41; 1960: 246)
	Country palaces	Ollantaytambo	Sarmiento (cap. 40; 1960: 245)
		Pisac (Cuyos)	Sarmiento (cap. 34; 1960: 238–239)
		Machu Picchu	Rowe (1990)
		Guamanmarca	Rowe (1990)
		Tambo Machay (hunting lodge)	Cobo (lib. 13, cap. XIV; 1964: 175)
Topa Inca	Town palaces	Pucamarca (possible)	Rowe (1967)
		Calispuquio	Cobo (lib. 13, cap. XIII; 1964: 171); Sarmiento (cap. 54; 1960: 259)
	Country palaces	Chinchero	Sarmiento (cap. 54; 1960: 258); Betanzos (parte I, cap. XXXVIII; 1987: 173)
		Amaybamba (possible palace)	Rostworowski (1963)
Huayna Capac	Town palaces	Casana	Sarmiento (cap. 58; 1960: 260); Cobo (lib. 13, cap. XIII; 1964: 172); P. Pizarro (cap. XIV; 1986: 87–88)
		Pomacorco	Cobo (lib. 13, cap. XIII; 1964: 171)
	Country palaces	Yucay (Quispiguanca)	Sarmiento (cap. 58; 1960: 260); Murúa (cap. 30; 1962, vol. I: 76–77); Cabello Balboa (cap. 21; 1951: 361–362); Betanzos (parte I, cap. XLIII; 1987: 187); Villaneuva (1971)
Huascar	Town palaces	Amarucancha	Sarmiento (cap. 63; 1960: 265); Murúa (cap. 39; 1962, vol. I: 111); Cabello Balboa (cap. 24; 1951: 395)
		Collcampata	Sarmiento (cap. 63; 1960: 260); Murúa (cap. 39; 1962, vol. I: 111)

TABLE 3.2. Inca Palaces (cont.)

Inca	Kind of Palace	Name of Palace	Sources
		"Huascar's fortress" (probably Collcampata)	Rowe (1967, fn. 2)
	Country palaces	Huascar (Muina)	Sarmiento (cap. 63; 1960: 265); Murúa (cap. 39; 1962, vol. I: 111)
		Calca	Betanzos (parte II, cap. III; 1987: 212); Niles (1988)
Atahuallpa	Nothing near Cuzco		
Curi Ocllo (queen)★	in Cuzco	Curi Ocllo	Cobo (lib. 13, cap. XIII; 1964: 171)
Mama Anahuarque (queen)	death house, outside Cuzco	Pumamarca	Cobo (lib. 13, cap. XIV; 1964: 177)
Rahua Ocllo (queen)	country palace	in Yucay	Villanueva (1971)
unnamed queen	near Cuzco	Manahuañuncahuasi	Cobo (lib. 13, cap. XVI; 1964: 184)

★Curi Ocllo was the daughter of Pachacuti and wife of Amaro Topa Inca, his oldest son and originally designated heir.

were moved from house to house, perhaps in part to maintain the old system of visiting various properties, but most likely in order to evade the Spaniards, who sought to confiscate the mummies and the treasure they thought was stored with them.

The disruption of normal Inca royal life occasioned by Huayna Capac's sudden death on the northern frontier and by the subsequent crisis over succession did not change the fundamental pattern of erecting commemorative architecture. The accounts of Atahuallpa's attempt to create a death house for his father show the way that commemorative architecture also fits into succession politics. When Huayna Capac died in the north, his embalmed body was sent to Cuzco, and many *bultos* were made there of his fingernail and hair clippings (Betanzos parte II, cap. I; 1987: 208). In the north, Atahuallpa made his own *bultos* of his father's fingernail and hair clippings and of a scrap of flesh that he had taken when the body was being prepared. He planned to carry one *bulto* with him and to leave the other in the house where his father had lived and died in the north, so that the customary rituals for the dead king could be carried out (Betanzos parte II, cap. II; 1987: 209).

Some properties are associated with other life events of the rulers, such as the birth or initiation of a king. In some cases the structures were built for the Inca-to-be. Pachacuti, for example, anticipating the initiation and ear piercing of his chosen successor, had four temples to the Sun built around Cuzco to be used for that ceremony (Sarmiento cap. 43; 1960: 247). In other cases buildings were created to mark a birth. The birthplace of Huayna Capac was commemorated by creating a building in which the placenta from his birth was kept (Murúa cap. 30; 1962, vol. 1: 81; Sarmiento cap. 60; 1960: 261; Pachacuti Yamqui 1950: 247; the sources differ on whether the building was created by his father or by Huayna Capac himself). Huascar, likewise, developed an estate at the town in which he was born (Murúa cap. 39; 1972, vol. 1: 111; Sarmiento cap. 63; 1960: 265; Betanzos parte I, cap. XLV; 1987: 192), building the palace after his accession to rule. Betanzos tells us that many people believed the house Atahuallpa commissioned in the north marked his birthplace (Betanzos parte II, cap. V; 1987: 215).

Most importantly, the installation of a new Inca was marked by his creation of the principal palaces in and around Cuzco. The act of assuming rule is described in the narratives as taking place after the *purucaya* ritual marking the one-year anniversary of the death of the old king. There would have been no need for property in the king-to-be's name until he formally succeeded, for until that time he was fully in his father's descent group and thus able to profit from his estate. The need for new property would have been evident at his accession, as this event ended his membership in the father's descent group (marked by completing the mourning rituals) and initiated the new descent group (marked by his marriage and the acquisition of independent property for his descendants). Before his marriage and installation, the new Inca could have lived on the property of his father's *panaca*, though rarely are we told about the properties that may have belonged to a prince before he assumed rule. Before his city palace was built, Huayna Capac lived in Ucchollo (Murúa cap. 30; 1962, vol. 1: 77), property that may have belonged to Amaro Topa Inca, brother of his father and member of his father's *panaca* (Pachacuti Yamqui 1968: 301). His city palace, the Casana, and his country palace at Yucay were built shortly after he assumed rule, as will be explored in a later chapter.

For the later Incas, the assumption was marked also by the marriage to the sister selected for the new king. This requirement is made most clear by Betanzos (parte I, cap. XVI; 1987: 78; parte II, cap. VI; 1987: 220) and by Pachacuti Yamqui in describing the marriage and installation of Huayna Capac (1968: 307) and of Huascar (1968: 312). This pattern is also described when Topa Inca ordains that Huayna

Capac must marry his sister Cusirimay at Topa Inca's death (Cobo chap. 14: 1979: 142), and when Huayna Capac's lords order Huascar's spouse-to-be to begin the fast necessary to the installation of the new Inca (Betanzos parte I, cap. XLVIII; 1987: 201). Murúa tells a story of one of Huascar's captains telling him to take a wife when the mourning for his father was completed (Murúa cap. 43; 1962, vol. I: 121).

The accounts of these royal marriages also make clear the association of the parties with properties. At his wedding and installation, Huayna Capac's entourage left from the house of Pacachuti, his grandfather; the party of his queen-to-be and sister, Cusirimay, left from the house of Topa Inca, their father (Pachacuti Yamqui 1968: 307). At the wedding and installation of Huascar, his sister-bride was taken from the house of their mother, Rahua Ocllo, which was in the compound belonging to her dead consort Huayna Capac; from that palace the bride moved to the lodgings Huascar had built at Amarucancha (Murúa cap. 43; 1962, vol. I: 123). Such accounts give us hints of the places where the unmarried sons and daughters of a ruling Inca might have lived, and where his wife or widow would live. They also show the importance of place in the founding of a descent group that is implied by the installation and marriage of the Inca: Both he and his bride, in essence, are removed from the property of the *panacas* of their predecessors and begin their lives in the new status of Inca and *coya* in property belonging to the *panaca* they would establish.

The relationship between buildings, succession, marriage, and filial duty that is hinted at elsewhere in the histories is made explicit in the accounts of Atahuallpa's hastening to build a palace at Carangue in the old Cayambi territory pacified by his father. He selects the site, traces out the plan for the buildings, and charges his associate, Unanchullo, with the task of building the structure (Betanzos parte II, cap. V; 1987: 214–215). He leaves a *bulto* that he had made with his dead father's fingernails and a scrap of his flesh at the building site—probably to assure the Inca overseers and their building crews that he has the authority to command the work. Unanchullo was ordered to build as quickly as possible, for Atahuallpa wanted to conduct his fast and the necessary rituals for taking the throne (Betanzos parte II, cap. V; 1987: 217). When work has not proceeded fast enough for Atahuallpa, Unanchullo is told to hasten the roofing of the palace so that Atahuallpa and his bride-to-be can carry out the necessary fasts and so that the *bulto* of Huayna Capac can see to Atahuallpa's installation as Inca and the blessing of his marriage (Betanzos parte II, cap. VI; 1987: 220).

Betanzos' mention of the presence of his father's *bulto* at the building site hints at tensions that Cieza de León spells out more fully in an account of building a palace in the north.[4] In this story, Atahuallpa has approached the Cañaris and some *mitimaes* living near Tomebamba to begin work on a palace for him that he would use as his father and grandfather had used theirs. Because a messenger from Huascar has arrived, spelling out his side of the succession dispute, the workers refuse to build, as they believe that Atahuallpa lacks the authority to command their work. Rather, as Cieza tells it, Atahuallpa is taken prisoner (parte II, cap. LXXII; 1985: 207). The symbolic importance of Atahuallpa's attempt to build a palace and thus to stake his claim to rule was not lost on his rival to the throne. Murúa tells the story of Huascar's reaction to his brother's construction activities:

> le llegaron en este medio mensageros del Gouernador de Tomebamba y del cacique principal de los cañares, llamado Ocllo Calla, diçiendo que Atao Hualpa hauía hecho grandes palacios para él y socolor destos hauía leuantado para sí otros de mejor fábrica y más sumptuosos, y que se trataba y hacía seruir como si fuera ynga y señor, con mucha magestad y aplauso. . . . Oydas esta nueuas por Huascar Ynga, recibió dellas, como estaba con mala voluntad, ynfinito enojo, y de nueuo començó a hazer pesquiça dela quedada de Atao Hualpa en Quito. (Cap. 46; 1962, vol. 1: 133)

> at this moment, messengers arrived, sent by the governor of Tomebamba and Ocllo Calla, principal *cacique* of the Cañaris. They told him that Atahuallpa had built large palaces for him and at the same time had built himself palaces that were even more lavish, and that he was acting as though he was Inca and making people serve him as their lord, with great majesty and reverence. . . . And when Huascar Inca heard this news, as he was displeased and had become extremely angry, he set out against Atahuallpa in Quito.

Cieza, who tells a similar story, notes succinctly: "Y cierto oy a muchos Indios entendidos y antiguos, que sobre hazer vnos palacios en estos aposentos, fue harta parte para auer las diferencias que ouo entre Guascar y Atabalipa" [I heard many wise and ancient Indians say that a large part of the differences between Huascar and Atahuallpa had to do with the business of constructing palaces] (parte I, cap. XLIIII; 1986: 148). Huascar, too, hurried to build palaces fitting his position and duties as Inca. Near Cuzco he built a palace at his birthplace (Muina) (fig. 3.8), where he carried out the fasts for his dead father. He also hurried to build his city palace at Amarucancha (fig. 3.9) because he knew many foreigners would be arriving with his father's funeral procession (Cabello Balboa cap. 24; 1951: 395). He also developed a country estate at Calca (fig. 3.10), which he settled with *mitimaes* from many provinces (Murúa cap. 46; 1962, vol. 1: 133).

We also have eyewitness testimony of the association of building with the installation of a new Inca. After they have killed Atahuallpa and realizing that, with his murder of Huascar, there is no legitimate

ruler in place, the Spanish invaders decide they need to install someone who will have native support while still not opposing their own
cause. When they make their choice,

> De inmediato se dispuso el nuevo Cacique a observer sus dos días de ayuno
> en lugar apartado del trato de las gentes en una casa que se aparejaba a tal
> objecto desde el momento en que el Gobernador le hizo saber sus desig-
> nios. La casa estaba próxima a su alojamiento y mucho maravilló al Gober-
> nador y a los demás españoles ver cómo en tan poco tiempo fue levantada
> casa tan grande y tan buena. (Arocena 1986: 70)

FIGURE 3.8. An overview of
the site of Cañaracay, on Lake
Muina, related to the estate
that Huascar built at his birthplace.

FIGURE 3.9. Wide niches and fitted masonry from an interior wall of Ama-rucancha, in Cuzco, the city palace claimed or built by Huascar.

> Immediately, the new *cacique* went to observe his two-day fast in a place re-moved from contact with others in a house that they had begun preparing for that purpose the moment that the Governor let him know his plans. The house was next to his lodging, and the Governor and the other Span-iards marveled how they could build such a large and good house in such a short time.

This report reminds us that, even with the disruptions that followed the disastrous encounter with the Spaniards at Cajamarca, royal tradi-tion was followed: A building was erected to facilitate and to com-memorate the installation of a new Inca. This monument would serve as the visible marker of the beginning of his history.

Conclusion

In many ways, the Incas sought to make history visible. Personal his-tories were manifested in the objects owned by a person and the places visited, used to inspire remembrance of that person's deeds in commemorative ceremonies. The objects and places served as mne-monics of an individual's life, used to forge the history that would be as carefully guarded by his descendants as were the mummy of their ancestor and the property owned by that individual. Public history—at least of male warriors and the spiritual forces that inspired them— was made visible in the celebrations of military victory that included reenactments of battle and displays of captives and booty brought back from war. The religious aspect of those battles was shown in the objects made from the captives and the spoils of war and their incorporation into places of devotion for the royal families. The link to both history (the victory in battle) and myth (the role of the gods in the Inca victory) was manifested in such objects.

FIGURE 3.10. Remains of a double-jambed doorway at Calca, the country estate developed by Huascar.

For the Incas, architecture was a way to give form to claims of mythical or legendary history. It could legitimate claims to kingship, to ownership, and to victory; it could validate claims to mythical descent or justify the usurpation of a mythical history, as at Titicaca, Tiahanaco, and Pachacamac. The placement of a structure, the story told about its construction, and aspects of its design all helped to give shape not only to a building but to the history which caused it to be made.

The accounts of the royal and ritual life of the Incas allow us to reconstruct, in general terms, the ways in which they remembered, performed, commemorated, and displayed their understanding of history. In the succeeding chapters I will turn to the specific case of Huayna Capac to suggest how the stories of his life and the works attributed to him might be seen as efforts to shape his history and to confirm his place in the Inca dynasty.

4

HUAYNA CAPAC'S HISTORY

The lives of most Inca rulers are known only through the formalized stories preserved by their descendants; the degree to which these stories approach a documentary history can merely be guessed at. In the case of one Inca ruler, however, we have other information to supplement the official histories of his life. For Huayna Capac (fig. 4.1), we have memories about him reported as anecdotes and elicited in legal investigations. We also have architectural remains attributed to him that give us insight into how he lived and how he chose to present himself to the world.

The histories of Huayna Capac are of particular interest because of his place in the Inca dynastic sequence. Huayna Capac ruled while the Spaniards were making their early explorations of the Inca world but died before they launched their major invasion of those lands. He assumed control of an empire that had been, for the most part, carved out in the lifetime of his grandfather Pachacuti and his father, Topa Inca. His position as a late member of the Inca ruling elite doubtless shaped his personal and political aspirations and had its reflection in the narratives that tell of his life and in the buildings he left. Because he ruled at the time of European contact, he figures in the narratives left by those writers, both the historical and the legal. Witnesses who testified to Spanish investigators a generation after Conquest remembered him and could recall with clarity actions that he had carried out that had repercussions for their lives. It is often possible to consult such testimony to fill in aspects of his life and character that are not addressed in the narrative histories or to cross-check on events that are mentioned.

Because he was the father of both Huascar and Atahuallpa, the principal disputants in the fratricidal war that was in process at the Spanish arrival in the Andes, Huayna Capac's history was recalled by both Inca parties. And because he was the father of several of the Incas set up to rule by the Spaniards, the Spanish writers, too, had cause to advance his history in order to give legitimacy to those descendants with whom they treated, such as Manco Inca and Paullu and eventually Sayri Topa and Titu Cusi Yupanqui. For Spanish men married to Inca princesses who claimed property due to their descent from or affiliation with Huayna Capac, it was also important to glorify him as legit-

FIGURE 4.1. Huayna Capac, depicted as a young man in full battle regalia (Guaman Poma f. 112 [114]; 1980: 92).

imate king in order to advance the claims of their wives. For all these reasons, Huayna Capac makes an interesting case to consider the ways in which the life of a ruling Inca was remembered and reported by his descendants and by their conquerors.

Although there probably was a formal royal narrative that told of the life of Huayna Capac, it has not come down to us in as cohesive a form as that of his grandfather. But we can discern episodes that must have been present in the narrative. We have several juicy retellings of the events surrounding his accession to office. We also have a series of stories about the wars on the northern frontier, including elaborate accounts of calling up and sending off the army, descriptions of the bloody battles against their enemies, and a dramatic story about a revolt by some of his generals during the northern campaign. Finally, we have accounts of his death in an epidemic on the northern frontier. The stories that told of Huayna Capac's life show many of the traits that can be discerned in other royal narratives: Episodes are framed by rituals, they include patterned repetition, and they are chosen to represent Huayna Capac in a favorable light.

There is remarkable agreement among the narrative sources that describe Huayna Capac's life, so much so that it is possible to reconstruct the sequence of the history that was created to account for this last pre-Conquest Inca. In the succeeding discussion, I draw from the multiple narrative sources that tell of Huayna Capac, noting variation where relevant and suggesting ways in which the facts of his life may have been altered to make a better story. Where possible, I suggest the ways in which sources other than the formal narratives—eyewitness accounts, legal petitions, and tribute records—might be used to enrich our understanding of the ruler's life.

Huayna Capac: Young Heir to the Empire

Huayna Capac was born Inti Cusi Guallpa (Callapiña, Supno y otros 1974: 41) or Tito Cusi Gualpa (Sarmiento cap. 54; 1960: 258), son of Topa Inca and Mama Ocllo. Of all the Incas to rule, he was the only one to be the product of a brother-sister union.[1] Huayna Capac was born on the northern frontier while Topa Inca was engaged in the Quito wars. His birth rituals were celebrated at Tomebamba, whence the name of the descent group he founded, Tomebamba *panaca*. As a very young child Huayna Capac traveled with his parents and the victorious Inca army to Cuzco, where he met his grandfather, the elderly Pachacuti Inca. According to Betanzos, Pachacuti at that time selected Huayna Capac to succeed Topa Inca on the throne, marking his choice by placing a small fringed headdress on the boy's head. At this time, the boy was also given the name Huayna Capac (Betanzos attributes the naming to Yamqui Yupanqui, his wife's ancestor) to indicate that he was young (Huayna) and to describe the rich and important legacy to which he was heir (Capac) (parte I, cap. XXVII; 1987: 131–132). Pachacuti Yamqui describes a ritual in which Pachacuti involved the little boy in the triumphal celebration of the Quito wars, giving him miniature weapons and putting him in charge of the symbolic reenactments of battles at the fortress above Cuzco (1968: 302–303).

These stories are important in affirming that Huayna Capac was the legitimate heir to his father's position: If the universally loved Pachacuti had favored him, there could be no dispute about it. There were at least two major threats to Huayna Capac's claim to rule when later he succeeded his father (to be discussed in a succeeding section); whether stories of his close association with Pachacuti are true or not, it would have been in the new Inca's best interests to circulate stories that supported his claim to rule. The stories are also in keeping with the image presented in other narratives about Huayna Capac's extraordinary devotion to his ancestors.

We know very little about Huayna Capac's youth. In contrast to most Inca princes, who went to battle with their fathers, uncles, or older siblings, Huayna Capac seems to have spent little or no time on the battlefield as a young man. The Inca empire had nearly reached its maximum extent by the close of Topa Inca's Quito campaign. There were no new programs of conquest initiated by Topa Inca after the northern wars and very few military interventions to consolidate Inca claims during the rest of his regime. There would have been few important military ventures during Huayna Capac's youth in which the young prince could have gained honor.

Although he did not spend his time with the army, the young Huayna Capac learned other skills he would need as ruler. Topa Inca left him as governor in Cuzco while he went to Collasuyu; Huayna Capac would have been a young man at this point (Cieza parte II, cap. LXI; 1985: 176). Ramos Gavilán, who knew stories about the shrine of Titicaca, reports that Huayna Capac was set up as governor there after his father's visit to the site (lib. 1, cap. XXIX; 1988: 179; Cieza also reports the visit but not Topa Inca's appointment of his son as governor; parte II, cap. LXI; 1985: 177).

Huayna Capac also had duties that prepared him for his religious obligations. Betanzos tells a story about Topa Inca naming him to be overseer of the herds of the Sun; his job was to include getting annual accountings of the herds of the Sun from throughout the empire and to personally mandate the sacrifice of animals for rituals (parte I, cap. XXXIX; 1987: 176–177; see also Sarmiento cap. 57; 1960: 260). Huayna Capac had one other job associated with religion. At some point he made changes to the shrine system of Cuzco, adding huacas and modifying the system put into place in his grandfather's lifetime (Rowe 1980); we do not know if this was part of the charge given him by Topa Inca or if these changes took place during his own administration.

Huayna Capac did not spend all his time working, however. Among the pastimes he enjoyed was hunting. Betanzos, for example, details episodes of hunting in Ayaviri and Oruro (parte I, cap. XLIV; 1987: 189; parte I, cap. XLV; 1987: 191). As will be discussed in a succeeding chapter, he had a hunting lodge built on his estate at Yucay, as well.

A Disputed Succession

As is typical for Inca royal histories, in the narratives that tell of Huayna Capac there is little attention to the life of the boy before he succeeds his father. In contrast to the stories of other Inca rulers, however, his include reports of plots against his succession, both within the royal houses of Cuzco and from the provinces. Versions of these plots are presented by a variety of writers, including Murúa (caps. 28–29; 1962, vol. 1: 70–75), Cabello Balboa (cap. 20; 1951: 357–360), Sarmiento (cap. 55; 1960: 259), Cobo (cap. 16; 1964: 88), and Pachacuti Yamqui (1968: 305–308). Brief allusions to succession disputes also appear in accounts by Cieza de León (parte II, cap. LXII; 1985: 179) and in the *Relación de Quipucamayos* (Callapiña, Supno y otros 1974: 41). Betanzos does not tell of the succession disputes but does associate some of the individuals named in the other stories with the life of Huayna Capac (parte I, cap. XXXVIII; 1987: 176–177). The story can be pieced together from these sources.

Though one version of the story in circulation asserted that Topa Inca died after being shot by an arrow (Murúa cap. 26; 1962, vol. 1: 67), most claim that Topa Inca died after an illness; Betanzos claims it was of four months' duration (parte I, cap. XXXIX; 1987: 177). There were suspicions that he had been poisoned or bewitched by one of his concubines, the Lady Chiqui Ocllo, who hoped to promote her son to succeed his father. She claimed that Topa Inca chose her son Capac Guari to succeed him out of love for the boy's mother. Sarmiento's version of the story includes an incitement to rebellion by a concubine he calls Cori Ocllo, a relative of Capac Guari, who lobbied her relatives to support the boy's case (cap. 55; 1960: 259).[2] The attempt by the concubine to place her son on the throne was supported by some of Topa Inca's highest associates; Murúa and Cabello both claim the plot was quashed by Huayna Capac's mother with the help of some of her loyal relatives. As a result of the plot, the enchantress was killed. The young boy at the center of the plot may not have fared so poorly. While one version of the story mentioned that he and his followers were captured and killed by one of Topa Inca's brothers, others claimed the boy was banished from Cuzco and given land, food, and servants at his father's estate at Chinchero, where he lived the rest of his life.

The stories about the attempt to do Huayna Capac out of his place invariably blame the ambitious mother either for taking the initiative of killing Topa Inca or for illegitimately extorting favors for her son through her charms. The quashing of the threat by Mama Ocllo, her brother Guaman Achachi, and other brothers seems somewhat surprising unless this is seen, at least in part, as a contest between women—or, perhaps more accurately, a *story* about a contest between women. What is more surprising is the relatively light punishment given to the would-be usurper himself: To live out a life in relative luxury on his father's pleasant and productive country estate would seem

to be mild punishment, one that would not necessarily discourage future similar attempts. We can only speculate that perhaps the son had
followers in Cuzco, politically powerful allies who could be placated
by sparing the boy and laying blame on the errant concubine. The dispute is not articulated in terms of the son's right to rule but rather as
the mother's attempts to place charm and favoritism—or even witch-
craft and poison—over the ties of kinship that made Huayna Capac,
by rights, the heir to the throne. If young Capac Guari had allies in
Cuzco, they might have been in his father's *panaca*, Capac Ayllu, for
that is the family that owned the land to which he was banished.

A second attempt on Huayna Capac's succession was initiated by
nobles who seemed to be loyal to him. Huayna Capac was served by
two kinsmen: Lord Hualpaya and Lord Achachi.[3] Hualpaya acted as
governor and coadjutor, regent, or advisor to Huayna Capac. Achachi
was an important and influential man, serving as governor of the rich
Chinchaysuyu quarter (Cobo lib. II, cap. XVI; 1964: 88; Sarmiento
cap. 57; 1960: 260). Despite his apparent loyalty, Hualpaya had designs on the throne for himself or for one of his sons. Using his influence and wealth, he planned a violent usurpation of power: He had
rulers of provinces loyal to him fill baskets with weapons, which he
planned to smuggle into Cuzco disguised as baskets of coca (Cabello
Balboa cap. 20; 1951: 358) or coca and peppers (Cobo lib. II, cap. XVI;
1964: 88) and tent poles (Murúa cap. 28: 1963, vol. I: 73). Achachi discovered the plan when thieves, upon discovering the baskets held
weapons instead of the legitimate contents, informed him. An alternative story claimed that the plot was discovered by a half-uncle of
Huayna Capac who discerned it in a vision (Pachacuti Yamqui 1968:
306). Achachi detained the arms smugglers and their overseers, tor-
turing them until they revealed the plot. He gave Hualpaya no indication that his treachery had been discovered, preferring to let him and
his party reveal their plans by apparently carrying through on their
mutiny. When the traitors launched their attack, Achachi and his
friends surrounded and killed them. Hualpaya had planned to carry
out his coup by inviting Huayna Capac to a party at the palace called
Quispicancha, where he would be killed. Men loyal to Lord Achachi helped Huayna Capac escape, and Hualpaya was captured and
imprisoned in the houses of Capac Yupanqui. Later, he and his followers were killed, along with the son on whose behalf the plot was
launched. In addition, the provincial lords who had joined in the conspiracy were killed, along with their children, and their property was
taken by Huayna Capac; the lower-ranked residents of these provinces
were taken as his *yanaconas*. Pachacuti Yamqui's version of the coup
attempt is a little different. In his story the treachery was set to take

place in the Temple of the Sun; Hualpaya therefore had to be ambushed outside of the temple. Again, in this version, Hualpaya is immediately beheaded for his part in the plot, while his associates are captured and brought to justice; the provincial conspirators are castigated by being struck three times on their backs with large rocks.

Can we make sense of these stories? There are two versions of the narrative of Hualpaya and Achachi, one which is reported in the common source of Cabello Balboa and Murúa and by Cobo and which probably was alluded to by Sarmiento's informants, and one version which was told by Pachacuti Yamqui. Pachacuti Yamqui includes no mention of a plot by a concubine, though a Capac Guari appears as a military hero in Topa Inca's campaigns (1968: 304). In the usurpation narrative told by Sarmiento, the two plots against Huayna Capac are woven into a single story. Sarmiento does this by making Guaman Achachi the hero of both and having Huayna Capac hide at Quispicancha during the first (rather than the second) attempt against him.

Assuming that the narratives were based on real incidents, the roots of these plots against Huayna Capac can perhaps be understood in terms of other aspects of Inca domestic and foreign political relations. The first plot, that which proposed to put Capac Guari on the throne, reveals one of the problems of Inca marital and domestic relations: A ruler could have many sons, though only a few who were borne by the principal wife. But the sons of favored concubines, or secondary wives, particularly those who lived at their father's court, could have a number of important youthful allies. In a story about the political advantage given to the son of the Lady Guayro, for example, the son is described as going through the initiation ceremonies in Cuzco (Cobo lib. 12, cap. XV; 1964: 86), which would have meant that he knew the highest nobles of his generation, and he may have gained allies during service in the Antesuyu campaign. A concubine who came from a politically important Inca family might have many powerful allies on her side willing to support the cause of her son. The rule of inheritance that said the legitimate son should be confirmed in his status by the dying Inca meant that there was a certain degree of discretion in the matter of naming a successor. Many of the tensions and problems of Inca succession that were revealed at the death of Huayna Capac can certainly be traced in this dispute. The stories of the plot for Capac Guari and the story of the Lady Guayro also give some insight—and not very flattering insight—into the character of Topa Inca, who is portrayed as being perhaps too easily swayed by the women in his life to sacrifice Inca ideals. Few descendants of Topa Inca escaped the slaughter by Atahuallpa's generals, and perhaps there was no one to expunge such anti–Topa Inca stories from the oral tradition.

The story of the treachery by Lord Hualpaya can best be understood as reflecting aspects of both foreign and domestic policy. Our best identification of Hualpaya is as the son of Capac Yupanqui, who was probably a brother of Pachacuti. This identification, presented by both Murúa and Sarmiento, is in keeping with the characterization of him as an uncle of Huayna Capac, offered by Cobo, and as a second cousin of Topa Inca, as mentioned by Cabello Balboa. There were several Capac Yupanquis in Inca history: There was, of course, the Capac Yupanqui who was one of the legendary Inca rulers and founder of Apu Mayta *panaca*. A more notorious Capac Yupanqui was a brother of Inca Yupanqui who, despite his impressive conquests in Chinchaysuyu, was killed by the Inca (Murúa cap. 21; 1962, vol. 1: 48–50; Sarmiento cap. 38; 1960: 244; *Informaciones de Toledo*, question XII; Levillier 1940) or by his own hand (Cieza parte II, cap. LVII; 1985: 161) or went on to serve with distinction in additional campaigns (Garcilaso parte I, lib. VI, caps. X, XII; 1609: 139 r.–140 v.). Another Capac Yupanqui, an uncle of Topa Inca, shows up in Cieza's account of Topa Inca's life as his advisor and general who accompanies him to Quito (parte II, cap. LVII; 1985: 161). We don't know which Capac Yupanqui is the father of the Lord Hualpaya who attempts to betray Huayna Capac. Perhaps it is a son burning with resentment that his father's military prowess was repaid with an Inca's anger and, ultimately, by his death. Or possibly the Capac Yupanqui implicated in the plot was an uncle and loyal general of Topa Inca who felt that he and his son were better equipped to run the empire than was the Inca's son. In any event, there must have been a conspiracy that involved a certain number of highly ranked peoples in Chinchaysuyu, as the conspirators brought weapons toward Cuzco through Limatambo, a point on the Chinchaysuyu road, and the plot was discovered by citizens who brought it to the attention of the governor of that quarter. All the requisite Capac Yupanquis made conquests in those lands and probably had a certain following among lords there.

Chroniclers differ in the timing of these attempts against Huayna Capac relative to his installation as Inca, though there is agreement that the attempts took place not long after Topa Inca's death. It is also difficult to know how disruptive the coup attempts were, though Cieza, who places the attempt immediately following the death of Topa Inca in those times when there was no ruling Inca, claims that it was the governors and the *mitimaes* alone who were able to keep order (parte II, cap. LXII; 1985: 179).

Huayna Capac as Inca

Although Huayna Capac inherited rule of an established empire, one whose boundaries had, for the most part, been determined by the conquests carried out during his grandfather's and his father's regimes, Huayna Capac was no stranger to turmoil. The threats to his succession that involved members of the royal families and that built on the disgruntlement of provincial lords merely foreshadowed attempts against him personally or against Inca rule that would plague his reign until his death. There would be rebellions among the Chachapoyas, the people of Puná, and the Chiriguanos; there would be a mutiny at Tomebamba led by the nobles from Cuzco and his trusted general; there would be claims that his death was due to poisoning by old enemies among the Chachapoyas. These disputes are important for what they tell us of the political climate at the time of his rule.

But for now, it is important to discuss the actions of Huayna Capac once the succession threats were quelled. When he succeeded, he removed the advisors who had served him and put his brother Auqui Topa Inca in that role (Sarmiento cap. 57; 1960: 260). He then completed the mourning rituals for both parents, as his mother, Mama Ocllo, died shortly after her consort. Murúa and Cabello concur with Sarmiento that Huayna Capac mourned both his mother and his father at the same time (Sarmiento cap. 57; 1960: 260); Betanzos places the death of Mama Ocllo around three and a half years after Topa Inca's death and credits Huayna Capac with preparing separate mourning rituals for each of his parents (parte I, cap. XLIV; 1987: 189). References to the death of Mama Ocllo are important in establishing the time of Huayna Capac's first military campaign.

By all accounts, Huayna Capac was extraordinarily close to his mother, Mama Ocllo. Cieza tells us that she often advised her son about business she had seen Topa Inca engage in (parte II, cap. LXII; 1985: 180). Betanzos comments that at her death, Huayna Capac was so upset that he did not leave his room for a month and cried constantly out of love for her (parte I, cap. XLIV; 1987: 189). The somewhat surprising fact that Huayna Capac did not go off to war until relatively late in life was, according to Cieza, due to a promise he had made to his mother: He promised not to go off to war in Quito or Chile as long as she was alive (parte II, cap. LXII; 1985: 180). When Mama Ocllo died, she was buried with many goods, including treasures, clothing, and servants (Cieza parte II, cap. LXII; 1985: 180). Among the treasures used in the death ceremony were spindles of gold and small beer pitchers of gold, which women were to use in the *purucaya* ritual to emulate Mama Ocllo's spinning and her pouring of beer for her husband (Betanzos parte I, cap. XLIV; 1987: 190). At her death, Huayna Capac made a *bulto* of her and put it in her house, decorated with a moon (Betanzos parte I, cap. XLIV; 1987: 190). The extraordinary veneration of his mother led Huayna Capac to create a gold statue of her to be placed in a temple in Tomebamba when he later went off for the long campaign on the northern frontier. The statue had its own speaker, a Cañari woman, and was venerated by the *orejones* of Cuzco (Murúa cap. 34; 1962, vol. 1: 92; Cabello Balboa cap. 22; 1951: 374). Acosta adds that when Huayna Capac's mummy was discovered by Spanish authorities, it was carried to Lima along with Mama Ocllo's (lib. 6, cap. XXII; 1954: 202).

Perhaps because of his experiences as a youth in the capital, or perhaps because he had a need to take greater control after the usurpation attempts, Huayna Capac took a particular interest in his relationship to his ancestors and to the gods. Shortly after he assumed rule, Huayna Capac began an inspection of his realm. He sent official visitors to each province to contact the governors and inventory the tribute established by his father, and he himself went out to the provinces near Cuzco to inspect and inventory the capital's surrounding area (Betanzos cap. XL; 1987: 179–180; see also cap. XLII; 1987: 185–186). Cieza specifies that the visit included the provinces of Xaquixahuana and Andahuaylas as far as the Soras and Rucanas (parte II, cap. LXIII; 1985: 181). Betanzos and Cieza tell that Huayna Capac sent out gifts to the provincial governors (Betanzos cap. XL; 1987: 180; Cieza parte II, cap. LXIII; 1985: 181), continuing the kind of diplomacy premised on royal reciprocity that his ancestors had used to reward past loyalty and insure future cooperation with Inca endeavors. Betanzos gives an indication of how an inspection tour near Cuzco was carried out (parte I, cap. XLII; 1987: 186). He notes that Huayna Capac was received in local costume on a special throne or *usnu* seat built for him in each town's plaza. His reception included song, dance, and feasting, along with camelid sacrifice. In return for the accounting of the town's property given by its lord, Huayna Capac offered clothing, women, and gold from Cuzco.

A second kind of inspection noted by Betanzos involved the reorganization of the Cuzco area (parte I, cap. XLI; 1987: 181). In this inspection, Huayna Capac, together with his lords, walked around the city, inspecting bridges, buildings, and canals and mandating necessary repairs. He then examined the lands of the Sun to inspect the irrigation systems and to order any repairs. This inspection also involved the priest of the Sun, who was to give an accounting of the property that belonged to the *mamaconas* and *yanaconas* of the Sun. After hearing the accounting, Huayna Capac augmented the property. As reported in chapter 1, Huayna Capac then elicited an accounting of the property of each of the dead Incas from the custodians of those mummies and increased the number of servants dedicated to some of them (Betanzos parte I, cap. XLI; 1987: 182–183).

We do not know if it was typical for a newly installed Inca to visit and inspect the provinces and the property of his ancestors and of the religion. Assuming that it was not, Huayna Capac may have felt the need to make an inspection of the provinces in person in order to reaffirm control of them. After all, the first provinces he inspected in person were the neighboring lands of Chinchaysuyu; these might well have been home to the people implicated in the attempt against him by Lord Hualpaya. The fact that he ordered new overseers and governors suggests that he felt the need of more loyal people in those positions. Certainly the fact that he killed some provincial conspirators and deprived others of their property meant that he or one of his loyal governors would need to reassign positions and property in some provinces. The inspection of the property of Cuzco and of the Sun and the mummies may have filled a similar need in terms of royal politics: Huayna Capac could affirm control of the state and the religion by making such an inspection. He could also check to see whether the advisors implicated in the conspiracy against him had deprived him or the Sun of any property. By inspecting the mummies and hearing their histories, he established his own place in Inca religious and political history. He also took the opportunity to enhance the estates of selected ancestors. Perhaps the mummies he chose to reward in this way were the ancestors of people who had been particularly loyal in supporting his cause against attempts by his half-brother and by his uncle.

Huayna Capac and War

Huayna Capac evidently made good on his promise to his mother that he would not go to war until she died. Although he was accompanied on this inspection tour by fifty thousand troops (Cieza parte II, cap. LXIII; 1985: 181), he first went off to fight while he was still in mourning for his mother. Immediately following his mother's death (and close on the heels of the second usurpation attempt that had some support in that province), Huayna Capac set off on a campaign against the Chachapoyas.

The Chachapoyas Campaign

It seems likely that this first Chinchaysuyu campaign was motivated by a need to punish those provincials who may have sympathized with the factions who attempted to usurp Huayna Capac's authority; his targeting of the Chachapoyas was certainly directed to quelling a rebellion there (Sarmiento cap. 58; 1960: 260). In the narratives of his life, however, the campaign is articulated in terms of Huayna Capac's devotion to his dead parents. Several sources note that the campaign was so close in time to his parents' death that he had to seek special permission from the Sun to celebrate their mourning rituals in Cajamarca (Cabello Balboa cap. 20; 1951: 360; Murúa cap. 29; 1962, vol. 1: 76); Cieza reminds us that his campaign against the Huancachupachos and Chachapoyas campaign was launched from that city (parte I, cap. LXXVIII; 1986: 229). As Betanzos presents the story of the campaign, Huayna Capac explains to his generals that he needs to go to Chinchaysuyu to get sufficient coca and *ají* for his mother's *purucaya* celebration; it is a story Betanzos frames in the context of repeating Pachacuti's decree that such goods be obtained by purchase. Nonetheless, Huayna Capac sets out to acquire the goods backed by an army of one hundred thousand men in what is clearly a military venture. During the three years he fought against the Chachapoyas, he wore mourning, and rather than enter Cuzco with victorious displays, he had his army return in mourning out of respect for his mother, whose *purucaya* ritual was not yet completed (Betanzos parte I, cap. XLIV; 1987: 190–191).

The Collasuyu Campaign

After his Chachapoyas venture, Huayna Capac turned his attention to Collasuyu. The appointment of generals for this campaign was accompanied by ceremony. As Cieza tells it:

> En la plaça del Cuzco se puso la gran maroma de oro y se hizieron grandes vayles y borracheras y, junto a la piedra de la guerra, se nonbraron capitanes y mandones conforme a su costunbre; y ordenado les hizo un parlamento Guaynacapa bien ordenado y dicho con palabras behementes sovre que le fuesen leales así los que yvan con él como los que quedavan. Respondieron que de su serviçio no se partirían, el qual dicho loó y dio esperança de le hazer merçedes largas. (Parte II, cap. LXIII; 1985: 181–182)

> They placed the big chain of gold in Cuzco's plaza and held great dances and drunken festivals, and next to the Stone of War the captains and commanders were appointed, as was their custom. And when this was done, Huayna Capac gave a formal speech and spoke with strong words, telling them that everyone should be loyal, those who went with him and those who remained in Cuzco. They answered that they would not leave his service. He praised their loyalty and promised them great rewards.

Accompanied by his huge army, he is described as taking account of the resources of that quarter and revising tribute requests while leaving many new buildings (Cieza parte II, cap. LXIII; 1985: 181–182). Ac-

cording to Betanzos, his visits included Cacha, where he dedicated a
new temple, and Cochabamba, where he reorganized the *mitima* colo-
nies established by his father (parte I, cap. XLV; 1987: 192; confirmation comes from Wachtel 1980–81 and Morales 1978). He continued
his march into Tucumán, Chile, and the Mojos region, where he established *mitimaes* and organized tribute, and he also sent captains to
maintain order on the Chiriguano frontier and to rebuild the fortress
of Pocona (Cieza parte II, cap. LXIII; 1985: 183–184; Murúa cap. 30;
1962, vol. 1: 77; Cabello Balboa cap. 21; 1951: 362; Sarmiento cap. 59;
1960: 260). While in Collasuyu, he announced his intention to go to
war on the northern frontier of the empire.

The Northern Campaign

The northern campaign was kicked off with elaborate ceremony and
pageantry in Cuzco, as was surely typical for other military endeavors.
It was to be an extended and bloody effort that would take Huayna Capac twelve years to resolve and that would engage him for the rest of
his life (fig. 4.2).

There was probably an elaborate story accounting for the declaration of the war and the assembling of troops. Fragments have come
down in Sarmiento, and especially Murúa and Cabello Balboa, which
give a sense of the sacred nature of Inca war (or at least of stories of
Inca war) and of the formalized way in which the army was assembled.
Huayna Capac had gotten news of the rebellion of the Cayambis, Car-
angues, Pastos, and Guancavelicas while he was in Collasuyu. He
learned that they had killed Inca governors and were preparing for
battle (Sarmiento cap. 60; 1960: 261). He chose to go to the sacred and
ancient city of Tiahuanaco to declare war on Quito, then visited the
shrines of the Island of Titicaca, where he consulted the priests, offered sacrifices, and formally called up troops (Sarmiento cap. 59;
1960: 261; Murúa cap. 30; 1962, vol. 1: 78; cf. Pachacuti Yamqui 1968:
308). He then returned to Cuzco to await the assembling of his army
and to carry out his own fasts and rituals.

As Pachacuti Yamqui tells it, the declaration of war while he was in
Collasuyu (which he places in Pomacanchis, in his own home province, rather than in Tiahuanaco) was designed to obligate local lords
to provide troops for the campaign:

> Y en Pomacanchi se junta toda el reyno de los curacas, yendo o veniendo a
> reçibir, y allí pregona armas contra Quito y Cayambis, porque la nueva ve-
> nía cadal día dando abissos que como estaban rebeldes. Y estando assí, re-
> parte las armas y bestidos y comida para la gente que avían de yr a la con-
> quista; y entonces por los curacas hazen juramento, y assí dan cargos a los
> oficiales de guerra. Al fin buelben los curacas cada una a sus tierras,

lleuando cajas y *unanchas* enarboladas, con las armas en las manos, y por el ynga promete grandes cossas a los curacas, con juramento solemne de cumplirlos mejor que sus passados. Al fin señala días para juntarse en vn día de todas partes con sus gentes de guerras y municiones y cosas necesarios. (1968: 308)

And in Pomacanchis he gathered together all the *curacas* of the land, and he asked for troops to go against the Quitos and Cayambis, because news had arrived that very day that they were in rebellion. So he divided weapons and clothes and food among the people who were going to go on the campaign. Then he swore in the *curacas* and installed the military leaders. At last the *curacas* returned to their lands, carrying drums and banners and weapons. The *curacas* promised the Inca they would do their best and pledged to surpass the contributions of their ancestors. Finally, he indicated the day on which the troops would meet with their weapons and supplies.

In Pachacuti Yamqui's story, the day on which troops are to assemble is set for a year and a half from the meeting, obligating the *curacas* to call up men for the campaign.

In an abbreviated story presented by Murúa, Huayna Capac makes a second declaration of war in Cuzco, soliciting the participation of Cuzco's noble families (cap. 31; 1962, vol. 1: 79–80). The soldiers from Collasuyu, Condesuyu, and Antesuyu are feted and then leave. The Chinchaysuyu soldiers then arrive, are feted, and urge the Inca army to embark. Finally, the noble soldiers from Cuzco leave. As in so many other stories, the arrival, celebration, and departure of the armies are reported individually and repeated (at least as Murúa tells it) three times, in order of increasing prestige. (As Cabello Balboa tells the story, only the Chinchaysuyu army appears in Cuzco, urging the Inca to leave soon; cap. 21; 1951: 363). Pachacuti Yamqui suggests that the ritual send-off lasted every day from sunup to sundown for a full three and a half months (1968: 308).

In making the arrangements for his departure, Huayna Capac appointed generals for his campaign. In one version, he named Michi or Mihi as captain of the Hanan Cuzco brigade and placed Auqui Topa Inca in charge of the Hurin Cuzco troops; in this version, Guaman Achachi remained in Cuzco as his governor. Other stories assert that his son Topa Cusi Gualpa (who would become Huascar Inca) remained in Cuzco to govern in his absence, along with his uncle Apu Hilaquito and brother Auqui Topa Inca. Another son, Tito Atauchi, remained in Cuzco to carry out fasts for the Inca's success (Sarmiento cap. 60; 1960: 261; Murúa cap. 31; 1962, vol. 1: 80; Cabello Balboa cap. 21; 1951: 363). Huayna Capac's son Atahuallpa accompanied him to war, as did his consort Rahua Ocllo (Sarmiento cap. 60; 1960: 261; Betanzos parte I, cap. XLVIII; 1987: 199).

FIGURE 4.2. Huayna Capac goes to war in a jewel-studded war litter (Guaman Poma f. 333 [335]; 1980: 307).

Cieza de León describes Huayna Capac's progress to the northern frontier (see especially parte II, cap. LXIV; 1985: 185–191). He reminds us that in advance of the campaign, the main Inca road was improved and provided with storehouses, lodgings, and other facilities to support the army, the Inca, and his mobile court. That court would have been sizable. As Cieza tells us:

> Hízose llamamiento general en todas las provinçias de su señorío y vinieron de todas partes tanta jente que henchían los canpos. Y despúes de aver hecho vanquetes y borracheras generales y puesto en horden las cosas de la çibdad, salió de allí Guaynacapa con "yscaypachaguaranga lunas", que quiere dezir con dozientos mill honbres de guerra, sin los anaconas y

mujeres de serviçio, que no tenía quento el número dellos. Llevava consigo
dos mill mugeres y dexava en el Cuzco más de quatro mill. (Parte II, cap.
LXIV; 1985: 186)

He put out a general call for troops in all the provinces of his land, and so
many people came from all parts that they swelled the fields. After holding
banquets and drunken festivals and having put Cuzco's affairs in order,
Huayna Capac set out with *iscaypachahuaranca runa*, which means two hundred thousand men of war, not counting the *yanaconas* and serving women,
of which I have no accounting. He took with him two thousand women
and left more than four thousand in Cuzco.

Pachacuti Yamqui, too, describes the order in which the army moved.
Each squadron of five hundred had a captain, and each group of one
thousand had a standard and officers. In order to assure that they
marched in formation and that the right number of soldiers was present and that they were well outfitted, an *usnu* was built every thirty
leagues, where the troops were inspected and food was dispensed (Pachacuti Yamqui 1968: 309).

It is difficult to imagine this juggernaut on the move, marching on
newly made roads through lands that had been provisioned for them.
If the story unfolded as the narratives told by Sarmiento, Murúa, Pachacuti Yamqui, and Cabello Balboa would suggest, that is, if the
northern rebellion began while Inca attention was focused on the
south, the people of the northern frontier would surely have gotten
wind of the Inca's plans and would have had several years to prepare
themselves for the onslaught and to worry about the inevitable encounter. Although Cieza's account of the northern campaign is somewhat different (the Inca settles a number of local skirmishes, estab-
lishes order, and only later has to contend with the alliance of the
native groups near Quito), he, too, notes that during the Inca march to
the north the Quiteño groups were forming alliances and building
forts to prepare themselves (parte II, cap. LXVII; 1985: 194).

Focusing on the logistics of travel, Cieza, himself a soldier and
traveler (parte II, cap. LXIV; 1985: 185–188), reports that the army
stayed at Vilcas, where the Inca reendowed a temple and made sacrifices. Pachacuti Yamqui adds that the Inca celebrated Capac Raymi
there (1968: 308). Huayna Capac proceeded to Xauxa (Jauja), where
he adjudicated boundary disputes, then the army rested at Bonbón
(Pumpu). During a stay at Cajamarca, the army engaged the Guan-
cachupachos and Chachapoyas, old enemies of the Incas; to mark his
army's victory, Huayna Capac sent many Chachapoyas as *mitimaes* to
live near Cuzco. A less successful incursion was attempted against the
people who lived in Bracamoros, though, as Cieza notes, the Inca nobles did not admit to their failure; he heard the story from dignitaries

from Chincha, Collao, and Xauxa who were not so reticent about telling of the Inca defeat at the hands of naked savages (parte II, cap. LXV; 1985: 189–190).

The temporal relationship of these events to the dramatic stories of the defeat of the allied groups of the northern frontier was a matter of debate even among the Incas. The accounts that focus on the northern wars (Sarmiento, Pachacuti Yamqui, Murúa, and Cabello Balboa) describe the army marching straight from Cuzco toward the battles in the north. However, as Cieza notes, "Some of the *orejones* claim that Huayna Capac returned to Cuzco from Quito, following the coast as far as Pachacamac, while others say that he remained in Quito until he died" (parte II, cap. LXVI; 1985: 192).

The former tradition was used by Cieza, who reports that the army reached Quito via Latacunga province. Exploring the coast, Huayna Capac settled a dispute between Puná and Tumbes, then proceeded to Chimu and then to the oracle at Pachacamac; this is the point, he notes, where some informants claim he returned to Cuzco, and others say he went back to Quito (Cieza parte II, cap. LXVI; 1985: 193). At some point the army marched down the coast to Chincha and built storehouses, lodgings, and temples, and at some point Huayna Capac went to Quito and embarked on the war. Pachacuti Yamqui presents a story of Huayna Capac being called to Pachacamac to consult the oracle and, on its advice, proceeding to Chimu. He constructed buildings at Pachacamac (1968: 309). The version that has Huayna Capac returning to Cuzco was the basis of the problematic accounts of Montesinos (1920) and Oliva (1895), who likely drew from Blas Valera's vanished history as well as the account by Zárate (cap. XII; 1947: 473). It may also have informed Garcilaso's confused account of the northern campaigns (Garcilaso relied on both Blas Valera and Cieza). Cobo seems to have included both traditions in his account (lib. 11, caps. XVI–XVII; 1964: 88–94). In this tradition, the army's work in the north was restricted to an inspection tour with a few bloody battles along the way.

Probably because it was his final campaign and fresh in the minds of veterans of the battles who reported it to the Spaniards as well as the historians who sang the victory songs, we have a fair amount of detail about Huayna Capac's victories in the north. The sequence of battles and the military strategy used in the conquests near Quito are based on accounts set down by Murúa (caps. 32–33; 1962, vol. 1: 82–90), Sarmiento (cap. 60; 1960: 261–263), Cabello Balboa (caps. 21–22; 1951: 361–379), Pachacuti Yamqui (1968: 308–311), and Cieza de León (parte II, caps. LXVII–LXVIII; 1985: 194–198).

Huayna Capac based his campaign at Tomebamba, the city located in modern Cuenca, Ecuador, the town of his birth. From here, he sent out armies to the land of the Pastos; as Murúa tells it, the honor of that *entrada* was left to the armies from Collasuyu and Condesuyu, as the Pasto lands were cold and mountainous like their own homelands (Murúa cap. 32; 1962, vol. 1: 82). The Pastos, seeing that the Collasuyu soldiers' favorite weapons were *ayllus*, staged their assault in a narrow canyon where these weapons would be useless. The conquest was hard-won, with much loss among the Collasuyu troops especially. After the victory, the Inca army invaded the vacated Pasto forts and towns, killing survivors, burning towns, and tearing down forts. An Inca governor was put in place, and the army prepared for the campaign against the Caranguis and their allies (Murúa cap. 32; 1962, vol. 1: 86).

For the Carangui campaign, Huayna Capac sent to Collasuyu for re-inforcements (Murúa cap. 33; 1962, vol. 1: 86; cf. Pachacuti Yamqui 1968: 309; the participation of conscripts from around Chucuito is confirmed by many of Garci Diez de San Miguel's informants [1964]). Huayna Capac wished to take charge of this campaign himself and fought his way down to the coast at Tumbes, which was the Carangui and Cochisqui frontier. After driving the enemies out of their fort at Cochisque, Huayna Capac faced dissension among his own generals on the best strategy for the final attack. Doubling back from Otavalo, the Inca army caused the Caranguis to retreat to another hilltop fortress, which they surrounded in hopes of starving out the enemy. When the Caranguis repelled an Inca raid and then launched their own attack, many Inca troops were killed, and Huayna Capac was injured and believed dead. After driving his enemies back to their fortress, Huayna Capac played the waiting game again, using his time in Tomebamba to select governors for the newly pacified provinces, to mandate worship of the Sun, and to select captives to be included in the victory parade to Cuzco (Murúa cap. 33; 1962, vol. 1: 89–90).

The third campaign was against the Cayambis, and it was the bloodiest of all the northern fights. The Cayambis took the initiative, attacking from their hilltop fortress, killing many Incas, and disheartening the Inca army so that it fled. In the Inca counterattack, both sides fought so valiantly that there was no place to stand except on top of other bodies. When the Inca captain Auqui Topa was killed, his troops fled across a river, but many drowned in it. In the final attack, Huayna Capac again led the army, which was divided into three parts (the Inca captain Michi was in charge of one third, and the other was a Chinchaysuyu army). The Inca siege lasted five days, and the surrounding area was burned. Huayna Capac faked a withdrawal to lure the Cayambis out of their fort, knowing that a portion of the Inca army was planning to come in from behind to destroy it. The Cayambis lost heart and fled to a nearby lake, while the Inca army came in to slay many of the troops that were hiding in the reeds or slitting the throats of the enemies and throwing them in the water. The lake turned red with their blood, for which it was called Yahuarcocha (blood lake). The Cayambi captains climbed up into the lake's willow trees and continued to fight to the death. Pinto, an especially valiant captain, fled to a forest, and when he was captured, Huayna Capac honored his bravery by using his skin for a drumhead to dance for the Sun in Cuzco.

The accounts of Murúa, Cabello Balboa, and Pachacuti Yamqui allude to the near-defeat of the Incas during their long campaign and to the political cost to Huayna Capac. In a story set after the Carangui victory and before the Cayambi campaign in Murúa's account, and probably in the middle of the Cayambi campaign in Pachacuti Yamqui's, the long siege resulted in great despair among the troops. In accounts by Murúa (cap. 34; 1962, vol. 1: 90–93) and Cabello Balboa (cap. 22; 1951: 371–379), Huayna Capac was angry that his troops had left him for dead at Carangui and so did not invite his generals to the victory feasts; rather, he ostentatiously celebrated with his *yanaconas*. Further, he cut the troops' rations. The Inca generals saw their troops going hungry, and, led by Michi, the *orejones* decided to march back to Cuzco, carrying the image of the Sun (in Murúa and Cabello Balboa) or Huanacauri (in Pachacuti Yamqui's story) from Tomebamba's temple. Huayna Capac could only counter their mutiny by sending the statue of his mother, Mama Ocllo, to meet them on the road, with a Cañari woman addressing the nobles in the Inca queen's name. She promised them clothes, sandals, and food if they would return to Tomebamba. They obeyed her, and Huayna Capac rewarded them by filling the plaza with food, clothing of rich *cumbi* cloth as well as *ahuasca* and cotton cloth, and other things that they wanted, including women. He then offered the *orejones* a public apology and invited them to take what they wanted from the goods piled up in the plaza. His reward was sufficient to buy the loyalty of the *orejones*, who remained with him and, with the help of reinforcements sent from Cuzco, finally defeated the Cayambis.

We have independent confirmation of the magnitude of the army mustered by Huayna Capac for his northern conquest and for the difficulties faced by the soldiers from Collasuyu. Informants to an investigation of the Inca tribute system in Chucuito in 1567 recalled that men from their villages had been sent with the Inca to fight in the north. Francisco Vilcacutipa, the elderly *cacique* of Ilave's Anansaya moiety, was one of the soldiers who went to Tomebamba with Huayna Capac; he claimed that the war lasted for twenty years. He reported that the first conscription included six thousand soldiers from Chucuito province, of whom five thousand died, along with all but two of the *caciques* who went with them. He added that a second draft included two thousand men, of whom one thousand died (Diez de San Miguel 1964: 105–106). Pedro Cutinbo, former governor of Chucuito, reported that two thousand young men from the province had gone to fight the wars in Tumbes (Diez de San Miguel 1964: 170). Huayna Capac had to redirect personal goods to the war effort, too. Witnesses reported that during the northern campaign he sent an overseer to his private reserves near Abancay to carry to Tomebamba all the cotton, ají, and other goods that had been harvested in order to sustain the war (testimony of Gonzalo Alvarez Caja; Espinoza Soriano 1973: 287). Pedro Llatacapa also reported that he sent from Tomebamba for cotton and ají, and that they also sent coca and *sacapa*, dance rattles worn by Huayna Capac's soldiers in battle and in celebrations (Espinoza Soriano 1973: 293).

Almost certainly, the story of the northern wars presented by Pachacuti Yamqui, Murúa, Cabello Balboa, and Sarmiento is based on a formalized history of the northern campaign, probably one of the *cantares* that told of Huayna Capac's victories. If, as is likely, the northern campaign included a great number of stops devoted to revision of the tribute system, provisioning of *tambos*, and quelling of local skirmishes, that sort of detail is edited out of the *cantar*. The story of the victory condenses what was likely to have been a large amount of time into a handful of episodes. Huayna Capac devoted at least twelve years to the Quito wars; some of this time was surely spent resting and establishing order in the wake of the victory. All of the routine and the tedium is edited out of the *cantar*. In many ways, the story is formalized. It includes allusions to rituals: In Sarmiento, the declaration of war is accompanied by sacrifices, and the campaign begins with a divination ceremony; in Murúa and Pachacuti Yamqui, the send-off includes a formal address by the Inca and a review of the troops; Pachacuti Yamqui reminds readers that the campaign begins and ends with Huayna Capac celebrating the feast of Capac Raymi. The story also names the valiant allies of the Inca and the brave enemy captains, offering public credit for the success of the troops. Pachacuti Yamqui's account includes closure of the sort that is more likely to be encountered in a formal construction of events than in real life: The *orejones* of Cuzco march as far as Vilcas and realize they have forgotten to bring their war idol, Huanacauri, and they return to Cuzco to get it; when Michi mutinies, the *orejones* grab the same idol and begin to carry it back to Cuzco. The structure of the remembered history also involves repetition in threes: Murúa's informants structure the departure ceremony of the Army of the Four Quarters into three events; the story divides the northern campaign into three major battles of increasing difficulty: against the Pastos, against the Caranguis, against the Cayambis.

Perhaps because they don't want to destroy the drama of the story of the Quito wars, the sources that describe the battles on the northern frontier include diminished reference to Huayna Capac's other accomplishments. Sarmiento and Cobo, for example, toss in abbreviated references to Huayna Capac's descent to the coast after victory and his conquests there, and Murúa and Cabello, though their accounts are more extensive, provide little detail on those campaigns. Cieza, who appears not to have based his account on a formal *cantar* of the northern campaign, provides an account which is more matter-of-fact and includes many more stops on the trip, where the Inca endows temples, settles petty disputes, and makes small conquests. It seems likely that Cieza's informants were basing their story on the more mundane reporting of a ruler's activities, something perhaps akin to accounts kept for tribute purposes or to plan provisioning of the army, rather than the more flamboyant accounts that praised the valor of a ruling Inca. Still, parts of the victory *cantar* show up in other sources. In particular, the story of the Inca rout of their enemies at Yahuarcocha existed in several versions, not just in those sources that seem to draw from the formal *cantar*, including Cieza, Betanzos, Garcilaso, and even the usually unreliable Montesinos and Oliva.

The Death of Huayna Capac

Most of the accounts of the northern campaign terminate with Huayna Capac's death from disease in the north. But as shouldn't, perhaps, be surprising in stories that take us to heart of the succession dispute between Huascar and Atahuallpa, there are varying versions of his death. Huayna Capac heard of an epidemic that was sweeping the empire and learned that many of the nobles of Cuzco, including the governors he had left there, had died; the epidemic was probably smallpox, sweeping from south to north in advance of the Europeans. While he was in Quito, resting from battle or preparing to return to Cuzco and deal with the epidemic, the disease struck the Inca camp, killing many of his trusted generals and catching Huayna Capac himself. On his deathbed Huayna Capac was asked to name his successor. He first named Ninan Cuyochi, who was an infant, but the choice was not acceptable because the divination did not augur well (Sarmiento cap. 62; 1960: 264), or because Huayna Capac was too ill to remember his selection of the infant when asked to verify it (Betanzos parte I, cap. XLVIII; 1987: 200), or because the boy had died in the interim (Cabello Balboa cap. 24; 1951: 394). The nobles asked for his second choice, and the dying Inca named Atahuallpa, who refused (Betanzos parte I, cap. XLVIII; 1987: 200), or he named Huascar (Sarmiento cap. 62; 1960: 265), or the nobles chose Huascar themselves, after divination. Some stories in circulation claimed that Huayna Capac divided the empire between Atahuallpa and Huascar, but the account is either not present in the most reliable sources or is dismissed by them (Cieza parte II, cap. LXIX; 1985: 200).

The accounts of the Inca's death existed in different versions. At least one version (accepted by Pachacuti Yamqui and dismissed by Murúa) asserted that when the epidemic hit his camp, Huayna Capac ordered that he be sealed up in a house (Pachacuti Yamqui 1968: 311) or below the ground (Murúa cap. 37; 1962, vol. 1: 103) so that he

FIGURE 4.3. Huayna Capac's embalmed body being carried to Cuzco from the northern frontier (Guaman Poma f. 377 [379]; 1980: 350).

wouldn't catch the disease. But his efforts were in vain. In Pachacuti Yamqui's colorful story, when his associates unsealed the house a week later, Huayna Capac's dead body was in it all alone. Pachacuti Yamqui also describes the plague as being brought by a dark-clothed supernatural messenger bearing a box full of butterflies; the escaping butterflies were the harbingers of the plague (1968: 311). Pedro Pizarro offers a story of three dwarves who came to Huayna Capac as auguries of his death (cap. 10; 1986: 48).

There were other versions of the death of Huayna Capac that have not been preserved in the Inca royal narratives. As late as 1574 members of a ruling family of Chachapoyas maintained the tradition that their ancestor Chuquimis sent medicinal herbs to cure the dying Inca, and that Huayna Capac's captain, believing that the Inca had been poisoned by the herbs, desecrated Chuquimis' grave and punished his sons for the crime by placing them in the Sancahuasi of Cuzco, from which they emerged unscathed (Schjellerup 1997: 71, and appendix 14, 335).

The sources do agree on the disposition of the body. It was embalmed by Huayna Capac's closest associates, dressed in its finest clothing, and placed in a litter to be carried back to Cuzco amid great displays of grief (fig. 4.3). As Cabello Balboa reports it, Huayna Capac mandated the commemoration of his death, which was recorded by the quipucamayos:

> Hallaron tambien por los Quipos el orden que se auia de tener en llevar su cuerpo á el Cuzco, y como se auia de entrar triumphando, y guardando ansi en esto (como en todo lo demas) lo mandado por el muerto Rey llevaron su cuerpo de Quito á Tumibamba y allí repararon hasta poner en orden el Goviemo de la tierra y lo necesario para tan largo viage probeyeron los Albaceas de el muerto Guaynacapac por Governador de la tierra a un Quigual Topa natural del Cuzco, y dejaronle las compañias de Soldados que parecio combenir, y tomando consigo las estatuas y figuras y Guacas (que del Cuzco auian traydo) se pusieron en camino para alla acompañando a la trieste viuda Mamaragua Ocllo llebando siempre el cuerpo en hombros de hijos primos, y hermanos los mas principales personages de todo el Ymperio. (Cap. 24; 1951: 394)

The quipus also told of the order they should follow in carrying his body to Cuzco and mandated that they should enter [the city] in triumph. Following this mandate (as in all other things), they carried his body from Quito to Tomebamba, and they stayed there until they had established the government of that region and made all the arrangements necessary for such a long journey. They placed Quigal Topa, a native of Cuzco, as governor there. Leaving him with the troops he thought were necessary and taking with them the statues and figures and huacas which they had brought from

Cuzco, they set off to accompany Mama Rahua Ocllo, the sad widow. The body was always carried on the shoulders of his sons, cousins, and brothers—the most important people in the Empire.

The mourning that marked his death also included the suicide or sacrifice of many of his retainers. Cieza claims that four thousand people accompanied him to the grave, among them women, pages, and servants (parte II, cap. LXIX; 1985: 199–201), while Acosta puts the number at more than one thousand (lib. V, cap. VII; 1954: 147). The Anonymous Jesuit reports as well that more than one thousand animals were sacrificed by dignitaries who named the animals for themselves and sent them to accompany Huayna Capac in their stead (1968: 159).

While it is surely a dramatic story to tell of the progress of the cortege from one end of the empire to the other, the tension is heightened by the fact that the procession is designed to mark the death of the divine king as well as to celebrate the Inca victories in the north. Murúa gives an account of the triumphant return of the army (cap. 41; 1962, vol. 1: 116–118). Assuming that this account is correctly placed relative to his death, a statue of Huayna Capac was carried with the troops, and the parade included day-long entrances of the army, divided into three groups and accompanied by the *orejones*—all richly dressed and carrying trophy heads, medallions, and loot—and parades of captives. Some of the army replayed the key battle scenes, and the nobles sang victory songs. It should be noted that the description parallels the military send-off ritual (the army in three parts) that he offers at the beginning of the campaign.

Huayna Capac's body escaped destruction in the Inca civil wars and eluded confiscation by the Spaniards for many years as well. The body was to be cared for by a group of *apoyanaconas* brought from the northern frontier to be its attendants. The custodians were settled on Huayna Capac's estate at Yucay, where they furtively worked to sustain the body for two decades. Atau Rimache originally served as manager of Tomebamba *panaca* and overseer of the mummy's custodians; he was succeeded in this job by Alonso Tito Atauchi, Huayna Capac's grandson (*Informaciones de Toledo*; Levillier 1940: 167, 169; see also Villanueva 1971, pregunta trece; Farrington 1995), who claimed to be a member of the *panaca* founded by Huascar (*Fe de la prouança*, Sarmiento 1960: 278). The mummy was finally confiscated by Polo de Ondegardo in 1559 at a house in Cuzco, where it was hidden and guarded by two attendants, Gualpa Tito and Suma Yupanqui (Sarmiento cap. 62; 1960: 265).

Wives and Sons

Because his death took place at the onset of the Spanish Conquest, many of Huayna Capac's descendants lived into the historical period. For a variety of reasons, we know about some of them. Among the royal ladies seeking land in the Spanish courts after the Conquest were several who traced their descent from him. Also, some of the highly placed Inca men with whom the Spanish treated were similarly his descendants.

Wives

Like his ancestors, Huayna Capac had a number of productive liaisons with women. One source claims he had more than fifty spouses (Espinoza Soriano 1976: 264). His legitimate wife, Coya Cusirimay, was his full sister, whom he married at the time he succeeded; her premarriage name may have been Pillcu Huaco (Garcilaso parte I, lib. VIII, cap. VIII; 1609: 205 v.). The marriage did not produce a living male heir, though sources differ on the nature of the problem: Garcilaso claims that Cusirimay produced no child (parte I, lib. VIII, cap. VIII; 1609: 205 v.–206 r.), and Sarmiento says she bore no son (cap. 60; 1960: 261). Pachacuti Yamqui claims that Ninan Cuyochi, the infant who was Huayna Capac's deathbed choice of successor, was her son, though this account contradicts his claim of Cusirimay's early death (1968: 308). Pachacuti Yamqui reports that Huayna Capac selected a second sister, Mama Coca, as wife, but that his father's mummy did not consent to the marriage. When lightning bolts also hit the fortress, Huayna Capac realized the wedding was not to be; he arranged her marriage to a disgusting old man, and later she entered an *adllahuasi*, while Huayna Capac later took another principal wife, Cibi Chimpo Rontocay (Pachacuti Yamqui 1968: 308).

Outside of his marriage to his sister-wife, Huayna Capac produced the sons who were to figure so prominently in succession disputes just before and just after the Spanish Conquest. The oldest of these sons was Atahuallpa. At least two stories circulated about his maternity: One version claimed that his mother was the daughter of a Cañari *cacique* and that Atahuallpa had been born on the northern frontier; the other claimed that his mother was a lady from Cuzco and that Atahuallpa had been born there. Betanzos identifies Atahuallpa's mother as Pallacoca, a lady of Cuzco who was a second cousin of Huayna Capac and great-granddaughter of Inca Yupanqui; he places Atahuallpa as a member of Capac Ayllu (parte I, cap. XLVI; 1987: 194). Some confirmation of this claim comes from Sarmiento, who identifies Atahuallpa's mother as Tocto Coca, a cousin of Huayna Capac and a member of Inca Yupanqui's lineage (cap. 63; 1960: 265). Pachacuti Yamqui simply identifies her as Tocto Ocllo Coca (1968: 308). On the other side, Guaman Poma identifies Atahuallpa's mother as a Chachapoya woman (f. 114; 1980, vol. 1: 83). Zárate says that Atahuallpa's mother was from Quito and that he had been born there during an early northern campaign (lib. I, cap. XII; 1947: 473). Cieza reports that the mother was a native of Quilaco, though he notes that others said she was a lady of Cuzco from Hurinsaya (parte II, cap. LXIII; 1985: 184).

Huascar, by contrast, was indisputably the son of an Inca lady from Cuzco, Rahua Ocllo. This son was born at the town of Huascar or Huascarquiguar (Sarmiento cap. 63; 1960: 265) on Lake Muina, not far from Cuzco, as Huayna Capac was returning from his inspection of Collasuyu (Betanzos parte I, cap. XLV; 1987: 192). His popular name was taken from the town of his birth (Sarmiento cap. 63; 1960: 265), though there was also a story that it referred to a rope or cable of gold that his father made to commemorate his birth (*huasca* means "rope" in Quechua; see, e.g., Cobo lib. 11, cap. XVIII; 1964: 94). His birth name was Tito Cusi Gualpa Inti Illapa (Sarmiento cap. 63; 1960: 265) or Inti Topa Cusi Huallpa Huascar Inca (Pachacuti Yamqui 1968: 311). Rahua Ocllo was among Huayna Capac's women. Her relationship with Huayna Capac must have lasted for at least twenty years; her privileged position in his bed is suggested by the fact that she accompanied him on his long campaign to Quito (Sarmiento cap. 62; 1960: 265), during which time she bore him a daughter, Chuqui Huipa, while her son, Huascar, had been born many years earlier.

Rahua Ocllo's family affiliation was also in dispute at the time of the Conquest, as was her exact relationship to Huayna Capac. Some stories simply asserted that she was his legitimate wife (Cieza parte II, cap. LXIII; 1985: 181 and cap. LXIX; 1985: 200). There was also a tradition circulating that she was a sister of Huayna Capac, taking the position as legitimate wife because of the first sister's death or barrenness (Sarmiento cap. 60; 1960: 261; Garcilaso parte I, lib. VIII, cap. VIII; 1609: 206 r.). If she was a legitimate wife, then Huascar was by rights his father's successor (see Guaman Poma f. 114; 1980, vol. 1: 83). There was a more plausible story that she was a descendant of a lord of Hurinsaya moiety of Cuzco (Betanzos parte I, cap. XLVI; 1987: 194). Still, Huascar was insecure enough about his own parentage so that when his father's preserved mummy was brought to Cuzco, he married it to his mother in order to legitimize his claim to rule (Pachacuti Yamqui 1968: 311). It was doubtless in Huascar's interest to do all that he could to promote his mother's cause. The stories that she was a full sister of Huayna Capac may have been circulated by Huascar and his party; alternatively, they may have been the product of reasoning by later Inca informants or Spanish chroniclers, based on Huascar's claim of legitimacy.

Claims and counterclaims based on kinship were central to most arguments about privilege, landownership, and, of course, succession, so it is not surprising that rival versions of the truth were in circulation. When Atahuallpa's generals captured Huascar and his family, they reviled his mother by saying that she was a concubine, rather than a wife, of Huayna Capac and that she was a base woman, not a queen (Sarmiento cap. 66; 1960: 271), thus casting aspersions on Huascar's claim to the throne. Zárate claims that Atahuallpa's mother was the daughter of a lord of Quito (cap. XII; 1947: 473). Garcilaso reports that his elderly noble kinsman whose family was especially hard hit by Atahuallpa's generals refused to mourn the death of a son of Atahuallpa and claimed that Atahuallpa was not the son of Huayna Capac but that his mother had conceived him by an adulterous affair with a native of Quito (parte I, lib. IX, cap. XXXIX; 1609: 262 v.). While doubtless untrue, this outburst shows the kind of aspersions cast on character in matters of reputation, fame, and succession.

The varying traditions about the disputants' maternity can be seen as propaganda pertaining to the son's right to succeed his father: Since Huascar expected the loyalty of the *orejones* of Cuzco, he had every reason to deny that Atahuallpa could have any legitimate tie to the Inca capital; by claiming that his rival was the son of a Cañari woman or a native of Quilaco, he denied his birthright to Cuzqueño or even ethnic Inca loyalties. In his pro-Atahuallpa account, Betanzos gives him claim to the throne by virtue of seniority (he was the older of the disputants), place of birth (he was born in Cuzco, rather than outside of town), and descent (his mother was a member of the higher-ranked Hanansaya moiety and was kin to Huayna Capac, while Huascar's mother was a nonrelative from the lower-ranked Hurinsaya moiety).

The maternity of other important sons is similarly clouded in some confusion. Manco Inca's mother is identified by Garcilaso as Mama Runtu, Huayna Capac's first cousin (daughter of Auqui Amaru Topa Inca, Topa Inca's second brother; Garcilaso parte I, lib. VIII, cap. VIII; 1609: 206 r.), while Guaman Poma identifies Manco Inca's mother as Cayac Cuzco and notes that she also gave birth to Ninan Cuyochi (Guaman Poma f. 114; 1980, vol. 1: 83). Pachacuti Yamqui calls her Cibichimporontocay and considers her the second wife of Huayna Capac (1968: 308). Manco Inca was born during Huayna Capac's inspection of Collasuyu (Pachacuti Yamqui 1968: 308), possibly at Tiahuanaco.[4] This son was first to be loyal to the Spanish invaders and then to be a thorn in their side, heading up the siege of the Inca capital and establishing the Inca government-in-exile at Vilcabamba. A fourth son, Paullu Topa Inca, was born to Osica (Guaman Poma f. 114; 1980, vol. 1: 83) or possibly to Añas Qolque (Temple 1937). This is the Inca whom the Spaniards set up as their puppet and who ruled in Cuzco until his death in 1551.

In addition to the four sons who achieved prominence after the death of their father, there were a number of other children of Huayna Capac, though rarely do we know much about their mothers. Sarmiento identifies a Tito Atauchi who was left in Cuzco during the Quito campaign to assist Huascar (cap. 60; 1960: 261); this was probably the father of Alonso Tito Atauchi, implicated in directing Huayna Capac's mummy custodians (see *Informaciones de Toledo*; Levillier 1940: 67). Guaman Poma identifies Tito Atauchi's mother as Lari, probably referring to the fact that she came from Lare or Lares (f. 114; 1980, vol. 1: 83). Guaman Poma identifies other sons sired by Huayna Capac, among them Illescas Inga, born to Chuquillanto; Uaritito, born to a lady named Anahuarque; Inquiltopa, born to a Cañari lady; Uanca Auqui, born to a lady from Jauja; and Quizo Yupanqui, born to the sister of Capac Apo Guaman Chaua (f. 114; 1980, vol. 1: 83). Cieza adds Nauque Yupanque, Topa Ynga, Topa Gualpa, Tito, Guama Gualpa, Cuxi Gualpa, Tilca Yupangue, and Conono (parte II, cap. LXIX; 1985: 200). Among the daughters of Huayna Capac were Chuqui Huipo, whose mother was Rahua Ocllo and who married her brother Huascar (Murúa cap. 43; 1962, vol. 1: 121; Pachacuti Yamqui 1968: 312), and possibly Coya Miro, who likewise had a child by her brother Huascar (Sarmiento cap. 67; 1960: 272), and Chimbo Cisa (Sarmiento cap. 67; 1960: 272). Daughters who survived the Inca civil wars and are known by their post-Conquest names may have included a Coya Doña Beatriz (Garcilaso parte I, lib. VII, cap. XI; 1609: 178 r., lib. IX, cap. XXXVIII; 1609: 261 r.), Doña Leonor Coya (Garcilaso parte I, lib. IX, cap. XXXVIII; 1609: 261 r.), and another daughter known as Doña Inés Huaylas Ñusta whose mother was a lady from Guaylas or Huayllas (Garcilaso parte I, lib. IX, cap. XXVIII; 1609: 261 r.; Espinoza Soriano 1976: 268).

Many of the children of Huayna Capac and possible claimants to the throne were killed by Atahuallpa in the butchery of the noble families during the Inca civil wars. Only two adult sons escaped: Manco Inca and Paullu Topa, who were of low birth on the part of their mothers and who hid from Atahuallpa's generals. Children under age ten or eleven were similarly spared (Garcilaso parte I, lib. IX, cap. XXXVIII; 1609: 260 v.). However, if Huayna Capac truly spent the last twelve years of his life on the northern frontier (and if children and concubines were not returned to Cuzco), there may have been few very young progeny in Cuzco for Atahuallpa's generals to kill.

The total number of children fathered by Huayna Capac was large, but there is little consensus on just how large it was. Garcilaso says there were about two hundred children (parte I, lib. IX, cap. XXXVIII; 1609: 261 v., lib. IX, cap. XXXVI; 1609: 259 r.), while Guaman Poma claims there were five hundred (f. 114; 1980, vol. 1: 83). Sarmiento asserts that there were more than fifty (cap. 62; 1960: 265). It is hard to choose among these estimates. Guaman Poma's claim of five hundred offspring is probably too high, as it assumes both extraordinary stamina and remarkable fecundity on the part of the Inca.[5] Sarmiento's number may be too low: He only mentions male progeny in his narrative, and it is quite likely that the "more than fifty" children meant "more than fifty living male children."

The pattern of maternity and the number of children attributed to Huayna Capac remind us that Huayna Capac had liaisons with many provincial ladies. Sixteenth-century documents seeking lands by the descendants of Doña Inés Huaylas Ñusta suggest how some of these relationships may have been contracted. Two prominent women from Huayllas were taken as concubines by Huayna Capac, perhaps in order to engender children with them and thus to assure a blood Inca in a position of inherited rule in that province. The women were Contarguacho, daughter of a *curaca* of Jatun Huaylla, and Añas Colque, daughter of Huacachillac, lord of Lurin Huaylla (Espinoza Soriano 1976: 249). The concubines were accorded certain privileges, among them land, *yanaconas*, and the right to live in Cuzco (Espinoza Soriano 1976: 258). Espinoza Soriano suggests that the goal of women taken from the ethnic lords' families and placed in the sexual service of an Inca was to bear one living descendant. This document suggests that Añas Colque was mother of Paulo Inquil Topa Inca, and Contarguacho was the mother of a son who died and a daughter named Quispe Sisa, later baptized Doña Inés, or Huaylas Ñusta (Espinoza Soriano 1976: 268–269).

The Narratives of Huayna Capac's Life

For all the detail that we can reconstruct as checks against the history of his life, there remain some curious features about the stories that tell of Huayna Capac: He is shown to be a skillful diplomat, using Andean rules of reciprocity to great effect in securing the loyalty of local dignitaries in his early inspection tours and in obligating the lords of Collasuyu to send him troops for the northern frontiers. Yet if we take the stories at face value, it is his failure to reward his most elite soldiers after the long and difficult siege of the Caranguis that causes a rebellion by the ethnic Inca soldiers and their generals (it is an Andean solution—the provision of clothes, food, and women, along with a little intervention by Huayna Capac's dead mother—that finally buys their loyalty again). The narratives also play on Huayna Capac's alleged youth and his inexperience as a warrior. Saddled throughout his adult life with the name Huayna Capac, he is depicted as so inexperienced at the time his father dies that he is utterly dependent upon the regents and advisors and the intervention of his uncles and his mother. There is no discussion of how Huayna Capac became an astute diplomat and successful warrior: All we have are examples of his skill, juxtaposed against a story of a boy who almost didn't become Inca.

We might ask whether, in fact, there was a single, formal narrative that told of Huayna Capac's life. After all, the Inca royal families were in a state of chaos at the time of his death as an epidemic swept the empire from its capital toward the northern frontier. And the crisis of succession that led within a few years to the Inca civil war meant that at least some of the men of his *panaca* who might be charged with remembering and performing Huayna Capac's history were dead. The arrival of the Spaniards and the brutal acts they carried out might also insure that the record of the great Inca ruler would not be remembered. Yet there is enough detail to the accounts of his life, and enough similarity among the varying sources we have, to suggest that a narrative was composed and that at least portions of it were officially remembered. We do not know in what contexts the story—in whole or in part—might have been performed. Huayna Capac's mummy was successfully hidden from Spanish officials for many years, and it seems difficult to believe that its custodians would not have been charged with repeating the story of his accomplishments. The prominent place of Mama Ocllo in the stories—she intervenes against usurpers at the time of her son's accession and she intervenes against the rebellious Inca generals and their followers in Tomebamba toward the end of her son's rule—may reflect the fact that her body was cared for and hidden along with that of her son. Perhaps in this case, the need to cling to Inca royal ritual in the face of great opposition led to especially elaborate praise of the dead Coya. The theme of her work with fractious members of royal families to insure legitimate succession and obeisance to the Inca ruler might have taken on special significance in light of the tensions between those members of Inca *panacas* dedicated to conserving Inca customs (a value presumably held by those who cared for the royal mummies) and those who sought to advance their own position through accommodation to Spanish authority.

The Problem of Chronology

That Huayna Capac was a real, rather than a mythical, personage is indisputable: At the time the Spanish scribes began to keep records, there were people alive who remembered him, described him, and could recall vividly those of his deeds which had affected them or their ancestors, such as his calling up of troops from their village, his pressing fathers into service as *yanaconas* on his estate far from their natal land, or his marrying women from highly placed provincial families. Despite the fact that he was a real person and that he lived up into the beginnings of the historic period for South America, it is remarkably difficult to construct a chronology of his life from the sources we have. Even the date of his death, which is likely to have occurred when the Spaniards were first exploring the coast of the Andes, cannot be reliably determined from the competing sources (Rowe 1978). Part of our lack of knowledge of his life is no doubt due to the fact that not all aspects of even an Inca's life were accorded equal importance in constructing his history by Andean historians. Further, Spanish chroniclers felt compelled to create dubious chronologies for the lives of the pre-Conquest rulers. Still, it is possible to consult some of the chronologies offered in different sources to see what points of convergence they might offer.

The most detailed chronology of the lives of Topa Inca and Huayna Capac is offered by Betanzos. He gives durations for many events in their lives, which allows us to reason backward from fixed reference points to suggest possible chronologies.

As a starting point, we will accept Betanzos' claim that Topa Inca went off with his brothers to conquer Chinchaysuyu when he was around twenty-five years old. Following the rest of the chronology he presents, we can derive an approximate timeline for the reign of Topa Inca, including dates that lead up to Huayna Capac's reign (see table 4.1).

Although it is superficially very precise, Betanzos' chronology is not completely internally consistent. For example, in order to have Huayna Capac be born in Tomebamba during the Quito campaign and be twelve years of age at the end of Topa Inca's Collasuyu campaign, we have to assume that Topa Inca's Antesuyu effort was either of very short duration or that it took place simultaneously with other events described for his life. Also, alone among the chroniclers who give a timetable for the building of Sacsahuaman, Betanzos claims it was built in six years. Others assume it was built over a much longer time, extending its construction into Huayna Capac's reign. Still, if we assume that there were six years in which Topa Inca focused his efforts on that endeavor, the chronology is not out of line. Making these assumptions, and assuming all the times attributed to his life and presented by Betanzos to be accurate, Topa Inca would have been about sixty-eight when he died; Betanzos gives us an age of seventy, which is quite close.

TABLE 4.1. Events in the Lives of Topa Inca and Huayna Capac Based on Betanzos' Chronology

Events in Topa Inca's Life	Duration of Events	Events in Huayna Capac's Life
Topa Inca is 25		
Conquest of Quito	5 years	
Topa Inca rests with his father	2 years	
Topa Inca returns to Tomebamba	3 years	Huayna Capac is born
Topa Inca rests in Cuzco	2 years	
Topa Inca's Antesuyu campaign	unknown	
Pachacuti dies	3 months	
Purucaya of Pachacuti	1 year	
Topa Inca's Collasuyu campaign	7 years	Huayna Capac is 12 years old
Topa Inca rests in Cuzco	4 years	
Topa Inca builds the fortress	6 years	
Topa Inca rests in Cuzco	2 years	
Topa Inca builds Chinchero	5 years	
Topa Inca rests in Chinchero	2 1/2 years	
Topa Inca dies at age 70	4 months	Huayna Capac is too young to rule

The Problem of Regents

In the chronology Betanzos provides for Huayna Capac's life, we have a few more gaps, along with additional problems to solve (see table 4.2). Again, if we assume Betanzos' timetable to be accurate, Huayna Capac would have been around thirty-two years of age when his father died. Yet Betanzos asserts that Huayna Capac was too young to rule without regents, and that he had two regents for the first ten years of his rule. This claim makes little sense within Betanzos' chronology, and it conflicts with several other statements about Huayna Capac's age. For example, Cieza reports that Huayna Capac's father left him in Cuzco (along with a trusted "lieutenant") to govern in his stead during the Collasuyu campaign (parte II, cap. LXI; 1985: 176). Another account suggests that Topa Inca placed Huayna Capac as his lieutenant in Lake Titicaca after the region was pacified (Ramos Gavilán lib. 1, cap. XXIX; 1988: 179). Although these could well have been symbolic appointments of a very young boy, they do affirm that the child was born at that time and thus must have been no juvenile when his father died some twenty years later. There is another contradiction if we assume a ten-year regency as presented by Betanzos. If that took place before the death of Huayna Capac's mother, as Betanzos claims, then Mama Ocllo would have outlived her husband by at least thirteen years. Other sources that address the date of her death assert that she died at the same time as or shortly after her husband (compare Murúa, Cabello Balboa, Sarmiento de Gamboa, Pachacuti Yamqui).

It is difficult to imagine that a thirty-something prince with several children would have been deemed too young to rule without regents. Sources other than Betanzos claim that Huayna Capac had close advisors (rather than regents) in his kinsmen Achachi and Hualpaya, and that it was treachery by the latter that made Huayna Capac name his

TABLE 4.2. Chronology of Huayna Capac's Life Based on Betanzos

Events in Huayna Capac's Life	Duration of Events	Events in Other Lives
First inspection of the realm	1 year	
Regents help Huayna Capac govern	10 years	
Second inspection of the realm	1 year	
Yucay estate is built	6 months	
Vilcas inspection	1 year	
Huayna Capac rests in Cuzco	6 months	
Huayna Capac hunts in Collasuyu	6 months	
Huayna Capac mourns for Mama Ocllo	6 months	Mama Ocllo dies
Chachapoyas campaign	3 years	
Mourning rites completed	6 months	
Huayna Capac rests in Yucay	unknown	
Huayna Capac hunts in Ayaviri	3 months	
Birth ritual of Atahuallpa	1 year	Atahuallpa is born
Huayna Capac visits Collasuyu	4 years	Paullu is born, Huascar is born
Inspection ordered	2 years	
Quito wars	unknown	Atahuallpa is 13 years old
Huayna Capac rests in Quito	6 years	
Huayna Capac dies		Pizarro arrives in Tumbes

full brother to that position. Pachacuti Yamqui asserts that it was three years between the death of Topa Inca and the full succession of Huayna Capac (1968: 307). If we assume that this statement meant that it took three years for the necessary rituals and for the quelling of two usurpations and the jettisoning of the disloyal governor to take place, his timetable makes sense: We would have Mama Ocllo outliving her husband by about three years in both Pachacuti Yamqui's and Betanzos' chronology if we omit Betanzos' unique—and problematic—reference to the ten-year rule by regents.

The Birth of Sons

The next adjustments to Betanzos' timetable come in reconciling two claims about Atahuallpa: that he was born sometime while Huayna Capac was resting in Cuzco or Ayaviri, and that he was thirteen years old at the beginning of the Quito wars. By Betanzos' timetable, Atahuallpa would have been only seven years old at the beginning of that northern campaign. However, he omits detail on the time taken by Huayna Capac to build and rest at Yucay. If we agree that Atahuallpa was born upon Huayna Capac's return from the Chachapoyas campaign and assume that there were six years during which Huayna Capac rested from the campaign, we can make the facts for Atahuallpa's life consistent. Further, that adjustment is necessary to accord with Betanzos' claim that Huayna Capac died at age sixty. Betanzos also doesn't give us an exact duration for the Quito wars. He mentions that they took place, and that after they were over Huayna Capac rested in Quito for six years. We can turn to other chroniclers for a bit of help here. Pachacuti Yamqui says that it took one and a half years to call up troops for that campaign and three and a half months to bid them farewell in Cuzco (1968: 308). Cieza says that the Quito campaign, from start to finish, lasted twelve years, and that Atahuallpa was thirty years old when Huayna Capac died (parte II, cap. LXX; 1985: 202). If we accept Betanzos' chronology alone, Atahuallpa would have been only nineteen when his father died; if we add another six years to Betanzos' timetable to allow for a longer stay in the north as described by Cieza, Atahuallpa would be at least twenty-five at his father's death. This makes more sense for Huascar's life as well. By Betanzos' timetable, Huascar would have been only a young boy at his father's death; Cieza claims that Huascar was about four or five years younger than Atahuallpa (parte II, cap. LLXX; 1985: 202), a fact which is consistent with the relative ages of the boys following Betanzos and with the ages for the two claimants established in Toledo's investigations (*Informaciones de Toledo*, esp. question XIII; Levillier 1940). By adding the extra six years that Cieza mentions for the Quito campaign, Huascar would have been around twenty, rather than an impossibly young thirteen or fourteen, when he followed his father on the throne.

Following the logic outlined in the foregoing paragraphs, we would (1) assume a short duration to Topa Inca's Antesuyu campaign; (2) omit the ten-year regency reported by Betanzos; (3) add six years early in the reign to account for Huayna Capac's work at and enjoyment of Yucay; and (4) add six years late in the reign to account for the Quito wars.

The chronology presented by Betanzos seems to represent an Inca way of remembering history, based on sequences of activities and the duration of each activity, rather than on an absolute chronology. It is easy to imagine a *quipu* designed to record information this way: Pendant cords could represent the activities, while the knots in the cords could indicate the amount of time devoted to them. Summary cords could show the amount of time devoted to whole episodes or to an entire life.

Still, it is tempting to impose an absolute chronology on the Inca record of Huayna Capac's life. In order to do this, we need to establish the date of his death. Various chroniclers fix this date by reference to the initial incursions of Francisco Pizarro's Isla de Gallo expedition, which brought Spaniards for the first time to the Andean coast in late 1527 and early 1528. Rowe argued, on the basis of sources available at the time, that the death dates they propose are 1524–25 (dates promulgated by Huascar's party to give him a longer reign) and 1527–28 (dates promulgated by Atahuallpa's party) but noted that the true date could not be established (1978). Betanzos' account of late Inca life is very pro-Atahuallpa, as his wife, Doña Angelina, was the bride designated for Atahuallpa, and it is not surprising that his dates, too, are in line with other pro-Atahuallpa accounts. Still, he provides so much plausible detail on Huayna Capac's camp and its reactions to the Spanish exploration of the coast that it is tempting to accept the dates he offers (Betanzos parte I, cap. XLVIII; 1987: 201). Accepting that placement, we come up with an approximate chronology of late Inca royal events which, though they are reckoned independently from the chronology given by Cabello Balboa and conventionally used to understand Inca culture history, are surprisingly consistent with his (see table 4.3). However, Betanzos' chronology would give a slightly longer reign to Topa Inca and a shorter life to Pachacuti.

Conclusion

The narratives that tell of Huayna Capac's reign are set in an empire plagued by problems: disputes over succession, rebellion by disgruntled provincials, disagreements among generals. But they also tell of a

TABLE 4.3. Possible Dates for the Lives of Topa Inca and Huayna Capac

Event	Dates Corrected from Betanzos	Dates Given by Cabello Balboa
Topa Inca begins to rule		1463
Full succession of Topa Inca		1471
Birth of Huayna Capac	1464	
Death of Pachacuti	1467	1473
Death of Topa Inca	1495	1493
Succession of Huayna Capac	1498	1493
Death of Mama Ocllo	1499	
Huayna Capac's war in Chachapoyas	1499	1496
Birth of Atahuallpa	1503	
Birth of Huascar	1507	
Northern campaigns begin	1516	
Death of Huayna Capac	late 1527 or early 1528	1525 or 1526

ruler who manages to resolve those problems by relying on his considerable skills as a diplomat, an administrator, and a warrior. The stories portray a man loyal to his mother and devoted to his ancestors. The narratives that tell of his life were part of the legacy he left to the Inca people—who could recall the glory of their past in the dark years after the Conquest—and to his descendants—who would use their link to this great ruler as validation for their own claims to prestige as they sought a place in Colonial society. But Huayna Capac also left a tangible legacy of his rule. Prominent in the stories of his life are accounts of the buildings he commissioned and the properties he developed. In the next chapters I will explore the ways in which we might consider the material evidence for Huayna Capac's role as a builder and shaper of his world.

5

HUAYNA CAPAC'S ROYAL ESTATE

Inca rulers had a duty to seek glory by carrying out valiant deeds. The formalized histories that told of an Inca's praiseworthy actions were the property that sustained the reputation he earned and passed on to his descendants. Important, as well, was the physical estate he developed to support himself and his court in his lifetime, for it, too, would sustain his mummy and his *panaca*. In this chapter I turn to the principal estate developed by Huayna Capac to show how we can understand its importance to the Inca and to his descendants.

Inca Royal Estates

As an Inca's successor carried out the ritual devotions preparatory to assuming rule, the simultaneous work of becoming an ancestor was begun. This included the ceremonial sanctioning of the marriage; the construction of the palace in Cuzco that would be his headquarters and the shrine for his mummy; and the creation of country estates to provide quarters for resting and the economic wherewithal to sustain the entertainment and private ritual commitments of the Inca, as well as to support his descent group (fig. 5.1). Because no Inca ruler could inherit property from his father, the obligation to acquire property was acutely felt. Pedro Pizarro reports of Huascar:

> enoxándose un día con los muertos, dixo que los auía de mandar enterrar a todos y quitalles todo lo que tenían, que no auía de auer muertos sino uiuos, porque tenían todo lo mexor de su reyno. (Cap. X; 1986: 54)

> becoming angry one day with the dead, he said that he should order them buried and should take all their belongings from them. [He said that] the goods should belong to the living, rather than the dead, and that the dead had all the best property in the kingdom.

The estates were the largest blocks of property held by living and dead individuals in the Inca empire, and their design—both the physical design and the social design implicit in their construction—was full of meaning.

Of all the estates that are identified as belonging to ruling Incas, we know most about the design, construction, and organization of Huayna Capac's estate in the Yucay Valley. We know its physical design from the remains that still stand, and we can reconstruct some of its

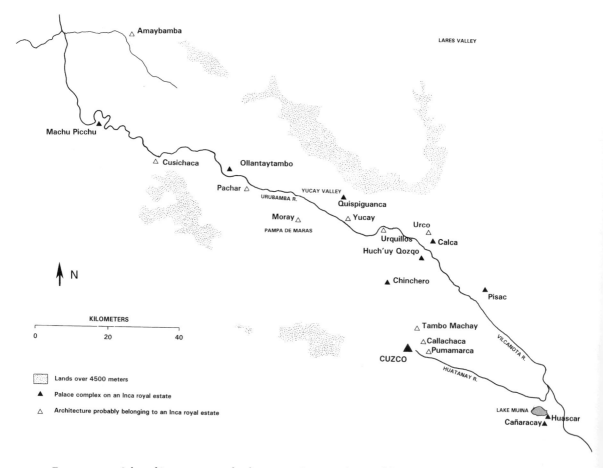

FIGURE 5.1. Selected Inca estates and palaces near Cuzco, redrawn with changes from Hemming and Ranney (1982: 66).

social design from a series of legal documents involving claims for its land or the workers who lived there. Further, because it was one of the later estates to have been built, there is reason to believe that the design we observe represents the original concept used to organize it. It wasn't under continuous modification or rebuilding, as may have been the case with sites maintained for decades by his descendants for a no-longer-living Inca. Since at Huayna Capac's death the Inca empire was plunged into chaos, his property was not substantially modified by his descendants. And while both sons who claimed the throne may have placed *mitimaes* on their father's land, neither disputant in the civil war expropriated his land, though they showed no such scruples about taking property from other ancestors.

History of the Estate

Huayna Capac's estate at Yucay was developed early in his reign when he had consolidated his rule. Betanzos places its construction before the death of Mama Ocllo, which would have been about three and a half years into Huayna Capac's reign (parte I, caps. XLIII, XLIV; 1987: 187–189). Sarmiento and Murúa date its construction to the time when Huayna Capac was engaged in the punitive campaign against the Chachapoyas. Its design was entrusted to Lord Sinchi Roca, one of Huayna Capac's half brothers and a man who was important enough to rule in his stead when the Inca was away from Cuzco (Sarmiento cap. 58; 1960: 260; Murúa cap. 30; 1962, vol. 1: 76–77; Cabello Balboa cap. 21; 1951: 361–362; Cobo lib. 12, cap. XVI; 1964: 89).

The royal narratives comment on the fact of the construction of the estate, but these are by no means our only sources of information on it. We have abundant physical remains which allow us to talk about its style (to be discussed in the next chapter). Further, we have rich documentation from the early Colonial Period that allows us to reconstruct aspects of its social organization and physical plan. Before considering the organization and design of the estate, it is important to address its history in the Colonial Period for what it tells us about Inca estates.

Historical Sources

The history of Huayna Capac's estate in the early Colonial Period shows the conflict between the Inca system of royal landownership with various Spanish institutions, such as individual title, the *encomienda* system, and the system of taxation. The Spaniards' interest in taking the desirable land of the Yucay Valley and in finding more tributaries for their own tax system helped to motivate legal claims for property within the limits of the estate. The men may have been encouraged in their actions by their wives, who complained that Cuzco was too cold and that their infants and young children would not thrive there: They wanted country homes in the valley. While the property platted out for the settlement demanded by the women was on Topa Inca's land (Urquillos, in the canyon adjacent to Chinchero), the *vecinos* of Cuzco also had their eyes on the rich farmlands and stands of forest adjacent to the estate that had been developed by Huayna Capac. The initial investigation of the land was motivated by a protest from the valley's *cacique*, Francisco Chilche, who was unhappy that the Spaniards of Cuzco were taking land within his domain. He argued that the land had long been the property of natives of the valley and that the Incas were tyrants who briefly expropriated that land. Chilche further argued that he was the legitimate *cacique* of the valley's residents. The Spanish investigation played ethnicities and competing histories against one another: To counter Chilche's claim, they had Inca notables testify that the land was the legitimate property of their ancestors and that the bulk of the estate's residents (Chilche included) were *mitimaes* brought in to work the land for their Inca lords. As might be expected, the Spanish investigations focused on which lands could be taken with the least native resistance and which properties would be the most productive.

There are a number of documents that are relevant to the discussion of the land. Most important is a series bound as the *Genealogía de la casa y descendencia de don Diego Sairitúpac, Manco Inca Yupanqui*, in the Archivo Histórico del Cuzco. Relevant portions of its contents have been published by Horacio Villanueva Urteaga, María Rostworowski, and others. The most useful documents in the series are enumerations of the properties made in 1551 and 1552 (Villanueva 1971: 1–54). In the 1551 investigation, court authorities (Mariscal Alonso de Alvarado, *corregidor* of Cuzco, accompanied by Juan Julio de Ojeda, Lic. Antonio de la Gama, and the scribe, Sancho de Orué) walked through the lands of the Yucay Valley accompanied by four Inca *orejones* (Juan Cari Topa; Tito Cogua; Quispe Gualpa, identified as a nephew of the Inca; and Bautista Ticsi). The Inca witnesses named the estates' properties and verified ownership of its parcels. In the narrative document, the locations of fields, terraces, fountains, and palaces are presented relative to features of the natural landscape, making it possible for modern researchers to follow the investigators' route from east to west in the valley. The resulting plan of the estate (a drawing apparently no longer preserved) was verified with the *orejones* and checked with Camiqui, a *cacique* of the natives of the valley, and with Francisco Chilche, *cacique* of the *mitimaes* of the valley. As a result of the 1551 investigation, the *mariscal* allotted property in the Urquillos canyon (on Topa Inca's estate) to Spanish residents of Cuzco. In 1552, the *mariscal* enumerated the properties that were to be made available in the valley (referred to here as the 1552 document). While it is briefer than the on-the-ground investigation, it contains some additional information about the land that supplements the earlier document.

Also of value is a census of the Indian residents of the Yucay Valley made by Damian de la Bandera in 1558 prior to resettling them in *reducciones* (Villanueva 1971: 55–82; referred to here as the 1558 census). It lists adult men by *ayllu* and provides summary census information on both men and women of different ages and marital statuses that were relevant to the tribute system. It can be compared with a later census of Urquillos published by Rostworowski (1990). Also in this series of documents is a 1574 *pleito* of Doña Beatriz Coya, daughter of Sayri Topa, who, together with her husband, Martin de Loyola, sought *yanaconas* and property on the estate (Villanueva 1971: 82–148; called here the 1574 *pleito*; see also Sayri Topa's will in Lohmann 1965). The request was prompted by Toledo's imposition of *reducciones* and the concomitant threat to Beatriz Coya's holdings (Rostworowski 1970: 156). The argument provided in that *pleito* includes a history of the estate for the eighty years that had passed since its creation, supported by the testimony of many native residents of the estate only too willing to testify about the hanky-panky that had taken place since their fathers and grandfathers had been moved there to build it. A copy of Beatriz's detailed *expediente* from the Archivo de Indias was published with valuable commentary by María Rostworowski (1970). The final coda to that case is found in a series of requests by Beatriz's daughter, Ana María Lorenza, to gain title to the land and, ultimately, a request by her husband, Juan Henríquez de Borja, marqués de Alcañices, seeking recompense for lost income from the estate made on the part of his wife which is dated around 1614 (Henríquez de Borja n.d.).

There are other less detailed land documents that help us to understand the estate. Doña Angelina Yupanqui, aided by her husband, Juan de Betanzos, sought title to a number of fields on the estate, which was granted in 1558 (Rostworowski 1962: 143–151; hereafter, 1558 *título*); her possession of these properties is confirmed in Betanzos' *expediente* of 1566, which transferred ownership to their daughter (published in part by Horacio Villanueva Urteaga in Betanzos 1987: xxxiv–xxxv). A small plot that had belonged to his wife, Beatriz, a daughter of Huayna Capac, was claimed by Martin de Bustinza in an *expediente* of 1567 (Rostworowski 1962: 151–153). A false *cédula* claiming title to property and *yanaconas* was filed by three Inca nobles, Alonso Tito Atauchi, Juana Marca Chimbo, and Felipe Topa Yupanqui, in 1552 (Rostworowski 1962: 157–164; hereafter false *cédula*). Tito Atauchi's widow claimed some of the property in a document dated 1594, which was included in a later petition for land on the part of her son (*Composición de tierras de Yucay y Amaybamba*, 1594). Finally, there are documents filed by Francisco Chilche, the Cañari who became *cacique* of the *mitimaes* of the estate (Heffernan 1995: 79–84).

While there are many other documents and commentary on the lands of the estate, these are the principal ones that make it possible to reconstruct its history in the turbulent (and litigious) Colonial Period and to reconstruct its physical and social plan in the years leading up to the Spanish Conquest.

Colonial History of the Estate

The 1551 and 1552 documents were concerned with ascertaining the ownership of land (both pre-Hispanically and in the Colonial Period) and its productivity. The Spaniards sought a legal argument to take the land they wanted in the Yucay Valley. If land could be proven to have been owned by the Sun, it was subject to seizure by the Spaniards, as a land devoted to a heathen deity was subject to expropriation. Further, if land had been owned by some person or entity but was not currently being used, it was subject to expropriation as abandoned or underused land.[1] Land that belonged to an Inca or *coya* was more problematic, as in the 1550s and 1560s there were still Inca notables claiming property because of their descent from a royal landowner, and there were Spanish men married to Inca princesses who were launching claims on behalf of their wives' descent. Perhaps fortunate for the land-hungry Spaniards, most of Topa Inca's *panaca* had been wiped out in the Inca civil wars, so his holdings at Urquillos had few royal claimants. The Yucay Valley was also populated by a mix of people whose tribute status and jurisdiction were the subject of much confusion—to the Spaniards as well as, it seems, to each other.

At the time of the Conquest, the valley was home to *mitimaes* from a number of ethnic groups, mostly from Collasuyu and Chinchaysuyu, as well as to ethnic Incas from Cuzco and natives of the valley. According to the Cañari *cacique* Francisco Chilche, there were eight hundred Indians living in the valley in 1551 (Villanueva 1971: 44), down considerably from the two thousand *mitima* households that had been part of the estate's permanent population under Huayna Capac. Some of these residents had two generations of roots in the valley at the time of conquest and told stories about their fathers and grandfathers having been brought to build or maintain the estate (1574 *pleito*; Villanueva 1971: testimony of Fernando Coataslla, 139; Alonso Chauca, 136: Lope Martín Condemayta, 133; Lucas Chico, 130; Martin Yupanqui, 126; *Informaciones de Toledo*; Levillier 1940: 130). A sizable number of the latest additions to the valley's population included Cañaris brought in from Tomebamba and Quito at the time of the Inca civil wars. Some of these settlers were surely *mitimaes* sent there by Atahuallpa as punishment for their support of Huascar in the succession dispute. Some informants merely stated that they or their fathers had come with Atahuallpa's generals, Quizquiz and Chalcuchima; whether as soldiers or as *mitimaes* is left unsaid.[2]

In Inca legal theory the residents of an estate were *yanaconas*, placed in perpetual service of the estate's owner. In the Colonial Period, many of the people living within the estate's boundaries claimed to be *yanaconas* (most of them probably with reason), a status that had repercussions for their tribute status in the Spanish system. And Cañaris in general were to be made exempt from ordinary *tasa* (the Spanish tribute) due to their loyalty to the Crown in the conquest of the Incas (*Ordenanzas para la ciudad del Cuzco y sus términos*, título XXIII: Del servicio de los cañares y chachapoyas; Toledo 1986, vol. 1: 199), as were the members of Inca royal families. Still, in 1552 Chilche, a Cañari *cacique* of *yanaconas*, many of whom were themselves Cañaris, complained about the difficulty of paying the *tasa* that would ensue if his property were granted to the *vecinos* of Cuzco (Villanueva 1971: 24). The legal disputes over tribute status continued into the Toledan era. In the reforms instituted by Viceroy Toledo in 1572, those *yanaconas* and ethnic Inca nobles who had not formerly been subject to tribute under the Spanish system lost their exempt status. The *yanaconas* and other *tasa*-exempt Indians of the Yucay Valley were henceforward to give silver, wheat, maize, and firewood to the Crown to be used specifically for the upkeep of the Spanish fort in Cuzco (Cook 1975: 213).[3]

There were also complex eddies and undercurrents to the Spanish plans. (The history of these claims was itemized by Beatriz Coya in her *pleito* of 1574; Villanueva 1971: 82–148). Francisco Chilche, who had entered the land with Quizquiz and Chalcuchima, at some point became *cacique* of the *mitimaes* of the valley. He may have been given the job as overseer of the estate's native workforce by Francisco Pizarro, who had taken the estate for himself when he took over Huayna Capac's holdings in Cuzco. Pizarro did not believe that *encomenderos* should spend time on their lands and required the Spaniards to leave the running of their property to native *caciques*. While his immediate concern was most likely defending Spanish settlements from the threats posed by native resistance, it may also have been motivated by his desire to see Spaniards living lives of apparent leisure in town and to have Indians, whom he felt properly belonged in the country, deal with other Indians (*Ordenanzas complementarias para el buen regimen interno del Peru y bienestar de los naturales*, 20 abril de 1540; F. Pizarro 1986: 157–159). Chilche may have made his claim on the basis of his wife's right to property: He was married to a Doña Inés Coya, an Inca princess (1574 *pleito*; testimony of Pedro Chinansila; Villanueva 1971: 138). In any event, when Pizarro was killed in July 1541, he left his property to his young son Gonzalo, who was only six years old at the time and who would die in 1546 (1574 *pleito*, pregunta 5; Villanueva 1971: 99 ff.; will of 1539; F. Pizarro 1986: 312–317; *Fundación del mayorazgo . . . de 1539*; F. Pizarro 1986: 318–320). Pedro de la Gasca considered granting the *repartimiento* of Yucay and some of his father's coca lands to Francisco, the son of Francisco Pizarro and Doña Angelina (by 1548 she was the wife of Juan de Betanzos), though King Charles evidently did not accede to the request (*Relación de la Gasca al Consejo de Indias*, 26 de septiembre 1548; Perez de Tudela Bueso 1964, vol. 2: 272). The Yucay *encomienda* was briefly managed by the Crown's treasurer and then by the marqués de Cañete, who validated Chilche's claim to be *cacique* but divided the rule between him and Garcia Quispicapi, an ethnic Inca who was placed as *cacique* of its non-*mitima* populations.

Chilche took his job of *cacique* to heart and proceeded to live the life of a native lord. He claimed the bulk of the estate's good land for himself, including the entire Chicón canyon, and had his own *mamaconas*. When queried by Spanish authorities in 1551 and 1552 about his property, he was vague and curt in an apparent attempt to obscure the extent of his holdings and the land's economic potential. He may also have been trying to keep the authorities from knowing how many potentially tribute-paying Indians he had hidden in the less accessible parts of the estate, as asserted in the 1574 *pleito*.

There were other Cañaris claiming to be lords of their domain on the estate, too. Ucusicha was a Cañari dignitary who may have been sent to the estate as a *mitima*. Betanzos tells a story that is probably about this man. The Cañaris had opposed Atahuallpa's cause on the northern frontier and caused enough trouble so that he sent his generals to put down their rebellion. At the end of a year's rest in Cajamarca, Atahuallpa received a message from his general, Chalcuchima, about the impertinence of a Cañari lord:

> le hacía saber . . . que el más valiente hallaban en los encuentros que tenían era un cañari que se decía Ucoxicha el cual les decía siempre que le pesaba porque no iba allí Atagualpa para él solo pelear con él y que qué mandaba que se hiciese deste Ucoxicha como fuese preso y Atagualpa como oyése esto deste cañari dijo sonriéndose ese debe de ser valiente y queríase ver conmigo no le maten procuren de le tomar a vida y háganle honra pues ha sido tan buen hombre y siempre aturado [*sic*] peleando contra mi el cual Ucoxicha después fue preso por Chalcuchima y le fue hecha la honra que mandó Atagualpa y este Ucoxicha fue después gran amigo de los cristianos. (Betanzos parte I, cap. X; 1987: 233)

> [Chalcuchima] informed [Atahuallpa] that the bravest acts they had seen were found in the encounters with a Cañari named Ucusicha, who kept saying that he was sorry that Atahuallpa wasn't there, because that was the only Inca he wanted to fight. And he asked Atahuallpa what he should do with Ucusicha, who had been captured. Hearing this, Atahuallpa said, smiling, that the fellow must be pretty brave if he wanted to fight with him. He told them not to kill Ucusicha but rather to honor him as he had been a good man and always brave in his fights against Atahuallpa. So he was taken prisoner and honored as Atahuallpa had ordered, and afterward this Ucusicha was a great friend of the Christians.

The friendship to Christians involved opposing Gonzalo Pizarro's an-
tiroyalist uprising, for which Ucusicha was killed by Pizarro's captains
(1551 document; Villanueva 1971: 39).

The honor that was accorded Ucusicha included the right to be
cacique of a *mitima* population on Huayna Capac's estate. He was *cacique* of a community called Coto, which was on forested lands belonging to the Sun. By 1574 he was accused of having trumped up permission from President Gasca to keep Indians as tax-exempt *yanaconas*; he
was charged with having hidden forty Indians from the tax collectors,
of ruling the land with little regard to its true ownership, and of having passed the *cacicazgo* to his son Alonso Ucusicha (1552 document;
Villanueva 1971: 52, lands of Coto; 1574 *pleito* of Beatriz Coya; testimony of Pedro Cochachín, 104; Sebastián Tenazela, 114; Juan Bautista Rucana, 119; Martin Yupanqui, 127).

The Cañaris were not the only ones to be claiming property under
false pretenses. Alonso Tito Atauchi, an ethnic Inca, was claiming
large holdings on the estate for himself. When he served as an informant to Toledo's investigations of native idolatry in 1572, Alonso Tito
Atauchi identified himself as a grandson of Huayna Capac and son
of Tito Atauchi; his father, he reported, had from time to time ruled
the Inca empire (*Informaciones de Toledo*; Levillier 1940: 167). In 1572
Alonso was around forty years old. He had succeeded Atau Rimache as
head of a group of forty *apoyanaconas* living on the estate who were
custodians of Huayna Capac's mummy. When Alonso Tito Atauchi
took over, the *apoyanaconas* acted as ordinary tribute-paying farmers,
though they were secretly caring for the mummy and hiding it from
the Spaniards. Of course, when questioned about the Inca practice of
caring for mummies, Alonso did not volunteer any firsthand knowledge of the practice (*Informaciones de Toledo*; Levillier 1940: 169). After
Huayna Capac's body was discovered and taken to Lima, Alonso Tito
Atauchi presented a false *cédula* claiming the *yanaconas* had been
granted to him personally (1574 *pleito*; Villanueva 1971: 96 and pregunta trece; testimony of Pedro Cochachín, 108–109; Juan Bautista
Rucana, 115–116; Martin Yupanqui, 128; Martin Yana, 129; Lucas
Chico, 131; Alonso Chauca, 136–137; see also the false *cédula* dated
1552 in Rostworowski 1962: 157–164). His Spanish wife, Doña Costanza de Castilla, continued claims for land in the valley after her husband's death (*Composición de tierras de Amaybamba y Yucay*, 1594).

Meanwhile, Inca royal women were also involved in the land grab
in Yucay. Doña Angelina—Atahuallpa's fiancée, Francisco Pizarro's
mistress, and ultimately Juan de Betanzos' wife—was one of these.
She had property there that she may have been given by Francisco Pizarro (1551 document; Villanueva 1971: 37) and sought title to a

number of fields she claimed as a descendant of Topa Inca (1558 título; Rostworowski 1962: 143–151). Juana Marca Chimbo Coya owned and claimed land on the estate (1551 document; Villanueva 1971: 39) and joined in the false *cédula* with Alonso Tito Atauchi (Rostworowski 1962: 157–164). Juana Tocto, identified as a *cacica*, is mentioned as a landowner in a 1567 claim for half a *topo* to grow *ají* (claim of Martin de Bustinza; Rostworowski 1962: 152).

There were also other natives who owned land on the estate, including sizable holdings belonging to Gualpa Roca and his sons (Doña Angelina's 1558 título; Rostworowski 1962: 144; 1551 document, Villanueva 1971: 36, 47; 1552 document, Villanueva 1971: 51, 53). The *cacique* Quispe Capi, an *orejon* of Cuzco and Chilche's Inca counterpart, had some lands (1552; Villanueva 1971: 51; 1558 título; Rostworowski 1962: 144), as did other Inca dignitaries, including the sons of Don García Cayo Topa (1551 document; Villanueva 1971: 36) and an unnamed dignitary from Cuzco (1552 document; Villanueva 1971: 53). There was land that belonged to Apaolomache, who is probably the Atao Rimache who confirmed the 1551 property lines for Spanish investigators (Villanueva 1971: 41) and who was in charge of the *apoyanaconas* who were caring for Huayna Capac's mummy. There were also Cañari dignitaries claiming land, including Vilca, a principal lord of Chilche (1552 document; Villanueva 1971: 51; Unoy Acosca) and two of his sons (1552 document; Villanueva 1971: 52). A Cañari named Palchichapara had land at Acosca that had belonged to Huayna Capac (1551 document; Villanueva 1971: 37), and unnamed Cañaris had fields at the mouth of the Chicón canyon (1551 document; Villanueva 1971: 38). Finally, there were a number of plots owned by natives who are mentioned in legal documents and sometimes in census lists, though their ethnicity and social standing cannot be determined.[4]

Complicating the whole matter was the fact that the Spaniards were using a grant of an *encomienda* involving lands of the estate as an incentive to induce the rebel Incas to come out of the jungle. Sayri Topa was promised the *encomienda*, though Garcilaso was cynical about whether in 1559 there was anything to give him. Garcilaso claims that the valley had all been divided among the Spanish citizens of Cuzco (his own father had received a grant there in 1552), so that all Sayri Topa really got was the title, lord of Yucay. Garcilaso also claims that the letter of agreement that Sayri Topa signed in Lima really did not grant him the property but only gave him immunity from unnamed crimes (parte II, lib. VIII, cap. IX; 1617: 283 r.). As meager as his grant may have been, Sayri Topa did live on the land for the few remaining years of his life until he died in 1561; the death was widely believed to have been poisoning at the hand of Francisco Chilche, who was released from prison after a year's stay when his guilt could not be proven.

After Sayri Topa's death, the *encomienda* passed to his infant daughter, Doña Beatriz Coya (see Lohmann 1965; Cook 1975: 137; Hampe 1979: 89). Her inheritance was briefly used as an inducement to Titu Cusi to leave Vilcabamba, so that his son Quispi Titu could marry Beatriz and receive control of the last good Inca estate (Hemming 1970: 302), a marriage which never took place. But Beatriz became such a hot property as a marriage prospect that she was placed in a convent by the viceroy and ultimately betrothed to Martín de Loyola. Suits for title continued by this couple in 1574 and into the next generation by their daughter Ana María Lorenza. It was 1610 before the title was clearly and indisputably granted to Ana María and her husband, the marqués de Alcañices, though by then there was little worth having. In 1614 they sued for payment of back tribute (Henriquez de Borja n.d.) and eventually won.

Social Plan of the Estate

The sad and confused history of the estate in the sixteenth and early seventeenth centuries was the result not only of the Spanish Conquest but of the odd cultural mix that was typical of Inca royal estates. Largely populated by *mitimaes*, the permanent residents of the estate had included the one thousand households from Chinchaysuyu and one thousand from Collasuyu noted in the 1574 *pleito* (testimony of Fernando Coataslla; Villanueva 1971: 139), along with ethnic Incas sent from Cuzco or elsewhere to oversee various projects.

The estate's population included many ethnicities, only some of which are identified in the available sources. In addition to the ubiquitous Cañaris, there are references to *mitimaes* who identify themselves as Soras (*Informaciones de Toledo*, Alonso Condor of Pomaguanca; Levillier 1940: 108), Guancabelicas (1558 *título*; Rostworowski 1962: 144), and Quichuas (1551 document; Villanueva 1971: 37); there are Luringuancas and natives from Guaylas (*Informaciones de Toledo*, Pedro Cachache and Domingo Achimec; Levillier 1940: 101; 1574 *pleito*, testimony of Martin Yana, Alonso Chauca; Villanueva 1971: 128, 136).[5] Among the residents from Collasuyu must have been natives of the Urinsaya moiety of Chucuito, for the dignitaries and *quipucamayos* of that community told Spanish investigators in 1567 that people from their town had been sent to Yucay as *mitimaes* (Diez de San Miguel 1964: 81).

The estate's population had important identities other than ethnic ones, too, that added to the colorful mix in the Yucay Valley. Some identified themselves as *yanaconas* and some identified themselves as *camayos*, workers having a very specific job to do (1574 *pleito*; Alonso

Chauca; Villanueva 1971: 136).[6] It is likely that many of the estate's residents were farmers, or *chacracamayos*, as was Marcos de Cayogualpa, a native of Chaoca (*Informaciones de Toledo*; Levillier 1940: 109). There were also more specialized *camayo* positions. For example, Martin Capta, a native of Cachi, served the Inca as *cachicamayo*, or salt maker (*Informaciones de Toledo*; Levillier 1940: 108). The estate also had people who built and maintained its houses, such as Martin Yupanqui's father, who had been sent from Cuzco to work on the estate (1574 *pleito*; Villanueva 1971: 126). Its population included house servants (father of Marcos de Cayogualpa; *Informaciones de Toledo*; Levillier 1940: 109; the town of Ayabica; testimony of Geronimo Chumpiri; *Informaciones de Toledo*, Levillier 1940: 114)[7] and pages (Alonso Condor; *Informaciones de Toledo*; Levillier 1940: 108).

Estates also had guardians for the storehouses (testimony of Antonio Pacrotica, whose father guarded maize storehouses in Xacxaguana; *Informaciones de Toledo*; Levillier 1940: 112), there were sentries, and there were spies (Martin Cuxipoma of Quylliscachi [Quilliscachi] was a spy who was supposed to keep Huayna Capac apprised of local events when he was in Tomebamba, *Informaciones de Toledo*; Levillier 1940: 78).

The estate at Yucay also had more exotic offices. Juan Gualpa, an *orejon* who lived on the estate, was in charge of quality control for Huayna Capac's clothing; he made sure it was the right size for the Inca's wardrobe (*Informaciones de Toledo*; Levillier 1940: 78). Domingo Malma reported that his father, Guaman Chambi, was Huayna Capac's servant and that he served in his house, guarding his weapons. He also remembered that when the Inca attended festivals and drank, his father looked after the sling that the Inca wore on his head (*Informaciones de Toledo*; Levillier 1940: 152).[8]

The towns on the estates also had internal stratification, with overseers for varying numbers of workers, whether as farmers or as more specialized producers of crafts. For example, Domingo Sucso reported that his father was an overseer in charge of ten workers, a post that went to his brother when the father died, as Domingo hadn't the aptitude for the work (*Informaciones de Toledo*; Levillier 1940: 152). Alonso Condor's father was brought as a *mitima* to be the *curaca* of Pomaguanca on the estate (*Informaciones de Toledo*; Levillier 1940: 108). Roldan Matara's father was *curaca* of a group of Huayna Capac's potters (*Informaciones de Toledo*; Levillier 1940: 60; these potters may not have been on an estate), while the fathers of Alonso Conchay and Juan Tarumaguia were *curacas* of *cumbicamayos*, or clothmakers (*Informaciones de Toledo*; Levillier 1940: 114, 159; again, it is unclear whether these *cumbicamayos* lived on the estate at Yucay).

The historical documents make it clear that an estate was based on a carefully planned social design that mixed together workers of diverse ethnic backgrounds who carried out a range of jobs in support of the royal owner of the estate. As will be seen, the physical plan of the estate at Yucay helped to reinforce this diversity. That plan can be discerned from the historical documents and compared with the evidence on the ground to locate building complexes and property lines.

Physical Design of the Estate

The estate was carved out of a stretch of land running for approximately 15 kilometers through the valley the Incas called the Yucay Valley; it is now known as the Vilcanota-Urubamba Valley, or the Sacred Valley of the Incas (fig. 5.2). The land claimed by Huayna Capac ran between a narrowing of the valley at Guayocollo (about 11 kilometers from Calca) to a narrowing at Patashuaylla on its western end. Socially, the estate included the lands between Topa Inca's developments at Huayllabamba (an extension of his Chinchero property) and Pachacuti's holdings at Pachar (considered as part of his development at Ollantaytambo). While Pachacuti may have had some buildings in Yucay (Sarmiento cap. 41; 1960: 236), the estate was in a part of the valley that had not, prior to Huayna Capac's reign, been substantially developed by the Incas.

When he took it over, the land was occupied by four native groups: On its eastern end were the Pacas and the Chichos; toward the western part were the Cachis and Chaocas. When the estate was developed, these people continued to live on their lands, though they may have become *yanaconas* on the estate. For example, Martin Capta of the town and *ayllu* of Cache (1558 census; Villanueva 1971: 3) had a father who was a "*criado*" of Huayna Capac (*Informaciones de Toledo;* Levillier 1940: 108); this term often referred to *yanaconas* (Rowe 1982: 97–98).

There is no reason to believe that the land was taken by force, as seems to have been the case for earlier estates (Pachacuti, for example, developed Pisac to mark the defeat of the Cuyos, Ollantaytambo to mark his defeat of the Tambos, and Machu Picchu to mark his successful Vilcabamba campaign; see Rowe 1990). However, the status of the towns' residents may have changed when they were incorporated into the estate. Hernando Conchuy of Chauca had a father who was an overseer or inspector for Huayna Capac, a job his more distant ancestors had done for Topa Inca (*Informaciones de Toledo;* Levillier 1940: 110). Pedro Atasco, another native of the town and *ayllu* of Cachi (1558 census; Villanueva 1971: 64), reported that his father, Llacta Chaperi, had served as a *curaca* in the town of Gualpa, placed there by Topa Inca, but that

despues en tiempo de guainacapac el dicho guainacapac dixo que auia ha-
blado con sus dioses e con el sol y que auia dicho al dicho su padre deste
testigo que no conuenya que el ny sus paryentes ningunos de su ayllo
fuesen curacas sino yndios comunes e que asy les quito el dicho cargo. (Informaciones de Toledo; Levillier 1940: 108–109)

later, in Huayna Capac's time, Huayna Capac said that he had consulted
with his gods and the Sun and that he had told the informant's father that
it was no longer right for him or his relatives or anyone else in his *ayllu* to
be *curacas*. Rather, they should be common Indians.

The land that Huayna Capac took for his estate was, in fact, probably
unclaimed for very good reason: It was swampy, with a river that
meandered across the valley and with irregular land in the valley bottom. Reclaiming that land and developing it into an estate was a monumental task, one on which Huayna Capac embarked in a big way. Betanzos describes the way in which this work was done:

mandó a todas las provincias y dentro de seis meses se juntaron ciento y
cincuenta mil indios en la ciudad del Cuzco y como el Ynga los viese
mandó a los señores del Cuzco que se fuesen con aquella gente y la llev-
asen al valle de Yucay y él ansi mismo fue con ellos y luego puso en obra en
aderzar del valle e hizo que el río fuese echado por la parte de hacia el
Cuzco haciéndole fortalecer y haciéndole madre por do fuese y por la parte
que el río iba hizo derribar los cerros y allanarlos y ansi hizo el valle llano y
de manera que en él se sembrase y cogiese y hizo que en él se edificasen ya
casas y aposentos do él se fuese a recrear en el cual valle dio estancias a los
señores del Cuzco ansi a los vivos como a los muertos que estaban en bultos para que allí pusiesen sus yanaconas mozos de su servicio para que les
labrasen sus verduras y hortalizas y cosas de sus recreaciones y allí hizo
Guayna Capac que se edificasen muchos pueblos pequeños de a veinte y a
treinta y cincuenta indios en los cuales pueblos puso muchos indios mitimaes de todas las naciones y provincias de la tierra. (Parte I, cap. XLIII;
1987: 187)

Huayna Capac ordered that one hundred thousand Indians, or as many as
possible, come from throughout the land. Then his order was sent out to
all the provinces, and within six months one hundred fifty thousand Indians assembled in the city of Cuzco. And when the Inca saw them, he ordered the lords of Cuzco to go with those workers and take them to the
Valley of Yucay. He himself went with them and started the work of im-
proving the valley. He had the river moved to flow along the side facing
Cuzco, making it stronger and making a bed where it went. Along the path
of the river the Inca had hills leveled. Thus he made the valley flat so that it
could be planted and harvested. He had houses and lodgings built where
he could go to enjoy himself. In this valley he gave farmlands to the lords
of Cuzco, both to the living and to the dead lords who were already in *bultos* so that they could put their *yanacona* servants there to cultivate their

vegetables and other things for their enjoyment. And Huayna Capac had them build many small towns of twenty, thirty, and fifty Indians. In these towns he put many *mitima* Indians from all the nations and all the provinces of the land.

The resulting landscape of the valley matches Betanzos' description. Where the Inca canalization is intact, the Urubamba River flows tight against the south side of the valley through the length of the estate. The architectural and agricultural developments are all located on the north side of the river. The canyons of the north side of the Urubamba Valley are water-rich, and the rivers that issue from them are used to irrigate the terrace systems of the estate. Terrace systems are

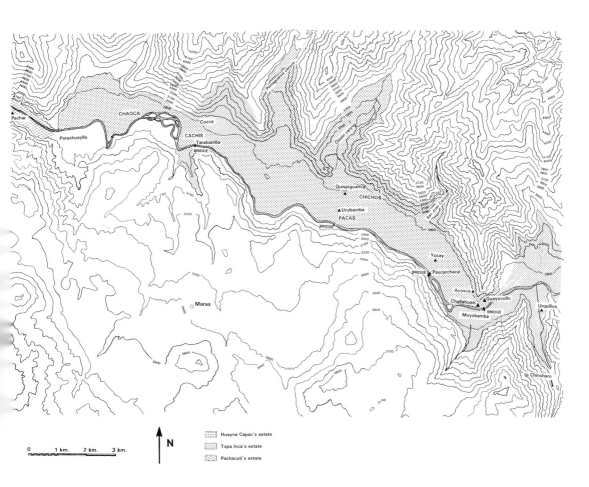

FIGURE 5.2. Map of the Urubamba-Yucay region showing the limits of royal estates and lands belonging to natives of the valley. Locations are derived from sixteenth-century documents published by Villanueva Urteaga (1971). The map indicates the name and approximate location of identified properties but does not indicate their size.

built on the alluvial fan that descends from the San Juan canyon (above Yucay) and on lands at the mouth of the Chicón and Pomaguanca canyons (north and northwest of Urubamba, respectively). There are also terraces against the slopes of the north part of the valley midway between Yucay and Urubamba and in the floor of the valley on the east end of Urubamba. The estate's main architectural complexes, too, are located on the north side, including standing remains that can be observed in modern Yucay, the palace of Quispiguanca on the north edge of Urubamba, the site of Cocha Sontor in the Chicón canyon, and the site of Inca Racay in the Pomaguanca canyon. Additional compounds are no longer standing, but their presence on the north side of the valley can be located on the basis of historical sources.

Roads and Bridges

The estate's complexes were linked by a network of roads and bridges. While some traces of this infrastructure can be seen today, the location of others is based on references to them in sixteenth-century *visitas*. In these documents, the dignitaries who walked the estate, pointing out lands to the legal authorities, followed Inca roads. They located properties by references to the road they followed, as well as to roads they crossed and bridges they observed.

There were several bridges on or near the estate. One was in the middle of Moyobamba, one of Topa Inca's fields (1551 document; Villanueva 1971: 36, 46). The bridge seems to have been related to his estate, rather than Huayna Capac's, as it linked Topa Inca's lands on the south side of the valley (Orquillos [Urquillos], Guayllabamba [Huayllabamba], and, ultimately, Chinchero) with his holdings on the north side (Guayoccari). More reliably associated with Huayna Capac's estate was a bridge at Guayocollo, the constriction of the valley where his lands started (1551 document; Villanueva 1971: 36). There was another at Paucarchaca, within the modern town of Yucay (1551; Villanueva 1971: 37, see also fn. 13). There was another in Urubamba (fig. 5.3), the foundations of which can still be seen from the modern bridge (1551; Villanueva 1971: 38–39). There was also a bridge at Taracachi near the western limits of the estate; almost certainly this is the Inca bridge at a place now called Tarabamba, seen in figure 5.4. This latter may have been important for linking Topa Inca's holdings on the south side of the river with a forest he owned at Cozca (1552; Villanueva 1971: 52) on the north side. The location of a bridge called Pacachaca is uncertain; it connected Huayna Capac's lands to Maras (1552; Villanueva 1971: 53), suggesting it might be the bridge near Taracachi where a road climbs to Maras by way of its salt works. Other locating information, however, would place it in the modern town of Urubamba, near lands that belonged to the Paca people and where one of the ancient roads to the estate may have crossed.

There were several Inca roads on the estate as well. One probably followed the course of the Colonial Period road, and now modern highway, paralleling the river and passing on the south edge of the modern towns of Yucay and Urubamba. There was also a road that passed north of Urubamba, heading to the palace of Quispiguanca (fig. 5.5). Its course can no longer be completely traced, but it is

FIGURE 5.3. The foundations of an Inca bridge in the modern town of Uru-bamba. It is possible to see part of the Inca canalization of the river in the lower portion of the photo.

FIGURE 5.4. The modern bridge at Tarabamba in 1987. It is built above the foundations of the Inca bridge in a stretch of river that is still canalized.

clearly the road walked by the *orejones* of Cuzco in the 1551 *visita*. It is probably the path that runs from the plaza of Yucay and around Lake Guachac. Its course around or over Chichobamba is no longer traceable. There was an Inca road running north-south somewhere east of the palace of Quispiguanca (the *orejones* crossed it in the 1551 visit; Villanueva 1971: 38); it is probably the foot road now called Pacacalle that climbs toward Quispiguanca from the Recoleta (fig. 5.6). There was also an Inca road up the Chicón canyon from Quispiguanca, at least, and a road west of Quispiguanca and south of the mouth of the Chicón canyon. This latter is probably near the course of a modern road that passes above a system of Inca fields and is now a car road that links Urubamba and Pomaguanca (fig. 5.7). There are traces of a road that most likely connected fancy architecture at Yucay with its terrace system. A short extension of raised causeway traverses a swampy area on the northeast edge of the modern town; continuing this line toward the east is a ramp that climbs a set of curvilinear terraces (see fig. 7.2). It is probable that the *orejones* walked along this road as they identified properties in the town of Yucay, but its full extent can no longer be traced. Pairs of roads run north-south within the Yucay terraces and within the field systems west of Urubamba. These will be discussed in chapter 7 as part of the design of those developments.

FIGURE 5.5. Portion of the Inca road at Chichobamba, heading west toward Quispiguanca. The prominent black hill in the background is Tantanmarca.

It is difficult to account for all the bridges. It is likely that the westernmost and easternmost bridges (at Moyobamba and at Taracachi) predated Huayna Capac's development of the estate. They seem more intimately tied to Topa Inca's holdings which, at exactly those locations, include property on both the north and south sides of the river. The bridges at Paucarchaca and Urubamba were definitely within Huayna Capac's estate. The Urubamba bridge, which seems to have been

FIGURE 5.6. Overview of the modern town of Urubamba, looking north toward Chicón. Pacacalle, probably following the course of an Inca road, runs diagonally from midright to center left in the photo, ending just below the palace of Quispiguanca. The small plaza in the foreground, planted with a large tree, is probably the original site of the Inca property called Urubamba.

FIGURE 5.7. The lower portion of the Chicón canyon road, looking south, adjacent to the modern cemetery of Urubamba. Like other north-south-running roads on the estate, this one was a double road with a deep canal between the two lanes.

the one that gave the best access to the palace compound of Quispiguanca, would have been the most logical ancient entrance to the estate. The bridge at Yucay, assuming it existed, might have been used to carry goods from the massive terracing systems of that town to storage facilities in Cuzco and, perhaps, at Huayna Collca (on the south side of the river, high above Yucay). The course of the Inca road linking the capital at Cuzco to Huayna Capac's estate is, unfortunately, not

known. Witnesses to Toledo's *informaciones* on idolatry in 1571 identify
Chinchero as "on the road to the Yucay Valley" (Levillier 1940: 48),
though whether they refer to the Spanish or the Inca road is uncertain.
There was an Inca road to Chinchero from Cuzco and from Chinchero
to the valley via the Urquillos canyon through lands that were part of
Topa Inca's estate. The modern highway to Urubamba from Cuzco
now goes via Chinchero and Huayna Collca. The latter was associated
with Huayna Capac's estate lands, as was Tiobamba, property on the
Pampa de Maras well to the west of Chinchero and the Urquillos
canyon and through which the old highway linking Urubamba and
Cuzco passed. (That highway was in use through the mid-1970s.) An
Inca road designed to link Cuzco and Quispiguanca might well have
passed over Huayna Capac's lands (Huayna Collca and Tiobamba),
rather than Topa Inca's (Chinchero and Urquillos). It is logical to assume that it came down the north face of the steep hills bounding the
river someplace where it would connect with a bridge. Nineteenth-
century traveler Ephraim George Squier reports going to Urubamba
from Chinchero on a steep road with Inca stone foundations supporting its switchbacks; it was broad enough to support six people walking abreast. Even in the early 1860s, he noted that the road was poorly
preserved (1877: 486–487). Although he does not clearly indicate its
course, the road appears to have run along the face of a steep hill,
rather than descending through a canyon. Squier writes of crossing
the river at Urubamba on a stone bridge (1877: 489), presumably the
one with the Inca foundations. From his brief description of the journey, it seems that, whatever its route from Chinchero to the edge of the
pampa, it probably dropped into the valley, following a course to the
east or near that of the modern highway.

Moyas

While the estate today feels overwhelmingly like a place devoted to agriculture, there were many parts of the property that were not used for
the large-scale production of crops. Such places include small gardens, parks, woods, and waterworks.

There is ample evidence in the standard histories of the Incas to
suggest that an Inca vision of an ideal province included its development to full economic potential. It is also clear that the country estates developed by Inca royalty included provision for production agriculture for themselves, for favored relatives, and for the Sun. But that
is not the only kind of agricultural landscape valued by the Incas. The
country estates especially were places where parks and gardens were
created and where forests were planted.

Huayna Capac's estate had a number of places that are described in the 1551 document as *moya* or *moya y prado* (fig. 5.8). In Inca the term *moya* meant "orchard or garden" (Gonçalez Holguin, *muya*; 1952: 254). In the context of the estate, *moya* lands appear to have been places devoted to enjoyment and relaxation. Some of them had architecture; several had water. Any agriculture that took place in the *moya* lands was considered separate from the production agriculture that took place on the estate's terraces. Some of the *moyas* had plots devoted to small-scale cultivation of relatively exotic crops. For example, Paucarchaca, specifically identified as a *moya*, had a pond or ponds and a few small fields of hot peppers and sweet potatoes (1551 document; Villanueva 1971: 37). The dedication of these fields to nonproductive agriculture is stressed in the 1552 document, which identifies the eight *topos* of land there as having been planted "for the doves" (Paucalchaca; 1552 document; Villanueva 1971: 53). An unnamed plot nearby had three buildings, plus some small fields planted in hot peppers, coca, cotton, and peanuts (1551; Villanueva 1971: 39).[9]

In these fields, the crops planted were special. Coca, peanuts, cotton, and sweet potatoes are crops that do well in zones that the Incas would have categorized as *yungas*: subtropical and coastal regions that had a lower altitude and generally warmer climate than the highland area around their capital. Though the Yucay Valley is noticeably warmer than Cuzco, cultivating such crops on the estate would have been a challenge and surely would not have been something practiced in large-scale agriculture. It is likely that these crops were grown as exotics much the way that people in the region today carefully tend tropical plants in their homes or ornamental gardens. It should also be noted that coca and hot peppers, at least, are products with strong ritual associations for the Incas. Few religious offerings took place without coca. Both coca and *ají* were needed for the *purucaya* ritual. Betanzos tells a story about Huayna Capac spending a full year acquiring the coca and *ají* needed to celebrate his mother's *purucaya* (parte I, cap. XLIV; 1987: 189). While an abundance of *ají* was desirable for the death commemoration, abstinence from hot peppers was required for certain Inca ritual fasts. The cultivation of coca and *ají* on *moya* lands may have been a way to enhance the garden with the presence of plants that had strong ritual associations. It is also the case that cultivating these exotics may have reminded the Incas that they controlled all the areas in which the plants were native—it was a microcosm of empire, in much the way that exotic animals from the Antesuyu campaigns were taken to Cuzco. We know that the Incas elsewhere demanded that *mitimaes* bring seeds from their native provinces to the lands they resettled at the behest of the Incas. Perhaps these plants were the product not only of the labor of forcibly transplanted people but of the seeds they brought with them from their homelands.

Recreational *moyas* did not necessarily have exotic plants. At least two of the *moyas* on the estate were devoted to water or water gardens. An unnamed *moya* near Yucay included fountains in which the Inca kept fish and grew the *totora* reeds with which ears were pierced (1551; Villanueva 1971: 38). This *moya* may have been located at the foot of the hill on which the Salesian agricultural farm is located (Villanueva 1971: 38, fn. 15). The area still has several confined ponds with *totora* growing in them and is bordered on one side by agricultural terraces and on the other by a causeway that leads to the town of Yucay. More likely, it was near the edge of Guachac, a swampy region and rainy-

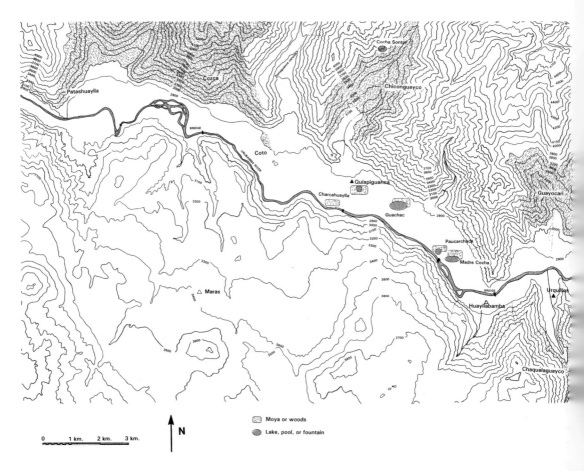

FIGURE 5.8. Map of *moya* lands on the estates of Huayna Capac and Topa Inca, based on sixteenth-century documents published by Villanueva Urteaga (1971), supplemented by my fieldwork. The map indicates the name and approximate location of *moya* properties, but their extent is not known.

season lake located midway between Yucay and Urubamba. Again, the strong ritual association of *totora* with the ear-piercing ritual of young men might have enhanced the experience of contemplating the fountains of this *moya*, whether or not these particular reeds were ever used to pierce ears.

Another water-based *moya* is one which contained a lake called Madre Cocha (mother lake), where Huayna Capac bathed (1551; Villanueva 1971: 37). The hybrid Spanish-Quechua name Madre Cocha is related to one of the shrines of Cuzco (Mama Cocha, Ch-Ex:1; Cobo book 1, chap. 16; 1990: 83); the goddess of the sea was also Mama Cocha (Cobo book 1, chap. 7; 1990: 33). Mama Cocha is one of the deities illustrated by Pachacuti Yamqui (1950: 226). Whether or not Madre Cocha was identified as an embodiment of a goddess or a place to communicate with a goddess, it is unthinkable that a lake where a divine king bathed would be considered merely ordinary. Again, bathing was associated with ritual cleansing in the *purucaya* and other ceremonies carried out by Inca royalty (see, for example, the conclusion of Huayna Capac's mourning for his mother; Betanzos parte I, cap. XLIV; 1987: 190). The additional use of this *moya* is unclear: As Villanueva transcribes the document, the *moya* is a place where the Inca went with his relatives ("una Moya del Inca que es su prado donde se iban con sus ayllus") (Villanueva 1971: 37). A transcription of this passage by John Rowe suggests it is where the Inca went to play a gambling game with dice ("donde se iban a jugar a ayllus") (John Rowe, personal communication). The former transcription suggests the likelihood that kin group-based rituals took place on the estate; the latter focuses more on its recreational use.

One *moya* on the estate was clearly associated with the activity of hunting. The Chicón canyon, which runs north from near the center point of the estate, is described in the 1551 document as one of Huayna Capac's *moyas* which was wooded and had no residents:

> A mano derecha de estos tambos [de Quispiguanca] hay una quebrada entre dos sierras que se dice Chicón la cual era Moya de Huayna Cápac y en ella hay arboleda y muchas tierras en los cuales en tiempos del Inca no había nunguna casa de indios y ahora hay ciertas casas del Inca y un cañari que tiene allí su casa y era esta arboleda y prado que nunca la sembraban. (Villanueva 1971: 38)

> To the right of these *tambos* [of Quispiguanca] there is a canyon between two mountains that is called Chicón. It was a *moya* of Huayna Capac. It is forested, and there are many lands where, in the time of the Incas, there was no home belonging to Indians. Now there are a few houses of the Inca, and a Cañari has his house there. And this was a forest and a park that was never used for agriculture.

The 1552 document explains that the canyon, owned by Huayna Capac, was used for hunting:

> Dicen que la quebrada de Quispehuanca que está una arboleda Chicón Guayco que era de Huayna Capac, solía tener venados y otras cosas de montería, dicen que hay mucha madera en ello y que ahora la tiene don Francisco [Chilche] por suyo y tiene en ello mamaconas suyas que lo guardan. (Villanueva 1971: 52)

> They say that the canyon of Quispiguanca was a forest called Chicón Guayco which belonged to Huayna Capac. It only had deer and other things for hunting. They say that there is much wood there and that now Don Francisco [Chilche] claims it and has some of his *mamaconas* [probably *sic* for *yanaconas*] guarding it for him.

Guaman Poma describes how these royal hunting preserves were used:

> Cómo el Ynga salía a cazar de uenados y de perdises a un jardín que ellos les llama moya. Que dallí ánima beuiente no les coxe nada, sólo el Ynga y la Coya coxen con lasos toclla y tira con su riui y ligas pucacon, llicacon. Y se huelga con su muger coya y auquiconas y nustas y capac apoconas, apoconas en el güerto, jardín que tenía para ese efecto señalado moya, pasto de fiesta del Ynga. (F. 330; 1980, vol. 1: 302–303)

> [This is] how the Inca went out to hunt deer and partridges in a garden they call a *moya*. No other living soul can take anything from that place except the Inca and the Coya, who hunt with lassos, traps, and throw their *boleadoras* and their *pucacon*, nets. And the Inca goes to enjoy himself with his wife and princes and princesses and all his lords in the garden which was reserved for that purpose. *Moya*: Party pasture of the Inca.

For the Incas, hunting was a royal privilege, and it is not surprising that the activity should take place on a royal estate. Pachacuti, for example, had a hunting lodge near Cuzco, probably the ruins of Puca Pucara (shrine An-1:9; Tambo Machay; Cobo book I, chap. 14; 1990: 63). The Inca ruins in the Chicón canyon, to be discussed in the next chapter, are best interpreted as a hunting lodge or as structures devoted to the ritual that surrounded Inca royal hunts. Huayna Capac's hunting preserve probably didn't have production agriculture, but it may have been planted. By 1552, investigators, desperate for timber, remarked on the trees to be found in the canyon. And Francisco Chilche, the Cañari who claimed control of the *mitimaes* of the estate and took over much of its property after the death of Francisco Pizarro, had six *yanaconas* caring for trees in that canyon in 1565; they also guarded the boundaries of his property (Heffernan 1995: 81–83). We do not know whether Chilche's tree guardians were his own solution to claims against his land by Spaniards or whether they were a contin-

uation of an Inca role for *yanaconas* on the estate. Arboriculture probably was a job practiced pre-Hispanically: Gonçalez Holguin reminds
us that the Inca language had a term for transplanting trees where
they were lacking (*ppittcta cassacta mallquipani*; Gonçalez Holguin 1952:
224).

In addition to the forested hunting preserve, Huayna Capac's estate—like those of other Incas—had stands of forests. The forested
lands were all toward the western edge of the estate near a patch of
forest at Cozca that Topa Inca owned on the north side of the Urubamba (1552; Villanueva 1971: 52). The two forested areas that belonged to Huayna Capac were known as Charcahuaylla (1552; Villanueva 1971: 53) and Patashuaylla (1552; Villanueva 1972: 53). These
lands were west of the modern town of Urubamba (both are preserved
as place-names and bus stops on the Urubamba-Ollantaytambo highway). The land known as Coto, west and south of the Pomaguanca
canyon, was also forested. But in contrast to the other lands, this forest belonged to the Sun (1552; Villanueva 1971: 52).

Although the Spaniards who wrote about the economic potential of
the estate's lands in 1552 were interested in noting which were fields
and which were forested, there is no information in that document
about how the Inca rulers used the forests on their estates. The fact
that Topa Inca claimed forest fairly far from his holdings on the south
side of the river suggests that there were forest products that he found
useful. Firewood was a necessary part of Inca ritual. The forest owned
by the Sun could well have provided fuel for the brazier called Nina
where Cuzco's sacrifices were burned (Ch-3:1; Cobo book I, chap. 13;
1990: 55). Topa Inca's forests could also have provided wood for the
fire used to cook the food that he ate or to burn the food that would be
sacrificed to his mummy. Timber would have been the most valuable
commodity to be found in a forest, and the amount of building activity
that took place on an Inca's estates and on his holdings in Cuzco
would have required a great deal of wood.

Wood was used for rafters, purlins, ridgepoles, and columns, as
well as for lintels on some doors and niches and corner braces on
some buildings. The wood used for lintels on the estate required
straight trunks about 30 centimeters in diameter, with a length of up
to 6 meters. The wood that is still preserved in one of the buildings at
Quispiguanca was identified by a local resident as *aliso* wood, a material that both Cobo and Betanzos describe as used in Inca buildings
and that Protzen observed in construction at Ollantaytambo (Protzen
1993: 162–163). Finding timber long enough and thick enough to
serve as rafters and columns would have provided an even bigger challenge to Inca builders.

During the Colonial Period, there was a crisis in finding building materials. The practice of looting Inca buildings for their cut stone and timbers, which continues in the area today, was sufficiently well established by 26 March 1534 so that Francisco Pizarro created an ordinance against it; the city had only been officially founded as a Spanish city three days earlier (*Ordenanza para los vecinos del Cuzco . . . ; 26 March 1534*; F. Pizarro 1986, vol. 1: 149–150). A year later, he was requiring Spaniards to plant trees both to serve as boundary markers of their lands and to be useful for firewood (*Ordenanzas generales sobre la conversió . . . ; mediadios de 1535*; F. Pizarro 1986, vol. 1: 154), a law that was extended to Indian communities by Viceroy Toledo (*Ordenanza para la vida comun en los pueblos de indios; 6 de noviembre de 1575*, Título IX, Ord. XIII; 1986: 258). Garcilaso notes that the Spaniards had removed the wooden beams the Incas had used to cover the canalized rivers in Cuzco to be used for house lintels (parte I, lib. VII, cap. XI; 1609: 177 r.). By 1565, the city of Cuzco was claiming stands of *aliso* trees planted in the Chicón canyon on the estate's lands (Heffernan 1995, appendix II: 81–82).

In addition to the fact that they probably managed their natural resources better than did the Spaniards, the Incas had ways to get the wood they needed when their economic system was intact. Firewood was one of the commodities that entered into the reciprocity between the Inca and a subject lord (*Informaciones de Toledo*; Levillier 1940: 94). Garcilaso claims that palaces made use of especially good wood (parte II, lib. I, cap. XXXII; 1617: 24 v.). It is not inconceivable that Inca incursions into tropical zones would have brought back woods from the jungle for use in especially complicated construction projects. The forest that belonged to the Sun at Coto may have been used as well for timbers for buildings devoted to the Sun or his custodians. Still, one way for an Inca to get wood was to grow it on an estate. Forests, like other kinds of economically useful lands (pastures, mines, fields), were individually owned by Inca rulers (segunda pregunta; Rostworowski 1970: 253) or by the Sun (lands of Coto on the estate).

The lands reserved as woods at the western edge of the estate were, for the most part, on regions of the estate that did not have readily available water for irrigation. It would surely have been possible to create canals to bring the lands into cultivation had the Incas wanted to do so. It has always been my impression that the estate developed from east to west. It may well be that the forested reserves on the west edge of Huayna Capac's holdings were places that hadn't yet been developed for other purposes and that would have been eventually developed further for Huayna Capac by his descendants.

Land Grants on the Estate

One striking aspect of the organization of Huayna Capac's estate is the presence of lands belonging to others within its boundaries, as shown on figure 5.9. It is clear from historical sources that royal estates, though individually owned, did not include land only for the developer of the estate. The sources do not make clear whether the land given in grants was owned by the *panaca* of the person to whom it was granted, or whether it was managed by the *panaca* of the Inca who developed the land and bestowed the grant.

The practice of including grants to others on a royal estate is not unique to Huayna Capac: His father, Topa Inca, included grants to the Sun, to his wife, Mama Ocllo, and to unnamed lords of Cuzco on his

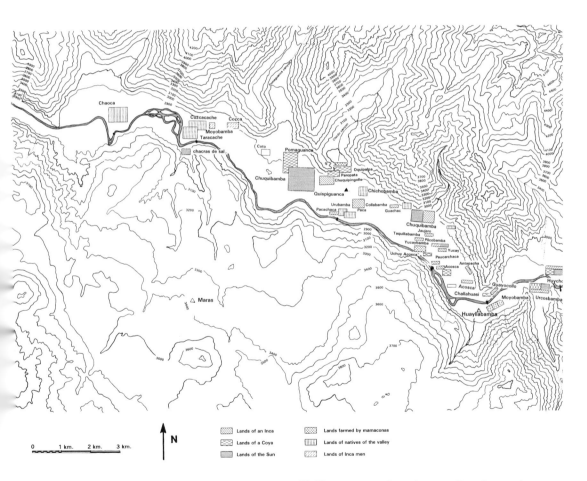

FIGURE 5.9. Map of fields on Huayna Capac's estate. Locations and ownership are based on sixteenth-century documents published by Villanueva Urteaga (1971), supplemented by my fieldwork. Properties are not drawn to scale.

estate at Chinchero (lands of Huycho, Urcosbamba; 1551 document; Villanueva 1971: 35, 45–46; see also Betanzos parte I, cap. XXXVIII; 1987: 173). Huayna Capac is reported to have given parcels "to the lords of Cuzco, to the living ones as well as to the dead ones" (Betanzos parte I, cap. XLIII; 1987: 187). Elsewhere we are told of specific grants made to his grandfather Pachacuti and the mummy of the first (and mythical) Inca, Manco Capac; these grants included *mamaconas* to serve the mummy and *yanaconas* who were settled on the lands (Betanzos parte I, cap. XLI; 1987: 182).

There are only two demonstrable parcels that may have been on Huayna Capac's estate that may have been grants to male relatives. Near Cozca there was land that had belonged to Inca Roca, identified as an uncle of Huayna Capac; in 1552 it was being farmed by Indians of the valley (1552 document; Villanueva 1971: 52). At Moyobamba was land that had belonged to Hachache, a nephew of Topa Inca (eight *topos* at Moyobamba now farmed by Doña Angelina de Betanzos; 1552 document; Villanueva 1971: 52–53). These parcels were near each other and adjacent to land that was owned by Topa Inca. It is possible that they got their grants through him, rather than through Huayna Capac.

The demonstrable grants within the estate were made to women associated with Huayna Capac. Huayna Capac gave a grant of fields and farmers to his mother, Mama Ocllo, at Antapacha (ten *topos*; 1551 document; Villanueva 1971: 37; Doña Angelina's título of 1558; Rostworowski 1962: 144), along with a small field at Unoy Acosca (*sic* for Uchuy Acosca, 1552 document; Villanueva 1971: 51) and a large terrace at Oquipalpa (1552; Villanueva 1971: 52). The Inca also made grants to his wives. His sister-wife, Coya Cusirimay, owned fields at Paropata (1552; Villanueva 1971: 52). Rahua Ocllo had ten households of workers at Challahuasi (1551 document; Villanueva 1971: 36), and more workers farther down the valley (1551 document; Villanueva 1971: 39). She also had land at Pomaguanca (1551; Villanueva 1971: 39, 48) which may have been farmed for the Sun (1552; Villanueva 1971: 52). There were other pieces of land on the estate that were farmed or owned by women but whose identities are not given. There were also lands associated with groups identified simply as "mamacunas del Inca" (the Inca's *mamaconas*) and "indias suyas" (his female Indians) (1551; Villanueva 1971: 38, 47, 51, 52). One of these properties, called Yucaybamba, was quite sizable: thirty *topos* in extent. The grants of large terraces made to his mother and his legitimate wife were adjacent to his palace of Quispiguanca, perhaps reflecting their closeness to him.

The grants that were specified as lands of Huayna Capac's mother and his wives, Cusirimay and Rahua Ocllo, deserve some discussion. Huayna Capac's mother, Mama Ocllo, was almost certainly dead by the time the grants were made. It is likely that the field was devoted to the upkeep of her mummy, including, probably, the sustenance of her attendants. Cusirimay did not bear sons who survived to succeed their father, and she herself probably died young. Like the grant of land to his mother, it is possible that this field was devoted to the maintenance of Cusirimay's mummy, rather than to the support of her living person. Rahua Ocllo was the mother of Huascar, the son who had the support of Cuzco's royal families in the succession wars that followed Huayna Capac's death. Although she came from a noble family of Cuzco, her position as a secondary wife was always a cloud over Huascar's claim of succession. He pulled many stunts to make himself appear to be the legitimate successor to his father, including marrying his mother to the mummy of Huayna Capac (Pachacuti Yamqui 1968: 311). It is not inconceivable that the relatively lavish grants to Rahua Ocllo were made by Huascar after his father's death, rather than being made at the time the estate was created.

Some support for this view comes from testimony made by a witness in Toledo's *informaciones* of 1571. Francisco Chachín, a native of Guaylas, was one of fifty *mitimaes* brought to Chinchaypuquio, near Cuzco, by Rahua Ocllo after Huayna Capac's death (*Informaciones de Toledo*; Levillier 1940: 112–113), a point he reaffirmed when he was a witness on idolatry (*Informaciones de Toledo*; Levillier 1940: 151–152; here he confuses Huayna Capac with Topa Inca). It is unlikely that Rahua Ocllo herself would have had sufficient clout even in Huayna Capac's lifetime to have commanded *mitimaes*. But it is not at all unlikely that her son, Huascar, could have made the order in her name. More problematic is the statement by witness Martín Caycha, a native of Guanuco, who claimed that his father, a *curaca* in his homeland, had been brought to the Cuzco region as *mitima* by Mama Ocllo, whom he identifies as Huayna Capac's wife (Levillier 1940: 142). The witness is clearly confused about the relation of Mama Ocllo to Huayna Capac. While it is possible that Topa Inca (Mama Ocllo's husband) gave her the right to take *mitimaes* (and there are stories to that effect in Cobo; see the story of her defeat of the *cacica* of Huarco, lib. 12, cap. XV; 1964: 87–88), that event would have taken place eighty to a hundred years prior to Caycha's testimony, which seems to be rather unlikely. Most probably, it was Huayna Capac who took Caycha's father as *mitima* to serve on lands dedicated to his (probably dead) mother, Mama Ocllo.

It is possible that the *mitimaes* who claimed to have been taken to estates by Mama Ocllo had been taken by a *bulto* of the dead queen. When ruling Inca men died, images or bundles were made of scraps of their flesh, clippings of their hair and fingernails, or clothes they had worn. These *bultos* were objects of devotion and also had as much authority as the real person of the ruler. When Mama Ocllo died, there was a *bulto* made of her by her son which was kept in her house in Cuzco (Betanzos parte I, cap. XLIV; 1987: 190), and we know that an image of her was kept in a temple at Tomebamba, too, where it figured in the quelling of the rebellion by Cuzco's nobles. It is not inconceivable that *mitimaes* taken by a statue of a dead queen might articulate their move in terms of their being taken by a still living queen. It is also possible that the *mitimaes* taken by Rahua Ocllo were taken by a statue of the living woman (the disruptions of the Inca civil war make it unlikely the grants to her were posthumous), though they could, alternatively, simply have been taken in her name.

In addition to the grants to humans and to mummies, there were lands on the estate dedicated to the Sun. These included the terraces known as Chuquibamba (golden plain), which included one hundred *topos* (1551; Villanueva 1971: 37). These lands, above Yucay, were divided between Huayna Capac and the Sun. There were additional parcels owned by the Sun in Yucay, including a house called Curicancha (1551; Villanueva 1971: 37) and an adjacent field two *topos* in size called Pilcobamba (Villanueva 1971: 37). Another thirty *topos* of land called Chuquibamba was located near the midpoint of the estate, just west of the mouth of the Chicón canyon (1551; Villanueva 1971: 39). There were fields at Pomaguanca which Rahua Ocllo may have farmed for the Sun (1952; Villanueva 1971: 52). Finally, there was the forest at Coto which belonged to the Sun (1552; Villanueva 1971: 52), which has already been discussed.

Conclusion

The physical plan that can be discerned from the historical sources shows us that Huayna Capac's estate was a place that included provision for his economic, social, ritual, and recreational needs. His country estate was a place where he could indulge in his favorite pastimes, including hunting and, perhaps, gardening, in the company of his courtiers, trusted male relatives, and miscellaneous women. The design of the estate shows an Inca view of a perfect landscape, one that juxtaposes economic productivity with recreational gardens, mundane activity with ritual, and balances agricultural fields with parks and irrigation canals with ponds. It is also a place that reflects the Inca view of a perfect social order: The Inca and the Sun are attended by fleets of *mamaconas* and served by workers, house servants, guards, and weavers from throughout the empire.

In the case of Huayna Capac's estate, we can chart the historical moment in which it was created and can consider its creation as a response to the events in play in the royal houses of Cuzco. The estate became a tangible marker of its builder's place in the historical and social order of the Inca dynasty. The documentary evidence gives us a starting point for understanding the design of the estate. It is by examining the architectural remains that we can begin to see how the design was put into place, and how the ideals set forth in its concept were realized in the distinctive architectural style at the site.

6

THE ARCHITECTURE ON THE ESTATE

The rich historical documentation on Huayna Capac's estate at Urubamba and Yucay makes it possible to trace the limits of that development, as well as to identify some of its component buildings, terraces, and other built features. There is no other case in the Andes
where we can so securely identify the date of construction and the
function of individual buildings or where we can understand the relationship of structures to other parts of the estate's design. From a
purely architectural standpoint, the constructions on the estate show
a unique style. In this chapter I present descriptions of the principal
remains on the estate, including the palace compound of Quispiguanca, the hunting lodge of Cocha Sontor, and buildings in and
around Yucay (fig. 6.1). I also include some discussion of remains that
no longer exist but whose location can be identified on the basis of
historical evidence.

Quispiguanca

Huayna Capac's main architectural compound was a palace called
Quispiguanca. Its location can be discerned from the historical
sources, particularly the 1551 and 1552 documents. We are told, for example, that

> Dicen que acabadas las tierras de Chichobamba de la otra parte de un cam-
> ino hay unos tambos que se dicen Quispeguanca que eran de Huayna
> Cápac. A la mano derecha de estos tambos hay una quebrada entre dos
> sierras que se dice Chicón . . . de esta quebrada sale un arroyo que viene
> derecho hasta dar al río. (Villanueva 1971: 38)

> They say that at the far end of the lands of Chichobamba on the other side
> of a road are some lodges that they call Quispiguanca which belonged to
> Huayna Capac. To the right of these buildings there is a canyon between
> two mountains that is called Chicón . . . from this canyon flows a stream
> that goes straight to the river.

As noted in chapter 5, the Chicón canyon is immediately north of
modern Urubamba and, indeed, has a stream that was canalized in
Inca times (as now) to run straight toward the Urubamba River. The
1552 document also places the palace near the mouth of the Chicón
canyon (Villanueva 1971: 52) and adds:

Encima de los tambos de Quispeguanca cerca de ellos está otra chácara que era de Mama Ocllo madre de Huayna Cápac que tiene cuatro topos de sembradura y se llama Oquipalpa. (Villanueva 1971: 52)

Above the buildings of Quispiguanca and near them is another field that belonged to Mama Ocllo, mother of Huayna Capac, which is four *topos* in extent and is called Oquipalpa.

Chichobamba, which delimited the palace property to its east, and Oquipalpa (Juk'ipalpa), which was just uphill from it are still in use as field names and are located in the proper position relative to a set of ancient ruins that must be identified as the palace complex.

The ruins are located near the midpoint of the estate on a slight hill on the north side of the valley. As suggested by the 1551 and 1552 documents, the complex is just south of the entrance to the narrow Chicón canyon and its impressive snow peak. Located within the San José

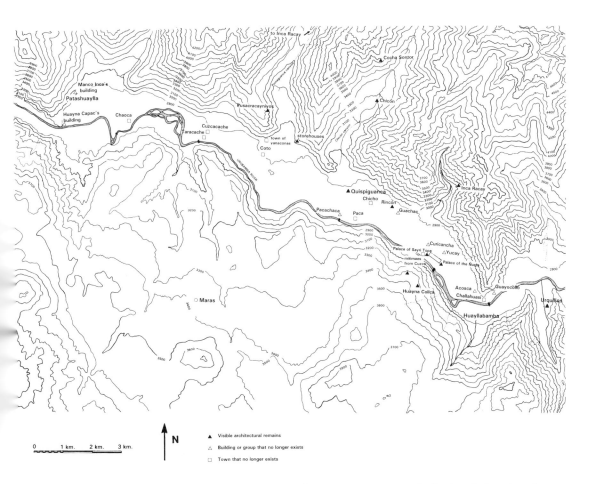

FIGURE 6.1. Map of Huayna Capac's estate, indicating the location of architectural groups based on Villanueva Urteaga (1971) and my fieldwork.

neighborhood on the north edge of the town of Urubamba, approximately a quarter of the site's area is within the boundaries of the modern cemetery, and the rest is on land which is cultivated (fig. 6.2). The Inca construction at Quispiguanca consists of a building terrace that supports the architectural space, a relatively well preserved surrounding wall on its east side, and a group of poorly preserved structures built along the north third of the site.

The Building Terrace

The main building terrace at Quispiguanca is a broad rectangle approximately 189 meters in length across its south face and approximately 125 meters wide, measuring to the face of the buildings that border its north edge (fig. 6.3). The original above-ground height on the well-preserved south and east sides of the terrace was at least 3.9 meters. Its top was finished level, as evidenced by a clearly preserved construction line. Above this line was a free-standing wall of less well fitted stonework which probably ran the full length of the south face of the terrace wall and in the interstices between buildings on the east wall. This wall may have stood as high as 1.5 meters to 2.0 meters above the modern ground level of the terraced surface. The carefully fitted stone masonry of the terrace's south face was provided with double-jambed niches with relatively wide proportions: 1.1 meters wide at the base, 1.1 meters at the height of the inner niches, and an estimated 1.3 meters as an overall height (fig. 6.4). One of the niches shows traces of a bright reddish-orange paint on top of its mud plaster. Despite the poor preservation of this wall and the displacement of many niches by vegetation, it is possible to observe the remains of twenty-eight niches. From their regular disposition on the wall, it is likely that the wall originally had at least forty niches along its length.[1] There are no corresponding niches on the east terrace wall and insufficient preservation of the west wall to discuss its design.

The East Entry

An architecturally elaborated wall delimiting the east side of the terrace served to mark access into and out of the palace's interior space. The east entry group consists of a symmetrical arrangement of buildings flanking an ancient, and now modern, footroad (figs. 6.5–6.7). On each side of the road there are remains of a small squarish building, here called a gatehouse (A and B on fig. 6.5); a narrow, probably rectangular building; and a tower with a nearly square footprint (C on fig. 6.5).

The gatehouses (A and B) are small structures with designs governed by strict symmetry. Exterior dimensions are 7.9 meters by 6.5

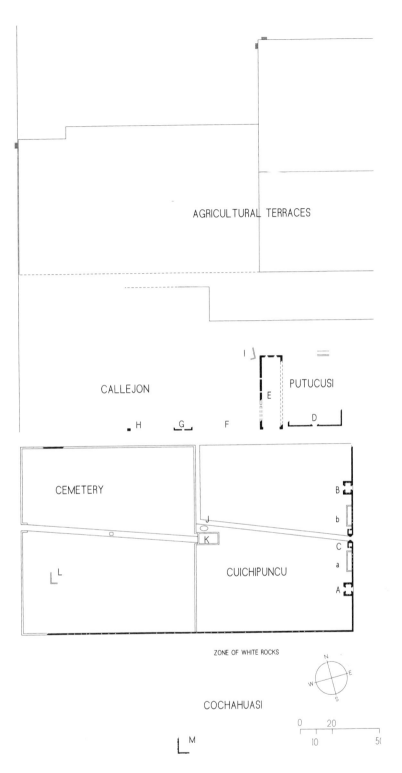

FIGURE 6.2. Plan of Quispiguanca, showing standing remains and modern features on the site. Ancient features include A, B: gatehouses; a, b: rectangular buildings; C: portal; D: Putucusi courtyard compound; E, H: great hall; F, G: small buildings; I: wall stubs and canals; J: white boulder; K: chapel; L: terrace wall stub; M: reservoir wall stub.

FIGURE 6.3. Overview of the south terrace wall at Quispiguanca, looking northwest.

FIGURE 6.4. Detail of the niched terrace wall at Quispiguanca, with double-jambed niche.

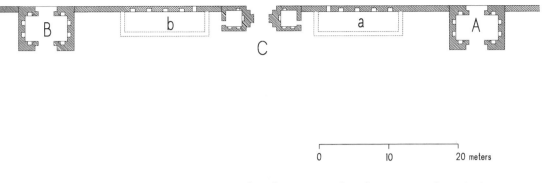

FIGURE 6.5. Plan of east entry to the palace compound at Quispiguanca. A, B: gatehouses; C: two towers of the central portal.

FIGURE 6.6. Existing remains of the east entry complex viewed from the plaza. Drawing by Robert N. Batson.

FIGURE 6.7. Existing remains of the east entry complex viewed from the exterior. Drawing by Robert N. Batson.

meters, and on each, the wall facing toward the plaza is 1.3 meters in thickness. The buildings have stone foundations—better fitted on the exterior than the interior—topped by upper walls of adobe brick. Gatehouse A preserves a wall portion that reaches 5.16 meters above modern ground level. Each gatehouse has two double-jambed doorways, one facing toward the plaza and the other facing away from the compound, oriented so that the double jamb is seen on the building exteriors (fig. 6.8). These doorways are huge: 3.2 meters tall, with a width of the inner jamb of 1.85 meters. The doorways still preserve traces of their original wooden lintels, comprising two parallel tree trunks, approximately 30 centimeters in diameter. Each doorway also has a pair of barhold devices on the interior of the building. Each gatehouse also had eight niches at the ground-floor level (figs. 6.9, 6.10). Like the doorways, most of the niches have wooden lintels and traces of mud plaster. The niches are about 1 meter in height, with 70-centimeter bases and 60-centimeter tops. One curious aspect of the niche construction is that the top of the niche slants upward noticeably from front to back; this slant is about 5 centimeters over the 50-centimeter depth of the niches. This feature was also noted on the single completely preserved doorway into this building, as well as at here and at some other buildings on the estate, to be discussed.[2]

FIGURE 6.8. West face of gatehouse A at Quispiguanca.

FIGURE 6.9. Interior of gatehouse A, showing a niche, barhold device, and interior of doorjamb. A thin topcoat of plaster is barely visible in the edge of the niche.

The upper walls include a small double-jambed niche centered about 80 centimeters above the top of the doorway on the west wall flanked by two standard-sized windows, now badly deteriorated. There is no ledge on the wall to suggest there would have been a second story in the gatehouse structures. The exterior of the west wall of gatehouse A also has a double-jambed niche centered between the windows about 4.7 meters above the modern ground level. There are also two small, double-jambed niches at this approximate height on the building's south wall. The relatively even weathering of the adobe walls suggests that the gatehouse structures originally had hip roofs, a style of roof appropriate for Inca buildings of this size and shape.

Each gatehouse is connected to its partner, the tower building by a wall (fig. 6.11). Shallow niches (70 centimeter base, 40 centimeter top,

FIGURE 6.10. Cross section of the remains of gatehouse A. Drawing by Robert N. Batson.

FIGURE 6.11. Photograph of Quispiguanca's south tower, C, niched wall, and small rectangular building, a, as they appeared in 1986, viewed from the southwest.

85 centimeters tall, 36 centimeters deep) show this to be, in part, the rear wall of a narrow building which is no longer standing (a and b on fig. 6.2). The building was approximately 12.7 meters in length and no more than 3.4 meters wide. One building still had a front wall in 1987, though it was probably not identical to the original Inca one.

The most unusual structures in the east entry façade are the pair of buildings that flank the road (C on fig. 6.5). Viewed from the inside of the compound, each appears to be a narrow tower with a single interior room that measures 2.40 meters by 2.33 meters on the ground floor. As is the case with the gatehouse structure, the tower on the south side of the modern road is the better preserved, reaching a height of 5.3 meters; it is likely that the building originally stood over 6 meters. Each tower has a single, narrow, off-center doorway on the side facing toward its gatehouse which provided entry to the ground level, and a second similarly sized opening at the second-floor level gave access to an upper story, presumably by using a ladder placed against the outside of the structure. As seen in figure 6.12, the building interiors have asymmetrical arrangements of architectural features: At the first-floor level, two niches on one wall face a single niche on the opposing wall; these niches have 52-centimeter bases and are 36 centimeters deep. The off-center doorway faces a centered niche that is 2.29 meters tall and has a base of 85 centimeters. The support ledge for the second floor can be observed about 2.75 meters above the base of the first floor on the east and west walls; there is no corresponding ledge on the north and south walls.

The second-floor interior features include wide openings centered on the east and west walls, narrow openings on the south and north walls, and a shallow niche on the south wall that is not symmetrical

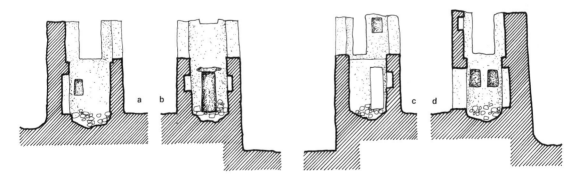

FIGURE 6.12. Cross section of the tower structure: a, west wall; b, north wall; c, south wall; d, east wall. Drawing by Robert N. Batson.

with respect to any feature on the north wall. The first-floor walls are made of mud-plastered stone, while the second-floor walls are entirely composed of mud-plastered adobe brick.

Taken individually, the tower buildings are unusual and oddly proportioned. But if they are viewed as a pair, they make more sense (fig. 6.13). The two towers flank the roadway that gave access to the ancient plaza. The walls that bracket the roadway define a triple-jambed portal which would have been about 2 meters wide. The ancient roadbed was approximately 1.3 meters above the modern road level and about 2.6 meters higher than the portal's base. Passage through the portal was

FIGURE 6.13. The two tower structures form a portal by flanking a stone-paved road.

probably by means of a ramp. Ramps are known for other nearby sites, including ramps in the terrace systems of Q'ellu Raqay at Ollantaytambo and Chinchero; there is also a stepped ramp at Chinchero that connects a broad plaza to the terrace on which the modern church is built.

If the towers are viewed as two parts of a single structure, the resulting portal obeys Inca principles of symmetry.[3] Figure 6.14 presents a possible reconstruction of that structure (see also plate 1). That reconstruction assumes a narrow chamber linking the two towers that is built above the lintel of the triple-jambed portal. The resulting building can be provided with a single and imposing roof, thus solving the problems of roofing what might otherwise be two independent structures that would require a covering to preserve their adobe walls.

The free-standing architecture and the upper portion of the terrace foundation show evidence of having been coated with multiple layers of mud plaster. In places it is possible to see three coatings, totaling around 5 centimeters in thickness. As is typical for Inca plaster, it shows abundant use of grass temper, which helps it to adhere to the surface of the wall and allows it to dry evenly without cracking.

The plastering seems to have been an integral part of the construction of the buildings. On the exterior wall of the north gatehouse, for example (B on fig. 6.5), it is possible to see that the initial coating of mud plaster was placed on the south and east wall faces before the surrounding wall was built against the gatehouse. Subsequent layers of plaster would have covered this join and given a smooth, overall surface to the buildings, thus obscuring this initial layer. The interior walls of buildings were plastered to the floor level, and the exterior walls facing toward the plaza seem also to have been plastered to the ground level. The exterior walls facing outward were probably plastered only above the level of the fitted masonry of the supporting terrace, as it is possible to see grooves worked into the stone just below the join of the good masonry with the less well fitted masonry above it. Presumably, these grooves would mark the point above which the wall was plastered and would result in a smooth plane of the finished wall. The plaster groove is a feature found at other Inca sites and observed in two other architectural complexes on the estate, as will be discussed.

The plaster traces visible today are about the same color as the adobe walls—a pinkish brown similar to the nearby soil. On one of the double-jambed niches of the south terrace wall there are still traces of a vivid reddish-orange color on top of this base coat.[4] The base coat of the upper portion of the west-facing door jamb on gatehouse A preserves a trace of creamy-colored plaster, though whether it

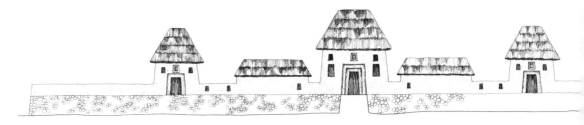

FIGURE 6.14. Elevation of the east entry façade as it may have existed in antiquity, viewed from the exterior. Drawing by Robert N. Batson.

is a base coat or a final coat is uncertain. The lower wall of the terrace, if it had been painted, could have been coated with the very thin top-coat of pigmented mud plaster that forms the painted coat of the plastered walls (see plates 2–3).

The east entry opens onto a broad terraced expanse that contains no above-ground remains of ancient buildings; it is an area that I consider to have been the site's plaza, and I will discuss it in a succeeding section.

The North Building Complex

The other region of the site with standing architecture is the set of buildings that defined the north edge of the Inca plaza. The ruins are visible now along the edge of a modern road that is bordered by badly weathered building foundations (B, E, F, G, and H on fig. 6.2). It appears that the entire complex was built on a low terrace that rose perhaps half a meter above the height of the main plaza.

The best-preserved building in the group was a great hall (fig. 6.15, E on fig. 6.2). Measuring approximately 14.2 meters by 43.8 meters (based on exterior measurements), the structure had fitted stone foundations and adobe upper walls. The building is oriented with one of its short sides facing south, toward the site's main plaza. This side has a single, broad opening that provided entrance into the building; only the base of the foundation is visible today (fig. 6.16). The interior corners of the structure are noticeably rounded. Traces of the adobe gable at the north end are preserved to a height of 2.83 meters. The bricks in this gable are 32 centimeters long, 10 centimeters wide, and 93 centimeters thick. The walled end also has two double-jambed doorways (the doorways have widths of 2.06 meters and 2.28 meters, respectively, to the outer jamb), with the double jamb visible from the building's interior. Today, the base of the door openings (and the building's interior) is about 50 centimeters lower than the ground surface on the north side of the structure. There are no barhold devices in

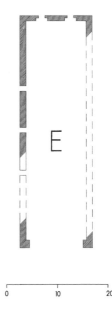

0   10   20 meters

FIGURE 6.15. Plan of building E, the great hall of the north building complex.

FIGURE 6.16. One of the remaining piers that define the wide opening in the south-facing end wall of building E.

evidence on the exterior wall. Two door openings are partially preserved in the long wall on the west side of the structure, and a third can be assumed to have existed to complete the symmetry. The opposite long wall is no longer visible above ground, hence any openings, if originally present, cannot be determined. The north wall and, especially, the northwest interior corner of the structure preserve traces of a vivid red-orange paint applied on top of the 4–5-centimeter-thick coating of mud plaster. I observed no paint preserved on the structure's exterior.

This structure was probably paired with a building of identical form built 63 meters west (H on figs. 6.2 and 6.19). This building is barely discernible: Only one pier of its door opening is visible in the modern wall that borders the fields. Still, this bit of wall is identical in style and size to the pier of the other great hall. Further, the wall that edges a modern road runs exactly where the east long wall of the building ought to have been. Since many field and architectural boundaries in and around Urubamba follow the walls of ancient buildings, this fact strengthens the identification of the remains as a second open-ended great hall.

In the area between these two large buildings there are remains of one, and probably two, smaller structures. It is possible to discern the corners of a building 11.3 meters in length with a door opening centered in the wall that faces toward the main plaza (G on figs. 6.2 and 6.19). A single building corner and a great deal of reused building stones continue in the modern wall that borders the road for an identical distance (F on fig. 6.19), suggesting there was a second, similar-sized building there. There are many acontextual building stones against the northwest corner of building E, indicating that there may have been other structures near that end of the building.

The ruins outline a small plaza defined on at least three sides by architecture. This small plaza is centered relative to the site's main plaza below it and shares its proportions (3:2). Its larger buildings, E and H, at least, both look out over the main plaza and, it is likely, in toward the more intimate plaza (plates 4–5).

The back wall of the best-preserved great hall (E on fig. 6.2) is about 21.2 meters from the beginning of tall agricultural terraces. This space, too, was an important part of the site, though its design remains elusive. The importance of this space is attested by the fact that the double-jambed doorways on the hall mark the entrance into that space rather than into the building. There are remnants of Inca fitted stone walls stubs, canals, and finished stones in this zone. Modern canals pass through this space, too, dropping down the front of the agricultural terraces and crossing just west of the great hall. While I cannot suggest exactly what it looked like, I think it is likely that these traces are remains of an architecturally elaborated water control structure. Given that entrance into the zone was by means of double-jambed doorways, it may have been a water shrine of some sort. The space may have been a place where carefully managed water was brought across the small plaza between the two great halls.

In addition to the buildings that define the small plaza group, the north building complex contains another compound, shown as D on figures 6.2 and 6.19. The compound is in a field called Putucusi, a name which does not appear in historical documents. The ruins are now also called by the Spanish name Buena Vista. Set back slightly relative to the great halls and small buildings, the poorly fitted stone foundations and adobe upper walls of its south-facing wall are still visible along the modern road, standing to a height of 3.15 meters above modern ground level. The visible walls have traces of niches on their north sides and appear to have been the rear walls of two buildings, 15.65 meters and 15.72 meters in length, respectively, separated by a narrow passage 2.3 meters wide with a formal doorway (fig. 6.17). (The doorway, very poorly preserved, may have been double jambed, with the double jambs facing inward, away from the main plaza.) Traces of the walling pertaining to this compound are visible on its east side (where the wall is preserved for about 9 meters from the southeast corner) and its north side (a wall is found about 41.9 meters from the front wall) and, 1.9 meters north of this, in a wall that defines a narrow passage in the north wall of the compound from the modern field boundary.

Although the above-ground information is minimal, the remains are most likely the exterior walls of a self-contained building group premised on the courtyard-house arrangement so favored by the In-

FIGURE 6.17. Exterior wall of Putucusi, the courtyard compound at Quispiguanca. The scallops are the remains of niches in the adobe upper walls of two of its component buildings.

cas. This field was excavated by Farrington, who provides a small plan of the compound (1995: 62, fig. 8). He interprets the remains as of a pair of rectangular structures 15.8 meters by 9.7 meters; a narrow building 19.4 meters by 3.2 meters at right angles to the pair and to their west; a large rectangular building 26.0 meters by 11.3 meters at right angles to the east; and a similarly sized (26.0 meters by 11.3 meters) building facing them on the north. All the structures face in toward a small plaza 25 meters on a side. While it is helpful to consider this reconstruction, there are some places where Farrington's interpretation of the remains seems to be in conflict with the above-ground information. Figure 6.18 presents a possible configuration for the buildings in this compound. It is based on Farrington's reconstruction of the group, with changes that bring his plan into line with observations made in the field. In particular, figure 6.18 indicates two buildings (rather than one) on the north side of the courtyard and suggests modifications in the building that forms its east side.

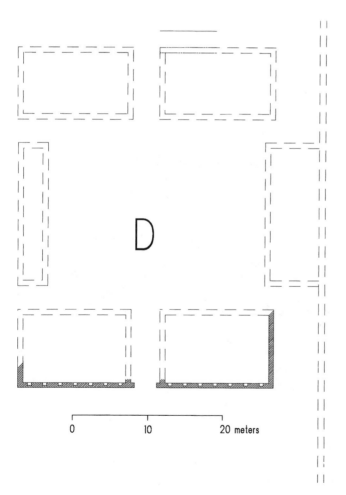

FIGURE 6.18. Possible plan of the Putucusi courtyard compound, Quispiguanca.

The west end of the group north of the great plaza is a mystery. Figure 6.2 indicates a blank space in this zone which preserves no aboveground pre-Conquest architecture. It is unlikely that this area was left open in Inca times. This space is exactly equal in size to the area covered by the buildings of compound D, the Putucusi complex, suggesting the possibility that a group matching its design might have been built on the west end of the site, as suggested in figure 6.19.

The Main Plaza

Nearly two thirds of the site was devoted to a great open plaza delineated on at least three sides by terracing or architecture. The fourth, or west, side of that space is poorly preserved, but guesses at its design can be made.

The west edge of the site is within the ground of the modern cemetery, and little that is attributable to Inca construction is observable there.[5] In a site so governed by principles of symmetry, it seems reasonable that there should have been a wall on the west side of the site that mirrored the formal entryway of the east. Unfortunately, the only traces of the original construction of the west side come from poorly preserved stretches of probable terracing (L on fig. 6.2; fig. 6.20). The 7.5 meters of walling are in line with the Inca corner of the south terrace wall and probably form a portion of that support terrace on the west side of the site. There is also a more mysterious 5.5-meter stretch of Inca walling at right angles to this one. Its masonry is similar to that seen in the support terrace, but it is hard to imagine that there should be terracing in this place. The masonry does not appear to be the style that would be seen in a free-standing structure, and though there are many isolated worked blocks within the cemetery (some of which have been placed to line up with this wall), the corner does not appear to have been from an Inca building.

One informant volunteered that before the construction of the modern cemetery wall there had been towers there that matched the structures on the east side of the site.[6] The better argument that there had been a gate comes from historical documents that locate fields that are to the west of the palace compound by reference to Otorongopongo (tiger gate), which is described as "at the entrance to Quispiguanca" (*Composición de tierras . . . 1594*).

Regardless of how it may have been bounded on its west side, the main plaza of Quispiguanca is a space displaying remarkable regularity, as seen on figure 6.19, which removes modern construction from the plaza. Its area takes up the lower two thirds of the site and is itself bisected longitudinally by the road that presumably passed through the portal of the east entry. The north-south axis of this space would

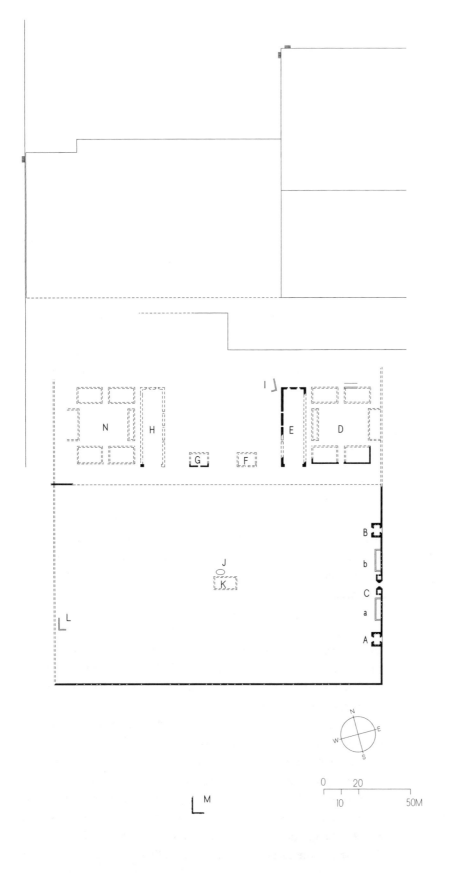

be bisected by a line that passed through the midpoint of the small plaza of the north building complex and that would pass immediately through a large white stone near the midpoint of the plaza (fig. 6.21).

The conspicuous white boulder, though near the center point of the plaza, is not on that center point. Rather, the center would fall within a Catholic chapel at the east end of the cemetery and adjacent to the white rock (K on figs. 6.2 and 6.19). It seems most likely that the Inca plaza was focused on the white rock but that the exact midpoint was at a shrine or platform now topped by a Catholic shrine; it seems reasonable to suggest that the devotions at that shrine would have been related to the rock.

The visual expression of the division of the plaza on a north-south line bisecting the rock is now a road and a canal; the canal may follow an ancient course. I have suggested that the area marked I on figure 6.2 may have included an architecturally elaborated treatment of water. It is possible that the water was transported from that space across the midline of the small plaza and over the midline of the main plaza. This would mean that the water would move over or around the point with the large white rock and its possible shrine. The association of stone with water is important in Inca design, giving some support for this interpretation. Further support comes from the observation that the entire terrace is graded at a consistent 1–2-degree slope from north to south; this is the same slope used on terraces at the site to carry water in irrigation canals across seemingly flat spaces. Thus water could have been transported from where it enters the north side of the site, across the plaza, and over the south terrace wall. Today the water drops down the terrace face, where it is collected and used as drinking water by farm animals and wash water by local residents of the San José neighborhood. In the Inca design of the compound, the water would probably have been collected into an artificial lake.

The sixteenth-century sources describe the buildings of Quispiguanca as being built beside a park with a lake: "On the left-hand side of this house of Quispeguanca alongside it is a park and lake that belonged to the Inca" (1551 document; Villanueva 1971: 38). Ironically, Quispiguanca is located on a natural high point which is almost the only part of the estate that wouldn't have been waterlogged. In con-

(facing page)

FIGURE 6.19. Plan of Quispiguanca as it might have been originally: A, B: gatehouses; a, b: rectangular buildings; C: portal; D, N: courtyard compounds; E, H: great halls; F, G: small buildings; I: wall stubs and canals; J, K: boulder and platform; L: terrace wall stub; M: reservoir wall stub.

FIGURE 6.20. Inca wall stub in the Urubamba cemetery, possibly from the west side terrace wall (L on fig. 6.2).

FIGURE 6.21. The white boulder near the center of Quispiguanca's main plaza (J on fig. 6.2).

FIGURE 6.22. The boulder-studded field south of Quispiguanca's terrace known as Cochahuasi, viewed from the west.

trast to other parts of the estate where we know that the natural water was managed into pools and fountains, here the lake that was made would have had to have been artificially constructed and maintained. The area adjacent to the face of the niched terrace wall is named Cochahuasi (lake house), a name applied to a field that used to run from the terrace down to the area where the public coed school was built in the 1980s (the area is now full of houses). Due to the pattern of drainage and the presence of this name, this is certainly where Huayna Capac's lake was located (fig. 6.22).

The limits and form of that lake are not reliably determined. Stubs of nicely fit wall are visible at ground level 72.3 meters south of the face of the terrace wall (M on fig. 6.2). Farrington's excavation of this feature revealed "an L-shaped Inka reservoir 2.05 m deep, whose maximum dimensions are 13.75 m wide and about 25 m long and whose inner corner was marked by a large granite boulder carefully sculpted to support a fine Inka wall" (1995: 63). He did not find any canals to account for the filling or emptying of the reservoir. It is somewhat surprising that this reservoir is so small relative to the rest of the standing buildings and architectural spaces of Quispiguanca. It is also surprising that the little reservoir is so far from the palace's south terrace wall. I suspect that the L-shaped reservoir identified by Farrington is just one part of a larger artificial lake that was located nearer the terrace wall; built much farther downslope from the terrace, the reservoir may have been related to the management of water being released from the lake.

The area where the larger lake could have been located is currently used for the manufacture of adobes. The soil is sterile and silty—just the sort of deposit one might expect from a lake bottom. Informants recall that prior to the 1980s the small pool of water there was much larger. The identification of this area as a lake makes sense of several other remarkable features. Part of the area in front of the niched wall is full of enormous white boulders—similar to the white rock that is the apparent focus of the plaza, though some here are even larger. Boulder fields are found all around Urubamba, where landslides bring a great deal of rock and debris down from the canyon and adjacent hillsides. A large lake would have offered an attractive surface to reflect the rocks and the forty red niches arrayed on the terrace wall above it (see fig. 9.19).

Cocha Sontor

While Quispiguanca is the architectural centerpiece of Huayna Capac's estate, there are other constructions that were part of its design. High in the valley of the Chicón canyon is an extraordinary site known today as Cocha Sontor (*cocha*, "lake"; *sontor*, "excellent, superior").[7] As noted in chapter 5, Huayna Capac had a hunting lodge and park in this canyon; it is possible that this complex was the lodge or that it was related to the lodge. There are no other extant ruins in the canyon that are better candidates for a hunting lodge. There is a small set of agricultural-style terraces in one of the sheltered patches on the west edge of the canyon much lower than Cocha Sontor, but no obvious architecture nearby. The Hacienda Chicón, fairly near to these terraces and below the ruins of Cocha Sontor, had a foundation wall that appeared to preserve Inca stonework in 1987; a decade later, residents spoke of a standing Inca wall that used to be on the hacienda grounds. This now-vanished complex may have been the hunting lodge, in which case Cocha Sontor would be some sort of facility that was subsidiary to it—related, perhaps, to the park and to surrounding features of the landscape.

The road to the Chicón canyon passes immediately west of the modern cemetery wall in Urubamba; that would also be just west of the Inca surrounding wall for Quispiguanca (see fig. 5.7). In its lowest courses, it runs alongside tall Inca agricultural terraces and a deep canal, similar in style to the Yucay terrace main canals, that carries water toward Quispiguanca. The entrance to the canyon is marked by a steep hill of unusual color and form that is prominent in views from the east end of the site. Known as Tantanmarca, this hill has a blackish color that contrasts with the color of the hills around it. There is a modern chapel on the north face of Tantanmarca and paths that zigzag up to it from the valley bottom. The top of the hill includes a knife ridge with Catholic crosses and paths that cut diagonally up the much steeper south face of the hill. From below, there appear to be terraces supporting a small platform on this hill.

In the well-watered Chicón canyon itself there is modern agriculture on broad terraces in the mouth and floor of the canyon, most of which have no obvious traces of Inca masonry. The canyon also includes modern waterworks that pool water in a concrete tank for release south and east to Chichobamba and a canal that probably follows the course of an ancient one that courses water due south toward Quispiguanca and Urubamba. The road itself is barely passable by vehicle and shows no traces of Inca-style paving, walls, or stairs. There are not too many choices for the course of a road up the canyon: It is likely that the Inca road would have been close to the course of the modern road, at least as far as the Hacienda Chicón. Above that point, a modern dirt road heads east, and a foot road cuts off toward the west side of the canyon and climbs steeply to reach the ruins of Cocha Sontor and settlements above it. Probably the Inca road would have done this, too, though whether it did so following the course of the foot road toward the site is not known.

The compound of Cocha Sontor is small but no less interesting and distinctive than the ruins at Quispiguanca (fig. 6.23). It consists of a single relatively well preserved building, square in footprint, facing onto a rectangular subground construction. A niched wall, probably the rear wall of a now-vanished building, runs at right angles to the square building and similarly faces onto the sunken rectangle (fig. 6.24).

The Square Building

The only standing building (A on fig. 6.23) also seems to be the principal structure at the site. In describing it I will refer to the side that opens onto the sunken rectangular area as the front and the wall that, on its outside, faces downslope and across the valley as its back. The building's foundations are of well-fitted masonry, with special attention to the finish and fit of blocks on the front wall of the structure and around a 1.7-meter-wide doorway centered in that wall (fig. 6.25). The doorway opens to the northeast. The building measures 6.32 meters by

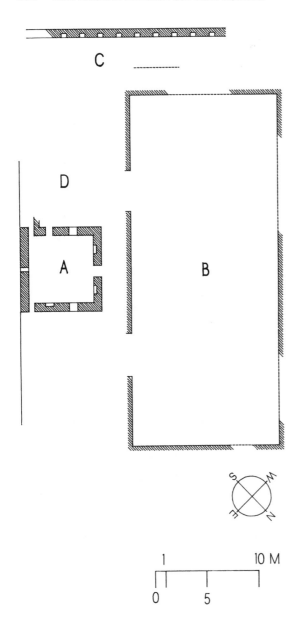

FIGURE 6.23. Plan of Cocha Sontor: A: main building; B: sunken rectangular area; C: niched wall; D: intriguing terraced space.

6.30 meters, based on interior dimensions. The front wall is 95 centimeters thick at the base. The building has a number of interior and exterior features that are of certain Inca construction and others that are questionable. But even the indisputably Inca features are a bit odd.

In addition to its central, single-jambed doorway, the building has two narrow openings in its side walls where they would join the rear wall. These openings are approximately 1.7 meters tall and about 70 centimeters wide near their base and 45 centimeters at the top. These openings are reminiscent of the narrow doorways on the first- and

FIGURE 6.24. View of Cocha Sontor from the north.

FIGURE 6.25. Detail, the doorway of building A, Cocha Sontor.

second-floor levels of the tower structure at Quispiguanca (C on fig.
6.2). There is a second tall, narrow opening in the northeast wall, opposite a tall, narrow niche in the wall that faces it on the building's interior. In the interest of symmetry I had originally thought this opening should also be a niche, but it is clearly finished on both edges as a
doorway. Between the two narrow doorways on the exterior wall is a
bit of beautifully worked wall stub coming out at right angles from the
foundation of the structure. From an examination of the foundation
on which the building is constructed, it does not appear that this is
part of a second building. Rather, it appears to be a nice bit of walling
that delineated a passage into and out of the structure through its narrow rear opening. I will return to this feature later. There is a niche in
the interior front wall adjacent to the door. In the relatively well preserved northwest wall of the structure, there is one body-sized niche
on the exterior of the building which matches the size of the rear-wall
openings (fig. 6.26) but is not symmetrically disposed relative to the
opening on that wall; the southeast wall is insufficiently preserved to
tell whether there would have been a matching oversize niche there.
About 3 meters above the ground there are remains of probable windows in the side walls and a definite window in the rear wall.

The structure has adobe above the well-fitted stone foundations and
an original wall height on the exterior of approximately 3.6 meters.
The interior, where cattle and pigs are penned, currently has a floor 40
centimeters lower than its original floor level. The original level can be

FIGURE 6.26. Exterior view of the north wall of building A showing its
oversize niches, narrow doorways, and battered walls.

discerned in several features: The mud that plasters the interior walls ends about 40 centimeters above the modern floor level, and stones from the wall protrude as well into that lowest 40 centimeters.

The above-ground stratigraphy of building A is rather interesting. There are no ledges or Inca beam holes to suggest that the structure originally had a second story, though it did have high windows. The building, however, was given a second story at some point. Figure 6.27 shows the building interior and the clear evidence that round beams were placed in the wall to support a second floor. However, changes in the color, size, and composition of the adobes at this point suggest that the second story is a post-Inca addition. It appears that the beams for this addition were placed just above the top of the high Inca windows. The same type of adobes are seen on the walls that delineate a structure (D on fig. 6.23) identical in form to the Inca building and placed alongside it. (The northeast wall of the Inca structure would become the central wall of the newer rectangular structure.) Because the post-Inca adobes are built right onto the Inca adobe walls, it seems likely that the Inca structure had an even top, meaning that it most likely had a hip roof. This is the style of roof that would be expected on an Inca building with these proportions. The post-Inca adobes converted this single-room, single-story, tall, square Inca building into a two-room, two-story, rectangular structure with gable roof.

The rear wall of the structure is built on a terrace that rises about 2.75 meters from the modern ground surface. The terrace is 51.4 meters long and approximately 53 meters in its maximum width. Its exact width is difficult to discern, as the field is an irregular shape and is apparently defined on only one side by a rough terrace wall. If the terrace was of Inca construction, it is not evident in the scant traces of masonry visible today.

As is the case of the structures at Quispiguanca, Cocha Sontor's building A has well-fitted masonry only on its exterior walls. The interior was coated with mud plaster to the floor level; traces of the plaster are up to 4 centimeters in thickness. The exterior walls were plastered at least above the stone foundations. Again, there is a noticeable groove near the join of the stone foundations with the adobe upper walls which seems to indicate a line to which the mud plaster was applied. Because it is not completely preserved, it is not possible to say with certainty how the Incas handled the problem of plastering around the doorjamb: The interior should have been plastered to floor level, but the outside might have been unplastered in its lower courses. As with Quispiguanca, the outside lower walls could have had a thin layer of plaster which would be flush with the upper wall's top coat.

FIGURE 6.27. Building A at Cocha Sontor viewed from the southwest. Various building epochs are clearly visible, including the most recent, represented by adobes drying in the foreground.

In contrast to the architecture at Quispiguanca, none of the architectural features preserved at Cocha Sontor have multiple jambs: Windows, niches, narrow doorways and main door are all single jambed. In this regard, they are reminiscent of the features of its portal building (tall, narrow niches and doorways; single-jambed niches; windows), with the exception that the latter structure defines, ultimately, a triple-jambed entrance to the site and the building at Concha Sontor is not associated with a road.

The Sunken Rectangular Construction

The square building is centered with respect to a rectangular construction sunk into the ground 2.9 meters from its front wall (B on fig. 6.23). This space measures 32.7 meters by 14.2 meters; the top line of its well-fitted masonry is 1.05 meters above modern ground level at the southeast end and 98 centimeters above the ground at its northwest end (fig. 6.28). Two wide (4.0 meters and 3.8 meters, respectively) openings are symmetrically disposed on the side nearest the square building; on the opposite side, the wall has deteriorated in the stretches opposite these openings, so it is not possible to say with certainty whether there was a similar pair of openings. The masonry of the sunken rectangular space is well fitted.

The Niched Wall

At right angles to the long axis of building B is a stretch of wall that preserves traces of nine niches (C on fig. 6.23). As is the case of building A, there is evidence of reuse of this wall. Just above the tops of the niches are adobe bricks that appear to be newer than those in the part of the wall that has the niches; this change in wall composition appears about 2.3 meters above modern ground level (fig. 6.29). The niches are relatively shallow, measuring 54 centimeters at the base and 46 centimeters at the top. Like the niches of the gatehouse at Quispiguanca, they are slanted upward, measuring 60 centimeters in height at the front and 64 centimeters in height at the rear of the niche. The attribution of these niches—and the wall—to Inca construction is based on the slanted niche profile, taken together with details of their construction. The lintels on the intact niches are made of wood wrapped with rope and vegetal fiber. The niches were evidently coated with mud; some of the niches preserve a creamy-colored plaster.

FIGURE 6.28. Detail, wall of the sunken rectangular reservoir (B on 6.23). In the center, one of the openings into the reservoir has been blocked by non-Inca masonry. To either side the original, relatively well fitted masonry is visible.

In technique, these niches are like the niches of the gatehouse at Quispiguanca. In shape, they are reminiscent of the shallow, nearly rectangular niche of the upper story of the tower (which, incidentally, preserves a creamy color, too).

The niches are disposed in a partial stretch of Inca walling modified by other, later construction. The wall is approximately 4.35 meters northeast of the short wall of rectangular space B. Parallel to the niched wall and 2.85 meters in front of it are traces of a thin fieldstone wall. It is insufficiently preserved to discern whether it is a modern wall or whether it is an ancient wall that formed the front of a building. If the latter, it would have defined an extremely narrow structure.

Discussion

In visualizing the built space of Cocha Sontor, it is important to note its orientation with respect to surrounding features of the landscape. The site is located high in the Chicón valley and built up against a hill on the valley's west side. The view to the southeast of the site is of the impressive snow peak of Chicón and adjacent high, bare mountains where local people still go to hunt deer (fig. 6.30). Somewhat surprising, perhaps, is the fact that building A is not oriented so that one

FIGURE 6.29. The niched wall of Cocha Sontor (C on fig. 6.23). The upper portion of the adobe wall is post-Inca.

FIGURE 6.30. View from the southwest at Cocha Sontor, toward the snow peak, Chicón. The peak may have been reflected in the rectangular reservoir.

would view that peak from its front door or—for that matter—from any of its ground-floor interior features. The peak could have been sighted from the high windows on the rear or northwest walls; however, without a second story, it is not obvious that it would be possible actually to see the peak when standing within the building were it roofed. The single, asymmetrical, human-height narrow niche on the northeast wall of the building is oriented to provide a view of the peak to a person or object placed in the niche or to permit the person or object to be viewed by the peak. From its front door, building A looks out onto the sunken rectangular space and across it to a scooped-out section in the hillside. This slope may have had a few narrow terraces, but any masonry that might originally have been present is no longer preserved. Looking higher up, the mountain, Cerro Sayhua, has a prominent, blackish, knob-shaped formation on top that would appear to be the most dominant feature of the natural landscape viewed directly from the square building.

The sunken rectangular space is exceptionally nicely made, and it is prominent in the viewlines from the square building, A (and, potentially, from the narrow, niched building or terrace, C, at its end). I have interpreted this space as an artificial lake, made to be filled with water, in the surface of which the impressive view of the snow peak could be seen from the architectural spaces, while the square building and its paired reflection could be seen from the far side of the pool (Niles in press). The openings in the wall that gave access to the space could have been stairs by which one could enter into the pool from the terraced spaces on either side of building A (figs. 6.31, 6.32).

FIGURE 6.31. Reconstruction drawing of the reflecting pond at Cocha Sontor. Drawing by Robert N. Batson.

FIGURE 6.32. Reconstruction drawing suggesting the possible relationship of buildings at Cocho Sontor. Drawing by Robert N. Batson.

PLATE 1. Reconstruction drawing of Quispiguanca showing the entry to the compound through the triple-jambed portal. Drawing by Robert N. Batson.

PLATE 3. Reconstruction drawing of Quispiguanca showing the great halls viewed from the rock at the center of the plaza. Drawing by Robert N. Batson.

PLATE 4. Reconstruction drawing of Quispiguanca showing the view from
the small plaza flanked by the great halls toward the center point of the main
plaza. Drawing by Robert N. Batson.

Although it is not currently full of water, the rectangular space is located where water could be coursed into it from above. In 1987 there were modern canals that ran along the hill just above and slightly east of the pool. In 1997 there were stone canal stubs visible just at the ground surface in the space just west of building A. While their course could not be followed, one leg of the Y-shaped pair was oriented directly toward the westernmost opening in the pool wall.

The interpretation of the rectangular space as a reflecting pond is strengthened by the modern place-name, Cocha Sontor, applied to the ruins. *Cocha* is a term applied to both natural lakes and artificial reservoirs. The association of an artificial lake with above-ground architectural spaces is analogous to the construction that Huayna Capac made at Quispiguanca. There, too, an artificial lake enhanced the park grounds and may have reflected the architecture (niches and terrace) adjacent to it.

The stub of wall on the south end of the side wall of building A is curious. Its construction is integral to that of the building, for it is of the same fine masonry, and, in fact, individual blocks of the side wall are worked with an interior corner to create the bend for the wall stub, proving that it was intentionally built and contemporaneous with the construction of building A. There is no corresponding wall stub on the other side wall, nor, given the condition of preservation, could there have been one that was made the same way. It is not possible to tell how long the wall made by the wall stub was or why it was there. I suggest that perhaps the wall was designed to screen off movement into or out of the narrow rear door of the square building. An arrangement with a narrow concealed entrance is reminiscent of the baffled false entrance into the back wall of building CH 2 at Chinchero (rear wall, fig. 203, Gasparini and Margolies 1980: 215). In that structure, the feature appears from the building's interior to be a double-jambed niche, though it is actually a narrow, L-shaped opening through the seeming niche. The opening permits access from a narrow passageway between the building and the terrace behind it and into the interior of the building without passing through its doors. A small, partially hidden entryway also appears on the east wall of building CH 1 in the same plan of the site.

Any of these doorways (the possibly screened one at Cocha Sontor or the screened and disguised ones at Chinchero) might have been important to pathways associated with rituals carried out in and around the building, though it is a little difficult to imagine someone togged out in feather headdresses or a lot of clothes fitting through these narrow spaces. Still, the openings could have been doorways for attendants to provide discreet service to a living or dead lord or to an image housed in the building's interior space.

Because we can only guess the shape of any possible building defined by the niched wall, it is not possible to say how, if at all, the narrow passage might have been linked to that structure. The stubs of wall lining the passage match the style of masonry seen in building A; it is quite different from the fieldstone masonry of the niched wall C. Thus it is unlikely that the two buildings were parts of a single structure.

The design of the complex leaves us with several intriguing spaces. Most curious is the space in the rectangle between the square building, the niched wall, and the pool (D on fig. 6.23) and the corresponding space on the opposite side of building A. These would have been flat, terraced spaces which likely provided a superb view across the canyon, down toward Tantanmarca, and up toward Chicón. The other curious space is the scooped-out and possibly terraced hill face across the pond from the doorway of the building. We know from documents that Huayna Capac maintained the canyon as a *moya*; that is, it was a park or garden. It seems reasonable to suggest that this small space was planted with flowers or decorative plants that could be viewed across the pool from the building. Such a modification of the landscape would have continued the estate's overall theme of viewing nature (the peaks and mountains) through the lens of culture (framed in a window or reflected in an artificial pool).

Yucay

Within the limits of the estate but not as reliably contemporaneous with its initial design and construction are the Inca-style architectural groups in the Colonial, and now modern, town of Yucay. The standing remains include the "Palace of Sayri Topa," the "Palace of the Ñusta," and the plazas of modern Yucay. In addition, there is a small group of structures called Inca Racay built above Yucay in the mouth of the San Juan canyon. The *tambo* of Yucay was a town of some prominence in the Colonial Period and probably did, in fact, serve as home to Sayri Topa and some post-Conquest Inca royalty. However, we have little clear understanding of the chronology of the construction and use of the architecture on this part of Huayna Capac's estate.

The Inca Plaza of Yucay

The twin plazas of modern Yucay are bounded on the south side by the modern Pisac-Urubamba Highway and on the north side by the fronts of buildings, some of which probably date to the Colonial Period. The plaza on the west side of town, called Plaza Manco II, is bordered on its west by a row of buildings that include the Palace of Sayri Topa and on its east by Yucay's church (fig. 6.33). The plaza on the east side of town, called the Plaza de Armas, is bounded on the west by the wall of Yucay's church and on the east by the row of buildings that includes the façade of the Palace of the Ñusta. Not quite centered between the two modern plazas is the church, oriented north-south (fig. 6.34). The two plazas are devoid of architecture, but each has an enormous double *pisonay* (probably *Erythrina* sp.; see Soukup 1970: 266, 126) tree planted in its center. Currently water is coursed in canals that run north-south along the west side of Plaza Manco II and the east side of the Plaza de Armas.

In considering the ancient plan of Yucay, I would expect the town to have had one, rather than two, plazas. Based on analogies to plazas at other Inca sites (including Cuzco, Calca, and Quispiguanca), I would expect that plaza to be large, to be rectangular rather than square, and to have had architecture around three of its four sides. In Yucay it is possible to find that sort of plan by removing the patently post-Inca construction, the Catholic church, which divides the two plazas. Without the church we are left with a space bounded on east and west by the two extant Inca-style buildings. The dimensions of the resulting plaza are approximately 365.1 meters by 113.6 meters, including the modern highway, and 365.1 meters by 102.5 meters, if we assume the ancient plaza ended at the near side of the highway. The dimen-

FIGURE 6.33. Yucay, Plaza Manco II from the east, with *pisonay* tree in the center and the Palace of Sayri Topa on the far edge of the plaza.

sions offered here are based on measurements taken from the fronts of non-Inca buildings on the north side of the plazas. It is certainly possible that the upper side of the Inca plaza was farther north than the current edge of the plaza: There is no extant Inca masonry on that side of the plaza.

The Palace of the Ñusta

The eastern boundary of the proposed Inca plaza is marked by the row of buildings that includes the Palace of the Ñusta (fig. 6.35). The wall that faces the plaza has exceptionally finely fitted masonry and an adobe upper wall that begins about 1.6 meters above modern ground level. The building has been modified and is still in use as a house. Clearly visible is an original Inca exterior corner (fitted into another wall), an Inca doorway (now blocked), and a stretch of original walling with a post-Inca doorway cut into it. The façade also includes a single large niche centered between the Inca doorway and the recut doorway (fig. 6.36). The now-blocked Inca doorway is 1.9 meters wide. The niche is body-sized (2.83 meters high, 1.16 meters wide at the base, and 60 centimeters deep) with a stone lintel. Neither the door nor the niche appears to have been double-jambed.

FIGURE 6.34. The twin plazas of Yucay, viewed from the south side of the valley.

FIGURE 6.35. Yucay, Palace of the Ñusta, overview of existing remains, with post-Inca door cut into the left side of the wall.

FIGURE 6.36. Yucay, Palace of the Ñusta, southwest exterior corner, showing a blocked Inca doorway that has been converted into a window.

From the angle of inclination that can be observed, it is clear that the surface that faces onto the plaza was the exterior wall of a structure, rather than an interior wall. Further, the building corner that is preserved must have been the southwest exterior corner of the original building. The northwest corner is not intact; indeed, it appears that much of the north end of the original exterior wall is missing. Thus, it is not possible to reconstruct with certainty the original dimension or form of the structure.[8] It is noteworthy that the building, similar to

Quispiguanca and Cocha Sontor, shows a groove near the join of the adobe and stone portions of the wall where, I argue, the upper portion had a thick coat of mud and the lower presumably did not (fig. 6.37).

The Palace of Sayri Topa

The only visible Inca-style remains on the west end of the plaza are the imposing (but now largely reconstructed) stone and adobe walls of the building popularly known as the Palace of Sayri Topa (fig. 6.38).

FIGURE 6.37. Plaster groove at the top of the fitted masonry of the Palace of the Ñusta.

FIGURE 6.38. Yucay, Palace of Sayri Topa, east wall exterior. Clearly visible are gigantic paired niches that flank an enormous door. Lines of pendant stepped triangle niches also decorate the façade.

According to Gibaja, when she worked there in the 1970s, elderly residents of Yucay called the building "Huaca Huasi," or "sacred house" (Gibaja 1982: 83).

Gibaja's study of the structure, based on observations made before it was reconstructed (Gibaja 1982), shows that the single room that comprises the building measures 11.0 by 12.0 meters. Walls are 1.2–1.5 meters at the base. The single doorway centered on the east wall is 2.5 meters wide and 6.0 meters tall and had a wooden lintel wrapped in rope and straw. Flanking the doorway are elaborate arrangements of exterior double-jambed niches not quite as tall as the door but, like that feature, topped by wood lintels wrapped with rope. Each niche is, in turn, flanked by a series of seven small niches, each shaped like an inverted stepped triangle, arrayed one above the other. Interior building features include two double-jambed niches on the interior west wall that are nearly as large as the exterior ones, flanked by a pair of smaller niches. The south interior wall had three small niches at the standard height (1.5 meters above modern ground level) with four stepped-triangle niches above them. There is also a smaller double-jambed niche in the south interior wall. The north wall of the building was no longer intact when Gibaja worked at the site. It is possible that the building had a coat of red mineral pigment as its final, all-over color (see the comment in Gibaja 1982: 89), with paint decorating some of its interior features at least. The stepped niches on the interior south wall conserve traces of bright paint in green, turquoise, red, and white. They depict an image that may have been a rainbow or a headdress. Gibaja interprets the image as an Inca *mascaypacha*, part of the insignia worn on a dignitary's headpiece (1982: 87–88).

Gibaja considers the Palace of Sayri Topa to be "Neo-Inca," or pertaining to an Inca style dating to the Colonial Period. Part of her argument is based on the discovery of Colonial Period objects in the material excavated from the building. She also finds support in a radiocarbon date of A.D. 1450 ± 100. Still, neither of these observations rules out a pre-Conquest construction and later occupation of the building. Perhaps the more convincing argument is Gibaja's observation that the majority of the stones in the foundation are recut fine Inca stones (1982: 84). This suggests that at least an earlier Inca structure was modified in the construction of the Palace of Sayri Topa. Gibaja's analogy to other buildings that she thinks are contemporary with this structure (buildings at Mañaraqui Plaza in Ollantaytambo, including that site's "Water Temple"; the site of Urco near Calca; and, possibly, Urubamba [by which I assume she means Quispiguanca]) is premised on stylistic arguments. While conceding that there are obvious similarities among the structures she notes, I cannot unquestioningly accept the stylistic argument that all date to postimperial Inca culture. Clearly, at Quispiguanca the architecture is reliably dated to the reign of Huayna Capac and probably to the early part of his reign. We know that both Huayna Capac and his son Manco Inca did some construction at Ollantaytambo, a site that is mainly the handiwork of their ancestor Pachacuti. Manco's half-brother Huascar built or rebuilt palaces at Calca in the years before the Spaniards arrived. Manco Inca, too, spent time in Calca; whether either of these rulers had anything to do with the construction of nearby Urco is unknown. I concur with Protzen that it is safer to characterize the distinctive style that clearly begins with Huayna Capac—and that may continue in the works built or modified by his sons and grandson—as "Late Inca" architecture (Protzen 1993: 261–264) without making assumptions about its placement relative to the Spanish Conquest. This point will be revisited in chapter 9.

Inca Racay (Yucay)

There is another extant set of remains near Yucay that reflects more traditional Inca design. The small complex is constructed roughly 1 kilometer north of the town of Yucay on the east side of the narrow San Juan canyon that is the source of water for the town and the terraces. The ruins of a nearby mill have given the name of Molinachayoc (place with a mill) to this part of the canyon. The site—like so many others in the southern Andes—is called Inca Racay (Inca ruins). For the sake of discussion, I will assume the ruins are contemporary with the construction of the estate, though they cannot be identified with any of the complexes mentioned in the historical documents. Valencia notes the presence of these structures in his discussion of architecture near Yucay, mentioning, too, the good view of the terraces that is afforded by the structures at Inca Racay (1982: 69–70).

The ruins consist of at least nine structures, with remains of building terraces or other structures nearby (figs. 6.39, 6.40). The extant buildings represent two forms: long, narrow, rectangular structures built into the hill and smaller, towerlike structures. The long structures (1–5 and 8–9 on fig. 6.39) are two-story buildings, built into the hill, with multiple doorways (probably four of them) on the downhill-facing long side of the ground floor and similar openings on the uphill-facing side of the upper level. The fieldstone foundations are topped by adobe brick upper walls, and the buildings have gable ends with neither windows nor doorways in them. Buildings 1–4 and 8–9 are constructed so that a 3.6-meter-wide terrace runs between the second floor of buildings 1, 2, and 8 and the first floor of buildings 3, 4, and 9. A similar distance (3.6–3.7 meters) separates the narrow ends of building 1 from building 2, building 3 from building 4, and building 8 from building 9. The structures vary slightly in size but have interior dimensions of 3.3–3.4 meters by 17.5–18.7 meters. Building 5 has a similar form, though it is a bit smaller (2.8 meters by 11.0 meters). The rear walls of the structures are insufficiently preserved to determine the size and number of second-floor openings that surely existed on those walls.

Although the Inca Racay structures lack the gable-end openings seen at many sites, in all other respects they resemble the rectangular storehouses I have observed near Cuzco at such sites as Sillkinchani and Tawqaray and near Chinchero at Machu Collca. They are also similar to the rectangular storehouses of Ollantaytambo analyzed by Protzen as Type II storehouses (1993: 111–135). It seems reasonable to interpret the long buildings of Inca Racay as storehouses. It should be noted that the placement of the long storehouses is rather unusual: They are built low on the slopes of the hill in the narrow canyon bottom near agricultural fields. Storehouses of this form are more often located on slopes that are higher, often windy, and usually unsuitable for irrigation agriculture.

Buildings 6 and 7 are more unusual (fig. 6.41). They are arrayed parallel to one another and set some 30 meters uphill from the long storehouses. Building 6 is a structure with two rooms, one built onto the front of the front of the other and about 80 centimeters lower than it. The rear (uphill) chamber may have had access to the exterior via a door on its north side, and movement between the two chambers was facilitated by a single narrow doorway. The uphill structure measures approximately 9.6 meters by 4.3 meters, based on interior measurements; the lower chamber is about the same size. Each had a second story, confirmed by the presence of second-story windows on the end wall of each and the front wall of the lower chamber. The upper chamber preserves the stubs of beams and has rafter holes on interior and exterior, indicating the location of the upper level's floor. Access to the second story of each chamber was presumably by means of the large openings found in the north-facing second-story wall of each. Building 7 is a single-roomed structure that measures 5.4 meters by 6.4 meters, based on interior dimensions. It has a single doorway centered in the wall that faces building 6 and high windows on the side walls. Both structures have fieldstone and mud foundations and noticeably rounded interior corners.

Building 7 has a plan similar to other Inca buildings, with its closest parallel in a set of square structures at the storage site of Machu Collca. Building 6, however, is quite unusual. It is reminiscent of the two-story double-houses of Ollantaytambo, but the pattern of

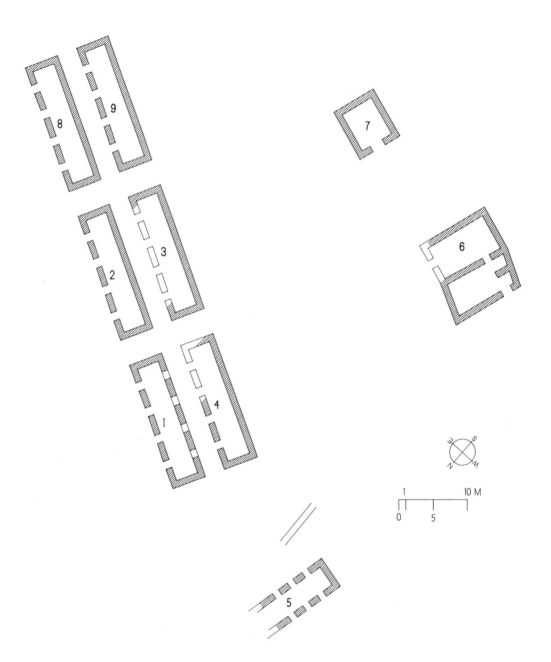

FIGURE 6.39. Inca Racay (Yucay), plan. Buildings 1–5 and 8–9: standard Cuzco-style rectangular storehouses; Buildings 6, 7: possibly modified storehouses or lookout points.

FIGURE 6.40. Reconstruction drawing of Inca Racay (Yucay). Drawing by Robert N. Batson.

FIGURE 6.41. Inca Racay (Yucay). Rear wall of building 6, showing the dramatic setting high on a hilltop in the narrow San Juan canyon. The Pampa de Maras is visible in the background.

doorways into and between its two chambers is unique. The pairing of structures 6 and 7 atop a ridge is reminiscent of the dual towers one sees on promontories overlooking the Urubamba-Vilcanota Valley that have been conventionally interpreted as lookout posts: From them one can see the entire Yucay terrace system to the south, the upper reaches of the San Juan canyon (the source of water for the terraces) to the north, and, toward the southwest, the edge of the Pampa de Maras as it drops down toward the town of Urubamba. This vantage point would allow close observation of the major routes into the lands of the estate.

The only other extant storage structures within the estate's boundaries are found in a small compound of Type I storehouses at the mouth of the Pomaguanca canyon (Huaycochea Nuñez de la Torre 1994: 251 and figs. 49–50, foto 32; Huaycochea calls the structures Pusacracayniyoc) that faced a handful of now-deteriorated structures that were probably Type II storehouses. The Pusacracayniyoc complex is a good example of the Type I storehouses that Protzen suggests were associated with the storage of root crops (1993: 111–113). Still, the identifiable groups of storehouses seem insufficient to store the agricultural goods and other items produced on Huayna Capac's estate. Some Inca informants testified that under the Inca, the goods produced on his lands were carried to Cuzco (1551 document, Villanueva 1971: 44). Huayna Collca, on the south side of the valley overlooking Yucay, has several large complexes of Type II storehouses. Although I have yet to determine the ownership of these facilities, lands at Huayna Collca may have been connected to the estate, as in 1586 descendants of the Cañari *cacique* who claimed much of Huayna Capac's estate in the mid– to late sixteenth century were attempting to sell land they had there (Heffernan 1995: 83–84).

Whatever storage facilities had been connected with the estate—at Huayna Collca or on the estate itself—may well not have made it intact through the turmoil of the Colonial Period. The land grab that took place on the estate, together with the loss of so much of its pre-Conquest *mitima* population, and its replacement by others, including Spaniards, probably meant that anything stored was looted and storage buildings likely burned. Documentary evidence suggests that as Manco Inca retreated downvalley from Calca toward Ollantaytambo he both built structures and burned them. It is conceivable that he built the storehouses at Inca Racay or that he modified existing structures to serve as lookout points. In addition to the vantage it gave of the principal road from Cuzco to the valley, the San Juan canyon is an access route to Lares, a jungle area that was important to Manco Inca's early resistance to the Spaniards.

For the time being, the complex at Inca Racay remains somewhat puzzling in design, function, and date of construction, and the issue of storage for the estate's products remains under study.

Other Architectural Complexes
Rincón

There is an isolated set of constructions of uncertain date and function found on the estate. A site called Rincón (corner or nook) is found just above the lake of Huachac, about midway on the path that runs between Yucay and Quispiguanca. Built on a piece of high ground, the site is now covered with eucalyptus and is in bad shape. I observed partial foundations of one structure which measured 3.70 meters in width and perhaps 29.70 meters in length. The proportions of the building, its orientation relative to the slope, and its construction of fieldstone and mud foundations with adobe superstructure are reminiscent of Inca rectangular storehouses, including the structures at Inca Racay. Still, the walls are thin, and my fieldnotes record my impression that the foundations did not look like Inca walls. There are traces of three terraces at Rincón, measuring perhaps 3.6 meters wide and perhaps 1.2–1.7 meters tall. The edge of the lake below Rincón has a number of worked blocks that look like they could have come from Inca constructions. Whether they are from buildings that might have been at Rincón or whether they are related to waterworks cannot be determined.

Inca Racay (Pomaguanca)

There are additional ruins that are probably related to the estate in and around the Pomaguanca canyon. This is one of the major valleys that runs north from the Urubamba within the estate's limits (Chicón is the other major valley, and the San Juan canyon, although it is narrow, is the third). Pomaguanca is a wide valley with a foot road leading northeast to the jungle at Lares (there is also a pass to Lares from Calca). Huayna Capac had coca-growing lands in the jungle beyond Lares, and it is likely that this was the main road linking those fields to the estate. The connection between Lares and this part of the estate continued into the Colonial Period. Diego de Trujillo had an *encomienda* that included Indians who worked coca fields in Lares and maize fields in Pomaguanca. The 1551 document notes Diego de Trujillo's holdings in a *quebrada* where he kept his Indians (Villanueva 1971: 39), along with six *topos* of land near the eastern edge of the estate which were farmed by Indians from Lares (1551 document, Villanueva 1971: 46). The name Larespampa (Lares plain) is still used for a soccer field just southeast of the mouth of the Pomaguanca canyon.

Before Conquest, the Pomaguanca canyon had land and buildings that belonged to Huayna Capac, his wife, and the Sun:

> Cerca de Pomaguanca el valle abajo está otra chácara que se llama Pomaguanca que era del sol y sembrábala Raba Osco-collo [sic] madre de Huascar Inca. (1552 document, Villanueva 1971: 53)

> Near to Pomaguanca, downvalley, is another field called Pomaguanca which belonged to the Sun. It was planted by Raba Oscollo-collo [sic for Rahua Ocllo], mother of Huascar Inca.

Compare to the 1551 document:

> Fuele preguntado que diga que un pedazo de tierra que están en el dicho valle a do dicen Panaguanca que era de Huaina Cápac y de Rahua-Ocllo su mujer. (Villanueva 1971: 47)

> [The elder] was asked what he could say about a piece of land in that valley which is called Panaguanca [sic for Pomaguanca] which belonged to Huayna Capac and Rahua Ocllo, his wife.

> hay un pedazo de tierra que se dice Tomahuanca [sic] que era de Huayna Cápac y dicen que la dio a una muger suya que se llama Raba-chula. (Villanueva 1971: 39)

> there is a piece of land which is called Tomahuanca [sic for Pomaguanca] which belonged to Huayna Capac and one of his wives named Raba-chula [sic for Rahua Ocllo].

Clearly visible on the west slope of the hill at the mouth of the Pomaguanca canyon is a row of Type I storehouses with their plaster preserved, the low openings at ground level, and conspicuous seams marking the multiple chambers. Although I haven't inspected the buildings, from a distance they are indistinguishable from similar constructions illustrated by Protzen (see, e.g., Protzen 1993: 118, fig. 5.8).

More important is a site high in the Pomaguanca Valley which, like the site above Yucay, has the noncommittal modern name of Inca Racay (Inca ruins). Described by Protzen (1993: 284–288), the architecture at the site includes structures of common Inca forms juxtaposed in unusual ways, as well as buildings of unique design (figs. 6.42–6.44). Pieces of the site have their counterparts at other complexes on the estate: Inca Racay's buildings B and C are roughly 8 meters by 10 meters and are separated by a passageway with a double-jambed doorway. This arrangement is reminiscent of the similarly sized structures at the Putucusi compound at Quispiguanca (see Farrington 1995: 62, fig. 8, structures B1 and B2). Inca Racay's buildings D and E are larger and face each other across an open courtyard. Their relative size and placement are a bit like the larger structures excavated by Farrington, also at the Putucusi compound of Quispiguanca (Farrington 1995: 62, fig. 8, structures C and D). Inca Racay's building A has a unique combination of features, including two stories, multiple chambers in a single structure, and an arrangement with a pass-through gateway. Protzen comments on the unusual relation between indoor and outdoor space in the structure (1993: 287). Although different even from the distinctive architecture of Quispiguanca, there are similarities there, too, in its strict symmetry and in its twinning of buildings. Further, Quispiguanca's gatehouses have tall walls (though not a second floor) and are designed as if they were a pass-through from inside into outside space. There are also analogies to the tower structures at Quispiguanca (C on fig. 6.2). As reconstructed here, the towers' two independent architectural spaces are united as a single structure on an upper-story level, similar to Inca Racay's building A. In contrast to the tower structure at Quispiguanca, the latter has a form that is bent into a U shape, a physical expression of Guaman Poma's *quenco huasi* style of palace (f. 330; 1980, vol. 1: 303). The arrangement of the Inca Racay's component buildings on a broad terrace overlooking a stream is also reminiscent of the arrangement of the palace of Quispiguanca with respect to the park and lake and the building of Cocha Sontor with respect to its lake.

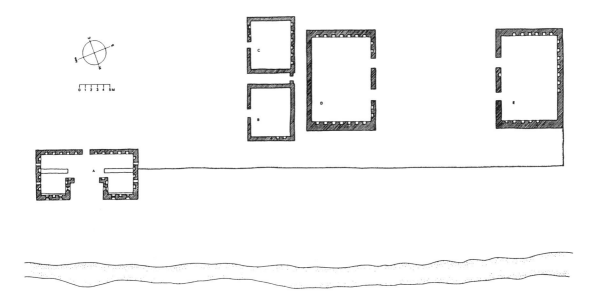

FIGURE 6.42. Plan of Inca Racay (Pomaguanca) from Protzen (1993: 285, fig. C.11), drawn by Robert N. Batson.

FIGURE 6.43. Inca Racay (Pomaguana). Reconstruction of the site as it may have looked, viewed from the river. Drawing by Robert N. Batson.

Huayna Capac is the only Inca to have had significant developments in and around Pomaguanca, and it is quite likely that the site of Inca Racay was one of the compounds related to his estate. Witnesses to Beatriz Coya's 1585 interrogatory noted that Huayna Capac had a palace at Pomaguanca, as well as palaces at Yucay, Quispiguanca, and Chicón (*Colección Betancur*, see fols. 1002 r. and 1008), though there is no indication of its precise location. The fact that Inca Racay has an unusual architectural style which is in many ways reminiscent of some of the distinctive features seen elsewhere on the estate strongly suggests that the complex was part of his development.

The Missing Buildings

The estate surely had additional buildings: Some are mentioned in documents, and others are suggested by reused cut stone. It is tempting to try to identify particular structures on the site with references to possible constructions mentioned in the historical and legal records. For example, Huayna Capac is said to have had a building at Acosca (1551 document; Villanueva 1971: 36). Another building belonging to

Huayna Capac is mentioned at Patashuaylla, as is a "large house" (1551 document; Villanueva Urteaga 1971: 39–40) or a group of *buhíos* constructed by Manco Inca (1552 document; Villanueva Urteaga 1971: 53; the latter construction may have included a large storage building that was still visible on the hillside in the mid-1980s). A *moya* near Pacachaca had buildings (1551 document; Villanueva Urteaga 1971: 39; 1552 document; Villanueva Urteaga 1971: 53), as did the *moya* at Guachac (1552 document; Villanueva Urteaga 1971: 53). There were also structures at Curicancha and Yucay (1551 document; Villanueva Urteaga 1971: 37–38). On the basis of locating information in the documents and the preservation of modern place-names, it is almost certain that these latter were constructed on some of the irregularly shaped terraces to the south of the main agricultural system of Yucay (see fig. 7.2), though there is no trace of above-ground physical remains that pinpoint their location or design. It is probably significant that Huayna Capac placed buildings at the major entrances to his estate along the valley road (Acosca, Challahuasi, and Guayocollo on the east and Patashuaylla on the west), near bridges (Guayocollo and Pacachaca), and on roads to mountain passes (the Inca Racays and

FIGURE 6.44. Inca Racay (Pomaguanca). Perspective view of the structures. Drawing by Robert N. Batson.

Cocha Sontor). Whatever their other functions, these buildings surely marked his territory and may have been associated with securing access to it.

Regrettably, the detailed inventories of the lands of the estate are quite vague on the structures comprising Quispiguanca or any other buildings on the estate. Farrington (1995) has suggested that the documents include neither mention nor description of Quispiguanca because the Incas kept the palace hidden from the Spanish while they cared for Huayna Capac's mummy there. There was an *obraje*, owned by the marqués de Alcañices y Oropesa, there in 1689 in which Indian-style clothing was made (Villanueva 1982: 276). The presence of an *obraje* adjacent to the palace grounds suggests that the palace must have been well known to the Spaniards, who had claimed the site since Pizarro took it at the Conquest. In any event, Quispiguanca, like Huayna Capac's buildings in Yucay, had been burned by Manco Inca in his retreat downvalley that took place around 1536, according to a number of witnesses who testified on behalf of Doña Beatriz Coya between 1585 and 1589 (*Colección Betancur*, vol. 8, fols. 906–1067 v.). Any structures left there by the early 1550s, when the legal record begins, would have been in poor shape. Most likely, the failure to describe the buildings on the estate reflects the Spaniards' greater interest in the agricultural potential of lands that were abandoned and could be brought into cultivation than in ruined buildings. The palace is simply described as *unos tambos* (some large houses or lodges) or *unas casas* (some houses); other structures on the estate are called *casas* (houses) or *buhios* (huts or houses made of adobe or unfitted stone).

In contrast to the lack of attention to the Quispiguanca compound, there are references to place-names in other documents that suggest the presence of architecture in its vicinity. A copy of a 1594 document includes claims for land by Doña Costanza de Castilla, the widow of Alonso Tito Atauchi, including lands in the vicinity of Quispiguanca; the copy was included in a 1613 petition for these lands on behalf of her son Don Alonso Ynga (*Composición de tierras . . . 1594*). The document shows that by 1594 the palace was probably in ruins. There is mention of the *corrales* and *corralones* (corrals or tall walls) of Quispiguanca. These references suggest that the buildings of the site no longer included roofs. It is also clear that by 1594 Quispiguanca was a name applied to fields, rather than purely architecture. Among the properties mentioned in the 1594 *composición* are (1) a field named Quispiguanca which was adjacent to the lands of the *mamaconas*; (2) two *topos* of land in Quispiguanca "adjacent to Yllaguaçi and lands of the mamaconas" (*Composición de tierras . . . 1594*: f. 3 v.); (3) property that abuts the lands of Roncoguaçi[9] and the lands of Quispiguanca;

and (4) "four additional *topos* called Chuquibamba which adjoins the lands of Otorongo pongo which is at the entrance to Quispiguanca" (*Composición de tierras* . . . 1594: f. 4 r.).

These field names suggest the presence of architectural features in or around Quispiguanca. It seems likely that the Otorongo pongo that is mentioned is a field name taken from a portal that formed an entrance to the palace compound. Chuquibamba is the name of lands west of the palace compound; thus, Otorongo pongo may have been the name of an entrance on the now-destroyed west side of the site. Gonçalez Holguin (1952) defines *otoronco* as *tigre* (tiger), by which he probably means jaguar, and *ponco* as "gate or door."

The document also mentions *yllaguaçi*, which includes the word *huasi* for "house" added to *illa*, a term which referred to lightning in early Quechua and refers to shiny things in modern Cuzco Quechua (Hornberger and Hornberger n.d.: 69) or to "stone which is considered sacred because it was struck by lightning" (Lira n.d.: 89). The name Illa Huasi is no longer in use but is suggestive of some architecture on lands so named; whether it refers to an actual structure and whether that structure was inside the palace compound or outside its boundaries cannot be discerned. The 1551 and 1552 documents locate fields of the *mamaconas* in the terraces just north and slightly above the architecture at Quispiguanca, and the proximity of Illa Huasi to the fields of the *mamaconas* might place the structure somewhere on the edge of the site.

The fields called Roncoguaçi or Runtuhuasi are less precisely located, though it is clear from the 1594 case that they are near Quispiguanca. Again, the inclusion of *huasi* (house) as part of the name is suggestive of architecture, though the first part of the name is uncertain. *Ronco* is defined by Gonçalez Holguin as "packets of coca or ají"; thus *ronco huasi* could mean, perhaps, "house for packets of coca or ají." *Runkhu* in modern Quechua means "cliff" (Hornberger and Hornberger n.d.: 221). Gonçalez Holguin defines *runtu* as "pebble" or "grain"; *runtu* in modern Cuzco Quechua means "egg."

A 1689 listing of the *doctrinas* of Cuzco includes reference to the haciendas of Yucay (Villanueva 1982: 273). One, Quencoguazi (*q'enko wasi*, zigzag house), is especially intriguing, as it includes the word for house, and Quencohuasi is one of Guaman Poma's types of palaces (f. 330; 1980, vol. 1: 303). Regrettably, the listing of the haciendas does not appear to be organized by topographic feature or geographic location, and it is not possible to locate it more precisely than to suggest that it is within the limits of the estate, somewhere around Yucay.

Of these names, only Quispiguanca is preserved today, where it is one name used for the field that forms the northwestern quadrant of the site—unfortunately, the only part of the site without any standing architecture. The name Cuichipunco (rainbow) is applied to the south gatehouse (A) that stands in an eponymous field. The south tower of the palace's east façade has no special name. I was told that the owner of the field in which the tower stands had dug around in the corners of that building looking for treasure because in his dreams he would see a big cat with glowing eyes walking there, so he believed there was treasure to be found in the tower. It is interesting that the owner's treasure marker was a big cat who walks around in a space that may have matched a now-vanished "Jaguar Gate."

The other buildings that must have been on the site originally but that can no longer be identified are the communities of workers who farmed the fields and maintained the estate. In support of Betanzos' claim that there were communities of "twenty, thirty, fifty" workers (parte I, cap. XLIII; 1987: 187), historical documents remind us that there were towns for the native groups of the region (Pacas, Chaocas, Chichos, and Cachis), there were, in the Colonial Period at least, towns in Coto and Yucay, and there were houses belonging to *yana-conas* adjacent to fields where they worked. For example, Chalahuasi, which had belonged to Rahua Ocllo, had ten houses (1551 document; Villanueva 1971: 36), and she had another community of *yanaconas* near the mouth of the Pomaguanca canyon (1551 document; Villa-nueva 1971: 39). Doña Angelina had a community with eight houses for ten male heads of household and their families near Cache (1558 *pleito*; Rostworowski 1962: 145).

Census inventories from the mid–sixteenth through mid–seventeenth centuries suggest that at least some of these communities may have been organized into idealized Inca units. In addition to the communities of ten households noted for Rahua Ocllo and Doña Angelina, the 1558 *visita* of Yucay gave the following numbers of adult males (presumably heads of household) for communities within the bounds of the estate: Guaro, 56; Chauca, 60; Cache I, 60; Cache II, 60; Paca, 56; Yucay, 49; Yanacona, 50; Acosca, 51; Chacho, 55; Machi, 50; Pomaguanca, 50; Chicon, 52 (Villanueva 1971: 59–82). These numbers strongly suggest that the communities were planned to include fifty households, and that they maintained that organization a generation after the Conquest.

Some of these communities are very precisely located in the 1551 and 1552 documents. For example, the ancient town of Chicho is almost surely located just east of the entrance to Quispiguanca on lands still called Chichobamba (1551 document; Villanueva 1971: 38). The town of Paca was probably located along the street now called Paca-calle in Urubamba near the river in what is now the town of Urubamba

(1551 document; Villanueva 1971: 38). The town of Coto was located near the mouth of the Pomaguanca canyon (1551 document; Villanueva 1971: 39). Cuzcacache, Taracache, and Chaoca were farther west in the valley, probably along the river (1551 document; Villanueva 1971: 39). Still, though their location can be approximated, there are no ruins that can be identified as the remains of farmers' homes.

Although the houses in which they lived cannot be located with certainty, the fields where Huayna Capac's *mitimaes* worked are well preserved. In the next chapter I will address the form and design of the terracing systems of the estate.

7

THE AGRICULTURAL WORKS
ON THE ESTATE

Huayna Capac's holdings in the Yucay Valley were important to his ability to maintain himself and his descent group. In addition, as Inca, he had ritual and entertaining obligations that required lavish expenditures of commodities. Integral to the design of the estate were systems of terraces which were devoted to the production of maize. There are terraces in several parts of the estate, but most are tucked against the hills on the north side of the valley (fig. 7.1). The most elaborate system is found in the lands north of Yucay, with less extensive systems found about midway between Quispiguanca and Yucay (above the community called Panteón Qepa), on the east edge of Urubamba, and above the palace of Quispiguanca. On the west side of Urubamba are fields that may not have been completely developed for agriculture.

I shall focus my comments on the terraces' design and their style of construction, as I did not measure carrying capacity, nor did I study in detail the management of water on those terraces. Some of these aspects of the terraces or their irrigation have been covered in a study by Valencia (1982) and have been mentioned in studies by Donkin (1979), Fioravanti-Molinié (1974, 1975), Molinié-Fioravanti (1982), and Farrington (1983, 1984).

Terraces at Yucay

Legal documents make a clear distinction between the Yucay that was built by Huayna Capac and the part that was known in the Colonial Period as the Tambo de Yucay; this latter name was apparently applied to a town roughly coterminous with the modern town. Referring to ancient terraces that are the most obvious Inca feature in Yucay, the 1551 document says:

> más adelante hay unos andenes de mucha tierra y muy buena que era del Inca y del sol por la mitad de los cuales baja un arroyo de agua y por la ladera de la sierra del mismo arroyo va otro. Entre los dichos andenes y el tambo, hay unos bohíos de Huayna Capac que fueron los antiguos donde se solían llamar Yucay y ahora también se llama así. Más hacia el tambo hay otro bohío que se llama Curicancha y ciertas tierras también del sol que se llama Curicancha y ciertas tierras también del sol que se llama Pilcobamba y también este Pilcobamba de la otra parte de la casa del sol hay

otro pedazo de tierra que era de Huayna Cápac que se llama también Pilcobamba. Del dicho arroyo que va por la ladera en la misma ladera hay ciertas
tierras que eran y son de los naturales del valle todos los cuales dichos andenes de Incas y del sol las tiene ahora el dicho Don Francisco cacique y
dicen que cada un anden de ellos tenía su nombre que no se acuerda de ellos y que de ciertas provincias venían cada uno sembrar su anden y con-
forme a la provincia que lo sembraba se llamaba el andén. (Villanueva
1971: 37–38)

farther on there are terraces with a great deal of good land which belonged
to the Inca and the Sun. In the middle of these terraces runs a canyon with
water, and through the slopes of the hill of that same canyon runs another.
Between these terraces and the *tambo* there are some *buhíos*[1] belonging to
Huayna Capac which were the ancient buildings that were the only place
named Yucay; they are still called Yucay. Farther toward the *tambo* is
another *buhío* called Curicancha and some lands of the Sun called Curicancha and certain fields that also belonged to the Sun called Pilcobamba. In
this Pilcobamba, on the other side of the House of the Sun, is another
piece of land that belonged to Huayna Capac that was also called Pilcobamba. From the canyon that runs through the side of the hill, on that very
slope there are certain lands which did and still do belong to the natives of
the valley. All of the terraces of the Incas and of the Sun now belong to the
cacique, Don Francisco [Chilche]. They say that each of the terraces had its
own name, though they don't remember them, and that workers came
from different provinces to farm the terraces, and according to which
province's workers farmed a terrace, that is what the terrace was called.

The 1552 document says:

Los andenes todos que están fronteros del Tambo de Yucay eran de Huaina
Cápac y para ellos sembraban sin tener en ellos indios cosa mucha, dicen
que cogían en ellos mil ciento y mil docientos fanegas de maíz y que ahora
después que los Incas dejaron de señorear se han metido indios principales del dicho valle en parte de ellos, y preguntado a los indios que por
qué han dejado las tierras que ellos solían sembrar dicen que porque eran
mejores las del Inca y que las suyas han dejado perder y que en estos andenes hay algunos que no se siembran por falta de indios, dice que cogen
de estos andenes don Francisco seiscientos setenta fanegas de maíz la cual
dice que es para la tasa. (Villanueva 1971: 51)

All the terraces that border on the Tambo of Yucay belonged to Huayna Capac, and the Indians farmed them for him without having much of anything else on them. They say that they harvested 1,100 and 1,200 *fanegas* of
maize, and that now that the Incas no longer rule, the Indian dignitaries of
this valley have taken over part of the terraces. Asking the Indians why they
have left the lands that were theirs to farm, they said that the Inca's fields
were better and that they had let their own go. Some of the terraces aren't
farmed because there aren't enough Indians. They say that Don Francisco

[Chilche] harvests 670 *fanegas* of maize from these terraces, which, they say, goes to pay the *tasa*.

These passages clearly refer to the main terrace system of Yucay, which, in fact, is good land, terraced and cut by canals of water that comes down from the canyon of San Juan. Several individual terraces still conserve names which could refer to ethnic groups placed on the estate as *mitimaes* (fig. 7.2).

The Inca terracing system at Yucay is built on the fan bounded by the entrance to the narrow San Juan Canyon on the north, or uphill, side and by the town of Yucay on its south, or downhill, side (fig. 7.3). The terraces are large, mostly rectilinear fields, contained by terrace walls up to 4 meters in height. The shape and size of the terraced fields vary. Lucmayoc, for example, the largest terraced field, is approx-

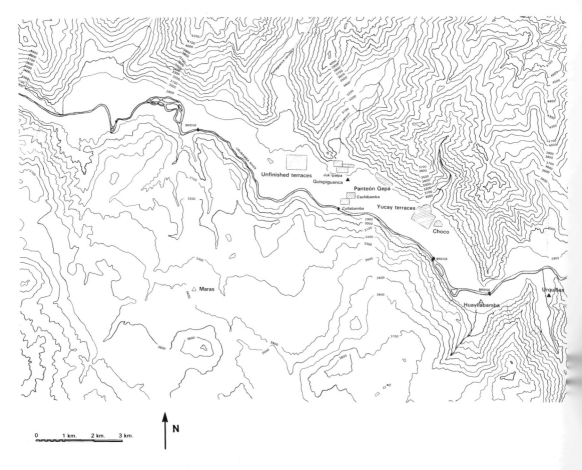

FIGURE 7.1. Map showing the location of major terrace systems on Huayna Capac's estate. Names and locations are based on fieldwork. Agricultural fields are not drawn to scale.

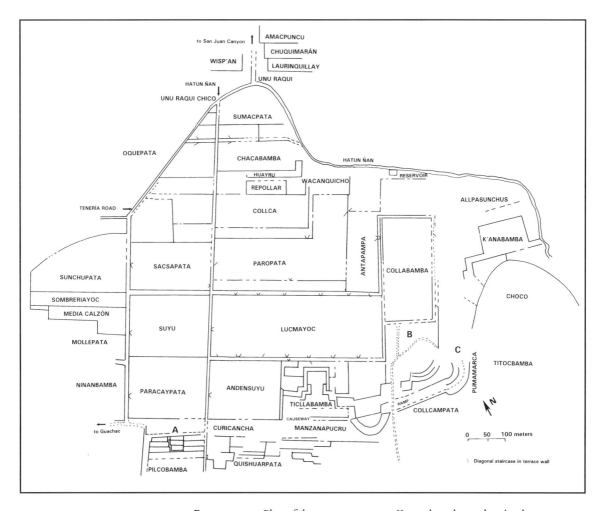

FIGURE 7.2. Plan of the terrace system at Yucay, based on a drawing by Valencia (1982), with additions from Molinié (1996) and incorporating observations from my fieldwork at the site. A: complex of terraces with peg-stone stairs; B: central zone of the Salesian agricultural school; C: the faux Late Inca structure.

imately 443.3 meters on its east-west axis and around 160.5 meters on its north-south axis. Most of the other terraces on the broad part of the alluvial fan have similar north-south widths, though most have somewhat smaller east-west dimensions. The fields are graded to slope slightly from north to south to facilitate the movement of water across the surface. Lateral canals running at the base of the terrace walls are similarly slightly graded to move water across each terrace.

The terrace system is built with two north-south-running roads that divide the system into subsystems and that facilitate movement of people, animals, goods, and water up and down the terraces. The two extant roads are today called Hatun Ñan (Quechua: big or great road)

FIGURE 7.3. Photograph of the terrace system of Yucay, looking north toward the San Juan canyon. The system's main roads are clearly visible running north-south through the system (Tenería is the broad road on the left, Hatun Ñan is the road to its right).

(fig. 7.4), which runs from just west of Yucay's plaza straight up near the mouth of the San Juan canyon, and Tenería (Spanish: tannery), which runs parallel to Hatun Ñan but west of it (fig. 7.5). The top of Tenería angles sharply to meet Hatun Ñan at a place called Unu Raqui (Quechua: division of the water). This is, in fact, where the main canals that supply the terraces divide (fig. 7.6). Hatun Ñan then continues across the top of the terrace systems (though it is not well preserved in these upper reaches) and drops down through the fields that belong to the Salesian agricultural school and down into Yucay. Although it appears to be a main road only on its west end, farmers told me that Hatun Ñan makes a large circuit of the terrace system and that it ultimately links Yucay's Plaza de Armas with its Plaza Manco II. As they conceive of the space, roads define the limits of the terrace system.

The design of the main roads is interesting. As it cuts north-south down through the terracing system (and, in the case of Tenería, as it angles northeast-southwest from Unu Raqui), each road runs perfectly straight. Hatun Ñan and parts of Tenería are double roads (fig. 7.7). Each is composed of two separate lanes, paved in stone and provided, in the steeper stretches, with stairs. While Tenería is a double road for most of its north-south extent, parts of Hatun Ñan appear to be a single road with a large canal on its west side. However, it is obvious that in those places where it does not seem to be a double road, it is because people have chosen to build their houses on one lane of the old road surface, perhaps to minimize the amount of good farmland used for their residences. Thus it is probable that Hatun Ñan, too, was originally double for its entire length, and the stretches that appear to be single lanes are the result of post-Inca constructions.

Dividing the lanes is a stone-lined canal that is both broad and deep. A German agricultural development project modified these canals in the early 1990s; they are now, in parts, lined with concrete. The

FIGURE 7.4. Hatun Ñan road, Yucay terraces, looking north toward the San Juan canyon.

FIGURE 7.5. Tenería road, Yucay terraces, looking south from a point just below Unu Raqui. The line of vegetation marks the canal centered between two lanes.

measurements presented here are based on observations of the roads in 1986 and 1987 before that reconstruction. In a section of Tenería road I measured one of the lanes as 3.2 meters wide, the other as 2.3 meters. The canal was 2.8 meters wide and 1.7 meters deep; in a portion of Hatun Ñan, the east lane was 3.1 meters wide, the west 2.4 meters wide, and the canal was 1.5 meters wide. Movement across the canal is possible only where planks have been placed across it: Even when it is not full of water, the canal beds are deep, and it is difficult to scramble down one side and up the other. There are places where each of the roads in the pair has a slightly different grade. Thus the two lanes that make up each of the main roads through the side are effectively separate, with each giving access to a different terrace.

The system of terracing is large; hence, the roads are more than a kilometer long. Because the roads run north-south and are immediately adjacent to terraces that step down from north to south and from east to west, a person walking through the terrace system experiences a rather remarkable disorientation. Climbing up from Yucay to Unu Raqui on either Hatun Ñan or Tenería, the road rises steeply. The terraces to the east (on the walker's right) will, at places, tower more than 4 meters above the surface of the road and several meters above the head of the walker. As the road rises relative to the nearly flat surface of the terraced space, the walker climbs to a point where her feet are at

FIGURE 7.6. Unu Raqui, at the mouth of the San Juan canyon, the point at which water is divided for the main canal systems of Yucay.

FIGURE 7.7. The lower stretch of Tenería, looking northwest. Its two lanes and central canal are easily visible.

the same level as the field. At the same time, looking west, the walker begins near the level of the field, then rises to a point several meters above the surface of the field (figs. 7.8, 7.9). The walker alternates between being dwarfed by the terrace walls and having sudden vistas open out across the fields. Always, one sees more terraces and, off in the western distance, the prominent black hill of Tantanmarca just beyond Huayna Capac's palace (fig. 7.10). The walker, too, is acutely aware that the terraces on the right and left side of the road, though they are part of a huge system that dominates the view, are separate.

It is, in fact, difficult to move between terraces across the road from one another both because the road can only be crossed by a bridge and because the terraced fields are not at the same level. Movement within a terrace, however, is facilitated by several strategies.

FIGURE 7.8. West lane of Hatun Ñan road. To the left, it rises above one terraced field to the level of the next. To the right, the terrace towers above the road.

FIGURE 7.9. Hatun Ñan. Viewed from the west, the road is clearly a ramp.

FIGURE 7.10. Tantanmarca hill and the west portion of the estate, viewed from the fields adjacent to Hatun Ñan road, Yucay.

At the foot of most large terraces is an east-west-running canal. In most cases, there is a path on a narrow and low terrace adjacent to it. Thus the system is designed to make it possible for pedestrians to move east-west just in front of the large terrace walls without stepping in the canal or on the planted fields. Modern farmers also walk around the perimeter of the fields, where they have worn footpaths in the soil; in these places, however, there is no formal construction to facilitate their movement in the work space.

Throughout the system there are constructions designed to move people—and in some cases water—between adjacent terrace levels. On the west-facing wall of each of the tall terraces in Yucay that is bounded on that side by a road, it is possible to see remains of a dual stair system. Inset into the terrace wall are two diagonal sets of stairs (they are arranged like a broad V) that climb from the road to the field above (fig. 7.11).[2] There are thirteen to seventeen stairs set into the terrace to climb approximately 4 meters. The two flights are arranged so that they do not meet in the center; rather, the inset staircases are separated by a column of masonry that is flush with the exterior surface of the terraced wall into which the stairs are set.

Similar arrangements are found on the south-facing wall of some of the largest terraces. In these cases, the column that separates the stairs may itself be bisected by a vertical groove down which water courses from one terraced surface to the next. In some cases the grooves are fully visible. In other cases, the groove is partially covered by stones placed across the groove on every other course of the masonry (figs. 7.12, 7.13). The effect is to have alternating squares of stone and water, which is beautiful when there is a good gush of silver water cascading down the groove. In the largest terraces these diagonal inset staircases may be disposed regularly across the wall. For example, across the face of the terrace that is the north boundary of Lucmayoc field there are seven sets of stairs preserved; they are approximately 64 meters apart in the center portion of the wall (63.8, 63.8, 63.9, 64.2 meters), with staircases spaced closer together toward the ends of the wall (28.7 meters from the west end; 14.2 meters from the east). The style of the stairs varies across the terrace, with some having simple stairs and at least one having a vertical groove with an alternating stones arrangement.

FIGURE 7.11. Photograph of a set of double stairs without irrigation groove from a west-facing terrace wall along Tenería road.

In a few cases (mostly in stairs on terraces at Urubamba) the paired diagonal staircases that run between field levels are placed into the inner corner where two terraces join at a right angle. In all the cases that I observed there was a vertical irrigation groove in the corner, and one set of stairs went up one terrace, while the other went up the wall at right angles to the other.[3] In essence, the V of the double staircase is folded into the corner where the two terraces meet.

This style of access is distinctive, and while it is not unique to the terraces on Huayna Capac's estate, it may well be characteristic of the architectural style that he devised. I have observed examples of this style at some of the agricultural terraces at the site of Urcos near Calca (Calca is 19 kilometers from Urubamba, about 15 kilometers from the terraces at Yucay). At Urcos, as at Yucay, there are other terraces in the system with peg stone stairs. Farrington says he has found this style of stairs at twenty-nine sites (1985: 59).

There is one set of often-discussed but unusual stairs at Yucay. On the east wall of Lucmayoc field there is a set of full double staircases set into the side terrace wall to provide access to the field. These stairs have been noted by others, including Donkin (1979: 111, fig. 3.71) and Gasparini and Margolies. The latter authors focus on stylistic analogies to other staircases, for example, at Ingapirca in Ecuador (Gasparini and Margolies 1980: 298).[4] Still visible in the 1970s and 1980s, by 1997 these stairs were no longer in use, nor were they well preserved. If they were contemporary with Huayna Capac's construction of the terrace, these stairs may have marked an important point of access onto one of the estate's most impressive fields. If, as I have suggested, there was an original Inca road and probably a canal dropping from Hatun Ñan through the terrace system toward lands now on the Salesian agricultural school grounds (the stairs are on the grounds of that school, too), the road would have passed along this terrace face, and the field onto which the stairs climb would have been the first (or the last) in the system.

Water, too, is moved through the terracing. The water gushes down the narrow San Juan canyon from a place known as Molinachayoc (place with a mill) or Jatunhuayco (great canyon). The point at the top of the terraces where the water is divided is called Unu Raqui (water division). While the main canals course down Tenería and Hatun Ñan roads, there are other branchings. Valencia offers names for other branches, including paired ones called Antapacha, which irrigates high lands east of Unu Raqui, and Perayocpata, which waters relatively high lands west of Unu Raqui. A second pair that divides at Unu Raqui Grande has branches called Choco, which heads to Choco and adjacent terraces, and Onoraque Chico (for Unu Raqui Chico); this

FIGURE 7.12. Elevation drawing of a set of double stairs with alternating-masonry irrigation channel, from the south face of Lucmayoc terrace, Yucay. Drawing by Robert N. Batson.

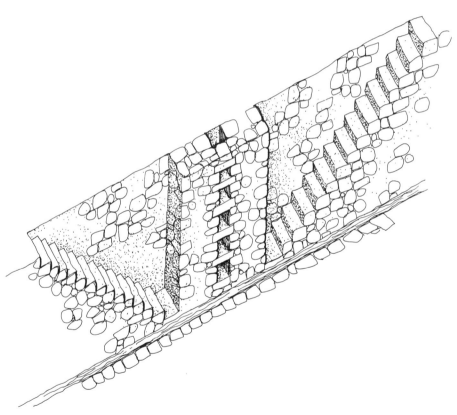

FIGURE 7.13. Isometric view of a set of double stairs with alternating-masonry irrigation channel, from the south face of Lucmayoc terrace, Yucay. Drawing by Robert N. Batson.

latter subdivides somewhat lower down into Tenería and Hatun Ñan (Valencia 1982: 75). There are additional branchings for which I elicited names, including, from higher to lower, Collabamba, Sunchupata, Sombreriayoc, Media Calzón, and Mollepata.

With the exception of the main canals (Unu Raqui, Tenería, and Hatun Ñan), the canal names that Valencia reports and that I elicited refer to the principal fields watered by each branch. Today water is diverted from main canals or branch canals by blocks of sod and rocks which people move into and out of the openings that go onto their fields or into the branch canals that form the main canals. Even though the German redesign of the system includes a mechanical apparatus to control the water at the main division point at Unu Raqui, I observed that people were still using dirt and rocks to divert water from the main canals into branch canals, even at this division point of the two main canals.

Unusual Terraces near Yucay

While most of the terraces in Yucay are clearly integrated into a single system, there are several sets of terraces that are distinctive and must be treated separately. Figure 7.2 shows that in the lowest tiers (that is, the terraces that abut or are within the modern town of Yucay, south of the terraces of Paracaypata, Andensuyu, Lucmayoc, and Collabamba), terraces are generally narrow and are built into small, self-contained systems (fig. 7.14). These terraces are generally no higher than 2.5 meters, are made with relatively small fieldstones, and, at least in the westernmost system, have peg stone stairs to provide access between terrace levels. In style, these terraces are not unlike terracing one might see on other Inca sites in the Urubamba-Vilcanota valley, for example, at Pisac or Machu Picchu. If they were built by Huayna Capac, they surely had a meaning different from the stylistically distinctive agricultural terraces on the site. It is likely that some of these terraces, at least, were used to support architectural groups, as they are in exactly the right position to have done so. For example, the buildings known as Yucay and Curicancha that are mentioned in the historical documents should have been near these terraces.

It is noteworthy that some of these lands were dedicated to the Sun, rather than to Huayna Capac. As terraces associated with architecture, they would be unlikely to share the stylistic attributes of the purely agricultural terraces. And terraces devoted to the Sun would not necessarily be of the same style as lands that supported an Inca. Perhaps, for example, the peg stone stairs and archaic style of terracing of the lands of the Sun on the southwest edge of Yucay's system are analogous to the archaizing architectural style of the palaces in Cuzco that

FIGURE 7.14. Low and narrow terraces with peg stone stairs form a discrete unit in the southwest portion of the terrace system of Yucay.

look like its principal temple of the Sun: It might have lent dignity to the Sun to have old-fashioned terraces. Perhaps, too, the use of peg stone stairs was thought to be more appropriate to Sun terraces than to the royal terraces, which have inset stairs. On peg stone stairs, shadows are cast as the sun moves across the sky. Perhaps this was evidence that the Sun was climbing the stairs or receiving the crops planted there on his behalf. Whether they were the property of the Sun or of another entity, the peg stone terraces could predate Huayna Capac's development of the estate: Perhaps they were built by his predecessors and incorporated into his estate, though not claimed by him for his private use. We can recall Sarmiento's claim that Pachacuti had developments in Yucay (cap. 41; 1960: 236). For all of these reasons, the sets of narrow terraces to the south edge of the main terracing system must be considered separately from the point of view of design, and probably function, of the main agricultural system.

There is a second area within the terracing system which needs to be treated separately. The massive parabola-shaped terrace that encloses a field called Choco is similarly unlike the rest of the terraces on the site. Valencia notes that, alone among Yucay's terraces, Choco has such features as a small inset niche to release water to the field and a canal that passes below the surface to move water from the main canal onto the field (Valencia 1982: 76). I would add that the top of the wall that defines Choco shows grooves in places, probably because it was used as an aqueduct to move water. Further, like the unusual terraces just described, the terrace that defines Choco similarly has peg stone stairs. However, close analysis of the terrace shows that it is probably not of Inca construction. Some of the blocks in the wall show the sharp edges and bright peck-marks of rocks cut with metal tools, rather than with the stone tools favored by Inca masons. Further, the peg stone stairs are not the kind of flattened, minimally worked stone one sees on other terraces; in Choco they are sharply rectangular and are set much closer together than are stones in other flights of Inca peg stone stairs. Taken together, it seems clear that the terrace that defines Choco is a construction that postdates the design of the bulk of the terracing at the estate. Whether it follows the course of an Inca terrace is unknown. There has been much reworking of the Inca canal that supplies Choco and the eastern terraces with water, and the Inca roads that otherwise pass through Yucay's terrace system do not include Choco terrace. I consider its construction to be a relatively recent event, one that reinvents aspects of Inca style without getting it exactly right. Overlooking Choco is another example of this reinvention of style: A wonderful faux Late Inca house copies aspects of the Palace of Quispiguanca and the Palace of Sayri Topa in modern materials but supports a gabled, corrugated tin roof (fig. 7.15). Its main structure has a nearly square footprint and proportionally tall walls. It also has exaggerated wall batter (it is more strikingly inclined than one would expect to see on a genuine Late Inca building) and three double-jambed niches in the upper portion of the wall.

Terraces near Urubamba
Terracing East of Urubamba

There are two places west of the Yucay system where large and elaborate terraces are built in a style similar to the massive terraces of Yucay. About midway between Yucay and Quispiguanca, within the community known as Panteón Qepa, is a set of tall and lovely terraces. In contrast to the large, rectilinear fields of the Yucay system, the fields here are mostly curvilinear. They nestle against the steep hills of the north side of the valley, and the uppermost terraces are fairly narrow. The lower terraces are broad and curved (see fig. 7.16). Like the Yucay terraces, the tallest is a little over 3 meters in height, and some are surmounted by diagonal sets of staircases with irrigation grooves. All of the names for the fields that I elicited were apparently post-Inca, as

FIGURE 7.15. Faux Late Inca building near Choco terrace, Yucay (C on fig. 7.2), photographed in 1987. Construction is modern but of uncertain date.

they referred to European-introduced crops planted in the area. Residents were emphatic that the water used for the canals came from the Chicón canyon and that the lands were within the district of Urubamba, rather than Yucay.

It is difficult to identify these terraces with any of the properties named in the early land claims. There is a property named Collabamba that belonged to Huayna Capac which is in about the right place (west of Yucay and east of Chichobamba), although the 1551 document does not mention that the land was terraced (Villanueva 1971: 38). The 1552 document mentions two large terraces named Cachibamba and Collabamba, presumably near each other, that belonged to Huayna Capac (Villanueva 1971: 51). I was told that Cachibamba is the name of a large terrace with 3-meter-tall walls that is adjacent to the Recoleta of San José on the eastern edge of Urubamba; if Collabamba is nearby, it is much too far south to be identified with the terraces I observed on the north side of the valley. For now, identification of the curvilinear terraces remains uncertain.

Immediately north of and above the palace of Quispiguanca are several large, rectilinear fields with 3.9-meter terrace walls and stairs. Bounded on the west by the canal that descends from Chicón, the terraces form the north edge of the Quispiguanca compound (see fig.

FIGURE 7.16. Curvilinear terraces above Panteón Qepa, between Yucay and Urubamba.

6.2). Both the modern name and the ancient descriptions make these fields rather easy to identify. The 1552 document notes:

> Encima de los tambos de Quispeguanca cerca de ellos está otra chácara que era de Mama Ocllo madre de Huayna Cápac que tiene cuatro topos de sembradura y se llama Oquipalpa. . . . junto a esta está otra que era de mamacunas de dos topos de sembradura. . . . cerca de esta está otra que se llama Paropata que era de una mujer te Huayna Capac que se llama Coya Coxiriman dicen que tendrá diez topos de sembradura. (Villanueva 1971: 52)

> Above the *tambos* of Quispiguanca and near them is another field that belonged to Mama Ocllo, mother of Huayna Capac, which was four *topos* in size and was called Oquipalpa. . . . Next to this was another that belonged to the *mamaconas* that was two *topos* in size. . . . Near this one was a field named Paropata which belonged to a wife of Huayna Capac named Coya Cusi Rimay. They say it was ten *topos* in size.

I elicited Juk'ipalpa as a name for one of the terraced fields, clearly the Oquipalpa of the 1552 document (see fig. 7.1). Clearly the tall terraced lands above the palace were devoted to the women (his mother and his sister-wife, both dead) in Huayna Capac's life.

Fields West of Quispiguanca

There is a second part of the estate that contains traces of a development similar in style to the terrace system at Yucay but by no means as completely built. The most visible stretches are near the mouth of Pomaguanca canyon, running from the road that passes at the edge of the hills down toward the Urubamba River. The visible remains include at least four roads that run straight downhill (approximately north-south). The roads—at least in places—seem to be double roads separated by a deep canal and bordered by large boulders. In a stretch of road that I measured, one lane was 3.6 meters wide; the other was 2.9 meters wide; the canal was 1.5 meters wide. The fields in this area may include some terracing, though fields bounded by large boulders on their downhill edge seem to prevail. The land west of Quispiguanca is full of huge rocks.

The fields near the roads that I observed may be part of the property which was known as Chuquibamba (see Doña Angelina's request of 1558; Rostworowski 1962: 144; *Composición de tierras . . .* 1594; 1551 document; Villanueva 1971: 47) or Pomaguanca (1552 document; Villanueva 1971: 52; 1551 document; Villanueva 1971: 47). When he was asked in 1551 about the ownership and use of the lands of Chuquibamba, Francisco Chilche said that

> no lo sabe qué tantos topos son y un indio viejo que estaba presente dijo que podía haver treinta topos y que en partes las siembras algunos indios del valle porque no son buenas tierras. (Villanueva 1971: 47)

> he didn't know how many *topos* the lands were and an old Indian who was present said they must be about thirty *topos* and that some Indians of the valley farm some of the lands, because they are not good fields.

When he was asked about Pomaguanca, which had belonged to Huayna Capac and Rahua Ocllo (elsewhere the document says the land belonged to the Sun and was planted by Rahua Ocllo [Villanueva 1971: 52]), Chilche answered that

> había cien topos de tierra y todo lleno de piedras y que algunos indios siembran algunos pedacillos de ello que todo no vale nada. (Villanueva 1971: 47)

> there were one hundred *topos* of land and full of stones; he said that some Indians plant little pieces of the holding which is worthless.

Properties with these names are also mentioned in a 1558 land claim, where they are described as having irregular shapes (1558 *pleito* of Doña Angelina Yupanqui, lands of Chiquibamba [*sic*] and Panaguanca [*sic*]; Rostworowski 1962: 144).

These references to poor and stony lands, located in the right part of the valley, seem to describe the fields I observed perfectly. When I visited the fields I had the impression that perhaps the land was still being converted into a terracing system that, when finished, might look like Yucay's. If this is the case, then the roads and water works had been laid out and the edges of the fields roughed out. Still remaining was the work of building the massive terrace walls and replacing the poor and rocky soil with useful earth. Informants told me that the lands west of Urubamba had been subject to repeated landslides, a fact that may account for the sparse visible remains in this area and the surplus of rocks in the fields.

There is reason to believe, in any event, that construction on the estate was proceeding from east to west. The eastern part of the estate's lands (the Yucay system and terraces as far west as the Chicón canyon) was quite well developed. By contrast, the lands at the westernmost edges of the estate (for example, the lands of Coto and Patashuayla) were, according to historical accounts, left as undeveloped forest land. There are no traces of terracing on them (the forests are gone, too). Topa Inca, too, had forest lands on this side of the valley near the western borders of his son's estate (lands of Cozca, 1552 document; Villanueva 1971: 52) and across the river from his own holdings. I suggest that the edge of the estate where it abutted the lands of his father were left undeveloped, in part as a buffer zone, in part as a source of raw materials and as a reserve which might be subject to later development.

Discussion

Because it is the best preserved, I will focus most of my discussion on the terrace system of Yucay, though many of the features seen there apply to the isolated terraces and smaller terrace systems mentioned. Taken together, the stairs in the terraces, the road system, and the system of paths that traverse the fields provide an apparently efficient way for people to move freely about the system. However, on closer examination, they only move people within selected parts of the system.

Following formal roads and paths, it is very easy to walk along a single, large terrace and to have architecturally unimpeded access to all of it. From a main road it is easy to climb up (or descend) onto the surface of a terraced field, but only at selected points. Terraces that are located one above the other can be reached via the stairs that are on the south face of most of the terrace walls. It is not, however, easy to move between terraces that are on different sides of a road, nor is it easy to climb between a road and a field other than in places where there are staircases provided.

In fact, if one reads the design of the system, it is all about control: Water and land are managed, to be sure, but so, too, are pedestrians and workers. Their movement around the system was circumscribed, and it could have been quite easily monitored by foremen or overseers placed at a relatively small number of locations throughout the system.

We know that in Inca times no workers lived on the terraces; rather, they went there from their residences to work. The large size of the terraces could have easily accommodated the groups of the "twenty, thirty, fifty" households that Betanzos claims were the residential groupings on the estate (parte II, cap. XLIII; 1987: 187). The historical documents assure us, too, that the workers on the estate represented a number of different ethnic groups, and that each group worked on a different terrace, named for that group. Thus the social design of the estate would also have facilitated control of the populations. Placing workers of different ethnic groups who spoke different languages on adjacent fields would also emphasize autonomy of the fields, of the work on those fields, and of the workers.

It is regrettable that the early historical documents do not distinguish the names of the individual terraces within the system. Some of the names in current use are clearly post-Inca because they refer to European introductions (Perayocpata, "pear tree terrace"; Repollar, "cabbage field") or include Quechified Spanish names (Sombreriayoc, "place with the sombrero") or fully Spanish names (Media Calzón, "briefs").[5] Other names may have referred to the populations that worked the lands. Collabamba (Colla plain) is a large field; we know that one thousand *mitimaes* from Collasuyu were settled on the estate. Antapacha (Anta land) is one of the terraces; Anta was a town near where Huayna Capac may have had holdings at another estate. Fields named Larispampa are said to have been built of stone carried to the site by the Indians from Lares (Villanueva 1971: 46, fn. 19). It is tempting to suggest that these were fields on which farmers from these places worked. Alternatively, it may be that the terraces were named for the origin place of the dirt used to create them: Lucas Chico testified that the terraces were made with dirt brought to the estate from elsewhere (1574 *pleito*; Villanueva 1971: 130).

As discussed in chapter 5, the population of the estate included *mitimaes* from a number of ethnic groups in Collasuyu and Chinchaysuyu, along with workers from Cuzco (presumably ethnic Incas) brought to maintain the buildings (1574 *pleito*, testimony of Martin Yupanqui; Villanueva 1971: 128). Although we cannot reconstruct where all the workers spent their time (nor, for that matter, do we know the ethnic identities of all of the estate's workers), the observation that each group had its own terrace to work is key to understanding how labor may have been organized and how the physical design of the estate is so intimately related to its social design. Both emerge from Inca ways of organizing and recording information.

The system also exemplifies control of time and view. Workers on the fields would always be looking at other fields and other workers.

They would not only be physically dwarfed by the high walls of the terrace but would probably feel like a very small and unimportant part of the social workings of the estate. Workers would see only the estate from almost any point in the terraces. (There is one point where they could look across to see unterraced land belonging to Topa Inca on the far side of the river, but it would presumably have had workers on it, too.) The most prominent feature of the landscape would have been the hill called Tantanmarca, the steep, black cliff located in the mouth of the Chicón canyon. Significantly, from most of the terraces it would be possible to look across fields and toward the rise of land on which Huayna Capac's palace would have been built. While I do not know if it would have been visible from their workplaces (there are now large stands of eucalyptus planted in the lands surrounding Quispiguanca which obstruct the view lines), it is possible that the workers could have seen the palace. At the least, they probably knew it was there but that the hour's walk that would bring them to its massive portal would have been an impossibly long journey.

The design of the terracing system, including its physical form, the way water is coursed through it, and the way that movement of people and goods is facilitated or discouraged may have an additional referent in the Inca system. We know that the Incas kept many of their records on *quipus*, knotted string cords, in which pendant cords with knots that conveyed, among other things, numerical information were suspended from a main cord. The physical design of the terracing system at Yucay looks a bit like a *quipu*, with a main road (Hatun Ñan, which even has the fluid, curved shape of a cord) from which other roads descend. Terraces could be recalled either by their relation to the road and staircases or by their relation to water and canals. Either way, they could be recalled as subsidiary to the major roads or canals that descend from the top of the system. Numerical information that would certainly have been relevant to the Inca workings of the terracing system could include the number of workers who were supposed to be present for any given day of work, the amount and kind of goods that were produced on each field, the order in which different fields were to be watered, and the duration of the irrigation. All of this information could have been easily stored on *quipus* and could also have been readily checked and verified against the physical design of the system.

Conclusion

The terracing systems of Huayna Capac's estate, no less than the architecture designed to house him and his courtiers, was a marvel of Inca engineering and design. Like the free-standing buildings, the terraces were orderly, imposing structures, serving the pragmatic end of increasing the economic potential of the land, as well as the symbolic end of consolidating and maintaining control over workers.

The principles of design that governed the style of architecture used on Huayna Capac's estate can also be seen in other constructions that date to his reign. In the next chapter I will consider some of the buildings and sites that can be attributed to him and explore the degree to which they, too, display the principles of design seen at Yucay.

8

HUAYNA CAPAC'S BUILT LEGACY

The architecture built on his estate at Yucay is the largest complex of constructions that we can attribute to the reign of Huayna Capac. But there are other sites where we have documentary evidence that he commissioned works that can be compared to the style of buildings seen there. We know that Huayna Capac built a town palace in Cuzco, he reendowed a temple at Cacha, and he commissioned architecture at Tomebamba. We do not always have the standing remains of buildings that we can directly attribute to his reign, but we can use historical sources to fill in some of the gaps.

Casana

The style of architecture seen at Quispiguanca has parallels to Huayna Capac's town palace, which was called Casana (Sarmiento cap. 59; 1960: 260; P. Pizarro cap. 14; 1986: 87; Rowe 1967; Murúa cap. 30; 1962, vol. 1: 77; Cabello Balboa cap. 21; 1951: 361). Casana, like the country estate, was built by Sinchi Roca (Sarmiento cap. 59; 1960: 260; Murúa cap. 30; 1962, vol. 1: 76–77; Cabello Balboa cap. 21; 1951: 361–362). We have no plan of the palace, nor do we have a full description. But there are intriguing references to it by several chroniclers that permit us to imagine aspects of its design.

The Casana was an especially impressive structure. Built on the northwest side of the main Inca plaza,[1] it would have been visible to all who gathered there, and aspects of its design were related to functions otherwise carried out in the plaza. It is probable that, like better-preserved or more fully described structures in Cuzco, the Casana had a plan that included a surrounding wall facing onto the plaza and many structures standing within its confines.

Pedro Sancho, an eyewitness to the conquest of Cuzco, reports that the house of Huayna Capac was the best of Cuzco's palaces (Arocena 1986: 135), an assumption we would otherwise have drawn from the fact that Francisco Pizarro, leader of the conquering party, took the palace for his own lodgings (P. Pizarro cap. 14; 1986: 69). Garcilaso, though he is mistaken in his attribution of ownership of the palace, comments on the beauty of the Casana and credits its impressive design for its unusual name:

La otra casa real que estaua al poniente de Coracora, se llamaua Cassana que quiere dezir cosa para elar. Pusieron este nombre por admiracion, dando a entender que tenia tan grandes y tan hermosos edificios, que auian de elar y pasmar al que los mirasse con atenciõ. (Parte I, lib. VII, cap. X; 1609: 176 r.)

The other palace, to the west of Coracora, was called Casana, which means "thing which freezes." It got this name because it was so admired, and it was understood that it had such big and beautiful buildings that anyone who gazed at it would be frozen in wonder.

The walls of the Casana were made of cut stone (Garcilaso parte I, lib. VII, cap. X; 1609: 176 r.). Among the most noteworthy structures in the compound was a huge hall, a building type that Pedro Pizarro and Garcilaso both call a *galpón*. In defining this type of building, Pedro Pizarro says:

Galpón quiere dezir un aposento muy largo, con una entrada a la culata de este galpón, que dende ella se ve todo lo que ay dentro, porque es tan grande la entrada quanto dize de una pared a otra, y hasta el techo está toda abierta. Estos galpones tenían estos yndios para hazer sus borracheras. Tenían otros cerradas las culatas y hechas muchas puertas en medio, todas a una parte. Estos galpones eran muy grandes, sin auer en ellos atajo ninguno, sino rrasos y claros. (Cap. 21; 1986: 160)

Galpón means a very large building with an entrance in the end wall from which you can see everything inside, because the entrance is so big, going from one wall to the other, and the ceiling is all open. The Indians have these *galpones* for their drunken festivals. They have others with closed ends and with many doors on the side walls, and the whole building is of a single room. These *galpones* were very big, without any divisions; rather, they are open and clear of obstacles.

It is clear from the context of the passage that the kind of *galpón* Pedro Pizarro saw in the Casana was the open-fronted style.[2] Garcilaso, too, saw the great hall of the Casana and reported that it was the largest of the four halls built on the main plaza of Cuzco:

En muchas casas de las del Inca auia Gaspones muy gãrdes de a dozientos pasos de largo y de cinquenta y sesenta de ancho, todo en vna pieça, que seruian de plaça, en los quales hazian sus fiestas y bayles, quando el tiempo con aguas no les permitia estar en la plaça al descubierto. En la Ciudad del Cozco alcançé a ver quatro Galpones destos, que aun estauan en pie en mi niñez. El vno estaua en Amarucancha, casas que fueron de Hernando Piçarro, donde oy es el collegio de la sancta Compañia de IESVS, y el otro estaua en Cassana, donde aora son las tiendas de mi cõdiscipulo Iuan de Cillorico, y el otro estaua en Collcampata en las casas que fueron del Inca Paullu, y de su hijo Don Carlos, que tambien fue me condiscipulo. Este Galpon era el menor de todos quatro, y el mayor era el de Cassana, que era ca-

paz de tres mil personas. Cossa increible que alcançesse madera que alcan-
çasse a cubrir tan grandes pieças. (Parte I, lib. VI, cap. IIII; 1609: 132 r.)

In many houses of the Incas there were very large *galpones*, some two hundred paces in length and fifty or sixty in width, all of one room, which they
used as a plaza for their festivals and dances in the rainy season when the
weather did not permit them to celebrate in the open air on the plaza. In
Cuzco I saw four of these *galpones* that were still standing in my childhood.
One was in Amarucancha, in houses that belonged to Hernando Pizarro,
where the Jesuit school is today, and the other was in Casana, where there
are now stores belonging to my schoolmate, Juan de Cillorico, and the
other was in Collcampata in the houses that belonged to the Inca, Paullu,
and his son Don Carlos, who was also my classmate. This *galpón* was the
smallest of the four, and the biggest was that in Casana, which would hold
three thousand people. It is hard to imagine they could find wood to roof
such big rooms.

The huge hall was merely one of many buildings inside the walls of
the Casana compound, though we lack descriptions of the others. The
complex had other kinds of constructions, too. Cobo mentions that
the palace was itself a shrine on the devotional circuit of Cuzco and
that within it "was a lake named Ticciviracocha which was an important shrine at which great sacrifices were made" (Ch-6:5; Cobo book
I, chap. 13; 1990: 58).

The side of the palace that presumably faced the plaza was also distinctive. Pedro Pizarro describes twin cylindrical towers that stood at
its two corners (cap. 21; 1986: 161–162). These latter had cut-stone
masonry, windows, and a thatched roof that was so thick, horsemen
could shelter themselves from the rain under its overhang. Pizarro
notes that when the roof was torched in the Inca siege of Cuzco, it
took a number of days for its wooden armature to collapse, because
the thatching was so thick that it did not burn quickly. Sancho includes a curious detail about the color of the entryway into the Casana,
which he claimed was made of white marble, red stone, and other
colors (Arocena 1986: 135). It is unlikely that the doorway was of such
colors of marble, a substance alien to Inca construction, but it is possible that the doorway was colored red and white. Sancho adds that
the walls of the Inca houses around the perimeter of the plaza (the Casana was one of these) were painted (Arocena 1986: 135).

The remnants of the wonder that was Casana exist today only in a
few stubs of beautifully fitted masonry inside the walls of offices on
the northwest side of the Plaza de Armas (fig. 8.1). In addition to the
destruction of its great hall in the Inca siege of Cuzco and in the
Pizarro-Almagro wars described by Pedro Pizarro, much of the Casana
was torn up in the Spanish reconstruction of Cuzco. Before he left

Cuzco in 1560, Garcilaso had seen some walls of the Casana torn
down to make a street. He saw the *galpón* remodeled as a convent and
then finally saw the *galpón* torn down to make way for stores and busi-
nesses (parte I, lib. VII, cap. X; 1609: 176 r.).

The now-missing twin towers of the Casana, along with the extant
wall stubs of the compound's surrounding walls, were apparently
made of exceptionally fine fitted stone in a style of masonry that is visually hard to distinguish from the walls built by Huayna Capac's ancestors. It is also a style that is very unlike that seen in most buildings

FIGURE 8.1. Fitted stone masonry of Huayna Capac's town palace,
Casana, on the Plaza de Armas in Cuzco. The battering visible on the
edge of the wall shows that this was an exterior corner of one of the
compound's component buildings.

on Huayna Capac's estate. It is likely that architecture built in the capital was in some ways more conservative than that seen in the country palaces. Perhaps this conservatism was an aesthetic decision: in order to look like the existing buildings of the capital, new structures had to retain something of their form and much of their substance. Huayna Capac's palace was, further, right on the main plaza at Cuzco, and retaining the style of masonry already in use in that important space would lead to a cohesive view of that side of the plaza. Possibly, too, the archaizing style of Cuzco's structures allowed a ruling Inca to draw on the power of his ancestors—including his spiritual father, the Sun—by presenting his home as fitting into their space and looking like their palaces, as well as looking like the city's most sacred building, the Coricancha. An Inca ascending to his position with the blessing of his dead ancestors might well have been looking ahead to the time when he, too, would be an ancestor and his mummy would be carried from its palace into the plaza along with the mummies of his predecessors and successors. In this regard, an Inca's palace was as much a shrine as a home and perhaps had to carry some of the visual weight of that function.

Still, in larger issues of design there are some striking similarities between the Casana and Quispiguanca. The descriptions we have of the Casana—admittedly sketchy, though made by eyewitnesses—are suggestive of the style of architecture seen at Quispiguanca. There, too, we see an entry façade with towers (though at Quispiguanca they are not round, nor are they made of fitted stone) and a portal that was probably colorfully painted. Quispiguanca, too, has among its structures an open-ended great hall that faces onto a plaza; one can easily imagine it being used as a rainy-season dance hall. And, like the Casana, Quispiguanca's design included a lake.

The Temple of Viracocha at Cacha (Raqchi)

The unusual architecture of the Temple of Viracocha at Raqchi continues to capture the imagination of students of the Incas.[3] Its distinctive style, for good reason, has much in common with the architecture at Quispiguanca.

The construction of the Temple of Viracocha is attributed to different individuals by different chroniclers. Garcilaso, in his famously confused account of the temple, credits its construction to Viracocha Inca (parte I, lib. V, cap. XXII; 1609: 120 v.–121 v.), an attribution followed by Cobo. Cieza de León, who provides some detail on an earlier shrine at the site, credits the Inca building to Topa Inca (parte I, cap. XCVIII; 1986: 269). The most plausible account, however, is that given by Betanzos. He concurs with Cieza that there was an earlier shrine at the site but claims that Huayna Capac reendowed the shrine and built the compound, including the great building and the surrounding structures.

It seems clear from the early accounts that at a place they called Cacha there was a shrine important to the Canas people who lived in that region and that later the Incas constructed their own shrine at the site. The original shrine commemorated an encounter with the creator god, Viracocha, a story told in detail by Sarmiento (cap. 7; 1960: 209), Cieza (parte II, cap. V; 1985: 9–10), and Betanzos (parte I, cap. II; 1987: 13–14). Viracocha created the sun and the moon and then created a race of people from stone who were to help to populate the world. As he wandered from Tiahuanaco (where he had created the stone people) toward Cuzco, he stopped at Cacha. There he encountered people who, not recognizing him as their creator, planned to kill him. Viracocha called down a rain of fire from the sky which completely burned up the mountain where the people had been. The people threw themselves on the ground in front of Viracocha, and he stopped the fire with a staff that he carried. He identified himself as the people's creator, and they built a shrine to honor him and to commemorate the rain of fire. The shrine received offerings of a great quantity of gold and silver. It had a stone statue that, according to Betanzos (parte I, cap. II; 1987: 14) was five *varas* tall. By the 1540s and 1550s, when Betanzos and Cieza visited the site, the wandering Viracocha was being equated with a Christian apostle (Cieza parte I, cap. XCVIII; 1986: 270). Proof was offered by the statue, which was believed to depict a white man in priestly garb. Betanzos interviewed elderly Indians about the statue and its shrine and was told that the sculpture depicted a tall man with a white dress that reached his ankles, that he had short hair and a crown on his head, and that he carried something that looked like the breviary carried by priests (parte I, cap. II; 1987: 14).[4] Cieza had heard that the image depicted a priest carrying rosary beads, an assertion he did not accept (parte II, cap. V; 1985: 10).

The Canas shrine that housed the statue may have been a small, open-air temple set apart from the more imposing Inca temple to Viracocha. Cieza and Betanzos both place it across a river from the Inca structure. It is possibly this earlier shrine that Garcilaso conflates with his description of the Inca temple, describing it as unroofed, with decorative entrances on all four sides and a true entrance on the east side (parte I, lib. V, cap. XXII; 1609: 120 v.–121 r.).[5]

Proof of the miraculous encounter with Viracocha was manifested in the burned rocks left by his rain of fire (fig. 8.12). As Sarmiento observed:

Mas el cerro quedó abrasado de manera que las piedras quedaron tan leves por la quemazón que una piedra muy grande, que un carro no la meneara, la levanta fácilmente un hombre. Esto se ve hoy; que es cosa maravillosa de ver aquel lugar y monte, que tendrá un cuarto de legua, abrasado todo. (Cap. 7; 1960: 209–210)

The hill was burned in such a way that the stones were so light after the burning that a very big rock which couldn't even be moved by a cart can easily be picked up by a man. This is still seen today, and it is a marvelous thing to see that place and that mountain, which is all burned for a quarter of a league.

Ephraim George Squier, a nineteenth-century visitor, offers a good description of the setting of the temple which gave the tangible proof of Viracocha's miracle:

Beyond the town, on the right bank of the river, and rising nearly in the centre of the valley, is the broad and rather low, irregular volcanic cone of Haratche. It has thrown out its masses of lava on all sides, partly filling up the hollow between it and the mountain, on one hand, and sending off two high dikes to the river, on the other. Between these dikes is a triangular space, nearly a mile in greatest length, literally walled in by ridges of black lava, heaped in wildest confusion to the height of many feet. (1877: 402)

According to Betanzos, Huayna Capac built the Inca shrine on the site during a visit he made to Collasuyu. It is a visit that Betanzos places after the construction of the palaces at Yucay, the death of Mama Ocllo, and the birth of Atahuallpa and before the births of Paullu and Huascar. This would place its construction early in the six-teenth century, perhaps between 1605 and 1610:

Como llegase a la provincia de Cacha diez y ocho leguas del Cuzco vio allí que en medio de un llana estaba la guaca del Viracocha que ya os contamos y preguntó que por qué estaba en aquel llano aquella guaca los de la pro-vincia le dijeron el milagro que allá hiciera el Viracocha y el fuego que cay-era del cielo y quemara el cerro y como esto oyóse y viese la quemazón quedo que hubiese de esto más memoria y luego mandó que le fuese edifi-cado junto aquel cerro quemado un galpón y casa grande y ansi fue hecho y es tan grande que otro mayor no lo hay en la tierra el cual galpón tiene de anchura ochenta pies y de largura otros cien pasos y el edificio del es en esta manera que porque para tan gran anchura no había madera que alcan-zase fue hecho por medio de esta galpón una pared de parte a parte con muy muchas puertas y ventanas muy bien labradas y desta pared a la pared del galpón hay anchura de cuarenta pies en el medio de la cual anchura hizo edificar unos pilares redondos y altos por los cuales y alto dellos fue puesta una cumbrera y ansi se cubrió este galpón y tuvo corriente porque la madera alcanzaba a aquella cumbrera de aquellos pilares y de los pilares iban puestos otros de maderos que alcanzaban a lo alto de la pared de en

medio y ansi fue hecho y acabado y allí le hacían fiestas y sacrificios al Viracocha ansi mismo hizo hacer en torno deste galpón otras muchas casas en
las cuales fueron puestas muchas mamaconas que él allí le dió y ofreció y
otros muchos yanaconas y todo servicio. (Parte I, cap. XLV; 1987: 191–192)

Approaching the province of Cacha, eighteen leagues from Cuzco, Huayna
Capac saw there on the plain the *huaca* of Viracocha that I have already told
you about, and he asked why that shrine was on the plain. The people of
the province told him about the miracle that Viracocha worked there, and
of the fire that fell from the sky and burned the mountain. And as he listened to this and saw the huge burned area, he decided that the miracle
should be commemorated. He ordered that they erect a hall and large
house adjacent to that burned hill, and so it was done. And it is so big that
there is none larger in this land. The *galpón* is eighty feet wide and one hundred paces long. It is built in such a way that there is no wood long enough
to span its great width, so they built a wall down the middle of the *galpón* so
that the width to span would be forty feet. In the middle of this span they
put some tall, round pillars. On top they placed the ridgepole, and thus
they roofed this hall. They could do it because the rafters were long enough
to reach [from the outside wall to] the top of the columns, and they put
more rafters to run from the top of the columns to the top of the middle
wall. And so this was done. And when it was completed they celebrated the
festivals and made the sacrifices to Viracocha. Around this *galpón* they also
built many other houses in which were placed many *mamaconas* that Huayna Capac gave to Viracocha and many other *yanaconas* and everything else
to serve the temple.

Betanzos' attribution of the construction to Huayna Capac has the
ring of truth. Alone among the chroniclers, he offers a detailed, accurate description of the Inca shrine and clearly indicates that he visited
the place personally and interviewed elderly residents of the area. This
is in contrast to Garcilaso, whose fanciful description of the temple
structure does not seem to have been written by anyone who ever saw
it, and Cieza, who visited the place but didn't describe it (Cieza parte I,
cap. XCVIII; 1986: 269–271; parte II, cap. V; 1985: 8–10).

The establishment of a temple at the site of a pre-Inca shrine of importance was typical of Inca religio-political strategy. Elsewhere in
Collasuyu, for example, the Incas staked an architectural claim on the
Lupaca shrines of Titicaca and Coati and the ancient shrine of Tiahuanaco. It is quite plausible that a *huaca* of importance such as the
Canas people had at Cacha—particularly one with such visible proof
of the god's rain of fire—would similarly be marked by the Inca presence. It is a little surprising that the earlier shrine would not have been
reendowed by an Inca prior to Huayna Capac. The Canas people were
brought into the empire fairly early. They were sufficiently loyal so that
they were taken in large numbers by Topa Inca's governors to estab-

lish order in Antesuyu, Chinchaysuyu, and Condesuyu while he was putting down a rebellion of Colla peoples (Betanzos parte I, cap. XXIV; 1987: 156).[6] It is possible that, as Cieza claims, Topa Inca did establish some Inca presence at Cacha. But it also seems clear that Huayna Capac built the structures that are relevant to this discussion.

Betanzos presents Huayna Capac's decision to build the temple in a way that echoes his description of other constructions. As he tells the story, Huayna Capac builds the temple in order to enhance the memory of the events that took place there, a decree which follows the reporting of the divine encounter. In structure, this episode mirrors the story in which the soon-to-be-crowned Huayna Capac listens to the deeds of his ancestors and then grants additional lands and servants to the care of their mummies (Betanzos parte I, cap. XLI; 1987: 181–183). In the Cacha story, too, the finale involves the provision of mamaconas and yanaconas for the upkeep of the temple.

In considering the design of the Temple of Viracocha at Cacha, we can supplement the early descriptions with observation of the substantial remains of the complex. The structures described so well by Betanzos (the great hall and the houses of the temple's custodians) are part of the complex, as are a series of round structures commonly identified as storehouses (figs. 8.2, 8.3).

The Great Hall

The great hall at Cacha is much as Betanzos described it (fig. 8.4). It has fitted stone foundations topped by adobe brick with a footprint of 92 meters by 25.25 meters (all dimensions are taken from Gasparini and Margolies 1980: 238–245). While its long side walls and one end wall no longer stand, one of its short ends is partially preserved and shows remains of at least one double-jambed doorway with the double jamb opening to the building's exterior (fig. 8.5). This doorway had barhold devices on the interior (fig. 8.6). The single preserved doorway is oriented on one half of one of the short walls; it seems likely that a second doorway was placed in the other half of the short wall so that the structure would be symmetrical. Because its outer walls are so poorly preserved, it is not possible to say with certainty whether it had doorways on any of the other three walls or what their form might have been.

The best-preserved part of the structure is its center wall. Unique among Inca great halls, this one was both tall enough and wide enough to require a center wall to support its roof structure. The center wall stands to a height of nearly 12 meters, and, as Betanzos' description suggests, it was pierced by ten door openings on the ground floor and large windows at a higher level (fig. 8.7). Also faith-

FIGURE 8.2. Overview of a portion of the Temple of Viracocha complex. In the center is the temple structure; immediately behind it is the zone of courtyard houses; and behind this are the circular storehouses. The lake is in the reedy area just below the near end of the temple building.

ful to Betanzos' description, the structure had enormous pillars of stone and adobe at the midline of each half to help support the rafters and beams. The lower part of the center wall was of fitted stone, and the upper walls were of adobe bricks.

Assuming the original height of the center wall to have been around 12 meters and assuming the now-vanished side walls of the structure to have been around 3 meters tall, the rafters that the build-

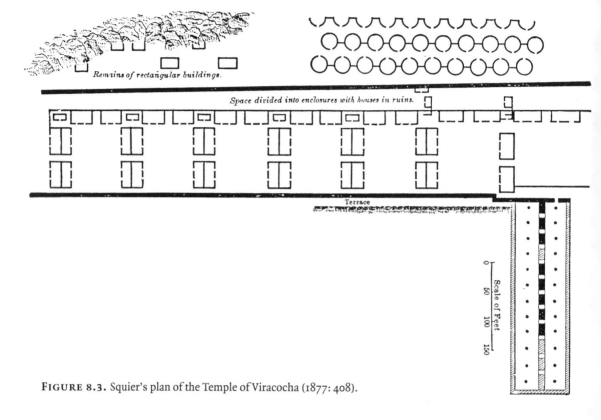

Remains of rectangular buildings.

Space divided into enclosures with houses in ruins.

Terrace

Scale of Feet

FIGURE 8.3. Squier's plan of the Temple of Viracocha (1877: 408).

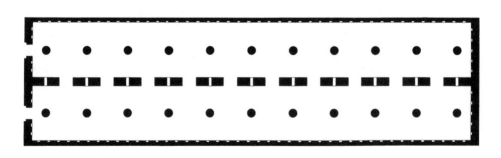

0   5   10   20 M

FIGURE 8.4. Plan of the great hall at the Temple of Viracocha (from Gasparini and Margolies 1980: 240, fig. 227).

ing would have required (if a single rafter spanned the width) would have been about 15 meters long. It is likely that the wooden columns of other Inca structures (e.g., Incallacta in Bolivia, the great halls at Huánuco Pampa) would have been at least this long. Thus neither the rafter length nor the height of the building would have been so great that it would have been physically impossible to span it with wood. The unique design of the structure using a standing central wall and wide stone-and-adobe columns must thus be seen as an intentional choice of the designer, not a design mandated by the size of the structure (fig. 8.8). It is possible that it was socially impossible to acquire wood of sufficient length and diameter to roof the building, that is,

FIGURE 8.5. Detail, exterior view of the double-jambed doorway with the column centered in it. Temple of Viracocha.

FIGURE 8.6. View down the length of the great hall of the Temple of Viracocha, showing column bases and the central wall as it appeared in 1998. Remains of barhold devices are visible adjacent to the doorway on the far end
wall.

the builders did not wish to divert laborers from other endeavors to
carrying logs from the regions where tall trees grew to the job site.
Perhaps the designer wished to avoid engineering problems that he
thought might have arisen in the structure, especially those related to
the buckling of wood columns from the heavy roof structure. Alternatively, it may have been that the innovative design simply appealed to
the designer and the Inca who commissioned the work.

There are some interesting points of comparison between this great
hall and the great hall at Quispiguanca. Both have the general width-

FIGURE 8.7. Remains of the center wall and columns of the Temple of Viracocha at Raqchi as it appeared in 1998.

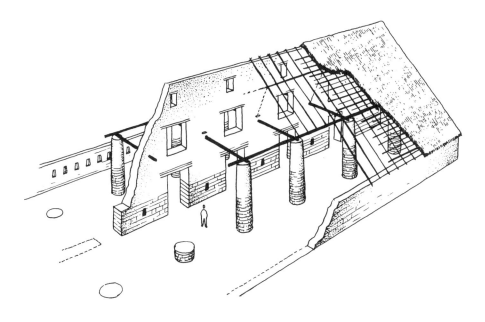

FIGURE 8.8. Reconstruction of the Temple of Viracocha (Gasparini and Margolies 1980: 248, fig. 234).

to-length proportions of Inca great halls (1:3 is standard; Quispiguanca is 1:3.06, based on exterior measurements; Raqchi is 1:3.64).
Both have at least one double-jambed doorway on one short end wall,
though at Quispiguanca the jamb faces the interior, and at Raqchi it
faces the exterior. Both the great hall at Raqchi and the surviving great
hall at Quispiguanca had stone foundations and adobe upper walls.
Both had plaster and, at Raqchi, traces of paint. The lower portion of
the center wall at Raqchi was painted with pendant stepped triangle
designs in a bright red paint which are still visible. The paint was applied directly on the foundation or as a thin layer of mud plaster that
adhered to the stone. If the lower foundations at Quispiguanca were
painted and plastered, it would have probably been done in the same
way. There is no plaster groove at Raqchi. The plaster grooves visible
on some structures at Quispiguanca and related sites make it clear that
any coating on the stone foundations was quite thin relative to the
thick plaster applied on the adobe upper walls.

In terms of design, the Temple of Viracocha has wide columns that
are placed immediately in front of the extant door openings on the
end wall. While possibly facilitating a processional route into the
building (see Gasparini and Margolies 1980: 242–243, following Garcilaso's description), the placement of the columns would seem to be
at odds with gaining a view into or out of the building through these
doorways. At Quispiguanca, there may have been wooden columns to
support the roof structure, but their size and placement are not noted
by the excavator (Farrington 1995: 62). Still, assuming they existed
and that they were fairly large in diameter, there is no axis in the building that would not intrude on a view into it, either through its wide
opening on the south wall (if there was one central line of columns) or
through its double-jambed rear doors (if there were two lines of columns). The presence of columns in both buildings—and their possible placement—seems to be at odds with Pedro Pizarro's description
that galpones were open and unobstructed. Columns also seem a surprising solution to roofing a building that might have been used for
dancing and festivities, as the early chroniclers report.[7]

Courtyard Buildings at Raqchi

A striking aspect of the plan of Raqchi is the highly regimented arrangement of structures south and east of the temple building (fig.
8.9). (Dimensions are taken from Gasparini and Margolies 1980:
234–239.) Disposed around six courtyards are groups of buildings arranged around three sides of each court. Each courtyard measures 27
meters by 31 meters, and, with but one exception, they include six
structures. Four are halves of Inca "double-houses" (that is, rectangu-

lar buildings divided longitudinally with a tall wall that serves as the apex for the gable roof and that separates the building into two non-communicating rooms); each of the rooms is 12 meters by 4.5 meters in area (fig. 8.10). The ground-floor room has niches on the interior walls; when Squier visited, the plaster on some of the niches retained traces of a bright purple paint (1877: 411). The other two buildings in each compound are slightly larger one-room rectangular buildings originally provided with a hip roof; Squier gives dimensions of 14.2 meters by 9.2 meters for these structures (1877: 411). The entire complex was walled on the north and south sides, and Squier noted smaller courtyard house structures within the walled zone, as well as some outside of it.

The courtyard complex is built on a terrace that rises about 90 centimeters above the surrounding building space (Squier 1877: 409). The flat building plane permits a very precise layout of structures. The

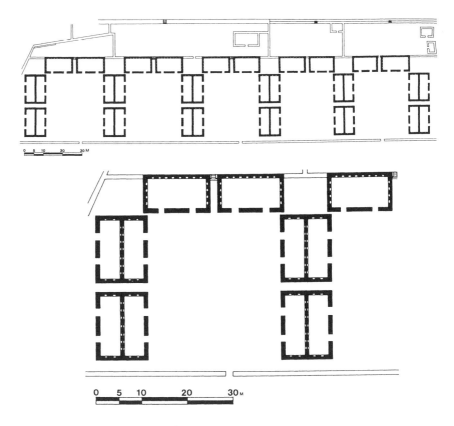

FIGURE 8.9. Plan of the courtyard house complex, Temple of Viracocha (Gasparini and Margolies 1980: 236, fig. 222).

FIGURE 8.10. Detail, one of the double-houses in the courtyard group, Temple of Viracocha.

plan is premised on right angles and precisely measured dispositions of buildings into groups which are, in turn, separated by passages of equal width. Like the temple structure, the courtyard buildings have stone foundations and (again, with one exception) adobe upper walls. The single exception is a building which has a stone wall built where the adobe would be. That this exception to the rule is not a modern reconstruction is shown by the mention of that structure by Squier, who visited in the nineteenth century (1877: 410–411) (fig. 8.11). Also like the temple building, the "double houses" of the compound have a central wall to support the roof and to divide the building into two chambers. In contrast to the temple structure, however, the "double houses" have no communication between the two sides; they are discrete rooms that face onto different courtyards.

The courtyard house arrangements at Raqchi are good candidates for the houses of the *mamaconas* that Betanzos tells us Huayna Capac gave to the temple. Their rooms would provide space for sleeping, sitting, and food preparation, and the courtyards would afford an area for dry-season weaving. The complex is screened from the rest of the site by a surrounding wall. Each compound also has access through a narrow opening to a small terrace or secondary courtyard behind it (see the detail plan by Gasparini and Margolies, fig. 222; 1980: 236).

Such a walled compound is what one might expect to see for women who were to have minimal contact with activities other than those associated with the temple and the upkeep of its deity.

Circular Buildings

In a walled zone south of the courtyard houses is a rigidly regular arrangement of circular buildings. The structures are about 8 meters in diameter and have stone foundations preserved to a height of up to 3 meters. Other than a single, narrow doorway in the stone foundations, the structures preserve no architectural detail. Squier noted that the buildings open onto formal passageways of equal width but are arranged so that doorways of facing buildings are not opposite one another (1877: 411). Squier observed 120 buildings when he visited and ruins of others; assuming a symmetrical arrangement of structures, there may have been upward of 150 such structures in the compound originally. The buildings are conventionally considered to be storehouses, following the identification of similar circular-plan buildings at such Inca administrative centers at Huánuco Pampa and Pumpú in the central highlands.

Terraces and Waterworks

One aspect of the site has received little attention from modern visitors, but, as shouldn't be surprising, the grounds of the Temple of Vi-

FIGURE 8.11. Squier's drawing of a pair of double-houses in the courtyard group, Temple of Viracocha (1877: 410).

racocha incorporated elegant waterworks. Squier wrote a clear description of them:

> At the upper end of this space, which has been widened by terracing up against the lava fields, and piling back the rough fragments on each other, is a copious spring, sending out a considerable stream. It has been carefully walled in with cut stones, and surrounded with terraces, over the edges of which it falls, in musical cataracts into a large artificial pond or reservoir covering several acres in which grow aquatic plants, and in which water-birds find congenial refuge. From this pond the water discharges itself, partly through numerous *azequias* that irrigate the various terraces lining this lava-bound valley, and partly through a walled channel into the Vilcanota.
>
> Overlooking the reservoir or pond, on a broad terrace, or rather series of terraces, on one side of a great semicircular area, rise the lofty ruins of the Temple of Viracocha, one of the most important ever built by the Incas, and which seems to have been unique in character. (1877: 402)

In Squier's commentary it is clear that he felt the artificial lake was an important visual focus of the site. He notes, for example, the orientation of the courtyard groupings relative to the water: "In arrangement every group or series is substantially the same, and consists of six buildings, two on each of the three sides of a court, the fourth side looking towards the artificial lake, etc., being left open" (1877: 410).

Always attentive to the landscape, alone among the visitors who describe the ruins of the temple compound, Squier notes the relationship of the architecture to terraces. He notes that broad terraces are used to widen the space provided for the waterworks, that a series of terraces are used to support the Temple of Viracocha, and that a terrace three feet high supports the courtyard houses. Surprisingly, Squier does not comment on the enormous wall that surrounds the site. Running from the crest of the ridge on the lava flows and town nearly to the Vilcanota River, a thick wall of dry-laid volcanic rock delineates the sacred precinct (fig. 8.12). The wall does not seem to be purely defensive, though there are few openings through it. The chronological and design relationship of the wall to the verifiably Inca constructions at Raqchi remain to be studied.

Discussion

The remains of the Inca temple compound at Raqchi represent a style that is distinctive but that has striking parallels to the structures built at Quispiguanca perhaps a decade earlier.

The design of the courtyards and their relationship to the temple is, in surprising ways, reminiscent of the constructions at Quispiguanca. Like the compound at Raqchi, Quispiguanca's courtyard group in-

FIGURE 8.12. The conspicuous lava flow that surrounds the Temple of Viracocha is surmounted by an enormous wall of dry-laid volcanic stone, seen here in 1998.

cludes structures enclosed by a surrounding wall, oriented around a courtyard (there perhaps 25 meters by 25 meters, rather than 27 meters by 31 meters), and built on a low terrace. As at Raqchi, adjacent courtyard structures at Quispiguanca are separated by precisely aligned passageways. As at Raqchi, entrance into the compound is through a small doorway built between two structures. And while Quispiguanca's plan probably did not include double houses, it should be noted that neither is its great hall large enough to require a central wall; thus any aesthetic parallel between buildings within a site that might have mandated provision of a central wall in Raqchi's courtyard house groups is absent there.

In overall design, the most obvious similarity is that each site has a courtyard complex adjacent to a great hall, and that each of the great halls at least has some access via one short end wall. Still, there seem to be major differences between the design of the great hall at Quispi-guanca and that seen at Raqchi. One of the great mysteries to me at Raqchi centers around the orientation of the temple structure. It is not clear how many doorways it had or where its major entrances would have been. For example, the easiest access to the zone of support houses is via the end of the building that still preserves a doorway. But this is also the direction that provides the least promising access to any kind of plaza or terrace. If the great hall at Raqchi was designed as were the *galpones* of Cuzco (that is, to provide roofed space for dances and celebrations in rainy weather), it likely had doorways on its long sides, which border relatively flat and unobstructed space. If it had a wide doorway on its north end wall, similar to the design of the great hall at Quispiguanca, it would face out on a fairly flat space. But that door opening would be obstructed by the central wall as well as the large columns.

The circular buildings of Raqchi are without parallel at Quispi-guanca. Assuming that they are storehouses, it is not surprising that there is no comparable large-scale storage facility at Quispiguanca. Raqchi was a major religious site adjacent to the principal Inca road to Collasuyu and deep within the heart of the territory of the Canas people. It was, moreover, a site endowed by an individual but not indi-vidually owned. Thus the functions of the state and the state religion could well have been part of the activities that took place at the site. By contrast, Quispiguanca was built and owned by an individual, and its surrounding fields supported him and his family. Produce from that site could have been carried to the nearby capital for storage or for consumption by the royal family. In any event, the storehouses seen in the Urubamba Valley are of different forms than the round store-houses, as noted by Protzen (1993: 111–135).

The most striking parallel between the two sites is the relationship of buildings to the constructed landscape. Both sites are built on ter-raced and flattened places, and both use a rigid right-angle plan (sur-prisingly rare for Incas, who usually accommodated their architecture to hill slopes). The early chroniclers do not talk about the lake Squier noticed, nor do they mention the masonry-lined catchment basin or terraces. But Squier's careful description of the waterworks is imme-diately reminiscent of the juxtaposition of the large lake, small reser-voir, and canal against the massive terraces supporting the hall and courtyards of the terraced space at Quispiguanca. There, too, a large and naturalistic lake may have been close to the terraced space that supports the architecture, and a smaller reservoir is located down-slope from where I assume the lake to have been. Squier's comment about the acoustics of the waterworks at Raqchi, as well as his mention of the birds and aquatic plants in the lake, similarly bring to mind the parks and the playfulness of water at Quispiguanca and, especially, the sound of the water coursing down the terrace faces on the estate.

Tomebamba

Huayna Capac's special affinity for the town of his birth, taken together with the amount of time he spent in his later years consolidating conquest of the northern frontier, led him to substantial building projects in Tomebamba. Unfortunately, the town was destroyed in the Inca civil wars (see Zárate's account of its burning by Atahualpa; lib. I, cap. XII; 1947: 473), and little was present for eyewitnesses to observe. Cieza de León, who passed through in the late 1540s, opined,

> Estos aposentos famosos de Thomebamba . . . eran de los soberuios y ricos que ouo en todo el Peru: y adonde auía los mayores y más primos edificios. Y cierto ninguna cosa dizen estos aposentos los Indios, que no vemos que fuesse más, por las reliquias que dellos han quedado. (Parte I, cap. XLIIII; 1986: 144)

> These famous buildings of Tomebamba . . . were among the finest and richest to be found in all of Peru, and [Tomebamba] had the biggest and best buildings. Whatever the Indians said about these residences fell short of reality, to judge by their remains.

The modern city of Cuenca, Ecuador, is built on the ruins of the Inca city, meaning that relatively little of the site is accessible to archaeologists (fig. 8.13). Still, it is possible to consider references to the site in several of the later chronicles and to compare what is known about the site's plan to other constructions.

We do not know how much of Tomebamba was Huayna Capac's handiwork. There had been an Inca presence there since Topa Inca's initial conquests in the north. Huayna Capac, in fact, was born there and may have spent his early years around Tomebamba.[8]

Miguel Cabello Balboa and Martín de Murúa, drawing on their common source, offer parallel accounts describing Huayna Capac's major construction efforts at Tomebamba in some detail. His work there is placed relatively late in his reign, when he is returning to Tomebamba on his way to the final conquest of the Cayambis and Caranguis with a huge army of conscripts in tow. The accounts suggest that Huayna Capac modeled the reconstruction of Tomebamba on the plan of Cuzco, using the same form and techniques on its buildings as were seen in the Inca capital and recreating some of its shrines and structures there. The buildings that Murúa and Cabello Balboa attribute to Huayna Capac are a temple of the Creator, temple of the Sun,

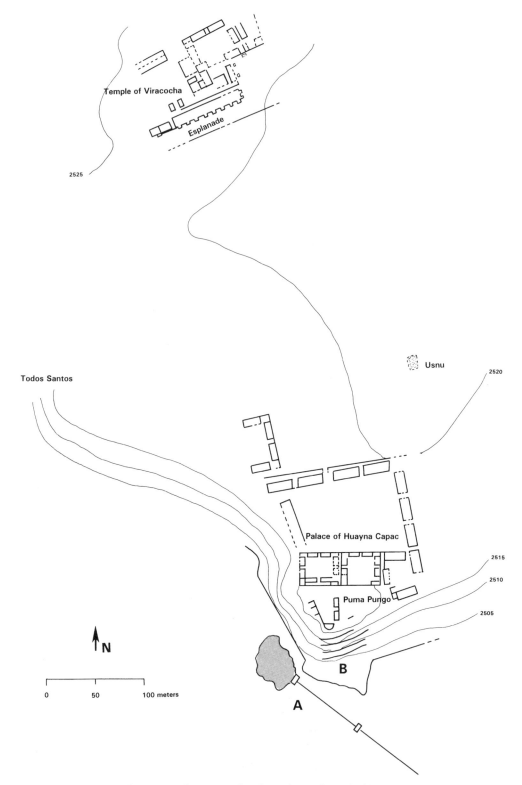

FIGURE 8.13. Plan of a portion of Inca Tomebamba, redrawn from Hyslop (1990: 141, fig. 5.8), with building attributions following Uhle (1923). A: waterworks, including an artificial lake, bath, and canal; B: zone of fancy terraces.

and temple of the Thunder. They also suggest that he built a great plaza with an *usnu* called Chuqui Pillaca (Murúa cap. 31; 1962, vol. 1: 81–82; Cabello Balboa cap. 21; 1951: 364–365).

Among the buildings that is a singled out is one called Mullu Cancha, which commemorated Huayna Capac's birth and honored his mother. As Murúa reports:

> y hizo por grandeça vna cancha que llamaron Mullo Cancha, a do hizo poner los pares en que hauía andado en el vientre de su madre con grandíssima reuerencia, y para ello mandó entallar vn bulto de muger y pússoselas en el vientre y grandíssima cantidad de oro y piedras preciosas con ellas. Las paredes de esta cassa eran de taraçea de Mulli y las listas de oro por toda la pared; hizo la figura de su madre Mama Ocllo toda de oro y púsola allí, llamábanla Tome Bamba Pacha Mama; los que seruían esta cassa y la guardauan eran los cañares, que decían que a ellos les tocaba porque Mama Ocllo era madre y tía y que Huayna Capac hauía nacido en este lugar quando su padre Topa Ynga Yupanqui hauía ydo a las guerras de Quito. Y en memoria desto y para çelebrar y authoriçar el lugar de su nacimiento hizo esta obra espantosa allí, pretendiendo hazerla cabeza de su señorío. Esta cassa tenía el suelo a manera de empedrado, que los yndios llaman rayçes de oro, de lo qual está todo cubierto el suelo. Las paredes del patio estaban aforradas por de fuerra en tallas de cristal, que fueron lleuadas para este efecto esde la prouincia de Huancabelica. (Cap. 31; 1962, vol. 1: 81–82)

and in order to enhance his greatness, he built a *cancha* called Mullo Cancha, in which he placed the placenta of his birth with great reverence. He ordered them to make a statue of a woman and to put the birth matter in her womb along with a great quantity of gold and precious stones. The walls of this house were inset with *mulli* and strips of gold for the whole length of the wall. He had the image of his mother, Mama Ocllo, made entirely of gold and put it here; it was called Tome Bamba Pacha Mama. The house was served and guarded by Cañaris. It is said that this was their duty because Mama Ocllo was the mother and aunt of Huayna Capac, and that he had been born in this place when his father, Topa Inca Yupanqui, had gone off to the wars in Quito. And in memory of this and in order to celebrate and legitimate the place of his birth, he planned to make it the head of his empire. This house had a floor entirely inset with stones which the Indians call "roots of gold." The outside walls of the patio were covered with sheets of crystal which had been brought for this purpose from Huancavelica.

The passage in Cabello Balboa is almost identical (cap. 21; 1951: 364–365). The *mulli* mentioned by Murúa is probably *mullu*, which Gonçález Holguin notes is pink shell or beads made from it, most probably spondylus (1952: 219).

While Murúa and Cabello Balboa attribute this work to Huayna Capac, Pachacuti Yamqui says the structure was built by Topa Inca:

Y en este tiempo nació Guaynacapaynga en Tomebamba, pueblo de los Cañares, y su padre Ttopayngayupanagui y su madre Cocamama anaguarque
y edifica la cassa y bohiyo muy grande, llamado Tomebamba pachamama:
quiere dezir, lugar naçido del benturosso infante; y en ello los perdona a
todos los hechiceros, por caussa del nacimiento del infante, por ruegos de
su madre, porque ya estauan sentenciados en secreto para empalarlos con
canganas de chunta de abajo, como un conejo. (1968: 301)

At this time Huayna Capac was born in Tomebamba, town of the Cañares.
His father was Topa Inca Yupanqui and his mother was Coca Mama Anaguarque. And he built the house and very big *buhío* called Tomebamba Pachamama, which means birthplace of the fortunate prince. In it they par-
doned all the wizards, in honor of the birth of the prince, at his mother's
request, for they had all been sentenced secretly to be impaled from below
on skewers of *chonta* palm, like rabbits.

Although confusing matters on the issue of who built the structure,
Pachacuti Yamqui does suggest its scale and, possibly, its building
material: as a "bohiyo muy grande," the building was probably a large
structure made of adobe.

It is hard to know what to make of the descriptions of Mullu Cancha or Tomebamba Pachamama, a building that would never have
been seen intact by any of the chroniclers who repeat its description.
The creation of a life-size gold statue of a woman is not implausible.
Eyewitnesses to the conquest of Cuzco report the discovery of statues
of life-size animals made of gold, along with images of divinities (P.
Pizarro cap. 15; 1986: 100–101; *Relación francesa* 1967: 75); a statue of
the creator god Viracocha in Cuzco was said to be solid gold and the
size of a ten-year-old boy (Cobo lib. 13, chap. 4; 1964: 156). The booty
sent back to Spain after Atahualpa's ransom included a woman made
of gold and silver and a gold man the height of a ten-year-old boy—
perhaps the image of Viracocha noted by Cobo (*Relación francesa* 1967:
76-77). The provision of a place to store the placenta of a divine ruler's
birth is likewise not improbable: The statues or bundles made at the
death of an Inca that would be venerated like his mummy included his
hair and fingernail clippings and were dressed in the clothes that had
touched his body in life (Sancho, in Arocena 1986: 142). Details of the
description of Mullu Cancha, however, are surprising at best, fanciful
at worst. Its decoration with bright red shells and crystal sounds
rather unlike what we observe in standing Inca architecture, though,
admittedly, our observations are based on the remains of buildings
long ago looted. Pachacuti Yamqui's suggestion that Tomebamba Pachamama (assuming it was the same building) was more impressive
for its scale than for its materials strikes a more plausible note.

Descriptions of other buildings at Tomebamba are much less detailed. Cieza reports that

> El templo del sol era hecho de piedra muy sutilmente labradas, y algunas destas piedras eran muy grandes, vnas negras toscas: y otra parescía de jaspe. (Parte I, cap. XLIII; 1986: 145)

> The Temple of the Sun was made of very smoothly worked stones, some of them very large. Some of them were black and rough, and others looked like jasper.

He adds that some of the stones used in the temple had been carried to Tomebamba from Cuzco at the behest of Huayna Capac by people who had attempted an uprising; the skepticism about the moving of the rocks that Cieza expresses in the first part of his chronicle is replaced by an unqualified repetition of the story in the second part (compare parte I, cap. XLIIII; 1986: 145 to parte II, cap. LXV; 1985: 190). Cieza also reports that doorways of buildings in Tomebamba were colorfully painted and set with precious stones. The walls of its temple of the sun and some of the palaces had thin layers of gold on the walls, with images of birds and animals worked on the walls or placed in the buildings' interiors (parte I, cap. XLIIII; 1986: 145). Pachacuti Yamqui includes a story about Huayna Capac's other works near Tomebamba. He reports that when Huayna Capac was marching with the army from Cuzco to the northern frontier, they arrived in Tomebamba and found people starving to death. Huayna Capac's response was to canalize a river and provide water for the region (the mazelike pattern of that canalization provided by Pachacuti Yamqui seems implausible), as well as to construct a Sun temple, Coricancha (Pachacuti Yamqui 1968: 309; 1950: 260). Tomebamba is also described as having lodgings for soldiers and many storehouses (Cieza parte I, cap. XLIIII; 1986: 146).

Although we know relatively little about the plan of Inca Tomebamba, what we do know suggests some intriguing comparisons to Huayna Capac's other works. In contrast to Murúa's assertion that Huayna Capac faithfully copied the style and technique of Cuzco's buildings here, the extant remains of Tomebamba appear to have relatively little of the fine cut stone that one might expect to see. Foundations that have been excavated and exposed are made of river cobbles, some of them worked, set in mud mortar. In his report on his excavation of the site, Uhle suggested that the locally available stones did not lend themselves to working as was the case for buildings in Cuzco (1923: 5), but the choice to make the walls in this style may have been intentional: The visible remains are not unlike the style and technique of the visible foundations at Quispiguanca, which similarly use locally available stone, much of it river cobble or fall from the region's land-slides. The architectural remains now shown to visitors (one group in Todos Santos Park and the other a group called Puma Pungo) were not adjacent to the Inca plaza of the site identified by Uhle, though they are near a structure that may have been a sun temple according to Id-rovo (reported in Hyslop 1990: 140). Perhaps their location away from the center of the site meant that these structures did not require the more conservative, Cuzco-style masonry, though we cannot discount the likelihood that any well-cut stones were reused in Colonial con-structions. Hyslop illustrates heaps of broken masonry blocks from Tomebamba (1990: 265), and Uhle shows reused cut stone in Colonial structures near the site (1923: lám. I), though an examination of their photos does not show blocks that appear to be as carefully worked as Cuzco's stones.

The Puma Pungo sector of the site, which has been partially exca-vated and restored, is located near the banks of the canalized Tome-bamba River. The remains of courtyard houses and an irregularly shaped plaza are built on a relatively flat terraced space overlooking the river and associated Inca waterworks (figs. 8.14, 8.15). The foun-dation of a courtyard house compound (which Uhle considered to be the Palace of Huayna Capac) is popularly considered to be a house of the mamaconas, based on the spinning tools found there in excavations (reported in Hyslop 1990: fig. 11.3, 296). The partially worked river cobbles that form their foundations outline a walled group of six or eight structures, arranged in pairs onto a common courtyard. Adja-cent buildings are separated by narrow passageways which align with similar passageways on the opposite side of the square. Relative to the size of the roofed area, the open courtyard is large. If we are seeking analogies to other buildings commissioned by Huayna Capac, we might find echoes of this design in the subsidiary structures at the Temple of Viracocha at Raqchi and possibly the Putucusi courtyard group at Quispiguanca.

A more intriguing parallel comes from an examination of water-works at Tomebamba. In an area adjacent to the Tomebamba River and below the Puma Pungo compound there is a large, irregularly shaped pool that drains from a canal, through a worked bath struc-ture, and then out, presumably to or toward the river (Hyslop 1990: 140–141). Quispiguanca, too, had a lake adjacent to the palace and likely had a large and possibly naturalistic pool immediately below the niched terrace wall which drained into a reservoir. This arrangement is strikingly similar to the relationship of terraced architectural space to waterworks at Tomebamba and similarly juxtaposes the apparently

FIGURE 8.14. Courtyard house group that has been excavated at Puma Pungo (Tomebamba), in Cuenca, Ecuador.

FIGURE 8.15. Curvilinear terraces of Puma Pungo (Tomebamba), viewed from below.

natural water of a large pool with the rigidly controlled water of a canal and bath. Regrettably, there isn't enough left of Inca Tomebamba
to examine such details as niche construction, door shape and proportion, and upper walls, as would be desirable for making a case that
its design fits within the canons of the architectural style attributed to
Huayna Capac's reign. The tentative comparisons that can be made
merely remind us how much of Inca architecture is no longer visible.

Other Sites

Historical sources confirm Huayna Capac's building activity at Yucay,
in the Casana, at Cacha, and at Tomebamba. There are other places
where he was also active but where we cannot reliably identify his
handiwork.

The great complex of Sacsahuaman overlooking Cuzco is one of
the sites that may, in part, have been credited to Huayna Capac. Most
chroniclers who comment on the site claim that work on the fortress
was begun by Topa Inca. All concur that it was a monumental task, involving the work of many laborers working over many years. Most
sources mention that work continued under Huayna Capac, though we
do not know whether this means that he finished a job begun by his
father or that he dedicated new buildings on a substantially finished
site. The original design of Sacsahuaman was a source of fascination
to early chroniclers, but despite several tantalizing descriptions and a
great deal of ongoing archaeology there, we do not know really what it
looked like, nor do archaeologists concur on what it was (fortress or
Sun temple or headquarters for Hanan Cuzco). The remains of Sacsahuaman that we see today are the terraces made of stones too big for the
Spaniards of Cuzco to carry away (see, e.g., Garcilaso parte I, lib. VII,
cap. XXIX; 1609: 196 r.). It is not possible to identify any construction
there that can reliably be attributed to Huayna Capac.

There are other places where Huayna Capac was active and certainly built. He is associated with the improvement and construction
of the road system, including the main road through the highlands
and the main road on the coast (Zárate lib. I, cap. X; 1947: 421; Murúa
cap. 37; 1962, vol. 1: 104; Murúa cap. XIII; 1946, vol. II: 75–76), a task
that apparently took place as he prepared for the military campaigns
on the northern frontier. He also constructed buildings and fountains
in Lares in the jungle not far from Urubamba (Murúa cap. 37; 1962,
vol. 1: 104; Murúa cap. XIII; 1946, vol. II: 75).[9] He also rebuilt a fortress
on the southern frontier that had initially been established by his
father and had been subsequently destroyed by the Chiriguanaes
(Murúa cap. 30; 1962, vol. 1: 77; Sarmiento cap. 61; 1960: 264; cap. 59;
1960: 260).[10]

Huayna Capac was also involved in reorganizing the *mitima* communities of the Cochabamba Valley, initially set up by Topa Inca (Murúa cap. 30; 1962, vol. 1: 77; Sarmiento cap. 59; 1960: 260; see also Morales 1978; Wachtel 1980–81). It is likely that formally planned Inca works attributable to his reign could be identified there. His activities in extending the northern frontier and consolidating the southern one also surely led to some administrative and military constructions at the ends of the empire.

Conclusion

The formalized stories that tell of the lives of the Inca rulers characterize Pachacuti as a tireless builder. Yet an examination of the evidence—historical as well as physical—suggests that Huayna Capac, no less than his grandfather, was an active reshaper of the Inca world. In addition to the innovative architectural style that he used in his country estate and, evidently, in parts of his city palace, the Casana, Huayna Capac consolidated control of the furthest reaches of the Inca empire, marking that control with architecture and building the infrastructure that made it possible to move the armies that kept the empire together.

The buildings he commissioned pushed the technical limits of Inca architecture and stretched, as well, the canons of Inca design. The little we know about the style of architecture used during Huayna Capac's reign gives us a tantalizing picture of the many now-vanished works he also commissioned. In the next chapter I will address the style that characterizes his buildings and its relationship to the works built by his ancestors and by his sons.

9

INCA ARCHITECTURE IN HISTORICAL CONTEXT

I have argued throughout that it is important to bear in mind the historical context of a work of architecture—to note who might have built it and what social and cultural factors might have helped to give it form and meaning. At the same time, the chronicles remind us just how difficult it is to attribute a date to a particular Inca construction. Still, it is possible to explore the development of aspects of Inca style in the context of Inca royal narratives.

Architecture and Chronology
Architecture

In cases where we have standing architectural remains and an historical record, it is possible to consider the way that particular substyles of Inca architecture pertain to different reigns. For example, in the case of the Temple of Viracocha at Raqchi, we are on firm ground in dating its construction to Huayna Capac's reign: We have the clear attribution of its construction by Juan de Betanzos, together with the many chroniclers who concur that Huayna Capac visited Collasuyu in the middle of his reign. Further, the relatively well preserved standing remains of the temple complex show us a coherent design for the compound that includes the great hall, courtyard houses, and circular structures at least. Examination of these remains allows us to make a stylistic argument that they pertain to the architectural style devised for Huayna Capac's country palace at Quispiguanca.

In other cases, we do not have the physical evidence that might allow us to determine the stylistic affinities of sites. There is little doubt that Huayna Capac's town palace, the Casana, contained innovative buildings. Its remarkable dual towers and enormous *galpón* alone were worthy of comment by several chroniclers, and if Garcilaso's etymology of the name is accurate, the palace must have been splendid. Contemporary with the construction at Quispiguanca and built, like that palace, by Sinchi Roca, the paltry physical remains that have lasted into this century show such conservative features of Cuzco-style masonry, niche design, and wall batter that it is visually indistinguishable from the remains other fine buildings in Cuzco, among them Coricancha (the Temple of the Sun) and Hatun Cancha. The wall stubs remind us that there were contexts in which even Late Inca buildings retained old-fashioned features of construction and design.

At sites where we have historical documents that attest to the commissioning of buildings by a particular Inca, we need to have careful observation and description of the physical remains. It should be possible to characterize the architectural style that prevailed during a particular reign, especially when we are looking at the works commissioned for royal use, such as those found in a palace or on a royal estate. This approach has informed the analyses of Ollantaytambo (Protzen 1993), Machu Picchu (Rowe 1990), Calca (Niles 1988), and, to a lesser extent, Callachaca (Niles 1987). It is also the argument advanced in general terms by Kendall (1976, 1985).

In reading Inca architecture, especially in considering the chronological setting for individual works, it is important to bear in mind the difference between works that were dedicated to the administrative and imperial needs of the state and those that were designed to serve the private needs of a ruling Inca (Niles 1993).

Projects of importance to the state, such as building roads, bridges, storehouses, forts, and, perhaps, terraces and houses for *mitima* populations on lands devoted to administrative projects, were probably built by conscripted *mita* labor. Though overseen by ethnic Inca inspectors, it is likely that the work responded to the needs of the expanding state. A discussion of the technical design and aesthetics of such functional constructions would be valuable and might help us begin to pinpoint the evolution of style in public works.

In the realm of religion, we have documentary evidence of Inca rulers reendowing existing shrines and temples and constructing new ones. We do not know the architectural requirements of Inca devotion, nor do we know whether the worship of different divinities might have required differently constructed spaces. We have a suggestion from historical sources that at least the Temple of the Sun at Tomebamba may have been built in a style reminiscent of the Coricancha in Cuzco and that stones from the capital may have been incorporated into it. We also have the clear evidence of the Temple of Viracocha at Raqchi, which has an innovative architectural style at once recognizable as a work datable to Huayna Capac's reign.

In the realm of royal architecture, it is likely that the official palaces of Cuzco retained much of the conservatism appropriate to the capital, but that in country palaces, architectural innovation could be freely expressed. It may well be that the styles appropriate for state constructions, religious constructions, and royal constructions developed at different paces and responded to different political and cultural pressures.

The historical accounts suggest that one element of Inca political strategy involved the rebuilding and improvement of places built earlier. The evidence is clear in cases such as Cochabamba, where Huayna Capac expanded the system of *mitimaes* placed in the region by his father and imposed a new order on the region's populations. It is also suggested in the cases where earlier works had been destroyed or proved inadequate, as was apparently the case in the fortresses on the Inca southern frontier. Huayna Capac's improvement of the road system established by his father and grandfather is another example of expanding what was there in light of new administrative necessity. In these cases we are dealing with sites of importance to the Inca state and to Inca political ambitions. We might interpret their reconstruction as relating to the changing needs of an expanding empire.

But other kinds of constructions seem to have had a different meaning for the Incas. The case of Huayna Capac's building activities at Tomebamba provides a good example. Whatever he may have built at the site begun by his father, we have to assume that his works were, in part, related to the increasing prominence of the northern part of the empire. Engaged as he was in the hard-won battle for the lands north of Quito, Huayna Capac had cashed in many political chips. He had called up reinforcements for the army twice, had redirected tribute to the war effort, and won the war only after twelve years and the loss of countless soldiers. Moreover, the wars had cost him the valuable support of some of Cuzco's nobles. He had paid dearly—in clothes, food, and *mamaconas*—to keep the Inca *orejones* from marching back to Cuzco with the sacred *huaca* of Huanacauri. And, as Cieza's story of the stones transported from Cuzco implies, there may have been trouble brewing back home. The creation of an impressive site to administer the north would have helped to remind everyone— vanquished Cayambi lords, loyal Cañari ones, conscripts from the provinces, and disgruntled nobles of Cuzco—of the Inca political agenda. And the construction of buildings in honor of his mother and his own birth (whether built by Topa Inca for his son or Huayna Capac for himself) would have been a reminder of the Inca's personal charisma and his divine charter to rule.

In a site such as Tomebamba, we need to bear in mind the model of Cuzco. That capital combined the functions of royalty, religion, and administration. Although it was formally planned, it was a work constantly under construction, with reserved spaces still to be filled in as generations of rulers added to its plan by building their palaces there, reendowing its main temple, and contributing their handiwork to the fortress on the hill above it.

Chronology

A feature which confounds our attribution of constructions to particular reigns is the Inca royal practice of reendowing earlier works. Cieza inadvertently pinpoints the problem:

> Era grande cosa vno destos palacios: porque aunque moría vno de los reyes: el sucessor no ruynaua ni deshazia nada: antes lo acrecentaua, y paraua más illustre: porque cada vno hazía su palacio, mandando estar el de su antecessor adornado como él lo dexó. (Parte I, cap. XLIIII; 1986: 144)

> These palaces were a wonderful thing, for when one of these kings died, his successor did not ruin or destroy anything. Formerly he enhanced it and improved it, because each king had his own palace, ordering that that of his predecessor remain as he had left it.

The passage shows the conflict inherent in Inca royal endowments: The new ruler could not touch anything that belonged to the former one, but he must improve it.

The mandate not to touch the property of the dead Inca was taken quite seriously. Several eyewitnesses to the first encounter of Inca and Spaniards note Atahuallpa's respect for his father's property. Ruiz de Arce reports that in amassing his ransom, Atahuallpa directed the Spaniards not to touch any of the property in his father's house (1955: 196, 198), and Pedro Pizarro adds that Atahuallpa was upset that the Spaniards had removed reeds from a palace where his father had slept (cap. 8; 1986: 33).

There are many examples of later rulers making grants to the estates of their ancestors, including Huayna Capac's grants of the Soras tributaries to Pachacuti's estate, and of gifts of estates to unnamed living and dead lords. We don't know exactly how these grants might have been expressed physically. For example, if Huayna Capac increased the number of *yanaconas* and *mamaconas* pledged to the service of a dead ancestor, were these workers settled on the existing holdings of the dead lord, or were new grants of real estate made? Who would have been responsible for ordering the construction of any houses or terraces needed for the expanded estates, the grantor or the head of the dead lord's *panaca*? If the grant were carved out of new territory (as may have been the case with some of the ones on Huayna Capac's estate), I can imagine that the new Inca might develop the land by providing architects and workers. The developed property might be managed by the *panaca* of the developer, or it could be transferred to the *panaca* of the dead lord, perhaps with the implicit understanding that the *panaca* had the job of maintaining an Inca presence in the region. But it is also possible to imagine that the grant was in essence a license for the dead lord's *panaca* to marshal the resources to develop the land in order to enhance the well-being and fame of its ancestor. In such a case, the head of the *panaca* would presumably be in charge of commissioning the works in the name of the ancestor. It is not inconceivable that structures created in this way might be built in the style devised by that lord or that prevailed in the architecture on his estate.

We are beginning to make progress on an understanding of the chronological development of Inca style. Kendall (1976) provided the general framework for attributing certain elements of Inca style to particular reigns, though her effort was hampered by the lack of detailed description of architecture available at the time and by the fact that some important sources that comment on the attribution of buildings were not available to her or were not used for her study. Gibaja's characterization of Neo-Inca style was a valuable effort as well (Gibaja 1982), though, as noted by Protzen, her characterization of the style was so broad that it certainly included pre-Conquest style well as post-Conquest (Protzen 1993: 261–263). Protzen's careful observations at Ollantaytambo and his clear description and illustration of his findings are the best attempt to date to distinguish the works commissioned by the early imperial ruler Pachacuti from those that date to the time of his great-grandson Manco Inca. The site's relatively good preservation makes it possible to observe traces of its clear modification on at least two occasions, and the historical sources are unambiguous on the fact of Manco Inca's presence and construction activities at the site. Nonetheless, Protzen notes that there are still many questions about the range of variation attributable to Inca style, both at a point in time and over time.

Antecedents to Huayna Capac's Style

As the foregoing discussion suggests, tracing the development of Inca architectural style is not a straightforward matter. But neither is it an impossible one. I shall argue that, under Huayna Capac's direction, Inca royal style changed in recognizable ways, responding to the historical circumstances that informed its creation. The re-visioning of earlier principles of design created a distinctive style that persisted into the years bracketing the bloody encounter between the Inca and Spanish empires.

While the cultural and stylistic antecedents to Inca imperial architecture are not well understood by archaeologists, there is no ambiguity in the narratives told by the Incas. Like so much of their royal and ritual life, the invention of their architectural style is credited to Pachacuti. It was a style devised for the temple that commemorated the divine grace that permitted the Incas to best their enemies and the capital fitting to be the seat of their nascent empire. In the narrative of his life presented by Betanzos and by Sarmiento, Pachacuti follows his victory over the Chancas with three episodes of construction: the rebuilding of the Temple of the Sun, the reconstruction of Cuzco, and the redesign of the agricultural works and support communities outside of Cuzco.

Betanzos credits Pachacuti with inventing the style used in the work and with very active participation in it. The design of the new capital city was one he had dreamed up himself, modeling it first in clay before laying it out on the ground (parte I, cap. XVI; 1987: 75–76). In the rebuilding of Cuzco, he ordered the existing structures to be abandoned and torn down, and "with his own hands, and along with the other lords of the city, had them bring a cord, and with it he laid out the blocks and houses that he had designed" (Betanzos parte I, cap. XVI; 1987: 77). Similarly, in the construction of the Temple of the Sun,

> E visto por el sitio do a él le paresció mejor que la casa debía de ser edificada mandó que allí le fuese traído un cordel le siéndole traído levantáronse del lugar do estaban él y los suyos y siendo ya en el sintido [sic] había de ser la casa edificada el mesmo por sus manos con el cordel midió e trazó la casa del sol e habiéndola trazado partió de allí con los suyos y . . . midío las piedras para el edificio desta casa. . . . y siendo ya allí pusieron por obra el edificio della bien ansi como Ynga Yupangue la había trazado y imaginado andando él siempre y los demás señores encima de la obra mirando como la edificaban y ansi él como los demás trabajaban en tal edificio. (Betanzos parte I, cap. XI; 1987: 50)

> Having chosen the site that he thought best for constructing the House [of the Sun], he ordered them to bring him a cord. And he got up from where he had been sitting with his lords and having decided to build the house himself, picked up the cord and measured and laid out the walls of the House of the Sun. Then he left with his lords and . . . measured the rocks for the walls of this house. . . . And when they were working on the building as Inca Yupanqui had laid it out and designed it, he and the rest of the lords were always walking around, seeing how they were building it. And he, along with the others, worked on the building.

The style devised for Cuzco's palaces and temples is one that Pachacuti put into place elsewhere; narratives report that it was used at Ollantaytambo (Sarmiento cap. 40; 1960: 245), as well as at temples, palaces, and fortresses in more distant parts of the empire (Cobo lib. 12, cap. XIII; 1964: 82).

One Inca tradition asserted that in the masonry style he devised for the structures of Cuzco and Ollantaytambo, Pachacuti was emulating the smoothly fitted stonework of the ancient structures of Tiahuanaco (Cieza parte I, cap. CV; 1986: 284; Cobo lib. 12, cap. XIII; 1964: 82).

Another tradition claimed that he pressed captives from that region to work the blocks in his palace at Ollantaytambo (Sarmiento cap. 40; 1960: 245). There is little archaeological reason to accept these claims at face value.[1] Still, as a motif in the narrative it is a fitting way to link Pachacuti's work as a builder (he creates a new style and imposes it on the landscape), a warrior (he is inspired in the work by his encounter with buildings or builders of Tiahuanaco during his conquest of Collasuyu), and son of the Sun (he devises the style to honor the divinity who appeared to him on the eve of battle). As with accounts of the lives of other Inca rulers, the architecture itself was the permanent legacy that helped to validate the claims of the royal history.

Although the stories of Pachacuti as a visionary architect were part of the formalized narrative that shaped a truth not necessarily verifiable through archaeology, it is the case that the architecture at sites where we know he was active has a stylistic uniformity. The Temple of the Sun, Pisac, Machu Picchu and related sites in the Cusichaca region, Tambo Machay, and parts of Ollantaytambo were all places designed by or for Pachacuti, and all show features that must be thought of as characteristic of early imperial Inca style (see figs. 3.2–3.4, 3.7). We see buildings that are more or less rectangular in shape with symmetrically disposed arrangements of doors, niches, and other features. Well-fitted masonry characterizes some structures at all the sites attributed to Pachacuti, though adobe walls and less well fitted stonework are also found in portions of the sites. Walls are generally battered, and niches and door openings may be noticeably trapezoidal, particularly in buildings with fitted masonry (fig. 9.1). Tall walls and door openings often show entasis, and double jambs may be present. Buildings may be arranged singly, in facing pairs, or in courtyard groups, and they may have gable, hip, or shed roofs. There are also certain characteristic features of site layout. At places such as Pisac and Machu Picchu, buildings are arrayed on top of mountains or ridges and, at these and other sites, are often oriented to give a direct view of a mountain or other prominent feature of the landscape (fig. 9.2). Systems for moving or displaying water in canals or formal baths may be a feature of site design. It is not uncommon at these early imperial Inca sites to find carved outcrops of rock near architectural groups or to find bedrock—carved or left in its natural state—incorporated into a wall or building. Further, though early Inca architecture is based on four-sided forms, it is rare for buildings to have 90-degree angles; rather, they are more often accommodated to the space available, which is, in turn, likely to be a terrace that follows the natural contours of the landscape (fig. 9.3).

FIGURE 9.1. A double-jambed doorway into a passageway at the Coricancha in Cuzco. The doorway shows the entasis and the narrow jamb that are characteristic of relatively early imperial Inca architecture.

All these features of Inca architecture were well established by the reign of Pachacuti and set the definition for the style that would have been known and responded to by his descendants. It would have been the basis of the style that was widely disseminated in the Andes due to the imperial ambitions of the Incas, realized by Pachacuti and his son Topa Inca. It was also the style that would have been familiar to Huayna Capac, who was installed as Inca in the temple built by his grandfather perhaps sixty years earlier.

FIGURE 9.2. Architecture at Machu Picchu is accommodated to the steep terrain of the site and is oriented to view prominent features of the landscape.

FIGURE 9.3. A building compound at Pisac is fitted onto a small terraced space that follows the natural contours of the hilltop.

Huayna Capac's Legacy

Huayna Capac's architecture responded to the canons of design established by his predecessors. The distinctive style devised during his reign became, in its own right, the basis for the works created by his sons and grandsons.

The Spanish advance party arrived in the Andes at a time when Huayna Capac had consolidated Inca control of the north and when his architectural style could be disseminated over the entire length of the empire, from the Chiriguano frontier in the south to Tomebamba in the north. Unfortunately, whatever developments he may have had in mind for the northernmost frontier were never realized.

Due to the disruptions of the Inca civil war and the arrival of the Spaniards, we know relatively little about the architectural styles that may have prevailed after Huayna Capac's reign. We know that Huascar built at Calca in the Yucay Valley, probably modifying a much earlier site (Niles 1988), as well as constructing Amarucancha in Cuzco and a palace at Muina in the Lucre Basin (see figs. 3.8–3.10). Atahuallpa's activities are less well documented. He successfully commissioned a building at Carangui that was readied for his marriage and installation as Inca (Betanzos parte II, cap. VI; 1987: 220); earlier, at Tomebamba, he had failed to convince the *mitimaes* that he had sufficient authority to command them to build him lodgings (Cieza parte II, cap. LXXII; 1985: 207–208).

There is an intriguing suggestion that Atahuallpa had access to a retreat near Cajamarca that may have incorporated some aspects of his father's style, though we do not know whether Atahuallpa himself built it. When the Spaniards arrived in Cajamarca, they did not find Atahuallpa there, as he was resting at a pleasure house a league and a half away by paved road, where he was carrying out a ritual fast (Ruiz de Arce 1955: 189). Some of his troops and retainers were there, too, in an enormous tent camp, and the compound itself housed the *mamaconas* who were attending the Inca. The compound had a hall and other constructions as well, as we are told by Pedro Pizarro, who heard about the first encounter from his colleagues:

> Pues llegado Soto donde estaua Atagualpa, que hera un galponçillo pequeño que allí tenían para el señor, con otros aposentos para quando allí se yba a holgar y bañar en un estanque grande que tenían hecho, muy labrado de cantería y al estanque benían dos caños de agua: uno caliente y otro frío, y allí se templaua la una con la otra para quando el señor se quería bañar y sus mugeres, que otra persona no osaua entrar en él so pena de la uida. (Cap. 8; 1986: 32)

[Hernando de] Soto arrived where Atahuallpa was, which was a small hall they had built there for the lord, with other buildings that he could use when he went there to enjoy himself and to bathe in a big pool that they had made. The pool was made of finely cut stone, and it was fed by two tubes of water, one hot and the other cold. And the one tempered the other so the lord and his ladies could bathe there, and no other person dared enter under penalty of death.

Ruiz de Arce has an even more intriguing description of a site he remembered well, as he was among the group who first encountered Atahuallpa:

fuimos zinco Adonde estava Atabalica, la casa de plazer hera De esta man-era. De quatro quartos tenia Dos cubos Altos y en medio tenia un patio En el patio estava hecho un estanque En el qual estanque Entravan dos caños de agua, uno caliente y otro frio Estos dos caños salian de dos fuentes y es-tas dos fuentes estavan juntas En aquel estanque lavavan El y sus mugeres A la puerta de esta casa estava un prado estava el con sus mugeres y alli lle-gamos De parte Del governador. (1955: 189)

five of us went to the place where Atahuallpa was. The pleasure house was like this: Among its four rooms were two tall towers, and in the middle it had a patio. In the patio there was a pool into which two tubes of water led, one warm and one cold. These two tubes came from two fountains which were next to each other. He and his women bathed in the pool. At the en-trance to the house was a park where he was with his women when we ar-rived, sent by the governor.

Other chroniclers comment, as well, on the trees planted around the compound. From these descriptions we take an image of a site with intriguing comparisons to the country palace of his father: a courtyard compound, a pool, two towers, and a parklike setting.

Near Cuzco, it is clear that the architectural style devised by Huayna Capac was continued by Manco Inca and, perhaps, by Sayri Topa Inca. The style that Gibaja (1982, 1984) identified as Neo-Inca, based on the Palace of Sayri Topa in Yucay and structures at Ollantaytambo, among others, may indeed have been built between 1535, when Manco Inca first opposed Spanish authority in Cuzco, and 1537 or so, when he retreated to the forested regions beyond Ollantaytambo. As Protzen notes, the evidence at Ollantaytambo suggests that this style has clear roots in Huayna Capac's buildings at Quispiguanca (1993: 261–265). Meanwhile, in Cuzco Colonial Inca dignitaries presumably continued elements of Cuzco-style architecture for another generation—and, by implication, the architecture helped them preserve elements of Inca ritual culture. Garcilaso describes the remains of Collcampata,[2] built by Manco Inca and then home to Paullu and his son Don Carlos Inca:

Yo alcançe en el un galpon muy grande y espacioso, que seruia de plaça en dias llouiosos para solenizar en el sus fiestas principales, solo aquel galpon quedaua en pie quando salí del Cuzco. (Parte I, lib. VII, cap. VIII; 1609: 173 r.)

I myself saw there a large and spacious *galpón* which they used as a plaza on rainy days to celebrate their important festivals. Only that *galpón* was still standing when I left Cuzco.

As he tells us elsewhere, Collcampata's *galpón* was the smallest of the four such structures in Cuzco (Garcilaso parte I, lib. VI, cap. IIII; 1609: 132 r.). The passage reminds us that the building form perfected by Huayna Capac was important in the political and religious life of his sons, even after the Conquest.

Huayna Capac's Style

The style of architecture devised for Huayna Capac's estate at Yucay represents a radical re-visioning of the existing canons of Inca design. We know that the estate was one of the first works commissioned when he assumed rule, so the date at which the new style was invented can be determined. Further, since so much of the estate is intact, we can talk about the way that individual buildings reflect the design, as well as complexes of buildings, and the relationship to the natural and built landscape.

Building Form

The buildings that form part of the estate of Huayna Capac, insofar as there are preserved remains that can be analyzed, are related to more widely known Inca building types. The site includes remains of *canchas*, walled architectural groups composed of buildings that face onto a common courtyard, an arrangement seen at countless Inca sites that had a royal presence. There are many variations in details of *cancha* groups. They may differ with respect to such features as the number of component buildings; the shape and roof style of its structures; the masonry of the buildings and, if present, its surrounding wall; the elaboration of its doorways; the treatment of space between and next to its component buildings. Regrettably, we do not know enough about the form of the courtyard compounds at Quispiguanca to make comparisons to the layout of better-preserved groups from other sites. Like other buildings at the site, the extant remains of Quispiguanca's courtyard house group include somewhat fitted stone foundations topped by adobe walls; the stones used in the foundations appear to be somewhat smaller than the stones chosen for the foundations of other groups on the site. Almost certainly, the interior and exterior walls of the courtyard groups would have been coated with mud plaster which would have obscured their foundations.

The *cancha* as a building type is found in some of the earliest imperial Inca constructions (e.g., the Coricancha and Pachacuti's developments in the Machu Picchu region and at Ollantaytambo; fig. 9.4), as well as the latest (Quispiguanca, Calca, and Amarucancha). *Canchas* are ideal arrangements for domestic units, providing both sheltered areas for protection from rain and wind and open space in which food can be prepared or meals can be taken. They also provide privacy for their residents, forming self-contained units in which any activity that takes place can be screened from the view of outsiders. While we do not know what activities took place in its buildings, at a palace such as Quispiguanca it would be likely that the domestic routines of the divine ruler or his favored associates would be sheltered from public view. The *mamaconas* who attended the Inca, too, would probably have lived or worked in a compound closed off from public access.

The Great Halls

The open-ended great halls of Quispiguanca provide more intriguing comparisons to other Inca buildings. The multidoored great hall that opens onto a plaza is a building type reported for a number of provincial sites of importance, including Cajamarca in the north highlands of Peru, Huánuco Pampa in the central highlands, and Incallacta in Bolivia. The unconstricted floor space, high thatched roof, and ample dimensions of such structures resulted in buildings with striking façades as well as impressive building volumes. For example, the now-vanished great halls of Cajamarca were two hundred paces long (Ruiz de Arce 1955: 190), and the great hall of Incallacta could have accommodated perhaps five or six hundred people (Lee 1992a: 15). The structures are intimately related to large plazas, serving to define them, as well as perhaps providing an imposing and identifiably Inca backdrop to the religious, administrative, or military activities that took place there. The provincial great halls are symbols, par excellence, of the "architecture of power" (Gasparini and Margolies 1980: 195 ff.).

The buildings at Quispiguanca are a special type of great hall. Like the provincial great halls, these have general width to length proportions of 1:3 and have one long side, pierced by multiple doorways, oriented toward a plaza (plates 3–4). They are distinctive, however, by having one end wall pierced with a broad opening. As suggested in chapter 8, the building type is one which is well documented in historical sources and is described by Pedro Pizarro (cap. 21; 1986: 160) and by Garcilaso (lib. 6, cap. IIII; 1609: 132 r.; lib. 7, cap. VIII; 1609: 173 r.; lib. 7, cap. X; 1609: 176 v.), who reports that the largest such structure

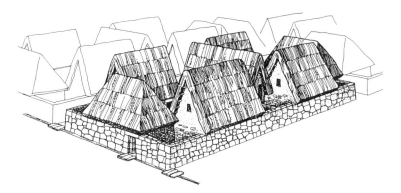

FIGURE 9.4. Courtyard house group from Ollantaytambo, reconstructed. Drawing by Robert N. Batson (Protzen 1993: 57, fig. 2.15).

was in Casana, Huayna Capac's palace compound. One of these structures was at the site of Cuzco's main Catholic church,[3] probably on the end near the Triunfo chapel, though its function and ownership under the Incas are not clear. Guaman Poma also shows this building being torched by Manco Inca in his siege of Cuzco (f. 400 [402]; 1980, vol. 2: 372) (fig. 9.5). His depiction clearly indicates the wide doorway in a gable end and the building's thatched roof.

Guaman Poma also illustrated the open-ended hall as one of the kinds of palaces known by the Incas (f. 329 [331]; 1980, vol. 1: 303). Shown on the far left of his drawing (fig. 9.6), the building is depicted from its front end, its wide doorway and gable end clearly visible; Guaman Poma calls it *cuyus manco*. The term *cuyus manco* also appears in early Quechua dictionaries. Gonçalez Holguin, for example, notes both the form and the function of such buildings in his entry for the *cuyusmanco huasi*, defining it as the "house of the *cabildo* or of judgment; with three walls and one open" (1952: 58). The 1603 *Arte de la lengva general del Perv* notes only the building type's function as the seat of the *cabildo* and its presence in Cuzco ("cuusmanco: casa de cabildo de los Indios del Cuzco"; *Arte de la lengua . . . 1603*). The function of the *cuyus manco* attributed by these early dictionaries may be supported by Pachacuti Yamqui, who, in the story of the quelling of a coup attempt against Huayna Capac, has the hero of the story go to the *cuyus manco* to share his vision of the conspiracy where the royal counselors, advisors, and judges were present (1968: 306).

Despite the fact that it is a building type so clearly documented in the historical record, the *cuyus manco* has not been given much attention by archaeologists. The great halls of Huánuco Pampa, though they have an opening in one of the short end walls (see, e.g., Gaspar-

FIGURE 9.5. Manco Inca, the son who led the Inca resistance against the Spaniards, here torching a building during the siege of Cuzco (Guaman Poma f. 400 [402]; 1980: 372).

ini and Margolies 1980: 205, fig. 189), can hardly be seen as representing this building type, as the opening is narrow. One extant example is well preserved in the foundations of the church at Chinchero, which was a royal estate of Topa Inca (fig. 9.7). Clearly visible in the church's foundations are the stone edges of the single doorway on the short end of the building (fig. 9.8). The doorway measures approximately 7 meters in width in a gable end wall approximately 12.74 meters wide. The building's length is approximately 44 meters. Inca fitted stone foundations are preserved to a height of about 1.95 meters and show even tops, suggesting that the upper portion of the original walls would have been made of adobe. Traces of an earlier gable can be discerned in the church's roof line; the earlier one, which may correspond to the Inca roof line, has a pitch of 45–47 degrees, in contrast to the 37–degree pitch of the current church's roof (fig. 9.9). The structure also preserves three doorways on the long wall facing what is now a plaza in front of the church and three doorways on the opposite long wall as well. (See the plan by Gasparini and Margolies 1980: 215, fig. 203; see also Alcina Franch 1976.)

The dimensions of Chinchero's great hall (12.7 meters by 44.0 meters) are similar to those of Quispiguanca's comparable structures (14.3 meters by 43.8 meters). The one striking difference, however, is

FIGURE 9.6. Guaman Poma's illustration of the types of Inca palaces, showing the open-ended *cuyus manco*, on the left, and the *carpa huasi*, an open-ended building with trusslike gable, behind it (f. 329 [331]; 1980: 303).

FIGURE 9.7. Overview, great hall (in the foundations of the church), fancy buildings, and terraces of Chinchero.

FIGURE 9.8. The end wall of the great hall at Chinchero, bracketing the Colonial doorway set into it, showing fitted masonry with sunken joints and the distinctive Inca wall batter.

the relative width of the opening in its end wall. At Chinchero the door opening is 7.0 meters in a wall 12.7 meters wide, yielding a ratio of door width to wall length of .55. At Quispiguanca, the door opening is 10.4 meters in a wall 14.3 meters wide, resulting in a door width to wall length ratio of .73.

While a small variation in the width or proportion of the doorway opening might not seem to be a major difference between the structures, it would have made a difference in the appearance of the two buildings. Subjectively, the great hall at Quispiguanca seems to be a big building with an entirely open end wall (fig. 9.10a), while the structure at Chinchero seems to be a big building with a wide doorway in one of its end walls. Further, the orientation of the end wall at Quispiguanca toward the site's main plaza makes the building an extension of that grand space; the building would surely have been brightened by the reflection of light off the plaza and through its wide doorway. By contrast, at Chinchero the end wall door opened onto a narrow terrace and provided views of the site's main plaza only over the roof of another building, or, from the terrace, through the ramped

FIGURE 9.9. The end of the church at Chinchero showing an earlier, steeper, roof line within the gable end.

opening between buildings. Perhaps more important, the difference in the end wall door-to-wall ratio may have occasioned an entirely different strategy of building design.

While the great hall of Chinchero would have posed no special challenge to builders accustomed to designing roof structures for Inca great halls without an open end wall, the great halls of Quispiguanca may have required special considerations (Niles, Batson, and Blechschmidt 1998). The steeply pitched thatched roofs of Inca great halls required support by wooden members such as rafters (diagonal members that supported a load-bearing ridge beam) or bipods (diagonal load-carrying members held in place by a ridge beam). Indeed, if the buildings at Quispiguanca had roofs pitched at 60 degrees with thatching 1 meter thick, the maximum width of the structure would have been just under 17 meters (Blechschmidt 1997). The roof support structure would have imposed a great deal of thrust on the long walls of the building, causing them, potentially, to push outward.[4] In most buildings, the end walls would help to tie the building together. In an open-ended building, however, there would be nothing to counteract the tendency of the walls to push outward at their ends, making the end of the side walls closest to the wide doorway particularly subject to failure.

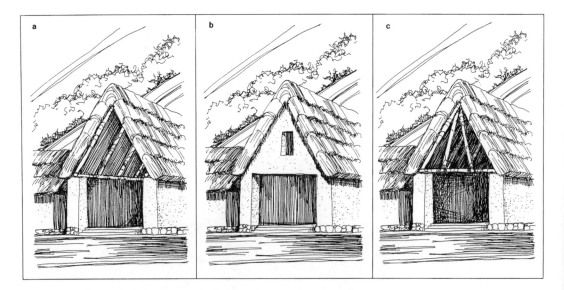

FIGURE 9.10. Reconstruction drawing of the open-ended great hall at Quispiguanca with possible end-wall constructions: a, with fully open end; b, with an adobe gable end suggested by Guaman Poma's drawing of the *cuyus manco*; c, with truss work on the open end, following Guaman Poma's drawing of a *carpa huasi*. Drawing by Robert N. Batson.

In a building with a relatively narrow end wall doorway, such as Chinchero, it would have been relatively easy to span the doorway with a lintel that would support an upper wall of adobe and that would serve to tie the end walls together and that would, not coincidentally, look much like Guaman Poma's depiction of the *cuyus manco* building type. By contrast, the wide opening of Quispiguanca's buildings, if it were similarly provided with a lintel and upper wall, would have been potentially subject to a great deal of bending stress from the weight of the gable end wall it supported (fig. 9.10b).

We do not know how the Incas, in fact, designed an end wall for Quispiguanca's great hall. One possible solution would have been to make a trusslike structure of wood that would tie the end walls together, reduce the thrust on the eave walls, and eliminate bending stress on the lintel (fig. 9.10c). The resulting structure would look much like Guaman Poma's depiction of the *carpa huasi* building type, the open-ended great hall depicted behind the *cuyus manco* in figure 9.6.

It is regrettable that we do not have the foundations of the great hall of the Casana to examine. That open-ended structure was supposed to have been the largest in Cuzco. As a building devised, like Quispiguanca, by Huayna Capac's architect, Lord Sinchi Roca, it is likely to have shown some of the technical and stylistic innovations of the country palace as well.

The great halls of Quispiguanca are clearly related in style to other buildings, especially, perhaps, the one at Chinchero built by Huayna Capac's father. It was a building type too that remained important into the Colonial Period, judging by the presence of great halls at Amarucancha and Collcampata in Cuzco. Although it is possible to see the origins of Quispiguanca's great halls in earlier buildings, the proportions of the Quispiguanca structures and the way that they pushed the limits of design suggest that they represented a quantum change from their predecessors.

Gatehouses and Portal

The gatehouses and portal structure at Quispiguanca are also buildings with possible parallels at other sites, but, like the great halls, they show a radical departure from their stylistic predecessors. The tall building with a squarish footprint and sometimes double-jambed doorways and external niches is seen in several of the building groups on the estate: Cocha Sontor, Quispiguanca, and the Palace of Sayri Topa at Yucay. As has been suggested, the closest stylistic parallels to these buildings are the "Water Temple" at Ollantaytambo and, possibly, the Q'ellu Raqay group at that same site (see, e.g., Sawyer 1980; Gibaja 1982, 1984; Protzen 1993: 263–265). Protzen (1993: 263–264) and Gibaja (1984) have identified the "Water Temple" (fig. 9.11) as part of the later epoch of activity at Ollantaytambo, while Protzen notes that Q'ellu Raqay (fig. 9.12) is less clearly attributed. We cannot say for certain whether the square buildings datable to Huayna Capac's reign represent his interpretation of an idea devised by his grandfather, or whether they represent his architect's invention of an idea that was continued into the next generation, though I incline to the latter explanation.

FIGURE 9.11. The Water Temple at Ollantaytambo, showing its oversize doorway and huge double-jambed niches as it appeared in 1977.

FIGURE 9.12. Body-sized double-jamb niches decorate the exterior of the main building at Q'ellu Raqay, Ollantaytambo.

Protzen has suggested that the oversize doorways, tall rooms, and relatively wide outer jambs of these structures are most likely characteristics of Late Inca architecture, a point with which I concur (Protzen 1993: 261–263). I would add that the style is first seen in Huayna Capac's reign and was probably first devised for the estate at Yucay. The illusion of massiveness of the gatehouses on that estate is augmented by their construction of one story with very tall walls and decorative features in the upper walls. The relatively small interior space of the buildings would have been made to seem grander by their tall walls and high roofs. (In a general sense, that is the principle that is seen in the design of the great halls, too: Although they are not very wide, the open end walls and surely the tall roof would have made the interior space cavernous. The view into the interior through the open end wall would have exaggerated the interior volume of the structure.)

A stone model of a structure built in the style of Quispiguanca's gatehouses and portal is displayed at the University Museum in Cuzco (fig. 9.13). Pertaining to Inca style, the model shows a tower with tall, double-jambed doorways on opposite sides that clearly indicate the building was a pass-through structure, like Quispiguanca's gatehouses and portal. The side walls are decorated with oversize double-jambed niches and the upper walls (or second story) with double-

FIGURE 9.13. Stone house model from the University Museum, Cuzco. Viewed straight on, the double-jambed pass-through doorway is visible.

jambed windows. Lacking archaeological provenience (Pardo 1936), it is not possible to tell whether the model is Early or Late Inca or if it was made in the Colonial Period. It is also not possible to tell whether the small building was a model of a structure that was to be built, a representation of a building that had been made, or a generalized depiction of a familiar building type. Still, there is no question that it looks like the gatehouses and portal at Quispiguanca and has affinities to other buildings that pertain to Late Inca style.[5]

One of the most apparently puzzling aspects of the gatehouses at Quispiguanca is the way in which their doorways—accessible from the interior of the compound—seem suspended nearly 4 meters above ground level when seen from the palace's exterior (see plate 2). There was apparently no formal means of access through these doorways in antiquity, as there are no traces of stairs, ramps, or peg-stone steps in the terrace wall beneath the doorways: From outside the compound, they are not functional as entrances.

There is no parallel yet reported for the hanging doorways. The palace of Topa Inca at Chinchero, however, may have offered an idea that took on a new interpretation in the design of the gatehouses of Quispiguanca. The main structures edging that site's main plaza (CH 1, CH 2, CH 3 on fig. 203; Gasparini and Margolies 1980: 215) lack ground-level approaches from the plaza. Rather, access to the building interiors is by means of doorways in end walls that open onto narrow ramps or terraces; in one building, CH 1, these end wall entrances are baffled. The long walls oriented toward the main plaza have wide, double-jambed openings that—like the doorways of the gatehouses at Quispiguanca—are high above the surface of the plaza (fig. 9.14; see also fig. 9.7). In contrast to Quispiguanca's gatehouses, where the opening is designed like and paired with a ground-level doorway from the palace interior, at Chinchero the openings have the proportions of windows. The general orientation of the buildings at Chinchero suggests they were built to discourage access but to afford views of the main plaza.

Still, it may be the case that Quispiguanca's architect was familiar with the design of his father's estate and took elements of it—an open-ended great hall, double-jambed openings placed high relative to ground level—and reinterpreted them in his own work, giving them a new design context.

Ramps, Alcoves, and Esplanades

While many of the architectural features characteristic of Late Inca style are seen at Quispiguanca, there are others that are more fully expressed elsewhere. Most intriguing is a feature seen in the Callejón

FIGURE 9.14. View across the plaza at Chinchero, showing the high windows on the buildings that face the plaza.

sector at Ollantaytambo (figs. 9.15, 9.16). (A full discussion of the complex is offered by Protzen 1993: 95–110.) Designed as a formal approach to the Q'ellu Raqay building group, the Callejón is delimited by a wall with at least sixteen small, niched alcoves separated from one another by piers about 1 meter thick. The wall borders the road as it slopes down toward the formal entryway into Q'ellu Raqay. On the basis of lintel holes and preserved sloping walls, Protzen has suggested that each alcove was roofed and that each had a floor raised slightly above ground level.

A remarkably similar feature is illustrated by Uhle (1923) based on his excavations at Tomebamba. In the compound he calls the "Templo de Viracocha," he identifies a region he calls the "Esplanada" that runs along the southeast exterior wall of the main building (fig. 9.17). As is the case with the Callejón of Ollantaytambo, Tomebamba's esplanade appears to be graded slightly downhill as it approaches the zone Uhle identifies as the plaza. Most striking, the rear wall of the temple structure and an adjacent building which form the border of the esplanade include remains of twelve small alcoves, separated from one another by piers (in Uhle's plan, these piers seem to be approximately 1.5 meters thick). The alcoves measure 3.10–3.35 meters in width but 2.0–2.25 meters in depth (Uhle 1923: 9). Like the alcoves at the Callejón, the Tomebamba alcoves have an open front facing onto the road. While Tomebamba's remains are not sufficiently well pre-

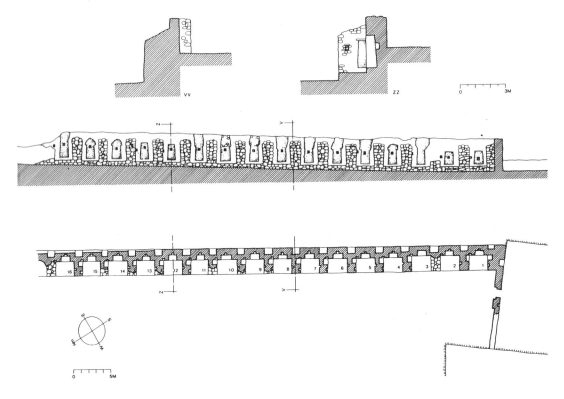

FIGURE 9.15. Plan of the Callejón, Ollantaytambo from Protzen (1993: 99, fig. 4.6). Drawn by Robert N. Batson.

served to indicate the presence of any niches or roofing features in the upper walls, Uhle must have thought the alcoves would have been roofed, as he calls them *casitas* (little houses). Their floors were paved with carefully selected pebbles (Uhle 1923: 9); Uhle does not comment on the height of the floor relative to the surface of the adjacent esplanade.

Both Tomebamba's esplanade and Ollantaytambo's Callejón serve as ramps that facilitated movement between important spaces. Adjacent to the Callejón and Q'ellu Raqay as well are smaller, steeper ramps that move visitors between levels in a small system of tall, elegant, and apparently self-contained terraces. While ramps are known for other Inca sites (see, e.g., Chinchero), it is tempting to draw a specific parallel between the ramps at Callejón/Q'ellu Raqay and those seen in the entrance to Quispiguanca (see plates 1 and 2) as well as in the agricultural roads of Yucay.

The presence of such distinctive architectural features as the ramps with alcoves at sites with a Late Inca component helps us to characterize an additional part of that style. While it is, perhaps, a feature that has its origin in the niched terrace walls of Tarahuasi, Tambo Machay, or the dubiously pre-Conquest construction at Chinchero, the formal processional way decorated with alcoves is qualitatively different from these kinds of constructions. We know that Tomebamba was rebuilt by Huayna Capac while he was active on the northern frontier, so it is likely that its "Templo de Viracocha" pertains to Late Inca style and, within that, to the modifications of the style that may have developed toward the end of Huayna Capac's reign, perhaps around 1520 or so. The Callejón is clearly related to Q'ellu Raqay, a compound with puzzling and unique architectural features that has eluded definitive chronological placement (see Sawyer 1980: 71; Protzen 1993: 263).[6] I would suggest that the presence of a similar architectural feature at Tomebamba, where we can more reliably attribute construction, helps us to posit a less tentative placement of Q'ellu Raqay within Late Inca style, though whether the compound is pre-Conquest or was built by Manco Inca remains an open question.

Material

The materials used in Quispiguanca's buildings are familiar from other Inca sites: fitted stone, fieldstone and mud, adobe brick, mud plaster, wooden lintels. The adobes used on the site are like other Inca adobes (Moorehead 1978). Visibly indistinguishable in color from the

FIGURE 9.16. A portion of the west face of the Callejón at Ollantaytambo, viewed from the southwest.

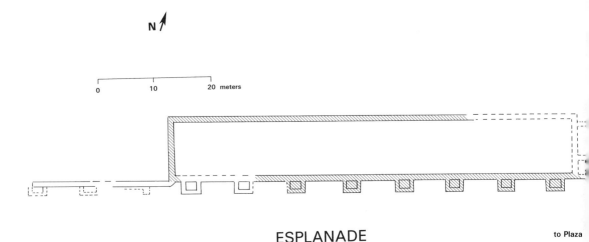

ESPLANADE

to Plaza

FIGURE 9.17. Detail, exterior wall of the Templo de Viraco-cha, Tomebamba. Redrawn from Uhle (1923).

surrounding soil, the adobes are hand made and have abundant inclu-sions of vegetal temper and grit. Typical of other sites, the adobes are laid header-stretcher. Bricks are long and loaf-shaped; I noted adobes that had length by width by thickness measurements of 50 centi-meters by 30 centimeters by 9 centimeters in gatehouse A and approx-imately 32 centimeters by 10 centimeters by 9 centimeters from the rear wall of the great hall E. At Ollantaytambo, bricks in the part of the site dating to its latest construction (probably attributable to Manco Inca) measured 110 centimeters by 20 centimeters by 15 centimeters and 90 centimeters by 20 centimeters by 40 centimeters (Gibaja, re-ported in Protzen 1993: 161); these bricks are not comparable in size to the ones I observed at Quispiguanca.

Judging by the gatehouses, the interiors of the buildings were plas-tered to floor level and the exteriors from ground to roof line in some structures (at Quispiguanca, the portal; the gatehouses facing the in-terior of the plaza) and, as noted, from a plaster line near the top of the join with fitted masonry in others (niched walls and gatehouses facing away from the plaza; Cocha Sontor; Palace of the Ñusta). The plaster was made of mud, with base coats matching the general color of the adobes. Multiple layers were applied to even out architectural features (such as niches) and to smooth the surface of the walls. The lower layers show abundant incorporation of vegetal fiber (visually, the fibers look like ichu grass), presumably so that the mud would ad-here better to the surface and would dry without cracking. In places, it was possible to observe up to three thick layers of mud plaster that together provided a 5-centimeter coating to the walls. The preservation of the walls did not permit me to investigate whether *ichu* was wrapped around adobe bricks, as Protzen observed at Ollantaytambo (1993: 160–161). Where adobe mortar or plaster was in contact with the wood used for lintels on doorways or niches, the lintel was wrapped tightly with rope made of twisted *ichu*, and bunches of *ichu* were generously packed around the rope.

The final coat of mud plaster was very thin—no more than a few millimeters, in contrast to the several centimeters of the base coats—and probably represented a different soil source, as visually the upper coat seems to be a different color from the base coats. The top coat is so smooth in places that it feels almost burnished; whether this sensation is due to the technique with which it is applied or the quality of the mud is not known. The gatehouses preserve some traces of this top coat in the sheltered interior niches and exterior door jamb; where it can be seen, the plaster appears to be a creamy white or very pale pink, in contrast to the darker pinkish-beige of the base coats.

The preserved traces of dark red-orange paint seen in the niched wall and interior of great hall E suggest that a colorful paint job was applied to interior and exterior wall surfaces on top of the upper coat of mud plaster. High-status Inca buildings were frequently painted. Traces of a red inverted stepped-triangle design are visible on the lower portion of the central wall of the Temple of Viracocha at Raqchi. And Protzen has observed a black band painted in a niche at Ollantaytambo and at Pachar (Protzen 1993: 237). In positing a color scheme for Quispiguanca, Robert Batson and I have suggested that the red of ornamental detail and possibly building interiors probably contrasted with another, most likely lighter color for the main wall surfaces. On the basis of a small ceramic house model from the University Museum in Cuzco (fig. 9.18), taken together with the tantalizing hints of a lighter color on the upper plaster coat of parts of the gatehouse, we have suggested that a cream color would have provided an effective contrast with the red of niches (Niles and Batson 1997). While we acknowledge that the color scheme is speculative, we have used it in our reconstruction drawings of the site (plates 1–4).

Kendall has suggested that Late Inca architecture is characterized by an increased use of adobe and paint, because, she claims, the idea was brought to the Cuzco region after the conquest of the coast or the Colla region, areas where adobe and painted building exteriors are reported (1985, part ii: 275–277). While there is no doubt that adobe and paint were used at Late Inca sites, there are many examples of adobe on important buildings near Cuzco that long predate these. For example, the site of Huch'uy Qozqo, begun by Viracocha Inca, in-

FIGURE 9.18. Ceramic house model from the University Museum, Cuzco. Its square form is reminiscent of the buildings at Quispiguanca. It is slip-painted in cream with maroon around the doorway and niches and black trim.

cludes adobe, as do structures at Pisac, built by Pachacuti; Callachaca, owned by Pachacuti's son Amaro Topa Inca; and Chinchero, built for Topa Inca. Further, eyewitnesses to the conquest of Cuzco comment on the brightly painted walls of the city (see Sancho in Arocena 1986: 135), suggesting that far from being associated with low prestige or late rulers, adobe and paint have a long and respectable tradition in Inca architectural style.

Landscape and Layout

While there are elements of Quispiguanca's component buildings that contrast with features characteristic of earlier Inca architecture, the most striking departure from earlier Inca design comes from the layout of the site and its relationship to the built and the natural landscape.

In surveying the architecture at Quispiguanca, I was repeatedly struck by how regular its layout was. In contrast to most Inca sites I had surveyed, Quispiguanca was built using precise right angles. Further, its major architectural units were to be found at points that were predictable: It is as though an invisible grid with units approximately 21 meters on a side had been laid over the ground and the buildings arrayed upon it (this unit shows up in the design of the terraces at Yucay, too). Other sites attributed to Late Inca style also appear to have impressed the archaeologists who have worked there with their regularity. Uhle reported that Tomebamba was built following very precise angles and straight lines (1923: 6), and his plans reveal that the component structures were based on right angles. Incidentally, the area comprising the structures Uhle considered to be the Palace of Huayna Capac measured 141 meters by 122 meters (1923: 6), measurements that are close to multiples of the nearly 21-meter unit observed at Quispiguanca.

In addition to the precision of its measurements, the style of architecture developed during Huayna Capac's reign was striking for the scale of its component buildings and the symmetry of site plans. The scale of the buildings devised at Quispiguanca and at the Temple of Viracocha at Raqchi was, as noted, an important part of what was impressive about the sites. Impressive, too, was the scale of the open space in the plazas of Quispiguanca and Yucay. Uhle noted the importance of scale in the architecture of Tomebamba in relating it to standard Inca style: "As big as [the Palace of Huayna Capac] was, and as original as its character was in many details, at core, it is nothing more than an enormous, logical, expansion of the plan of a common Inca [courtyard] house" of the sort seen at many other sites (1923: 5).

The symmetry seen in the plan of Quispiguanca is noteworthy. The architect paid careful attention to balancing the structures of the east entry façade (two gatehouses and two rectangular buildings flank a two-part portal) and, possibly, mirroring that wall with a similar, now-vanished construction on the west. In the northern complex of the site there are two great halls, two small buildings defining the edge of a plaza, and, possibly, two courtyard house arrangements. Similar principles of design are seen clearly at Raqchi in the orderly and regular arrangement of courtyard houses and circular buildings, the former arrayed also in matched pairs. Symmetry and pairing are also found at Tomebamba. There, Uhle comments on how surprised he was to find two identical courtyard complexes adjacent to each other in the compound he identified as the Palace of Huayna Capac. He could only offer the suggestion that, while one compound must have been reserved for the ruling Inca, the other may have housed the provincial governor, or, perhaps, the statue of Mama Ocllo that was kept at Mullu Cancha (Uhle 1923: 7). Sawyer, too, remarked on the "highly developed use of symmetry" at Q'ellu Raqay (1980: 71), and his plans indicate successive groups of paired structures. While symmetry and balance characterize standard Inca architecture to a degree, in the style devised during Huayna Capac's reign these principles seem to be much more fully expressed than they are at sites attributed to earlier reigns.

At a very gross level, there are points of similarity between the layout of Huayna Capac's buildings and those of his ancestors. Quispiguanca, like the main residential sector of Ollantaytambo and like the ceremonial sector of Chinchero, is oriented so that its plaza opens at the base of the site in the direction of a river. But in other regards the relationship of the site to the landscape is quite different from that seen in other Inca sites.

Quispiguanca is a walled compound built on an artificially flattened terrace. In contrast to Inca country palaces such as Pisac or Machu Picchu, which include architecture that echoes the form of the terrain and frames views of prominent features of the landscape, at Quispiguanca the buildings of the compound turn their backs to the snow peak, Chicón, and are oriented to frame views of other built or modified features within the palace's perimeter. Courtyard houses face onto the center of their shared courtyard; the great halls face onto their plaza; the portals and great halls frame views of the main plaza (plate 4). Where other sites are oriented to natural features of the landscape, the buildings of Quispiguanca relate to space which is shaped by culture. Even the views of the surrounding parklands and lake represent not a natural view but a view of a landscape that is itself an artifact, incorporating planted trees and artificially managed water. The lake itself was probably oriented to reduplicate the constructed world by reflecting its niches in the surface of the water (fig. 9.19). Alone among the architectural compounds on the site, Cocha Sontor is oriented to make reference to a snow peak. But there, too, the buildings turn their back on a direct view of the mountain; its image is approached only as a reflection in a carefully built pond (see figs. 6.31, 6.32).

FIGURE 9.19. Reconstruction drawing of the niched terrace wall and adjacent lake at Quispiguanca. Drawing by Robert N. Batson.

I do not mean to imply that the view of the natural landscape was not important to the design of the estate. The placement of the estate between two constrictions in the Urubamba Valley also tells us something about Huayna Capac's view of the natural world. These constructions form natural hydrological as well as physical boundaries, but more to the point, perhaps, they form view boundaries. From almost any point on his estate, Huayna Capac was embraced by views of his lands—and his lands only—looking to the east and to the west (fig. 9.20). Only in the highest parts of the estate can one get a glimpse of lands that might have belonged to Topa Inca high on the pampa across the river and in some unterraced fields above Huayllabamba. Looking to the east and west, the valley is seen as a sharp V; this is an inversion of the tall and impressive mountain one might expect to see on lands developed by Huayna Capac's ancestors. But the V shape furthers the impression of the extent of the estate: Looking especially to the west, it appears that the world just drops off beyond the closing of the valley. It is as though Huayna Capac controls everything to the horizon, and there is no world past that horizon.

We know that view, including view of the horizon, was an important feature of delimiting Inca districts (an examination of the limits of the *ceques* of Cuzco is one example). At Quispiguanca, it is also a principle that was put into practice in the choice of land on which to build and in the orientation of the views from the palace compound, as well as the views toward the palace from work areas on the estate. The same view of the lands would have been experienced by any visitors to the estate and by all who lived or worked there. It is likely that view was part of consolidating control of the lives of those who maintained the estate for its owner. It may also have helped to reinforce the image of Huayna Capac's autonomy in the eyes of royal visitors or diplomats who were entertained in the palace.

Revolution or Evolution?

The architecture on Huayna Capac's estate at Yucay, although it grows from Inca principles of design, is notably different from that seen on other royal Inca sites in the region. The buildings are massive, the spaces are open and flatter, their arrangement is more regular, and they orient to features of the built and natural landscape in characteristic ways. Rather than representing an end point of a steady evolution of Inca style, the style might better be seen as a radical re-visioning of it: The style plays with Inca notions of proportion and volume, it pushes the design of buildings to their technical limits, and it makes exaggerated use of architectural markers of high prestige.

FIGURE 9.20. View to the west from Lake Huachac. All that is visible is part of Huayna Capac's estate.

As we know from historical sources, the construction of Huayna Capac's estate is credited to his half-brother Sinchi Roca. In looking at the site he designed, one sees why he was considered to be a gifted and innovative architect, skilled at geometry (Murúa cap. 30; 1962, vol. 1: 76–77; Cabello Balboa cap. 21; 1951: 361–362). More than most Inca sites, Quispiguanca is a model of mathematical precision, with equal attention to the arrangement of open spaces and building volumes. The estate is also conceived as a coherent whole, with similar principles of design informing the mundane work spaces of subject populations of farmers, the hunting lodge where visitors relaxed, and the palace spaces reserved for royal ritual.

The architectural style Sinchi Roca devised responds in a very intentional way to the canons of Inca architecture. By incorporating an enormous plaza, Quispiguanca (and, perhaps, Yucay) brings to mind the most impressive Inca spaces: the main plaza at Cuzco, as well as plazas at important provincial sites like Cajamarca and Huánuco Pampa. The great halls of Quispiguanca (and probably, according to historical accounts, the great hall of the city palace at Casana) were surely taller and had broader openings than did buildings constructed for Huayna Capac's predecessors. The Temple of Viracocha at Raqchi, built not long after the palace at Quispiguanca, is also an innovative structure, requiring a central wall and seemingly unique adobe columns to support the massive roof that spans the unprecedented width of the structure. Far from choosing to adhere to the tried and true standards of Inca construction, Sinchi Roca devised technical solutions that made it possible to build and roof the largest great halls known in the Inca heartland. Impressive in their own right, the larger buildings and their plazas would also make it possible to hold even larger celebrations.

It is likely that the form of building seen in the gatehouses and portal of the palace is one of Sinchi Roca's inventions; in any event, the creation of a triple-jambed pass-through into the compound must be credited to him. As with the great halls, the buildings and their oversized doorways and tall walls are impressive structures that would dwarf any human standing near or passing through them. The double-jambed doorway is a marker of high prestige in Inca architecture, used sparingly at most Inca sites. Perhaps it was a doorway that could be used only by personages of a particular rank or one that marked a zone that required special comportment of visitors. Even sites known to have been associated with royalty or with the state religion (e.g., Machu Picchu, Coricancha) do not use double-jambed doorways lavishly. At Quispiguanca, the enormous double-jambed doorways of the gatehouses seem to be used wastefully: From the compound's exterior, they are no longer functional doorways but rather decorative elements, showing, perhaps, the specialness of the entire zone delimited within the compound's walls and suggesting that the status associated with that zone was out of reach to most people. Further, the site uses a triple-jambed portal to control actual access into the site. Here, the extra jamb must have suggested to visitors that the denizen of the palace was of even higher rank than would be a person approached through a mere double-jambed door.

As I have suggested throughout my discussion of the plan of the estate, much of its design was about control, both of access into and through the site and of views afforded to its workers and its visitors. While the site clearly reflects Sinchi Roca's talent and vision and his willingness to innovate, the particular kind of innovations it includes reflects the historical circumstances that led to its construction and the personal taste of the man who commissioned it. Huayna Capac was a man devoted to luxury, and the architecture attributed to him reflects his taste, a point made by Uhle (1923: 6) and repeated by Rowe (1990: 144). But early in his reign, the young Inca faced challenges. The site was commissioned by Huayna Capac after he withstood two coup attempts and consolidated his claim to be Inca. It is possible that the act of construction was, as with other rulers, a necessary prerequisite to his installation as Inca. The attempts against Huayna Capac's right to rule pitted powerfully placed members of the royal families against one another. There was sufficient support among the noble families of the capital so that a half-brother and a cousin could be seen as potential successors to Topa Inca. The second coup attempt had support as well among provincial governors. Quelling this attempt led to the execution of most of the conspirators and punitive raids on the provinces implicated in the plot. When Huayna Capac finally exerted his right to rule, he needed to display his authority in his actions (inspecting Cuzco and the provinces, replacing his regents or advisors, reendowing his ancestors' mummies) as well as in his architecture.

The placement of his estate in the valley where his ancestors had built their own country palaces showed his resolve to take his place in Cuzco's dynasty. The creation of productive fields and lush gardens on swampy and formerly worthless lands was an act worthy of his grandfather Pachacuti and much in keeping with the metaphorical duty of Inca rulers to convert underpopulated and underused lands into economically important properties. The fact that Huayna Capac conscripted 150,000 laborers from throughout the empire to build the estate was surely an assertion of political control that would have been convincing not only to the workers brought in to move the river but to the provincial governors and nobles of Cuzco as well.

The design devised for his earliest works—the estate at Yucay and, probably, the city palace of Casana—reflects the social and political circumstances that prevailed at the time of Huayna Capac's accession. By commissioning enormous structures that pushed the technical limits of Inca design, he was demonstrating his ability to create works appropriate to the grandeur of an Inca. By creating structures such as the great halls of Quispiguanca and the Temple of Viracocha, he was showing his willingness to improve upon the architectural legacy of his ancestors. The lavish use of double jambs and the nearly unprecedented use of a triple-jambed portal would similarly have resonated with noble visitors who understood that multiple jambs indicated higher prestige. Working from an aesthetic tradition which equated bigger buildings with higher prestige, Huayna Capac's architect devised a way to build the biggest buildings ever known and incorporated tricks (constructing them on tall terraces, entering them by means of ramps, juxtaposing big buildings with more intimate terraced spaces) that would make them seem even larger.

While it is possible to see the roots of Huayna Capac's architectural style in structures built by his father at Chinchero and, more distantly, by his grandfather in Cuzco, the buildings he devised for his country estate incorporate a new, visually revolutionary, and immediately recognizable style. Huayna Capac's constructions became an assertion of his place in history—not merely his right to serve as ruler but his place as a future ancestor.

Conclusion

Inca rulers were obsessed with creating monuments to perpetuate their memory. A work of architecture endures and becomes a way to prove the accomplishments of an ancestor. A work built in an immediately recognizable style is a mnemonic of history, analogous to the knot on a *quipu* that helped an Inca historian remember the deeds of a dead ruler. No less than the partisan narratives maintained by an Inca's *panaca*, a work of architecture created by and for a king becomes his version of history, a piece of visual propaganda designed to sustain his claims to eternal glory and his descendants' claims to prestige.

In the palace he created in the Yucay Valley Huayna Capac shaped a space that was suitable for his role as ruler of the greatest American empire. And in devising a style of architecture that was uniquely his, he built a permanent place for himself in Inca history.

Notes

Introduction

1. For a discussion of competing views of Inca history, see Urton (1990: 1–17 and 1996) and Zuidema (1990).

2. In distinguishing among broad categories of folk narrative I follow the characterizations conventionally used by folklorists. Legends are told as true, believed as true, and set in an historical world that obeys physical and social laws as we know them. Their protagonists are humans, sometimes with superhuman attributes. Myths are told as true and believed as true but are set in a time before the world and humans took on their present form. Protagonists of myths may be gods, demiurges, and ancestral forms of humans and animals. Under these criteria, the stories about the Incas' founding ancestors (Manco Capac and his siblings who emerged from the ground and established Cuzco) are myths. Narratives that tell of Sinchi Roca and his successors are legends. By considering them as legends, I do not mean to suggest that Inca royal histories are necessarily untrue but that our understanding of them can be enhanced by approaching them as folk narratives. For discussions of similar genres in other regions, see, for example, Finnegan (1992b) and Vansina (1985) on theoretical issues; Finnegan (1970), Opland (1974), and Vansina (1985) on the historicity of traditional narratives; Tedlock (1983) and Hymes (1981) on style; Foley (1988, 1995) and Finnegan (1992a) on the relationship between memory and performance. For examples from a narrative tradition contemporary with the Inca, see Hernãdez de Oviedo (lib. V, cap. I; 1547: XLV v.).

1. Genre and Context in Inca Historical Narratives

1. Archaeological work is beginning to provide dates for Inca influence in the provinces that suggest somewhat greater antiquity to the Inca empire than emerges from the historical record (see, e.g., the discussion in Pärssinen and Siiriäinen 1997). I focus here on what Inca royal traditions asserted about their history; therefore, I provide the dates and dynastic succession conventionally used by Andeanists based on written sources.

2. Bertonio's Aymara dictionary includes the cognate term *hayllitha*, adding that it was sung call-and-response style and extending its meaning beyond military celebrations and planting the fields to include the song sung by a group of people carrying wood to make rafters for a building (1984: 116).

3. This interesting account deserves further study. It is best seen as a large-scale Andean work party: Pachacuti invites everyone to the celebration but tells the *caciques* that he expects their people to help canalize the river and build

terraces in the Cuzco Valley. He plies them with food and drink, gives them clothing to wear, and—arguably—at this point makes the neighboring people into Incas-by-privilege.

4. *Borla* is a Spanish word that means tassel or fringe. Betanzos uses it in this passage to refer to the *llauto*, the headband with a long fringe or tassel that covered the forehead, that was equivalent to a crown for the Incas. In other passages the term is used to describe a decoration on certain garments. Because the referent is somewhat unclear (are *borlas* isolated tassels or continuous fringe?), I retain the Spanish term *borla* throughout.

5. It may be that the Incas in Vilcabamba had time to reflect more positively on Atahuallpa's life and death. The narrative prepared by Titu Cusi Yupanqui for Licenciado Lope Garcia de Castro in 1570 includes an account of Atahuallpa's capture and murder that contains many of the stylistic elements of formal narratives to be discussed in chapter 2 (repetition of events, incorporation of direct speech, and repeating metaphors, here likening the Incas to the quarry in a royal hunt and comparing the captured Atahuallpa to a tethered dog). As they attempted to keep their culture and religion alive, the Incas-in-exile, led by one of the surviving half-brothers of Atahuallpa, doubtless could have prepared a revisionist *cantar* that would focus on his tragic death at the hands of their common enemy and diminish the butchery that he instigated against his siblings and their allies.

6. Murúa also mentions Yamqui Yupanqui, noting that he was the oldest son of Pachacuti and that he made great conquests in Amaybamba (cap. 21; 1962, vol. 1: 51). In 1570 the *cacique principal* in Amaybamba was named Juan Yanqui Yupanqui, though he made no assertions about descent from Doña Angelina's grandfather. Rather, he identified his father as Rimache Yupanqui, who in turn descended from Pachacuti (Rostworowski 1963). The royal lands at Amaybamba belonged to Topa Inca, Mama Ocllo, and Pachacuti. In Cabello's parallel account the man elsewhere called Yamqui Yupanqui is identified as Auqui Yupanqui and is said to have been the ancestor of Don Juan Yupanqui from Amaybamba (cap. 16; 1951: 318). Cabello (or his modern editor) seems to have transcribed the elder Yamqui Yupanqui's name incorrectly.

7. It is possible that Doña Angelina, as his former mistress, was given some of the property by Francisco Pizarro, who had taken control of the estate for himself. However, the argument made to the court frames the request purely in terms of her descent from Inca royalty.

8. There was debate among the Incas about whether Inca Urcon had descendants. Cieza claims that he had many extramarital liaisons but no child by his legitimate sister-wife (parte II, caps. XLIV, XLVI; 1985: 129–131, 135–136). At the time of the Conquest there was no *panaca* that claimed Inca Urcon as its founder.

9. During the Colonial Period the preferred forum for competition among Inca elites moved from the battlefield to the courthouse. A 1603 dictionary of Quechua defines the word *atini* as "to dominate in battle or in a lawsuit" (*Arte de la lengua general* . . . 1603). Francisco de Toledo despaired of the Andean propensity to file legal documents and in his *Ordenanzas para la ciudad del Cuzco y sus*

términos of 18 October 1572 noted that "one of the things that causes the greatest damage in the republics are lawsuits, both in occupying people's attention and in the loss of their wealth. This is especially true in these parts, where it seems people are more accustomed to lawsuits than are people anywhere else" (1986, vol. 1: 178). Title IX of his *Ordenanzas* mandated the peaceful settlement of disputes and avoidance of legal battles.

2. Structuring Remembered History

1. The device of pairing similar phrases or sentences is called "semantic coupling" and is thought to be characteristic of Inca sacred invocations. Its presence in the royal histories suggests it is more broadly found in Inca narratives. See the review of this subject by Salomon ("Introduction" in Salomon and Urioste 1991: 35–36).

2. Other chroniclers, too, give examples of texts that involve Inca poetry, though not in the context of royal histories. Pachacuti Yamqui, whose first language was Quechua, includes several Inca texts in his account of the lives of the kings, including prayers, speeches, and songs. The structure, form, and verse patterns of these prayers and speeches is remarkably similar to that of the prayers presented by Molina and analyzed by Rowe (1953). There is also a useful comparison to a prayer to the Moon (Guaman Poma f. 285 [287]; 1980, vol. 1: 202) and the text of a song sung on the occasion of punishment of forceful corruption of virginity (Guaman Poma f. 309 [311]; 1980, vol. 1: 220–222).

3. In modern Quechua, the speech of others is indicated by the marker *-nispa* (which might be translated as "saying") appended to the utterance (Cusihuaman 1976: 280–281; Harrison 1989: 72–73). Salomon notes that direct speech and dialogue are common in the narratives collected by Francisco de Avila in the late sixteenth or early seventeenth century ("Introduction" in Salomon and Urioste 1991: 35).

4. The text written by Cabello Balboa in 1586 and Murúa's 1611 revision of his history of the Incas (compare Murúa 1962–64 and Murúa 1946) contain very similar passages, almost surely taken from a common source, now lost (Rowe 1987: 754).

5. Quechua uses a reportive marker to indicate events said to have happened but outside of the personal experience of the speaker, including events described in myths and legends (Cusihuaman 1976: 170–171; see also Harrison 1989: 73). The reportive contrasts with a "witness validator" marker which, in the transcribed narratives from Huarochirí, may represent redaction by the seventeenth-century editor of the stories (Salomon, "Introduction" in Salomon and Urioste 1991: 32–33). Salomon also notes the contrast between passages with the reportive (or "hearsay") marker and those which present direct speech in the Huarochirí stories.

3. Making History Visible

1. This type of performance at indigenous funerals persisted well after the Conquest. The second Provincial Council of Lima convened in 1567 to report

on the "superstitions" that persisted among Andean native peoples, including the observation that "when they bury the corpses they cut their hair and dress themselves in a certain kind of clothing. They play the drums and cry, singing. They carry the clothing of the dead to all those places where they walked about while they were alive. They put food and drink for them on their graves; they make sacrifices to the sun and to the rest of the idols" (Polo apendice B, cap. 105; 1916, vol. 1: 208). Juan de Betanzos and Pedro Cieza de León were both in Cuzco in 1550 to witness the death rituals of Paullu, a Colonial Inca and collaborator with the Spaniards. Although he had been baptized, Paullu's funeral was an Inca one (Cieza parte II, cap. XXXII; 1985: 98–99; cap. LXI; 1985: 178; Betanzos parte I, cap. XXXI; 1987: 145–148).

2. The discussion of Cuzco's shrines in the succeeding section uses numbers following Rowe (1980) as presented in Hamilton's translation of Cobo (1990). Rowe's article describes the logic of the system, as well as presenting information on Polo's and Albornóz's lists of shrines.

3. Murúa reports great numbers of skulls stored at Sacsahuaman in an account unfortunately lifted from sources on Mexico (Rowe 1987: 756). Although the passage sounds nearly plausible as a description of an Inca war monument, his "Inca" trophy head displays are, in fact, Aztec skull racks.

4. When informants from Cuzco talk about events that took place on the northern frontiers of the empire, they often conflate locations. It is not clear whether Cieza is talking about the same palace that Betanzos describes or a different one.

4. Huayna Capac's History

1. Brother-sister marriage had been established as the rule for Inca royal families by Pachacuti, who himself had a sister as one of his wives but not as the principal one. His queen, Mama Anahuarque, like other early Inca royal brides, had come from a ruling family of a neighboring town, in this case Choco (Cobo lib. 11, cap. XII; 1964: 77); she was mother of both Topa Inca and Mama Ocllo. The later Incas, Huayna Capac included, selected their principal wives from among the set of sisters, as decreed by Pachacuti. Coya Cusirimay, Huayna Capac's first sister-wife, left no living son and probably herself died young; his choice of a second sister, Mama Coca, was not sanctioned by the gods. Huascar also chose a sister as wife but did not live long enough to produce an heir to the throne. Sayri Topa may have married either a sister or a cousin (María Manrique), but they had only one child, Doña Beatriz, who married a prominent Spaniard, Martín de Loyola.

2. Cobo does not refer to Lady Chiqui Ocllo's plot but rather describes a gambling game staged by Topa Inca to humor a favorite concubine, a lady from Guayro. When her son won, he was rewarded by the gift of five towns in Urcu-suyu province, near Lake Titicaca (Cobo lib. 12, cap. XV; 1964: 36). While it is not the same story, it gives some insight into the character of Topa Inca, who could be bedazzled by a concubine and give possibly unfair advantage to her son at the expense of his legitimate sons.

3. Hualpaya is identified as an uncle of Huayna Capac (Cobo lib. 12, cap. XVI;

1964: 88). Sarmiento (cap. 57; 1960: 259) calls him a son of Capac Yupanqui, brother of Inca Yupanqui. Other sources call him Topa Inca's second cousin (Cabello Balboa) or nephew (Betanzos parte I, cap. XXXIX; 1987: 176). Lord Achachi is called an uncle (Cabello Balboa cap. 20; 1951: 359). Sarmiento identifies this man as Huaman Achachi, the brother of Topa Inca who helped quash Capac Guari's attempted usurpation; this may be the same Lord Achachi whom Topa Inca designated as general inspector to conduct a census after Topa Capac tried to cheat him (cap. 52; 1960: 256). Betanzos identifies him as Otoronco Achachi, the brother of Topa Inca who distinguished himself in the Antesuyu campaign and served as governor of that province (parte I, cap. XXXIX; 1987: 176). Alone among the chroniclers who mention these men, Betanzos characterizes them as coregents who remained loyal to Huayna Capac throughout his early reign.

4. Betanzos omits Manco Inca from the list of sons and claims that Paullu was born in Tiahuanaco (parte I, cap. XLV; 1987: 192). Other sources assert that Paullu was born in the town of Paullu in the Urubamba Valley (Espinoza Soriano 1976: 262).

5. Peter Palmieri, personal communication. Peter suggested I take these claims with a grain of salt and ran some numbers to show me their implications. Assuming he had sex with one woman per month, Huayna Capac could have sired more than five hundred children only if he was sexually active for forty-five years and that in at least 95 percent of the months there was a conception that led to a birth. If he had sex with two women per month, a mere twenty-five years of activity with 85 percent fertility would result in over five hundred conceptions; having two partners per month over forty-five years, assuming a 95 percent fertility rate, would result in over 1,000 conceptions. The numbers do not take into account months or years when the Inca may have been required to abstain from sex for ritual purposes, nor (as Joan O'Donnell suggested to me) do they factor in any possibility that a conception credited to Huayna Capac might have resulted from an encounter with someone else.

5. Huayna Capac's Royal Estate at Yucay

1. This was a point that especially disturbed Francisco Chilche, who argued that the Andean system of crop rotation required that some fields lie fallow between plantings. He was worried that lands not in continuous cultivation would be deemed to be abandoned and subject to seizure by the Spaniards (1552 document; Villanueva 1971: 24).

2. Zárate claims that Atahuallpa sent thirty thousand Cañaris to Cuzco with his generals (lib. I, cap. XII; 1947: 473). It is not unreasonable to think that some of this huge number may have been settled on the estate with their compatriots who had been moved there a generation earlier.

3. Many of the Indians of Yucay affected by this decree would have been ethnic Cañaris whose traditional exemption came from their tribe's loyalty to the Spanish cause during the Conquest and in the Spanish incursions into Vilcabamba. At the same time that the exempt Indians of Yucay and Cuzco were made subject to the tasa, Toledo decreed that the sole tribute owed by Cañaris

and Chachapoyas was personal service: They were to serve as guards for the Spanish fort at Sacsahuaman, they were to guard prisoners in Cuzco's jail, and they were to serve the *corregidor* of Cuzco (*Ordenanzas para la ciudad del Cuzco y sus términos*, 18 de octubre de 1572; título XXIII, Del servicio de los cañaris y chachapoyas; Toledo 1986, vol. 1: 199). Their service in the fort was confirmed in 1575 (*Título e instrucciones extendidos a Luis de Toledo Pimentel como castellano de la fortaleza de Sacsahuaman*, 19 de junio de 1575; Toledo 1986, vol. 2: 93–96). It is not clear how the mandate that the Indians of Yucay pay *tasa* to support the fort was reconciled with the exemption of the Cañaris from all but personal service.

4. The 1558 *título* of Doña Angelina lists fields owned by a number of Indians who also appear on the 1558 census lists (cf. Rostworowski 1962: 144–145; Villanueva 1971: 55–82). Names that appear on both lists include Caxana/Casani and Cupipullo/Cusipullo in *ayllu* Acosca; Condor Poma and Yupari in *ayllu* Machi of Yucay; Cochiguayman/Cochaguaman of *ayllu* Yanacona of Yucay; and Limachi/Rimache and Condor, names which appear in several *ayllus*.

5. Pedro Cachache and Domingo Achimec testified in 1570 that Topa Inca, rather than Huayna Capac, had brought their grandfathers from Guaylas and Luringuanca, respectively, to live in the Yucay Valley (*Informaciones de Toledo*; Levillier 1940: 101). In the famously leading questions posed in Toledo's investigations, their questioners made it clear that they were supposed to say that Topa Inca brought their ancestors to the region, rather than any other Inca. Pedro Cochache is listed as head of Ayllu Machi of Yucay on Huayna Capac's estate in 1558 (Villanueva 1971: 72). In 1574 a Pedro Cochachín testified that he was brought as *mitima* by Huayna Capac's captains (1574 pleito; Villanueva 1971: 104). There is a Domingo Achimec listed as head of Ayllu Chicón of Huayna Capac's estate in 1558 (1558 census; Villanueva 1971: 75).

6. The statuses of *yanacona* and *camayo* are explored by Rowe (1982), who observes that individuals could simultaneously be both. While in theory all male residents of a royal estate would have been *yanaconas*, it is unclear in documents describing Huayna Capac's estate whether that term was applied to the natives of the four indigenous towns within the estate's boundaries.

7. The location of this informant's town, populated by Huayna Capac's chamber servants, is not certain. If it is on the Yucay estate, it is probably in the Pomaguanca canyon. It may, however, be on one of Huayna Capac's other estates, probably the one at Sacsaguana (Xacxaguana).

8. We have confirmation of the fact that Huayna Capac could have needed someone like Guaman Chambi to watch after his headdress during festivals. Guaman Poma includes several drawings of Inca men in royal garb having laid their fringed headdress on the ground as they worship (f. 238 [240]; 1980: 212; f. 240 [242]; 1980: 214; f. 248 [250]; 1980: 222; f. 264 [266]; 1980: 238).

9. This property may be the same as one identified on the 1552 document as Pacachaca, which was still devoted to hot peppers in the Colonial Period, planted by Francisco Chilche and his associate, Gualpa Roca (Villanueva 1971: 53).

6. The Architecture on the Estate

1. Farrington (1995: 60) reports thirty-two extant niches on this wall and estimates there were originally forty-two. He also measured the terrace's length at 206.8 meters. I determined the size of the terrace by observing what I consider to be its original Inca corners. I believe that Farrington includes in the terrace length the corner of the modern cemetery. The extra distance he allows for the terrace accounts for the two extra niches he posits in the wall.

2. I am grateful to Robert Batson, who drew my attention to the unusual slant of the niches and door on gatehouse A and who diligently checked out other niches on the site.

3. Robert Batson turned his architect's eye to solving the problem posed by the two towers and devised the ingenious solution presented here. A fuller discussion of the design of this structure is presented in Niles and Batson (1997).

4. Gibaja suggested that the architecture in Urubamba was painted dark red (Gibaja 1982: 89), a comment echoed by Farrington (1995: 60). I have observed red paint only on a protected niche in the terrace wall and on a portion of the interior wall of great hall E.

5. Farrington (1995: 62 and fig. 3, 60) indicates the presence of Inca structures in the north and northwest side of the modern cemetery wall (J and H on his fig. 3). The style of masonry, angle of inclination of the walls, and details of niches, windows, and doors do not suggest pre-Conquest construction. Further, these buildings are outside the bounds of the area terraced for the Inca site. I do not consider them to be walls from Inca structures.

6. This comment was made to John Rowe in 1986 when he visited the site, though it is not certain that the informant was old enough to have seen the construction of the cemetery wall. I am grateful to John for sharing the comment with me.

7. I have discussed Cocha Sontor in a paper written earlier (Niles in press). The site plan and architectural observations presented here differ somewhat from the previous version and should be taken as an improvement upon it. The earlier paper was based on observations made in 1986 and 1987; in a visit to the site in 1997 I was able to see features that had formerly been obscured by modern construction. In particular, the earlier site plan notes a window (rather than a niche) on the front wall of building A; it does not include discussion of the wall near the rear entry to the building; one of the rear doors was considered to be a window; and the niched wall (structure C) was considered of dubious antiquity. Comments on the nature of the site made in the earlier paper are still valid.

8. Alfredo Valencia reports the presence of side walls on this building with three symmetrically disposed doorways and notes that only the rear wall of the structure was missing (Valencia 1982: 70). He does not give dimensions for the building.

9. The false *cédula* of 1552, which includes some properties of Doña Costanza's husband, calls this field Rondoguasi.

7. The Agricultural Works on the Estate

1. *Buhío* is a problematic word that appears in many sixteenth-century ac-counts of Inca culture and in legal documents. Probably from an Arawakan word picked up by the conquerors, the word is used in highland Peru to con-trast with *casa* (house), *tambo* (lodge or palace when used in the plural), and sometimes *aposento* (lodging or dwelling of a king and his court). A *buhío* is not a hut, but it surely is not as large or as grand as the main structures com-prising a palace. In some documents the homes of *yanaconas* are more likely to be called *buhíos* than are the homes of the Inca. But rulers also had *buhíos* in their palace compounds. In this passage the term refers to buildings that were owned by the Sun and hence must have been of some importance. In this con-text the term probably has to do with size (relatively small) and medium (per-haps adobe).

2. The dual staircases are a style apparently called DRPS (double recessed par-allel staircases) by Farrington (1995: 59).

3. This is a style apparently called RPS (recessed parallel staircase) by Farring-ton (1995: 59).

4. In addition to the similarity that Gasparini and Margolies note between Yu-cay's staircase and the stairs at Ingapirca in Ecuador, there is a close-at-hand model. The outside staircases on the dormitory compound at the Salesian ag-ricultural school (the Inca staircase and parts of Lucmayoc terrace are on Salesian property) similarly echo the diagonal form of these and the other staircases on the site.

5. Molinié, who has studied the ethnographic use of the terraces, elicited many of these names as well, along with others, to refer to topographic fea-tures near Yucay (1996). She has suggested that the native conception of the landscape reflects a gendered universe, an interpretation that she substanti-ates with an analysis of some of the names now given to terraces; her etymol-ogy of some of the names differs from my own.

8. Huayna Capac's Built Legacy

1. Murúa claims that one of the principal buildings of the Casana was where the main church of Cuzco was at the time of his writing (cap. 30; 1962, vol. 1: 77). He probably is confusing the great hall of the Casana with the great hall of Cuyus Manco, which was, in fact, used as the church for many years. He has a strange reference to the hall being used by the Colla peoples to hand out meat as ordered by the Inca. Murúa describes the hall as a "buhío muy grande," by which he probably means that it was made of adobe. Regrettably, we cannot know for certain whether he is in fact referring to the great hall within Casana or the hall that was used for the church.

2. The general description of *galpones* is followed by description of the conflict between Diego de Almagro and Hernando Pizarro. The latter holed up with his men in a *galpón* because of its wide end door (P. Pizarro cap. 21; 1986: 160).

3. Chroniclers refer to the location of this temple as Cacha, a name I have pre-served in my discussion of sixteenth-century accounts of the site. Its location

is most often called Raqchi by modern researchers, a convention I use in discussing the architectural remains of the site.

4. Juan de Santa Cruz Pachacuti Yamqui, a native of the region between Canas and Canchis, offers a different version of the story. Like the other chroniclers, he begins with a wandering creator god whom he identifies as the apostle St. Thomas. The rain of fire happens when he comes to Cachapucara, a tall mountain, where there is a female idol to whom children are sacrificed. The creator god causes the fire in order to burn the idol and her mountain (1950: 212). Pachacuti Yamqui mentions the burned hill but does not describe the Inca temple nor any prior temple to the creator god that may have been there.

5. Garcilaso's description of the temple at Cacha, seemingly very detailed, is actually internally inconsistent. He seems to describe both the Inca great hall with its pillars and center wall and a smaller unroofed structure with doors on all four sides. There seems little reason to believe that Garcilaso actually visited the site. But it is intriguing to speculate that perhaps he conflated the descriptions of two shrines that might have been there, the well-known Inca temple which more or less matches his description, and a second one that might be the Canas temple that is noted but not described by Betanzos and Cieza.

6. According to Polo de Ondegardo, the Canas and their neighbors the Canchis came to the aid of Pachacuti in repelling the Chanca invasion of Cuzco. He notes, however, that in contrast to the other people who came as vassals, the Canas and Canchis participated as mercenaries (Polo, "Del linage de los ingas . . ." 1917: 46). It is also possible to interpret this passage as Topa Inca sending off thousands of *mitimaes* from Canas and Canchis, near the homeland of the troublesome rebels of Collasuyu, to make sure that there weren't many people around to join in the mischief.

7. It is possible that columns in great halls had a ritual as well as a technical function. Earlier in this century Julio C. Tello made ethnographic observations in San Pedro de Casta in Peru's central highlands. During the annual ceremonies designed to elect officials, clean canals, and announce marriages, troupes of dancers led by ritual specialists celebrated in large buildings called *galpones* in Spanish and *waironas* in Quechua (Tello and Miranda 1923: 538). Although Tello does not provide a good description of the *wairona*, he observes that the large structures had a pillar erected in the center (he does not note whether it was integral to the structure of the building) that, like the walls and doorways, was profusely decorated with plants, flowers, and fruit. I am grateful to Frank Salomon for bringing this reference to my attention.

8. Our best evidence that Huayna Capac spent his childhood in Tomebamba comes from testimony elicited for Toledo's *informaciones*. In 1571 Tomas Pilpe reported that his father had been taken by Topa Inca to guard the land conquered in the north; he added that when Topa Inca returned from Quito, he left Pilpe's father there guarding Huayna Capac, the son that had been born in the north (*Informaciones de Toledo*, Levillier 1940: 113).

9. It is probable that Huayna Capac had a coca estate in Lares. It is accessible from his holdings in Yucay, and one of the terraces on that estate is said to

have been built by the Indians of Lares, suggesting a pre-Conquest tie to the region. An estate would probably have a palace and waterworks, especially an estate devoted to the production of a ritually charged commodity. In the Colonial Period Diego de Trujillo had a *repartimiento* of Indians who worked the coca fields in Lares as well as working corn fields within the boundaries of Huayna Capac's estate.

10. There are a number of fortresses near the southern frontier that could have been among those rebuilt at this time (see Hyslop 1990: 176; Lee 1992b, 1992c). Further, the Inca site of Incallacta may have been related to defensive or administrative activities in the area, though there is no documentary evidence to link the site to Huayna Capac or to any other Inca king or builder. Incallacta has a great hall second in size only to the Temple of Viracocha at Raqchi but quite different in design from it (Hyslop 1990: 176; Lee 1992a; Gasparini and Margolies 1980: 207–211).

9. Inca Architecture in Historical Context

1. Despite the claims expressed in the narratives and superficially seen in aspects of the two traditions, Inca stonemasonry and building design are quite different from what is seen at Tiahuanaco, as Protzen has convincingly argued (1997).

2. Collcampata had pre-Conquest shrines (Ch-4:3 and Ch-4:4; Cobo chap. 13; 1990: 56), though the relationship of those structures to Manco Inca's palace is uncertain. That Paullu retained an interest in native religion despite his conversion is also suggested by the fact that at his death a statue was made of him, incorporating his fingernails and hair clippings; it was venerated as were images and mummies of the pre-Conquest Incas (Cobo lib. 12, cap. XX; 1964: 103).

3. Francisco Pizarro gave the order to establish a new church in Cuzco in 1534 (*Acta de la fundación española de Cuzco*, 23 marzo de 1534; 1986: 163), locating the church on the site of an Inca building on the plaza. When Toledo arrived on the scene, he immediately gave the order to replace the existing adobe building with an appropriately grand structure (28 agosto de 1571, *Disposición sobre la construcción de la catedral* . . . ; 1986, vol. 1: 131).

4. Christopher Blechschmidt generously shared his insights on force and thrust in the great hall at Quispiguanca, and the following comments are drawn from our conversations. His ideas are explored at length in his thesis (Blechschmidt 1997) and have been incorporated in a paper as well (Niles, Batson, and Blechschmidt 1998) which contains a fuller argument about the design of the great halls at Quispiguanca.

5. We have depicted the gatehouse and portal structures with hip roofs, a style that is plausible for Inca buildings of those proportions and that matches all the available architectural evidence. We tried modeling the buildings with the flat roofs that might be suggested by a literal interpretation of the stone model and concluded that there was no architecturally sound method to account for such a roof type in the seasonally rainy climate that prevails at Quispiguanca. We assume that there may have been reasons having to do with the model's

use, possibly as a receptacle (the model has a shallow depression on its top surface), that account for the fact that it seems to depict a structure without a roof or with a flat roof.

6. I had suggested at one point that Q'ellu Raqay might be derived from a local Late Intermediate Period style in the region (Niles 1980: 60, fn. 1; see also Sawyer 1980: 71), a suggestion that I no longer believe to be true.

Glossary

ají   A hot pepper native to the Andes. Used in the *purucaya* ritual, its consumption was avoided during ritual fasts.

ayllu   A patrilineal descent group, whether royal or not. By the Colonial Period, the term had a territorial referent. The word also referred to a kind of dice used in an Inca gambling game and to a weapon made of stones tied to leather thongs that could be thrown around the feet of a fleeing or charging person or animal.

borla   A Spanish word used to refer to the *llauto*, the headband with pendant fringe that was the Inca equivalent of a crown, as well as to fringes or tassels such as those decorating the tunics worn by prisoners of war.

bulto   A Spanish word meaning bundle or statue. It is used to refer to portable images of Inca rulers that stood in for them in life or in death. Images reported for the Incas included full-size statues, bundles of clothing worn by the Inca in his lifetime, and statues or bundles incorporating the fingernail clippings or a scrap of flesh of the deceased ruler.

cacique   A term introduced to the Andes by the Spaniards and used to refer to a male native dignitary (female dignitaries were referred to as *cacicas*). Used broadly in Colonial documents, the corresponding Inca word is *curaca*.

camayo   A worker having an occupational specialty that contributed to an Inca or to the state economy, such as a *chacracamayo* (field maker) or *cumbicamayo* (*cumbi* cloth maker). For a discussion of the *camayo* status, see Rowe (1982).

cancha   A Quechua term that refers to a compound with or without a surrounding wall, comprising several buildings that face onto a courtyard.

cantar   A Spanish word that refers to an historical epic in poetry, prose, or song. The term was commonly applied to Inca royal histories and accounts of battles.

cédula   A grant of land made by the king of Spain. *Cédulas* were forged in Colonial times by Inca dignitaries eager to claim land.

ceque   An imagined line that connected a series of shrines in the pre-Columbian Andes. Each was maintained by a royal *panaca* of Cuzco.

coya   An Inca term for the principal wife of the ruling Inca. From Topa Inca's generation onward, the *coya* was supposed to be a full sister of the Inca. It was applied more broadly in the Colonial Period to Inca women of prominence.

galpón   A term introduced to the Andes by the Spaniards to refer to huge buildings with or without an open end wall and to buildings with multiple doorways on at least one long side. Some researchers call these structures *kallankas*. They may have been equivalent to Inca building types called the *cuyusmanco* and *carpahuasi*.

huaca   A shrine. In the ritual circuit of Cuzco, *huacas* were arrayed on *ceques* that radiated from the capital outward to its surrounding district.

huauque   An Inca term for brother, used to refer to the statue or image taken as an alter ego by the ruling Inca during his lifetime.

mamacona   The women chosen to serve the Inca or the state religion. Among the duties they carried out was the preparation of food, drink, and clothing for an Inca or for a deity. *Mamaconas* assisted in caring for mummies and in performing the histories that recounted their deeds.

mitimaes   People who were permanently removed from their homeland and resettled to another part of the Inca empire. Estates were among the Inca installations populated by *mitimaes*.

moya   A private reserve of the Inca or the Sun, sometimes maintained as a hunting preserve or forest.

orejones   Spanish term used to refer to the "big-ears," or noble men, of Cuzco. Piercing the ears at puberty and inserting a large ear plug that distended the lobes was a mark of nobility.

panaca   An Inca royal descent group. Each Inca founded his own patrilineal descent group, which was devoted to the care of his mummy and the custody of his history. At the time of the Conquest, there were twelve *panacas* in Cuzco, each tracing its descent from a real or mythical ruler.

purucaya   The ceremony held to commemorate the first anniversary of a death and to close the official period of mourning. The invention of the ritual is claimed by Pachacuti Inca.

quipu   A set of knotted string cords used widely as a mnemonic device in the pre-Columbian Andes and into the Colonial Period. *Quipus* were used to record historical facts, census, and tribute information, among other things. They were made and read by trained experts known as *quipucamayos*.

yanacona Before the Conquest, the term referred to a person in permanent, hereditary service to an Inca, including the residents of royal estates. After conquest the term was applied broadly. *Yanaconas* dedicated to the care of an Inca mummy were called *apoyanaconas*. For a discussion of *yanaconas*, see Rowe (1982).

Bibliography

ACOSTA, JOSÉ DE

1954 *Historia natural y moral de las Indias* [1590]. Biblioteca de Autores Españoles . . . vol. 73. Madrid: Ediciones Atlas.

ALCINA FRANCH, JOSÉ

1976 *Arqueología de Chinchero.* 2 vols. Madrid: Misión Científica Española en Hispanoamérica, Junta para la Protección de Monumentos y Bienes Culturales en el Exterior, Dirección General de Relaciones Culturales, Ministerio de Asuntos Exteriores.

ANONYMOUS JESUIT

1968 *Relación de las costumbres antiguas de los naturales del Pirú* [1594]. Biblioteca de Autores Españoles . . . vol. 209, pp. 152–189. Madrid: Ediciones Atlas.

AROCENA, LUIS A.

1986 *La relación de Pero Sancho* [1534]. Traducción, estudio preliminar, y notas por Luis A. Arocena. Buenos Aires: Editorial Plus Ultra.

Arte de la lengua general del Perv, llamada Quichua

1603 Sevilla(?): Casa de Clemente Hidalgo.

Arte y vocabulario de la lengua general del Perv llamada Quichua, y en la lengua Española. El mas copioso y elegante que hasta agora se ha impresso

1614 Lima: Francisco del Canto.

ASCHER, MARCIA, AND ROBERT ASCHER

1981 *Code of the Quipu: A Study in Media, Mathematics, and Culture.* Ann Arbor: University of Michigan Press.

BERTONIO, LVDOVICO

1984 *Vocabvlario de la lengua aymara* [1612]. Cochabamba: CERES (Centro de Estudios de la Realidad Económico Social), IFEA (Instituto Francés de Estudios Andinos), MUSEF (Museo Nacional de Etnografía y Folklore).

BETANZOS, JUAN DE

1987 *Suma y narración de los incas* [1551–57]. Transcripción, notas y prólogo por María del Carmen Martín Rubio. Madrid: Ediciones Atlas.

1996 *Narrative of the Incas* [1551–57]. Trans. and ed. Roland Hamilton and Dana Buchanan. Austin: University of Texas Press.

BLECHSCHMIDT, CHRISTOPHER

1997 Kallanka Construction in the Inca Empire. Unpublished senior honors thesis, Department of Civil and Environmental Engineering, Lafayette College, Easton, Penn.

CABELLO BALBOA, MIGUEL

1951   *Miscelánea antártica: Una historia del Perú antiguo* [1586]. Lima: Universi-
        dad Nacional Mayor de San Marcos, Facultad de Letras, Instituto de Et-
        nología.

CALLAPIÑA, SUPNO Y OTROS KHIPUKAMAYUQS

1974   *Relación de la descendencia, gobierno y conquista de los incas* [1608]. Edición
        de Juan José Vega. Lima: Ediciones de la Biblioteca Universitaria.

CIEZA DE LEÓN, PEDRO DE

1985   *Crónica del Perú. Segunda parte* [1553]. Edición, prólogo y notas de Fran-
        cesca Cantù. Lima: Pontificia Universidad Católica del Perú, Academia
        Nacional de la Historia.

1986   *Crónica del Perú. Primera parte* [1550]. Lima: Pontificia Universidad Catól-
        ica del Perú, Academia Nacional de la Historia.

COBO, BERNABE

1964   *Historia del Nuevo Mundo* [1653]. Biblioteca de Autores Españoles . . .
        vols. 91–92. Madrid: Ediciones Atlas.

1979   *History of the Inca Empire.* Trans. and ed. Roland B. Hamilton. Austin:
        University of Texas Press.

1990   *Inca Religion and Customs.* Trans. and ed. Roland B. Hamilton. Austin:
        University of Texas Press.

COLECCIÓN BETANCUR

1585–89 *Interrogatorio.* Part of a document presented by Martín García de Loy-
        ola and Doña Beatriz Coya in Cuzco. Archivo Departamental de Cuzco.
        Colección Betancur, vol. 8. Transcription by John H. Rowe.

Composición de tierras de Yucay y Amaybamba

1594   Archivo departamental de Cuzco. Beneficiencia. Becerro 15, 1649.
        Transcription by John H. Rowe.

COOK, NOBLE DAVID

1975   *Tasa de la visita general de Francisco de Toledo.* Versión paleográfica de No-
        ble David Cook. Lima: Universidad Nacional Mayor de San Marcos, Di-
        rección Universitaria de Biblioteca y Publicaciones.

CUSIHUAMAN G., ANTONIO

1976   *Gramática quechua: Cuzco-Collao.* Lima: Ministerio de Educación.

DAMIAN, CAROL

1995   From Pachamama to the Virgin Mary: What the Spanish Never Saw. In
        Penny Dransart, ed., *Andean Art: Visual Expression and Its Relation to Andean
        Beliefs and Values,* pp. 109–130. Aldershot: Avebury.

DIEZ DE SAN MIGUEL, GARCI

1964   *Visita hecha a la provincia de Chucuito por Garci Diez de San Miguel en el año
        1567.* Versión paleográfica de la visita y una biografía del visitador por
        Waldemar Espinoza Soriano. Documentos Regionales para la Etnolo-
        gía y Etnohistoria Andinas, vol. 1. Lima: Casa de la Cultura.

DONKIN, R. A.

1979   *Agricultural Terracing in the Aboriginal New World.* Viking Fund Publica-
        tions in Anthropology, no. 56. Tucson: University of Arizona Press.

DUNDES, ALAN

1980 The Number Three in American Culture. In *Interpreting Folklore*, pp. 134–159. Bloomington: Indiana University Press.

DUVIOLS, PIERRE

1979 Datation, paternité et idéologie de la "Declaración de los Quipucamayos a Vaca de Castro" (Discurso de la descendencia y gobierno de los Ingas). In *Les Cultures ibériques en devenir, essais publiés en hommage à la mémoire de Marcel Bataillon (1895–1977)*, pp. 583–591. Paris: La Fondation Singer-Polignac.

ESPINOZA SORIANO, WALDEMAR

1973 Colonias de mitmas multiples en Abancay, siglos XV y XVI. Una información inédita de 1575 para la etnohistoria andina. *Revista del Museo Nacional* 39: 225–299. Lima.

1976 Mujeres secundarias de Huayna Capac: Dos casos de señorialismo feudal en el imperio Inca. *Revista del Museo Nacional* 42: 247–298. Lima.

FARRINGTON, IAN S.

1983 Prehistoric Intensive Agriculture: Preliminary Notes on River Canalization in the Sacred Valley of the Incas. In J. P. Darch, ed., *Drained Field Agriculture in Central and South America*, pp. 221–235. BAR International Series 189. Oxford: BAR.

1984 Medidas de tierra en el Valle de Yucay, Cuzco. *Gaceta Arqueológica Andina* 3 (11) (September): 10–11.

1995 The Mummy, Palace, and Estate of Inka Huayna Capac at Quispeguanca. *Tawantinsuyu* 1: 55–65.

FINNEGAN, RUTH

1970 A Note on Oral Tradition and Historical Evidence. *History and Theory* 9: 195–201.

1992a *Oral Poetry: Its Nature, Significance, and Social Context.* Bloomington: Indiana University Press.

1992b *Oral Traditions and the Verbal Arts: A Guide to Research Practices.* London: Routledge.

FIORAVANTI-MOLINIÉ, ANTOINETTE

1974 Tendances actuelles de la communauté rurale péruvienne. *Sociologie du Travail* 16: 174–190.

1975 Contribution à l'étude des sociétés étagées des Andes: La vallée de Yucay (Pérou). *Etudes Rurales* 57: 35–59.

FLORES OCHOA, JORGE

1995 Tres temas pintados en queros incas de los siglos XVII–XVIII. *Revista del Museo e Instituto de Arqueología, Museo Inka* 25: 127–146. Cuzco.

FOLEY, JOHN MILES

1988 *The Theory of Oral Composition: History and Methodology.* Bloomington: Indiana University Press.

1995 *The Singer of Tales in Performance.* Bloomington: Indiana University Press.

GARCILASO DE LA VEGA, EL INCA

1609 *Primera parte de los commentarios reales, qve tratan del origen de los Yngas, reyes*

que fueron del Peru, de su idolatria, leyes, y gouierno en paz y en guerra: de sus vi-
das y conquistas, y de todo lo que fue aquel Imperio y su República, antes que los
Españoles les passaran a el. Lisboa: Officina de Pedro Crasbeeck.

1617   *Historia General del Peru. Trata el descubrimiento del; y como lo ganaron los Es-*
pañoles. Las guerras ciuiles que huuo entre Piçarros, y Almagros, sobre la partija
de la tierra. Castigo y leuantamiento de tiranos: y otros successos particulares que
en la Historia se contienen. Cordoua: Por la Viuda de Andres Barrera, y à su
costa.

1966   *Royal Commentaries of the Incas and General History of Peru.* Trans. Harold V.
Livermore. Austin: University of Texas Press.

GASPARINI, GRAZIANO, AND LUISE MARGOLIES

1980   *Inca Architecture.* Trans. Patricia J. Lyon. Bloomington: Indiana University Press.

GIBAJA, ARMINDA

1982   La ocupación neoinca del valle de Urubamba. In Italo Oberti, ed., *Ar-*
queología de Cuzco, pp. 81–96. Cusco: Instituto Nacional de Cultura.

1984   Sequencia cronológica de Ollantaytambo. In Ann Kendall, ed., *Current*
Archaeological Projects in the Central Andes: Some Approaches and Results, pp.
225–243. BAR International Series 210. Oxford: BAR.

GONÇALEZ HOLGUIN, DIEGO

1952   *Vocabulario de la lengua general de todo el Perú llamada Qquichua o del Inca*
[1608]. Lima: Imprenta San Martín.

GUAMAN POMA DE AYALA, FELIPE

1980   *El primer nueva corónica y buen gobierno* [1614?]. Edición crítica de John V.
Murra y Rolena Adorno; traducción por Jorge L. Urioste. 3 vols. Mexico
City: Siglo Veintiuno.

HAMPE, TEODORO M.

1979   Relación de los encomenderos y repartimientos del Perú en 1561. *Histo-*
ria y Cultura 12: 75–117. Lima.

HARRISON, REGINA

1989   *Signs, Songs, and Memory in the Andes: Translating Quechua Language and Cul-*
ture. Austin: University of Texas Press.

HEFFERNAN, KEN

1995   Paullu, Tocto Usica and Chilche in the Royal Lands of Limatambo and
Quispeguanca. *Tawantinsuyu* 1: 66–85.

HEMMING, JOHN

1970   *Conquest of the Incas.* New York: Harcourt Brace Jovanovich.

HEMMING, JOHN, AND EDWARD RANNEY

1982   *Monuments of the Incas.* Boston: Little, Brown and Company.

HENRÍQUEZ DE BORJA, JUAN

N.d.   *Por el Marques de Oropesa, como marido de Dona* [sic] *Ana Maria de Loyola*
Coya. Sobre la satisfaction que pretende le haga su Magestad por los derechos y
pretensiones en que viene informado por la Real Audiencia de Lima [1614?]. Biblioteca Nacional, Santiago.

HERNÃDEZ DE OVIEDO Y VALDES, GONÇALO

1547   Corónica de las Indias. La hystoria general de las Indias agora nueuamente im-
        pressa corregida y emendada. Salamanca: N.p.

HORNBERGER, ESTEBAN, AND NANCY H. HORNBERGER

N.d.   Diccionario tri-lingue: Quechua of Cusco/English/Spanish. 3 vols. Sicuani: Im-
        prenta Prelatura de Sicuani.

HUAYCOCHEA NUÑEZ DE LA TORRE, FLOR DE MARÍA

1994   Qolqas: Bancos de reserva andinos. Almacenes Inkas. Arqueología de qolqas.
        Cusco: Universidad Nacional San Antonio Abad del Cuzco.

HYMES, DELL

1981   Discovering Oral Performance and Measured Verse in American Indian
        Narratives. In "In Vain I Tried to Tell You": Essays in Native American Poetics,
        pp. 309–341. Philadelphia: University of Pennsylvania Press.

HYSLOP, JOHN

1990   Inka Settlement Planning. Austin: University of Texas Press.

JEREZ, FRANCISCO DE

1947   Verdadera relación de la conquista del Perú y provincia del Cuzco, llamada la
        Nueva-Castilla, conquistada por Francisco Pizarro capitan e la sacra, católica, ce-
        sárea majestad del Emperador nuestro señor; enviado a su majestad [1534]. Bib-
        lioteca de Autores Españoles . . . vol. 26, Historiadores Primitivos de
        Indias, vol. 2, pp. 319–343. Madrid: Ediciones Atlas.

JULIEN, CATHERINE

1982   Inca Decimal Administration in the Lake Titicaca Region. In George A.
        Collier, Renato I. Rosaldo, and John D. Wirth, eds., The Inca and Aztec
        States 1400–1800: Anthropology and History, pp. 119–151. New York: Ac-
        ademic Press.

KENDALL, ANN

1976   Descripción e inventario de las formas arquitectónicas inca; patrones
        de distribución e inferencias cronológicas. Revista del Museo Nacional 42:
        13–96. Lima.

1985   Aspects of Inca Architecture: Description, Function and Chronology. 2 vols. BAR
        International Series 242. Oxford: BAR.

LARREA, CARLOS M.

1918   Documentos. El descubrimiento y la conquista del Peru. Relación iné-
        dita de Miguel de Estete [1536?]. Boletín de la Sociedad Ecuatoriana de Estu-
        dios Históricos Americanos 1: 300–350. Quito.

LEE, VINCENT R.

1992a   Reconstructing the Great Hall at Inkallacta. In Investigations in Bolivia.
        Wilson, Wyo.: The author.

1992b   Cuzco-tuyo: The Search for a Lost Inca Fortress. In Investigations in Bo-
        livia. Wilson, Wyo.: The author.

1992c   Seven "Inka Pucaras" on the Bolivian Frontier. In Investigations in Bo-
        livia. Wilson, Wyo.: The author.

1996   Design by Numbers: Architectural Order among the Incas. Wilson, Wyo.: The
        author.

LEVILLIER, ROBERTO
1940   Don Francisco de Toledo, supremo organizador del Peru. Su vida, su obra
       (1515–1582). Tomo II: Sus informaciones sobre los incas (1570–1572). Bue-
       nos Aires: Espasa-Calpe.

LIRA, JORGE A.
N.d.   Breve diccionario kkechuwa español. Edición popular. Cusco: N.p.

LOHMANN, GUILLERMO
1965   El testamento inédito del Inca Sayri Tupac. História y Cultura 1 (1): 13–18.
       Lima.

MACCORMACK, SABINE
1991   Religion in the Andes: Vision and Imagination in Early Colonial Peru. Prince-
       ton, N.J.: Princeton University Press.

MENA, CRISTÓBAL DE (ANÓNIMO SEVILLANO DE 1534)
1967   La conquista del Perú [1534]. In Raúl Porras Barrenechea, ed., Las rela-
       ciones primitivas de la conquista del Perú, pp. 79–101. Lima: Universidad
       Nacional Mayor de San Marcos.

MOLINA, CRISTOBAL DE
1916   Relación de las fábulas y ritos de los incas . . . [1571]. Colección de Libros y
       Documentos Referentes a la Historia del Perú, vol. 1. Lima: Imprenta y
       Librería San Marti y Cia.

MOLINIÉ, ANTOINETTE
1996   The Spell of Yucay: A Symbolic Structure in Incaic Terraces. Journal of the
       Steward Anthropological Society 24 (1–2): 203–230. Urbana.

MOLINIÉ-FIORAVANTI, ANTOINETTE
1982   La Vallée sacrée des Andes. Société d'Ethnographie, Recherche Améri-
       caines 4. Paris.

MONTESINOS, FERNANDO DE
1920   Memorias antiguas historiales del Peru [seventeenth century]. Trans. and
       ed. Philip Ainsworth Means. New York: Hakluyt Society.

MOOREHEAD, ELISABETH L.
1978   Highland Inca Architecture in Adobe. Ñawpa Pacha 16: 65–94.

MORALES, ADOLFO DE
1978   Repartimiento de tierras por el inca Huayna Capac. (Testimonio de un documento
       de 1556). Segunda edición. Cochabamba: Universidad Boliviana Mayor
       de San Simon, Departamento de Arqueología, Museo Arqueológico.

MURRA, JOHN
1982   The Mit'a Obligations of Ethnic Groups to the Inka State. In George A.
       Collier, Renato I. Rosaldo, and John D. Wirth, eds., The Inca and Aztec
       States 1400–1800: Anthropology and History, pp. 237–262. New York: Ac-
       ademic Press.

MURÚA, MARTÍN DE
1946   Historia del origen y genealogía real de los Incas del Perú [1615]. Edición de
       Constantino Bayle. Biblioteca "Misionalia Hispánica," vol. 2. Madrid:

Consejo Superior de Investigaciones Científicas, Instituto Santo Toribio de Mogrovejo.

1962–64 *Historia general del Perú, orígen y descendencia de los incas* [1590–1611]. 2 vols. Edición de Manuel Ballesteros-Gaibrois. Madrid: Colecciones Joyas Bibliográficas, Bibliotheca Americana Vetus.

NILES, SUSAN A.

1980 Pumamarca: A Late Intermediate Period Site near Ollantaytambo. *Ñawpa Pacha* 18: 49–62.

1987 *Callachaca: Style and Status in an Inca Community*. Iowa City: University of Iowa Press.

1988 Looking for "Lost" Inca Palaces. *Expedition* 30 (3): 56–64.

1993 The Provinces in the Heartland: Stylistic Variation and Architectural Innovation near Inca Cuzco. In Michael A. Malpass, ed., *Provincial Inca: Archaeological and Ethnohistorical Assessment of the Impact of the Inca State*, pp. 146–176. Iowa City: University of Iowa Press.

in press *Moya* Place or Yours? Inca Private Ownership of Pleasant Places. *Ñawpa Pacha* 25–27 (1987–1989).

NILES, SUSAN A., AND ROBERT N. BATSON

1997 Sculpting the Yucay Valley: Style and Technique in Late Inca Architecture. Paper presented at the Dumbarton Oaks Symposium on Expressions of Power in the Inka State. Washington, D.C.

NILES, SUSAN A., ROBERT N. BATSON, AND CHRISTOPHER BLECHSCHMIDT

1998 Big Buildings and Small Plazas: Shifting Perspectives in Inca Ritual Space. Presented at the 38th Annual Meeting of the Institute of Andean Studies. Berkeley, Calif.

OLIVA, ANELLO

1895 *Libro primero del manuscrito original del R. P. Anello Oliva, S.J. Historia del reino y provincias del Peru, de sus Incas reyes, descubrimiento y conquista por los españoles de la corona de Castilla, con otras singularidades concernientes a la historia* [early seventeenth century?]. Lima: Imprenta y Libreria de S. Pedro.

OPLAND, JEFF

1974 Praise Poems as Historical Sources. In Christopher Saunders and Robin Derricat, eds., *Beyond the Cape Frontier: Studies in the History of the Transkei and Ciskei*, pp. 1–37. London: Longman.

PACHACUTI YAMQUI SALCAMAYGUA, JOAN DE SANTA CRUZ

1950 *Relación de antigüedades deste reyno del Pirú* [early seventeenth century]. In *Tres relaciones peruanas*. Asunción: Editorial Guaranía.

1968 *Relación de antigüedades deste reyno del Peru* [early seventeenth century]. Biblioteca de Autores Españoles . . . vol. 209, pp. 279–319. Madrid: Ediciones Atlas.

PARDO, LUIS A.

1936 Maquetas arquitectónicas en el antiguo Perú. *Revista del Museo y Instituto Arqueológico* 1 (1): 6–17. Cuzco.

PÄRSSINEN, MARTTI, AND ARI SIIRIÄINEN

1997 Inka-Style Ceramics and Their Chronological Relationship to the Inka Expansion in the Southern Lake Titicaca Area (Bolivia). *Latin American Antiquity* 8 (3): 255–271.

PEREZ DE TUDELA BUESO, JUAN

1964 *Documentos relativos a don Pedro de la Gasca y a Gonzalo Pizarro.* Contribución al XXXVI Congreso Internacional de Americanistas. Archivo Documental Español, vol. XXI. 2 vols. Madrid: Real Academia de la Historia.

PIZARRO, FRANCISCO

1986 *Testimonio. Documentos oficiales, cartas y escritos varios.* Edición preparada por Guillermo Lohmann Villena. Madrid: Consejo Superior de Investigaciones Científicas, Centro de Estudios Históricos, Departamento de Historia de América "Fernández de Oviedo."

PIZARRO, PEDRO

1986 *Relación del descubrimiento y conquista de los reinos del Peru* [1571]. Edición de Guillermo Lohmann Villena. Segunda edición. Lima: Pontificia Universidad Católica del Perú, Fondo Editorial.

POLO DE ONDEGARDO, JUAN

1917 *Tratado y auerigación sobre los errores y supersticiones de los indios* [1559]. In Horacio H. Urteaga and Carlos A. Romero, eds., *Colección de libros y documentos referentes a la historia del Peru,* vol. 3. Lima: N.p.

PROPP, VLADIMIR

1965 *The Morphology of the Folktale.* Austin: University of Texas Press.

PROTZEN, JEAN-PIERRE

1993 *Inca Architecture and Construction at Ollantaytambo.* New York: Oxford University Press.

1997 Who Taught the Inca Stonemasons Their Skills? A Comparison of Tiahuanaco and Inca Cut-Stone Masonry. *Journal of the Society of Architectural Historians* 56 (2): 146–167.

RAMOS GAVILÁN, ALONSO

1978 *Historia de Nuestra Señora de Copacabana* [1621]. Segunda edición. Academia Boliviana de la Historia. La Paz: Cámara Nacional de Comercio, Cámara Nacional de Industrias.

Relación de Chincha

1934 Relación y declaración del modo que esta valle de Chincha y sus comarcanos se gobernaban ántes que hobiese ingas y después que los hobo hasta que los cristianos entraron en esta tierra. Valle de Chincha, 22 de hebrero de 1558. In Horacio H. Urteaga, ed., *Colección de libros y documentos referentes a la historia del Perú,* vol. 10 (2a serie), pp. 134–149. Lima: N.p.

Relación francesa

1967 Relación francesa de la conquista del Peru 1534. Noticias verdaderas de las islas del Peru 1534. In Raúl Porras Barrenechea, ed., *Las relaciones primitivas de la conquista del Perú,* pp. 69–78. Lima: Instituto Raúl Porras Barrenechea.

ROSTWOROWSKI DE DIEZ CANSECO, MARÍA

1962   Nuevos datos sobre tenencia de tierras reales en el incario. *Revista del Museo Nacional* 31: 130–164. Lima.

1963   Dos manuscritos inéditos con datos sobre Manco II, tierras personales de los Incas y mitimaes. *Nueva Corónica*. Organo del Departamento de História, Facultad de Letras, Universidad Nacional Mayor de San Marcos 1: 223–239. Lima.

1970   El repartimiento de Doña Beatriz Coya, en el valle de Yucay. *História y Cultura* 4: 153–268. Lima.

1990   La visita de Urcos de 1652: Un kipu pueblerino. *Historia y Cultura* 20: 295–317. Lima.

ROWE, JOHN H.

1944   *An Introduction to the Archaeology of Cuzco*. Papers of the Peabody Museum of American Archaeology and Ethnology, Harvard University, vol. 27, no. 2. Cambridge, Mass.

1953   Eleven Inca Prayers from the Zithuwa Ritual. *Kroeber Anthropological Society Papers* 8–9: 82–99. Berkeley, Calif.

1967   What Kind of a Settlement Was Inca Cuzco? *Ñawpa Pacha* 5: 59–75.

1978   La fecha de la muerte de Wayna Qhapaq. *Histórica* 2 (1): 83–88. Lima.

1980   An Account of the Shrines of Ancient Cuzco. *Ñawpa Pacha* 5: 59–76.

1982   Inca Policies and Institutions Relating to the Cultural Unification of the Empire. In George A. Collier, Renato I. Rosaldo, and John D. Wirth, eds., *The Inca and Aztec States, 1400–1800: Anthropology and History*, pp. 93–110. New York: Academic Press.

1985a La constitución inca del Cuzco. *Histórica* 9 (1): 35–74. Lima.

1985b Probanza de los incas nietos de conquistadores. *Histórica* 9 (2): 193–245. Lima.

1987   La mentira literaria en la obra de Martín de Murúa. In *Libro en homenaje a Aurelio Miró Quesada Sosa II*, pp. 753–761. Lima: Talleres Gráficos P. L. Villanueva, S.A., Editores.

1990   Machu Picchu a la luz de documentos del siglo XVI. *Histórica* 14 (1): 139–154. Lima.

RUIZ DE ARCE, JUAN

1955   Una nueva relación de la conquista [1543]. *Boletín de la Academia Nacional de História* 35: 179–200. Quito.

SALOMON, FRANK, AND GEORGE L. URIOSTE

1991   *The Huarochirí Manuscript. A Testament of Ancient and Colonial Andean Religion*. Austin: University of Texas Press.

SANCHO DE LA HOZ, PEDRO

1557   *Repartición que hizo el Marques don Fr⁽ᶜᵒ⁾ Pizarro en Caxamarca, del tesoro que se tomo el año de 1533 Años al Cazique Atabalipa señor que era de estos Reynos* [1533].

SARMIENTO DE GAMBOA, PEDRO

1960   *Historia índica* [1572]. Biblioteca de Autores Españoles . . . vol. 135, pp. 193–279. Madrid: Ediciones Atlas.

SAWYER, ALAN

1980   Squier's "Palace of Ollantay" Revisited. Ñawpa Pacha 18: 63–73.

SCHJELLERUP, INGE R.

1997   *Incas and Spaniards in the Conquest of the Chachapoyas. Archaeological and Ethnohistorical Research in the North-eastern Andes of Peru.* GOTARC Series B. Gothenburg Archaeological Theses, No. 7. Göteborg: Göteborg University, Department of Archaeology.

SOUKUP, JAROSLAV

1970   *Vocabulario de los nombres vulgares de la flora peruana.* Lima: Colegio Salesiano.

SQUIER, EPHRAIM GEORGE

1877   *Peru: Incidents of Travel and Exploration in the Land of the Incas.* New York: Harper & Brothers Publishers.

TEDLOCK, DENNIS

1983   On the Translation of Style in Oral Narrative. In *The Spoken Word and the Work of Interpretation,* pp. 31–61. Philadelphia: University of Pennsylvania Press.

TELLO, JULIO C., AND PRÓSPERO MIRANDA

1923   *Wallalo:* Ceremonias gentílicas realizadas en la región cisandina del Perú central (Distrito de Casta). *Inca* 1: 475–549. Lima.

TEMPLE, ELLA DUNBAR

1937   La descendencia de Huayna Cápac. *Revista Histórica* 11: 284–323. Lima.

TITU CUSI YUPANQUI, DIEGO DE CASTRO

1992   *Instrucción al Licenciado Lope García de Castro* [1570]. Edición de Liliana Regalado de Hurtado. Lima: Pontificia Universidad Católica del Perú, Fondo Editorial.

TOLEDO, FRANCISCO DE

1986   *Disposiciones gubernativas para el virreinato del Peru.* Tomo 1: 1569–1574; Tomo 2: 1575–1580. Transcripción por María Justina Sarabia Viejo. Seville: Consejo Superior de Investigaciones Científicas, Monte de Piedad y Caja de Ahorros de Sevilla.

UHLE, MAX

1923   *Las ruinas de Tomebamba.* Conferencia leída por el Dr. Max Uhle en el Centro de Estudios Históricos y Geográficos del Azuay. Quito: Julio Sáenz Rebolledo.

URTON, GARY

1990   *The History of a Myth: Pacariqtambo and the Origin of the Inkas.* Austin: University of Texas Press.

1995   A New Twist in an Old Yarn: Variation in Knot Directionality in the Inka Khipus. *Baessler-Archiv. Beiträge zur Völkerkunde.* Neue folge Band XLII (LXVI. Band) Heft 2: 271–305. Berlin.

1996   R. Tom Zuidema, Dutch Structuralism, and the Application of "the Leiden Orientation" to Andean Studies. *Journal of the Steward Anthropological Society* 24 (1–2): 1–36. Urbana.

1997   *The Social Life of Numbers: A Quechua Ontology of Numbers and Philosophy of Arithmetic.* Austin: University of Texas Press.

VALENCIA, ALFREDO

1982   Complejo arqueológico de Yucay. In Italo Oberti, ed., *Arqueología de Cuzco,* pp. 65–80. Cusco: Instituto Nacional de Cultura.

VANSINA, JAN

1985   *Oral Tradition as History.* Madison: University of Wisconsin Press.

VILLANUEVA URTEAGA, HORACIO

1971   Documentos sobre Yucay en el siglo XVI. *Revista del Archivo Histórico del Cuzco* 13 (1970): 1–148. Cuzco.

1982   *Cuzco 1689. Documentos. Informes de los párrocos al obispo Mollinedo. Economía y sociedad en el sur andino.* Transcripción por Horacio Villanueva Urteaga. Cuzco: Centro de Estudios Rurales Andinos "Bartolomé de las Casas."

WACHTEL, NATHAN

1980–81 Les Mitimas de la vallée de Cochabamba. La Politique de colonisation de Huayna Capac. *Journal de la Société des Américanistes* 67: 297–324. Paris.

ZÁRATE, AGUSTIN DE

1947   *Historia del descubrimiento y conquista del Peru* [1555]. In Julio Le Riverend, ed., *Crónicas de la conquista del Perú.* Mexico City: Editorial Nueva España.

ZUIDEMA, R. TOM

1991   *Inca Civilization in Cuzco.* Austin: University of Texas Press.

Index

Boldfaced numerals indicate pages with illustrations.

PLATE 2. Reconstruction drawing of Quispiguanca, exterior view, from the southeast. Drawing by Robert N. Batson.